The Principle of Legality in European Criminal Law

School of Human Rights Research Series, Volume 75

The titles published in this series are listed at the end of this volume.

The Principle of Legality in European Criminal Law

Christina Peristeridou

intersentia
Cambridge – Antwerp – Portland

Intersentia Ltd
Sheraton House | Castle Park
Cambridge | CB3 0AX | United Kingdom
Tel.: +44 1223 370 170 | Fax: +44 1223 370 169
Email: mail@intersentia.co.uk
www.intersentia.com | www.intersentia.co.uk

Distribution for the UK and Ireland:
NBN International
Airport Business Centre, 10 Thornbury Road
Plymouth, PL6 7 PP
United Kingdom
Tel.: +44 1752 202 301 | Fax: +44 1752 202 331
Email: orders@nbninternational.com

Distribution for Europe and all other countries:
Intersentia Publishing nv
Groenstraat 31
2640 Mortsel
Belgium
Tel.: +32 3 680 15 50 | Fax: +32 3 658 71 21
Email: mail@intersentia.be

Distribution for the USA and Canada:
International Specialized Book Services
920 NE 58th Ave. Suite 300
Portland, OR 97213
USA
Tel.: +1 800 944 6190 (toll free) | Fax: +1 503 280 8832
Email: info@isbs.com

Cover image: Pieter Bruegel the Elder, The Tower of Babel (Vienna, 1563).

ISBN 978-1-78068-357-7
D/2015/7849/137
NUR 828

British Library Cataloguing in Publication Data. A catalogue record for this book is available from the British Library.

Acknowledgements

I have found almost everything ever written about completing a PhD to be true. Most people describe it as a lonely, difficult and humbling endeavour, while those who are more optimistic call it challenging and exciting. My supervisor once said that I would only have to do it once – this I sincerely hope is true. Those who reach the end finally admit that, amidst the lonely academic research, they met great people. This I know to be true.

I would like to thank Gerard Mols, Taru Spronken, Monica Claes, Tineke Cleiren and Klaas Rozemond for reading and approving the manuscript, and their valuable feedback. I also thank Maastricht University for creating such an enjoyable atmosphere, and the NWO for generously financing my research, and the publication of this book. The criminal law department has, most hospitably, given me a home throughout my academic endeavours for which I am grateful.

I have been blessed with supervisors of exceptional calibre and spirit, namely André Klip and David Roef. I thank André for trusting me with this challenging research, which is part of a project close to his heart. His straight-to-the-point view of law has shaped my legal thinking and writing. André's approach to European criminal law, often dynamic and against dogmatic stagnation, has been inspiring. I thank him for giving me the opportunity to be part of academia and for teaching me everything there is to know about it. Every single time I knocked his door I found a calm and supportive force – with an often wicked sense of humour – and he remained supportive even after I left his office. This gave me the confidence to continue.

I want to express my gratitude to David for his astute comments and sharp feedback which had a defining influence on my research. His passionate pursuit of reason(s) in law, and his intellectual ability to carve windows into the cement walls of legal doctrine are an inspiration. The early suggestion to get myself acquainted with legal philosophy and, later on, to use the models of justice have had an immense impact on the approach I chose in the following pages. And despite my difficulties in successfully achieving this, I will always remain indebted to him for pushing me to explore well outside my comfort zone.

I would like to thank Erik Claes for his comments on my presentation at a conference in Maastricht, and for his work that has been very instructive for my understanding of the legality principle. I am thankful to Peter Alldridge, Andrew Ashworth and John Spencer for their help with English criminal law. At Oxford,

Andrew Ashworth's insightful comments on my report on English law gave me much needed confidence. I also appreciate the warm welcome and excellent tour of Oxford University's grounds. The stimulating discussion that I had with John Spencer at Cambridge was most useful as it helped me draw comparative connections between civil and common law systems that transcend the legality principle.

I am happy to have been part of a research team with Jeroen Blomsma, Johannes Keiler and Anne-Sophie Massa. I found teachers and friends in them. I am grateful for the great sense of humour, support and contribution in my development as a researcher. Though often unconsciously done, each one helped me improve in different ways.

I owe my deepest gratitude to my friend Gabriela Belmar-Valencia for editing and proofreading with admirable patience an earlier version of the manuscript and kindly sparing the reader from some exotic vocabulary. My thanks should also go to Craig Eggett for proofreading my manuscript towards the end and giving me great tips. I also thank the different language centres in Maastricht, Düsseldorf and Frankfurt that helped me reach the desired level of Dutch and German.

I am indebted to all my friends and colleagues here and in Greece who helped me through difficult times and especially to Kei Hannah Brodersen, Liesbeth Baetens, Dorris de Vocht, Marrelle Attinger, Eleni Mantziou and Constantina Mitliagka.

I am awed by my parents' faith in me, and their unflinching support in helping me to continue doing what I love. My brother, Kostas, has been a solid, calm force by my side, enduring long phone calls and never uttering the slightest criticism, even when deserved.

Michael, your devotion and patience for a seemingly never ending project has been remarkable, despite all the untravelled trips that I kept promising. Thank you for sharing with me a love for creativity, for generously allowing me the space to exercise it in silence, and for always showing me, with kindness, the bigger picture whenever I lost sight of it.

Düsseldorf,
4 September 2015

Contents

ABBREVIATIONS

AC	Appeal Cases
AFSJ	Area of Freedom Security and Justice
AG	Advocate General
All ER	All England Law Reports
App.	Application
BGH	Bundesgerichtshof
BVerfG	Bundesverfassungsgericht
Cr App R	Criminal Appeal Reports
CS	European Coal and Steel Community Treaty
DCC	Dutch Criminal Code
EAW	European Arrest Warrant
EC	European Community
ECHR	European Convention of Human Rights
ECJ	European Court of Justice
ECLI	European Case Law Identifier
EComHR	European Commission of Human Rights
ECtHR	European Court of Human Rights
EPPO	European Public Prosecutor's Office
ER	The English Reports
EU	European Union
EWCA Crim	Court of Appeal Criminal Division
EWHC	High Court of Justice
EWHC Admin	High Court (Administrative Court)
GCC	German Criminal Code
HR	Hoge Raad
KB	Law Reports King's Bench Division
Law Com	Law Commission (UK)
LJN	Landelijk Jurisprudentie Nummer
NJ	Nederlandse Jurisprudentie
NJW	Neue Juristische Wochenschrift
OJ	Official Journal
OLG	Oberlandesgericht
Para.	Paragraph
QB	Law Reports Queen's Bench Division
RG	Reichsgericht
RGSt	Entscheidungen des Reichsgerichts in Strafsachen
Stb	Staatsblad van het Koninkrijk der Nederlanden
TEU	Treaty on European Union
TFEU	Treaty on the Functioning of the European Union

The Charter	Charter of Fundamental Rights of the European Union.
UK	United Kingdom
UKHL	House of Lords
WLR	Weekly Law Reports
ZaöRV	Zeitschrift für ausländisches öffentliches Recht und Völkerrecht
ZIS	Zeitschrift für Internationale Strafrechtsdogmatik
ZStW	Zeitschrift für die gesamte Strafrechtswissenschaft

Part 1

Setting the scene

Chapter I
Introduction

When Europe made the historic decision to set aside its internal borders, the national jurisdictions of the Member States – in areas as varied as tax law, product liability, criminal or family law – changed for good. As individuals, their businesses, products, cars and families began to cross national borders, they began to move between national legal orders. While this development sought to abolish boundaries in relation to individuals and the market, it also facilitated transnational crime. Cross-border crime and the lack of borders across the EU required the development of new legal instruments, including instruments of mutual recognition, harmonisation of definitions of criminal offences, trans-European institutions, arrest and evidence warrants, and soon, an EPPO.

A European criminal justice system cannot, and should not, only exist to battle cross-border crime. The EU has transformed from a union promoting economic interests towards *'an ever closer union among the peoples of Europe'*,[1] which shall *'offer its citizens an area of freedom, security and justice without internal frontiers'*.[2] It is a legal order based on democracy and the Rule of Law, human dignity, solidarity and freedom.[3] Any creation of a European criminal justice system raises questions regarding its legitimacy and purpose. Hence, European criminal law must be armed with legal principles that reflect the values of the EU, a union of the nation states built upon the Rule of Law and fundamental rights. One of these principles is the principle of legality, a doctrine deeply rooted in most national systems. While this principle already exists within the European legal order, it is still in its infancy.

1. The principle of legality and the criminal law

The principle of legality is a cornerstone of criminal justice systems around Europe. It is codified in international instruments, e.g. Article 7 ECHR and Article 22 of the Rome Statute of the International Criminal Court, national constitutions and criminal codes, such as Article 1 GCC, Article 16 of the Dutch Constitution. The essence of this principle is that no person can be punished for an act that is not criminalised by law, in other words, 'there is no crime without law'. The legality principle outlines certain substantive requirements of what can be considered a legitimate criminal norm and how it should be applied and interpreted. For example, the principle dictates that only parliamentary statutes can be a source of criminal

1 Article 1 TEU.
2 Article 3 para. 2 TEU.
3 Article 2 TEU.

liability; that criminal liability should be precisely defined in a written form; that criminal norms may not be applied retroactively; and that courts should interpret criminal liability only within the limits of the statute. Traditionally, the principle of legality belongs to the so-called general part of criminal law, namely a set of principles and general rules of criminal liability that permeate the criminal justice system and apply to all criminal offences.[4]

The legality principle is wide-ranging and may be present in a criminal justice system in a number of practical forms. If one uses the classical distinction between rules and principles developed by Dworkin, then it can be considered a principle – as its name denotes – because it is abstract, open textured and does not operate in an 'all or nothing' fashion.[5] However, some of its more concrete aspects, such as the prohibition of retroactivity, may function more as a rule if one applies the criteria of the aforementioned distinction. In addition, the legality principle also exists as a human – or fundamental – right, e.g. Article 49 of the Charter. As a human right, this principle may acquire qualities common to other human rights, such as a less absolute character that requires a balancing or weighing exercise in its application, and a tendency towards generalisation.[6]

What is the importance and role of the legality principle in criminal law? Often in scholarship different answers are found depending on whether one considers its functions to be internal or external to the criminal law system.[7]

The external role of the legality principle lies with its legitimising function.[8] Legitimacy is a concept difficult to define. As a virtue of political authority and institutions, it may receive various definitions. A descriptive account of legitimacy refers to people's beliefs about authority and political decisions. Such legitimacy may be found in tradition, charisma or trust. A normative account of legitimacy introduces thresholds or standards that must be fulfilled.[9] Separation of these two

4 M. Fincke, 'Das Verhältnis des Allgemeinen zum Besonderen Teil des Strafrechts', J. Schweitzer Verlag, 1975, p. 90. Although in English criminal law there is no official distinction between a general and special part, see S. Shute, A.P. Simester, 'On the General Part in Criminal Law' in S. Shute, A.P. Simester (eds), 'Criminal Law Theory: Doctrines of the General Part', Oxford University Press, 2002, p. 1; J. Gardner, 'On the General Part of the Criminal Law', in A. Duff (ed), 'Philosophy and the Criminal Law: Principle and Critique', Cambridge University Press, 1998, pp. 207–209.

5 R. Dworkin, 'Taking Rights Seriously', Duckworth, 1977, pp. 24–28.

6 E. Claes, 'Criminal Justice, Legality and Human Dignity', in E. Claes, R. Foqué, T. Peters (eds), 'Punishment, Restorative Justice and the Morality of Law', Intersentia, 2005, pp. 41–44; this is similar to its characteristics as a principle, R. Dworkin, 'Taking Rights Seriously', Duckworth, 1977, p. 26.

7 W.J.M. Voermans, 'Legaliteit als middel tot een doel', in W.J.M. Voermans, M.J. Borgers, C.H. Sieburgh, 'Controverses rondom legaliteit en legitimatie', Kluwer, 2011, pp. 10–14.

8 Ibid., p. 12; also somewhat similarly, L. Besselink, F. Pennings, S. Prechal, 'Introduction: Legality in Multiple Legal Orders', in L. Besselink, F. Pennings, S. Prechal (eds), 'The Eclipse of the Legality Principle in the European Union', Kluwer, 2011, p. 7.

9 P. Fabienne, 'Political Legitimacy', The Stanford Encyclopedia of Philosophy (Winter 2014 Edition), E.N. Zalta (ed), URL http://plato.stanford.edu/archives/win2014/entries/legitimacy/.

accounts can be blurring. Especially in criminal law, legitimacy can be loosely defined as the justification of coercive power or defining what use of coercive powers is permissible. The legitimising function of the principle of legality is to generate specific standards for acquiring legitimacy in criminal law. In particular, it sets the standard of what can be considered legitimate criminal *law* and defines the concept of law as opposed to pure state force. As criminal law is an invasive state action, the legality principle provides certain qualitative standards through which the otherwise illegitimate state power is transformed into *law*. Thus, the first question that the legality principle deals with is: how is criminal law legitimised? There are various ways to approach this question.

Within its legitimising function certain background values, such as individual autonomy, democracy, separation of powers, play an important role, as the legality principle becomes the mechanism by which these values find their way within criminal law. These values are often considered as the theoretical rationales of the legality principle. Hence, authors often associate this principle with the Rule of Law,[10] or as providing democratic legitimacy,[11] attributing legitimised powers to different state-actors,[12] and honouring the communicative value of the law.[13] Consequently, an issue to be considered in any analysis of the legality principle is: what are the principle's theoretical bases and how are these interpreted? By way of example, if the principle of democracy is regarded as the central value, then the legitimacy of criminal law means that parliamentary statutes can be the only source of criminal liability. Thus identifying the theoretical rationales behind the legality principle highlights the ideological character of a state's criminal justice system. In this regard, the legality principle is a meta-principle.[14]

Identifying the theoretical rationales of the legality principle is, however, not enough to explain the legitimising function of this principle. An additional question is to examine how the theoretical rationales can be combined in concrete and structured criminal law theories of legitimacy. It is a different exercise to examine the meaning of the theoretical rationales from discovering how these can inform criminal law legitimacy in particular. Thus, it is also important to engage in an analysis of possible legitimation theories that are based on particular interpretations of the theoretical rationales of this principle.

Alongside the external element, there is a normative internal element to the legality principle that is consequential to the external one.[15] It concerns internal

10 For example F.A. Hayek, 'The Road to Serfdom', Routledge, 1976, p. 61.

11 B. Schünemann, 'Nulla poena sine lege? Rechtstheoretische und verfassungsrechtliche Implikationen der Rechtsgewinnung im Strafrecht', Walter de Gruyter, 1978, p. 2.

12 G. Grünwald, 'Bedeutung und Begründung des Satzes nulla poena sine lege', ZStW, vol. 76, 1964, p. 1.

13 M.J. Borgers, 'De communicatieve strafrechter', in W.J.M. Voermans, M.J. Borgers, C.H. Sieburgh, 'Controverses rondom legaliteit en legitimatie', Kluwer, 2011, p. 162.

14 P. Asp, 'The Substantive Criminal Law Competence of the EU', Jure, 2012, p. 30.

15 W.J.M. Voermans, 'Legaliteit als middel tot een doel', in W.J.M. Voermans, M.J. Borgers, C.H. Sieburgh, 'Controverses rondom legaliteit en legitimatie', Kluwer, 2011, pp. 11–12.

normative questions of criminal justice. Who can make criminal norms? Should such norms be written or unwritten? How precisely should criminal behaviour be described and in which language? Thus, from a normative point of view, the legality principle offers answers to important questions. It is the internal and normative function of the legality principle that authors refer to when they discuss the codifying function of this principle,[16] or the *Gesetzesvorbehalt* (the German doctrine that criminal liability may only be based on statute).[17] The normative and legitimising functions are interconnected. If, for example, one accepts democracy as the main theoretical rationale then, consequently, the parliamentary statute is the primary normative source of criminal liability.

The legality principle's scope of application can be broad. Depending on the situation at hand, it may be defined further. This principle is multi-facial, from which more sub-principles or aspects can be drawn. It may also be approached from different angles.

A first approach is to look at the different qualitative requirements that the legality principle sets for criminal law: 1) there is no crime without a written criminal norm *(nullum crimen sine lege scripta* – or *lex scripta)*, 2) there is no crime without a pre-existing criminal norm *(nullum crimen sine lege praevia* – or *lex praevia)*, 3) there is no crime without a precise criminal norm *(nullum crimen sine lege certa* – or *lex certa)* and 4) finally, there is no crime without a strictly applied norm *(nullum crimen sine lege stricta* – or *lex stricta)*.[18] These four sub-principles are well-known aspects of the legality principle and they are usually the manner in which it is described in criminal law systems.

A second approach is to re-group its above four aspects depending on the state-actor to which they are addressed. For the legislator it provides certain requirements on how the criminal liability should be constructed (a principle for construction of criminal liability). For the executive, it defines the limits of their powers (a competence rule). For courts, the principle defines the scope and limits of judicial interpretation (a principle for judicial interpretation).

A third approach is to look at the dichotomy between the definition of criminal liability and the criminal sanction. As the principle applies to both the definition of criminal liability *(nullum crimen sine lege)* and the criminal sanction *(nulla poena sine lege),* both these elements must be applied and constructed in compliance with the legality principle. Therefore, in addition to the different aspects of the legality principle addressed to state-actors, the principle can be subcategorised further applying to the definition of criminal liability and to punishment.

It is important to clarify the terminology used. The term 'legality principle' is often used in continental systems in accordance with linguistic translations. Thus, one can find the Dutch term *legaliteitsbeginsel* or in German the term, *Gesetzlichkeitsprinzip.* The ECJ also usually refers to the term 'legality principle'

---

16 Ibid., p. 12.

17 BVerfG 1 BvR 718/89, 10 January 1995.

18 H.-L. Schreiber, 'Gesetz und Richter', Alfred Metzner Verlag GmbH, 1976, p. 102.

in its judgements.[19] The principle is also known by its Latin maxim as *nullum crimen nulla poena sine lege*. One should keep in mind that due to the generality of the principle of legality and its various aspects, different terms have been employed by authors and courts, such as *lex certa,* 'there is no crime without law', legal certainty, and non-retroactivity. Often these terms may denote a particular aspect of this principle, but they may also denote the principle of legality as such. To avoid any confusion, I shall adopt the term 'legality principle' instead of the Latin maxim *nullum crimen sine lege*. I shall, however, make use of the Latin maxims *lex scripta, lex certa, lex praevia* and *lex stricta* to denote the different aspects of the legality principle, instead of legal certainty or non-retroactivity.

2. A European *ius puniendi*

European legal integration has reached a point where criminal liability is no longer determined at a national level. There has been a transfer of competence to construct and interpret criminal liability to European state-actors, namely the European institutions. This competence is currently shared with national authorities. Consequently, there are two constitutional levels where two different state-actors function: the European and the national level.[20] In addition, there is also a directly enforceable system in sight, with the planned establishment of the EPPO.[21]

The term substantive European criminal law refers to a cluster or blend of national and European rules.[22] There are definitions of criminal liability found in European instruments (Directives, and formerly Framework Decisions) based on Article 83 para. 1 and 2 TFEU, which aim at the harmonisation of national definitions of criminal liability and the creation of European criminal norms. Regarding Article 83 para. 1 TFEU, the offences for which the EU shares competence with national legislators are specifically listed and are considered serious offences, often with a cross-border dimension, requiring pan-European cooperation and harmonisation of criminal norms. As far as Article 83 para. 2 TFEU is concerned, approximation instruments may be created for the proper enforcement of other EU policies such as the environment or the internal market.[23]

---

19 C–308/06 The Queen, on the application of International Association of Independent Tanker Owners (Intertanko) and Others v Secretary of State for Transport, 3 June 2008, para. 70.

20 Similar in A. Bernardi, 'Nullum crimen, nulla poena sine lege between European law and national law', in M.C. Bassiouni, V. Militello, H. Satzger (eds), 'European cooperation in penal matters: issues and perspectives', Cedam, 2008, pp. 87–117 and 114, where he refers to three levels of law-making process; the ascending, autonomous and descending where national and European rules blend together.

21 Commission Proposal for a Council Regulation on the establishment of the European Public Prosecutor's Office COM (2013) 534 final, 17.7.2013.

22 A. Klip, 'European Criminal Law: An Integrative Approach', Intersentia, 2012, p. 1.

23 C–176/03 Commission of the European Communities v Council of the European Union, 13 September 2005.

The EU is itself employing *ius puniendi* to either combat serious cross-border offences, which have benefitted from the abolition of internal borders, or as a tool to effectively enforce EU policies when deemed necessary.

One of the characteristics of the European *ius puniendi* is that there is shared competence regarding the criminalisation of certain conduct: the EU as a legislator defines the minimum scope of criminalisation (minimum scope means what should be at least criminalised).[24] National legislators are obliged to implement these provisions into national law, but they retain a margin of appreciation: the concept of implementation entails that they are allowed to adjust these rules to national law without, however, making the criminal norm more lenient or narrow in scope. They may also broaden the scope of criminal liability. This distribution of tasks between the European and national legislators means that vital decisions regarding the scope of criminal liability (i.e. what to criminalise and its minimum scope) are in the hands of the European legislator.

The interpretation of criminal norms outlined in Directives is mainly in the hands of European state-actors, namely the ECJ according to Articles 19 TEU and 267 TFEU. The ECJ has a guiding and supervisory role regarding the interpretation and implementation of European criminal legal instruments. Its guiding role consists of the competence to interpret the scope of criminal liability found in Directives for the assistance of the national courts. National courts may interpret the provisions of Directives themselves but it is the ECJ that provides an independent and autonomous interpretation of the terms used and the scope of criminal liability in those instruments.[25]

The supervisory role of the ECJ consists of assessing the validity of Directives and whether Member States have met their obligation to implement the legislation. In particular, decisions regarding the validity of Directives are solely in the hands of the ECJ and therefore a Directive can be declared void if it violates principles of European legal order, including the principle of legality (Articles 263, 264 and 267 TFEU). Furthermore, the ECJ is also competent to assess whether a Member State met its obligations regarding the implementation of a Directive on criminal law (Articles 258–259 TFEU).

The scope of national criminal liability and choices made can be reviewed by European actors differently. The implementation of criminal law Directives is to be guided not only by national law but also by EU law. According to the principles of

24 H.G. Nilsson, 'How to combine minimum rules with maximum legal certainty?', Europättslig Tidskrift, 2011, pp. 663–675.

25 Recommendations to national courts and tribunals in relation to the initiation of preliminary ruling proceedings 2012 OJ C 338, 6.11.2012, pp. 1–6; an example of such autonomous interpretation can be seen in C–308/06 The Queen, on the application of International Association of Independent Tanker Owners (Intertanko) and Others v Secretary of State for Transport, 3 June 2008.

sincere cooperation[26] and effective application of EU law,[27] national legislation must be in line with EU law and enforce it effectively. A vague criminal provision found in national implementing legislation can compromise these principles and, thus, the principle of legality has been included in the guidelines of the Commission and in ECJ case law as a principle with which the ECJ can supervise national implementation efforts.[28]

Conclusively, one can argue that there is a distinctive European *ius puniendi* where: (i) there seems to be a will for distinct policy choices regarding criminalisation; (ii) criminal liability per se is construed and interpreted to a great extent at the European level; (iii) national implementing legislation is evaluated in the context of European standards by the ECJ and national courts; (iv) to these one should add the forthcoming EPPO, which shall be a system of direct enforcement.

3. The need for a European legality principle

As explained above, the principle of legality has a legitimising and a normative role for a criminal system. Its application reflects certain legal theories and values, which define the ideological character of a criminal justice system. The ECJ has already recognised the legality principle – and its various aspects – as a general principle of EU law.[29] However, it is unclear how the principle of legality legitimises the European criminal justice system, whereas, its normative role presents lacunae and inconsistencies.

3.1. The legitimacy of the European *ius puniendi*

The establishment of a European *ius puniendi* raises many questions as to its legitimacy, purpose and compliance with the Rule of Law.[30] As the European state-actors create and define criminal norms, they become accountable to European citizens regarding the use of their respective powers. A persistent criticism is the lack of a consistent and coherent common European criminal policy, common understanding of the principles guiding the construction, and application of EU criminal legislation.[31]

---

26 A. Klip, 'European Criminal Law: An Integrative Approach', Intersentia, 2012, pp. 16–17.

27 M. Ross, 'Effectiveness in the European Legal Order(s): Beyond Supremacy to Constitutional Proportionality?', European Law Review, vol. 31, 2006, pp. 476–498; M. Accetto, S. Zleptnig, 'The Principle of Effectiveness: Rethinking its Role in Community Law', European Public Law, vol. 11, 2005, pp. 375–403.

28 Report from the Commission of the Council Framework Decision of 28 May 2001 combating fraud and counterfeiting of non-cash means of payment, COM (2004) 346 final, 30.4.2004.

29 E.g. Case 80/86 criminal proceedings against Kolpinghuis Nijmegen BV, 8 October 1987.

30 European Criminal Policy Initiative, 'A Manifesto on European Criminal Policy', ZIS, vol. 12, 2009, pp. 707–716.

31 Ibid.; Commission Communication, Towards an EU criminal policy Ensuring the effective implementation of EU policies through criminal law, COM (2011) 573, 20.09.2011, pp. 3 and 12.

The motivation to effectively combat crime or enforce European policies has resulted in the use of criminal law as a tool for public policy. The current legitimacy of European *ius puniendi* seems to be largely based on instrumental goals.[32] This results in the absence of a properly defined and coherent view of European criminal law.[33] The fact that the Treaties establish EU competence of *ius puniendi* is not necessarily a sufficient reason to consider such power legitimate.[34] What is missing is a debate about the legitimate basis of European criminal law and the roles of principles such as democracy, separation of powers, and individual liberty.[35] Is there a protective aspect to European *ius puniendi?* Or does it only facilitate the enforcement of EU law? Does it aim to protect individual autonomy from the arbitrary use of criminal law by state-actors? As such, the development of an autonomous European concept of the principle of legality would greatly facilitate the legitimacy of the European *ius puniendi* and the place of the Rule of Law in the EU's legal order.

What is more, it was mentioned that the legality principle has an important normative function within criminal justice systems: who can legitimately create criminal norms within the EU? Can the ECJ change or extensively interpret criminal norms? Should Directives creating criminal liability satisfy certain requirements regarding precision and retroactivity? The European criminal justice system functions at two-levels (the European and national); this element further complicates the application of the legality principle. There are questions regarding the interrelation of the two levels and the distribution of obligations that this principle generates. What qualities regarding certainty and retroactivity should national implementing measures have in order to be considered correct? Are there any methods for implementation that are better than others? Is a Directive prescribing criminal liability valid even if it is not published? In what languages should decisions be published? Some of these questions have already been answered by the ECJ, though in a fragmented manner not forming a coherent theory on a European legality principle. For example the ECJ has stated that the definition of criminal liability can be determined via judicial interpretation,[36] yet when it comes to implementation it usually favours statutory implementation.[37] The application of the legality principle in EU law is fragmented and there is no clear picture of the normative role of the principle of legality in the European criminal justice system.

---

32 Chapter VII para. 3.2.

33 European Criminal Policy Initiative, 'A Manifesto on European Criminal Policy', ZIS, vol.12, 2009, pp. 707–716.

34 M. Kaiafa-Gbandi, 'Approximation of substantive criminal law provisions in the EU and fundamental principles of criminal law', in F. Galli, A. Weyembergh, 'Approximation of substantive criminal law in the EU: the way forward', IEE, 2013, p. 88.

35 J. Blomsma, C. Peristeridou, 'The way forward: a general part of European criminal law', in F. Galli, A. Weyembergh, 'Approximation of substantive criminal law in the EU: the way forward', IEE, 2013, pp. 123–124.

36 T–99/04 AC Treuhand AG v Commission of the European Communities, 8 July 2008.

37 Report from the Commission of the Council Framework Decision of 28 May 2001 combating fraud and counterfeiting of non-cash means of payment, COM (2004) 346 final, 30.4.2004.

3.2. An autonomous European legality or national concepts?

Whereas the legality principle in EU law is important, one could question whether the existence of a distinct and autonomous principle, specific to EU criminal law, is necessary. Could national legality principles suffice? Could a national legality principle adequately deal with the tensions created by the partial transfer of the *ius puniendi* to the European level?

Whether one decides to use national interpretations of the legality principle as opposed to a purely European one, due to the recognition of the legality principle as a general principle of EU law, it is bound to have a European autonomous meaning in practice.[38] In any case, the problem is whether national concepts of legality could even legitimise and normatively influence the European *ius puniendi.*

First of all, there is the problem of binding EU institutions to nationally-based principles and meta-norms. This problem results from the independence and autonomy of the European legal order and system.[39] European institutions and rules cannot be governed by principles that belong to a different constitutional legal order. The national interpretation of the legality principle as such is inappropriate in the context of the EU: the Dutch perception of the limits of judicial interpretation cannot bind the ECJ, when for example it interprets the term 'serious negligence' found in a Directive. Neither can a German concept of *lex certa* be applied by the European legislator unless such a principle is recognised at the European level. Even when European instruments are applied within a national system, national conceptions of legality can only have a limited effect.[40] The European and national orders are separate in this regard, and unless the principle of legality has its own European standing and context, the existing national concepts cannot bind the actions of the European bodies. EU institutions function in conformity with EU norms, and their acts comply with European principles and rules.[41]

Secondly, the legality principle as it is understood in national systems may be incompatible with the existence of a European supranational criminal justice system; it is ultimately an issue of compatibility. For example, the German approach towards the legality principle emphasises the democratic source of criminal liability. Within the EU, criminal norms, which used to be solely produced by the Council, were thus considered problematic under the German legality principle. Now that the European Parliament has decisive control in the decision-making process, this problem has been remedied somewhat although it is not totally

38 C–261/09 Gaetano Mantello, 16 November 2010, para. 38.

39 Case 26/62 NV Algemene Transport- en Expeditie Onderneming van Gend & Loos v Netherlands Inland Revenue Administration, 5 February 1963.

40 M. Verhoeven, R. Widdershoven, 'National legality and European Obligations', in L. Besselink, F. Pennings, S. Prechal (eds), 'The Eclipse of the Legality Principle in the European Union', Kluwer, 2011, p. 69.

41 Ibid., p. 56.

solved.[42] This does not necessarily mean that a German concept of the legality principle cannot be adopted at the EU level. The issue of compatibility means that such application cannot happen automatically. Ultimately, the problem lies with the interpretation of the theoretical rationales of the legality principle. One would need to either adjust the legality principle to the European constitutional framework and/ or adjust this constitutional framework to the legality principle. As the institutional dynamics and existing decision-making in the EU are relatively inflexible, the legality principle, as understood in national jurisdictions, may not be capable of adoption at EU level without modifications.

Thirdly, the national concept of the legality principle has its own limitations and it may struggle to deal with the legitimacy problems created by a supranational system. A national concept of legality addresses the conflict of the particular nation state and individual autonomy. Issues with foreseeability due to the discrepancies in criminal provisions amongst states or due to different linguistic regimes cannot be fully managed. In a supranational regime additional questions may arise.[43] For example, is it a problem that individuals may not know which criminal code to consult when there are conflicting rules of jurisdiction?

These problems arising from cross-border activity cannot be covered by the legality principle as it is used at the national level. One cannot help but wonder whether the European *ius puniendi* can result in a different understanding of concepts such as individual autonomy and democracy, which cannot be addressed by national ideas on legality. It is important to point out that the Treaties have created certain rights for individuals regarding freedom of movement. Respect for these rights has been very closely observed and enforced by the ECJ. One could wonder for example whether freedom of movement could inform the protective functions of European criminal law. Can one expect from individuals who regularly cross borders to be acquainted with national legislation and, even more, jurisprudence? These questions cannot be answered within a national setting. One should consider the possibility that the Treaties and the European *ius puniendi* may create a different theoretical basis for this principle, inspired by the four freedoms and the principle of non-discrimination on the basis of nationality, a type of protection that transcends nation states.

Conclusively, a European legality principle seems not only necessary but, most importantly, desirable. The legitimacy of the European *ius puniendi* is neither an automatic result of the Treaties, nor can it result from the application of the national legality principle. What is more, the creation of an autonomous European legality principle shall contribute significantly to the much needed shift of European criminal law, from a piece-meal system, to a structured and principled system. In such a shift, the powers of EU actors would be based on an interpretation of

---

42 M. Kaiafa-Gbandi, 'Approximation of substantive criminal law provisions in the EU and fundamental principles of criminal law', in F. Galli, A. Weyembergh, 'Approximation of substantive criminal law in the EU: the way forward', IEE, 2013, pp. 99–100.

43 F. Meyer, 'Strafrechtsgenese in Internationalen Organisationen', Nomos, 2012, pp. 642–643.

European democracy, a European separation of powers, and a European conception of individual autonomy.

4. Research questions

4.1. General research question

The aim of this book is to present a European theory of the legality principle. The starting point is that the principle of legality in EU law has an independent (from national systems) and distinctive context and function. However, this research builds upon the existing status of the principle: such an independent interpretation has already been partly outlined by the ECJ. Existing jurisprudential fragments on the application of the legality principle in EU law will be gathered, criticised and further developed so that the European legality principle will be the result of a coherent and complete analysis of the European context. Therefore the general research question shall be:

> *'How should a European legality principle be constructed and applied in European substantive criminal law?'*

This contribution shall deal with the principle of legality as a meta-norm determining the scope, application, and interpretation of criminal liability in EU law. As explained, the legality principle has legitimising and normative functions. Because they are interrelated, both roles of the legality principle shall be investigated. For discovering how this principle legitimises the use of the European *ius puniendi,* the theoretical rationales and the characteristics of European criminal justice shall be dealt with. Is the principle of legality a doctrine that can function in single-systemic level, or is it possible that it can also be applied in a multi-level system? Moreover, this research shall also focus on the normative application of the legality principle in EU law, by reference to its specific constituent elements and the obligations resulting from them.

It should be noted that this research is part of the project 'Towards a General Part for Criminal Law for the EU', which has been taking place at Maastricht University since 2007 and is comprised of the independent work of researchers on the elements of a proposed European general part of criminal law. This research shall contribute to the on-going dialogue regarding the function of principles of justice and other fundamental rights in European criminal law.[44]

---

[44] For example, A.B. Schaut, 'Europäische Strafrechtsprinzipien', Nomos, 2012, pp. 125–177; P. Beauvais, 'Le principe de la légalité pénale dans le droit de l'Union européenne', Thèse, Université Paris X Nanterre UFR, 1 December 2006; European Criminal Policy Initiative, 'A Manifesto on European Criminal Policy', ZIS, vol. 12, 2009, pp. 707–716.

Certain clarification regarding the scope of application of the principle in EU law is in order. A European legality principle would apply to European substantive criminal law. But what does this term encompass?

Firstly, a European legality principle would apply to European instruments (Directives) and it would guide their construction and interpretation. This includes Directives based on Article 83 para. 1 and 2 TFEU, and Regulations based on Article 325 TFEU regarding fraud (if such a provision can generate competence regarding criminal law Regulations, something which is rather debated).[45] This means that the legality principle would be a principle guiding the construction of criminal liability for the European legislator and a principle guiding the interpretation of those instruments by the ECJ. It would bind both the European legislator and ECJ.

Secondly, a European legality principle would generate guidelines regarding the proper implementation of Directives into national criminal law (whether these are criminal law Directives or not), and therefore it shall also guide national legislators and courts when dealing with implementing legislation. This is because national authorities are obliged to respect all European rules, including the general principles of EU law and the Charter, when they implement EU obligations.[46] One may argue that there is a conflict between national conceptions of the legality principle and the proposed European legality principle. This may certainly be the case. A system where the national legality principle allows for judicially made criminal liability might have to apply different standards when it implements EU legislation into criminal law. The European legality principle therefore might impose some further obligations on some national systems. However, this is not something new when it comes to EU law.

Having said that, it should be made clear that this research does not aim to replace the national concepts of the legality principle. Maintaining national legal cultures is an important thesis for any project of integration. However, the coexistence of European and national legal orders could imply the cohabitation of two different interpretations of the legality principle within one system. Certainly, the question of what falls within the scope of EU law is not always clear.[47] However, one should keep in mind that the principle of legality is broadly similar amongst Member States. It will be seen that the interpretation of this principle in the chosen national systems of this research has been converging significantly, especially due to the influence of the ECtHR jurisprudence.[48] In any case, if different applications of the legality principle exist in one system, this might increase the chance of a

---

45 R. Sicurella, 'Some reflections on the need for a general theory of the competence of the European Union in criminal law', in A. Klip (ed), 'Substantive Criminal Law of the European Union', Maklu, 2011, p. 239.

46 C–112/00 Eugen Schmidberger, Internationale Transporte und Planzüge v Republik Österreich, 12 June 2003.

47 N. de Boer, 'Addressing rights divergences under the Charter: Melloni', Common Market Law Review, vol. 50, 2013, pp. 1094–1096.

48 Chapter IV para. 9.2.

cross-fertilisation and incremental alignment of legal cultures and national conceptions of the legality principle and its EU counterpart. However, this depends on whether the national systems accept such a course. It should be kept in mind that national legal traditions are not stable or static.[49] They are themselves products of various historical influences and are constantly in flux. In a cohabitation of two different legal orders, the European and the national, a bottom-up and top-down cross-fertilisation is inevitable.

Finally, this research aims at balancing continuity with change. The EU criminal justice system is still evolving. It should be noted that the whole EU project of an ever-closer Union is characterised by fluidity. There is a tendency towards further European integration and yet there are hiccups along the way.[50] This research and its conclusions shall be based on the current Treaties and their institutional framework. Hypothetical futuristic possibilities (such as the complete abolishment of national criminal orders for example) will not be dealt with.

4.2. Limitations of the research

There are certain limitations to this research that should be explained regarding the scope of the principle of legality.

Firstly, by principle of legality I refer to the principle that determines the scope, interpretation and application of criminal liability. This is to be distinguished from a procedural principle of legality, which governs the prosecution of criminal offences and the discretion of the prosecutor, something that is not a part of this book.[51] Questions regarding whether the EPPO should prosecute, or what the limits of discretion are in this regard, are of procedural nature and shall not be dealt with.

Secondly, in this research I shall focus only on the application of the legality principle to the definition and imposition of criminal liability and not to sanctions. Hence questions regarding the retroactivity or precision of sanctions fall outside the scope of this research. Criminal sentencing requires a different kind of research into the vast systemic particularities of national legal orders, the influence of procedural law, and the analysis of statistics on sanctioning and of judicial practice, something which cannot be accomplished within the time-frame of this project.

Thirdly, this research shall focus mainly on the application of the principle of legality to courts and the legislature. Therefore I will approach legality as a

49 J. Blomsma, C. Peristeridou, 'The way forward: a general part of European criminal law', in F. Galli, A. Weyembergh, 'Approximation of substantive criminal law in the EU: the way forward', IEE, 2013, p. 130.

50 E. Baker, 'The United Kingdom and its Protocol 36 Opt-out: Is Police and Judicial Cooperation in Criminal Matters within the EU losing Momentum?', European Journal of Crime, Criminal law and Criminal Justice, vol. 21, 2013, pp. 237–245.

51 It goes without saying that it is the principle of legality in criminal law that is the topic of this research and not its application to administrative or tax law, G.P. Fletcher, 'Basic Concepts of Criminal Law', Oxford University Press, 1998, pp. 206–214.

principle for the guidance of the construction of criminal liability and judicial interpretation.[52] An investigation regarding the role of the executive in criminal law and the conditions under which the executive might have legislative function shall not be included. This is justified not only due to the complexities and differences of the position of executive bodies in national systems, but also due to the lack of any current, directly enforceable EU system comparable to the one of national systems.

Finally, the principle of retroactive application of more lenient penalties or criminal liability, the so-called *lex mitior,* also falls outside the scope of this research. This principle is often associated with the legality principle, however, they are different principles. *Lex mitior* is interpreted from Article 7 ECHR,[53] and codified in Article 49 of the Charter, yet its relationship with the legality principle is debated.[54] Its *ratio* is also debated; for example, it may be based on the idea that the newer legislation is 'better law', as well as on grounds of equality and fairness.[55] Often in national law, it is discussed as a principle guiding rules of transition. The main difference from the legality principle is that, whereas the legality principle protects against arbitrariness, the *lex mitior* provides a benefit to the individual. Including the *lex mitior* would make it necessary to establish why this principle could be one of the constituent elements of the legality principle. However, such an analysis shall not be carried in this book.

4.3. Outline

This research shall be divided into two main parts. Part 2, shall deal predominantly with national legal systems and how the principle of legality is approached and applied in national law. Part 3 shall deal with the principle of legality in EU law by illustrating current problems, making certain doctrinal choices, and elaborating on how it should be conceived and applied.

4.3.1. The application of the principle in national law

Part 2 is comprised of Chapters III, IV and V. The aim of Part 2 is to identify an approximation of the principle of legality in national systems, which can be employed as a backbone for a European legality principle. In doing so, this part will be divided into three Chapters, each with a different purpose.

Chapter III analyses the theoretical rationales of the legality principle and its development from the birth of this principle in the Enlightenment era. As explained, analysing the legitimising function of this principle requires first that the theoretical

52 See above para. 1.
53 ECtHR Scoppola v Italy, App. 10249/03, 17 September 2009.
54 Opinion AG Kokott of 14 October 2004 in joined cases C–387/02, C–391/02 and C–403/02 criminal proceedings against Silvio Berlusconi *et al.*, 3 May 2005, para. 154–168.
55 J. de Hullu, 'Materieel strafrecht', Kluwer, 2012, pp. 125–126.

rationales of the principle be examined. The aim of this Chapter is twofold: first to identify the theoretical justifications for this principle and second, to discuss their various interpretations. As it will be seen, the legality principle is not a mere collection of 'do's and don'ts' in criminal law, but it carries with it certain values: individual autonomy, democracy, the separation of powers and *Rechtsstaat*. This Chapter delves deeper into the interpretation of these concepts and the different ways to approach them. Starting with an exposition of the possible interpretations of the theoretical rationales of this principle is important as the national systems may approach these concepts differently. The main question to be answered in this Chapter is: what are the theoretical rationales of the legality principle and how could they be interpreted?

With regard to individual autonomy, the question that arises is what exactly the meaning of individual autonomy is. Is individual autonomy only considered as an individual sphere to be protected from the intrusiveness of the state? Or, is there a reason to protect violations from other members of society? The concept of individual autonomy shall be analysed alongside similar concepts, such as liberty, human dignity and its importance in the formation of society. Regarding the principle of democracy, two different interpretations of democracy shall be presented. Is democracy a mere procedure? Or does it also entail a certain substantive mirroring of the individual's participation in the social contract? As far as the principle of separation of powers is concerned, the main question shall be to decipher Montesquieu's contribution, which has inspired the legality principle, and juxtapose different interpretations of his theories. Is the separation of powers a doctrine about separating state-actors or balancing them? Finally, with regard to the Rule of Law, different approaches and definitions shall be analysed in an attempt to understand the core of this concept.

Chapter IV shall be about the current *modus operandi* of the principle in national law. The aim is to observe how the principle is conceived and applied and what the existing problems are in national law. The research question to answer in this Chapter shall be: how is this principle interpreted and applied in national law and what problems arise in its application? This Chapter starts with an analysis of how the principle of legality is conceived in national systems and the main differences therein. It will continue with an analysis of the ECtHR's jurisprudence and its influence on national law. In the final part of this Chapter, the application of this principle will be observed in practice. It will be shown that the legality principle in national systems faces erosion with certain well-documented oxymora and paradoxes. In other words, the principle does not operate as it is theoretically conceived. The current issues shall be presented in a problem-based fashion so that the nature of the difficulties can be better understood.

In Chapter V, the *modus operandi* will be put into the perspective of the current philosophical trends regarding the legitimacy of criminal law. Three abstract models of criminal justice will be presented (the classical, instrumentalist and relational). These models are artificial, philosophical constructions that answer the question of how criminal law is legitimised. They are constructed based on different assumptions regarding the legitimation of criminal law and law in general. For each model, the theoretical rationales of the principle of legality may be interpreted differently. Thus, the different interpretations of individual autonomy, democracy, the Rule of Law and separation of powers as illustrated in Chapter III, shall be of use for Chapter V. These models shall be evaluated based on merit and in relation to the practical and theoretical problems that the legality principle faces, as these are explained in Chapter IV. The necessity for using different models of legitimacy stems from the assumption that the legality principle may elicit different interpretations and functions. In order to identify what type of legitimacy this principle should offer, one must consider what type of criminal justice must be defended. As will be explained, these models of criminal justice are based on existing theoretical models found in scholarship.[56] However, they are only philosophical constructs and they do not represent reality. Packer, who engaged in a similar intellectual exercise, explains that creating different models of legitimacy helps to *'perceive the normative antinomy at the heart of the criminal law. These models are not labelled Is and Ought, nor are they to be taken in that sense.'*[57]

Their purpose in this contribution is threefold. First, they facilitate the understanding of the development and problems of the legality principle, as these are identified in Chapter IV. Second, they provide for remedies in order to solve existing problems. Third, they offer a critical and, most importantly, transparent philosophical framework within which the legality principle operates. The advantage in using models of legitimation in addition to the theoretical rationales in Chapter III is that the models offer transparency regarding, for example, the influence that every version of democracy or individual autonomy has on the function of the legality principle. They also reveal how the theoretical rationales interact with each other. Most importantly, as these models are based on existing theories of legitimacy, they reflect different perspectives on the purpose and nature of the law. For example, if the assumption is that criminal law finds legitimacy in its effectiveness and contemporary value, then courts should be able to have more increased powers than the courts in another system where criminal law finds legitimacy in its already agreed context. Contemplating these possibilities within the structured environment of artificial models of legitimacy is more transparent and open to critical review. Therefore the main research question in Chapter V is: How does the principle of legality legitimise the criminal justice system? In this Chapter, the results of both Chapters III and IV shall be discussed. Is criminal law legitimised only when the principle of legality assumes the protection of individual autonomy *vis-à-vis* arbitrariness? Is this what makes a pure state force something which is called law? Or, is criminal law also legitimised through the protection of

56 For example, R. Foqué, A.C. 't Hart, 'Instrumentaliteit en Rechtsbescherming', Gouda Quint, Kluwer, 1990, p. 17; H.L. Packer, 'The Limits of the Criminal Sanction', Stanford University Press, 1968, p. 153; R. Dworkin, 'Law's Empire', Hart Publishing, 2006, pp. 114–275.

57 H.L. Packer, 'The Limits of the Criminal Sanction', Stanford University Press, 1968, p. 153.

individual autonomy from horizontal conflicts? Are principles of justice, such as legality, simply important public policies?

4.3.2. A European legality principle

Part 3 is comprised of Chapters VI, VII, and VIII and deals with the legality principle in EU law. Chapter VI shall explain the current position of the legality principle in EU law and its challenges. The approach of Chapter VI is similar to Chapter IV as its aim is to understand the current *modus operandi* of the legality principle but in EU law. As the EU system is far from comprehensive, the current picture of the legality principle shall be only fragmentary. The problems that occur shall be also presented in a problem-based fashion in order to illustrate the deficiencies.

Chapters VII and VIII aim to reconstruct the principle of legality at the EU level. In Chapter VII the legitimacy of European criminal law shall be discussed. Such legitimacy is interrelated with the legitimacy of the European legal order in general. Questions such as the concept of statehood, the possibility to have a criminal justice system transcending the nation state and the interrelation between the two levels of decision-making shall be analysed. Furthermore, I shall reconstruct the European criminal justice system with view to the different models presented in the end of Part 2. Accordingly, the different theoretical rationales and consequences of a legitimate European criminal justice system shall be analysed.

Chapter VIII shall delve deeper into the nature and function of the European legality principle in a legitimate European criminal justice system. Questions and problems identified in Chapter VI shall be answered and further functions of the legality principle shall be elaborated upon. What are its core constituent elements? How should it be applied? What obligations should it address to the EU and national state-actors? In particular, the legitimising and normative function of the legality principle shall be analysed and further important questions regarding the distribution of the *ius puniendi* between the European and national levels shall be answered. This Chapter shall end with general conclusions of this book and final considerations for future developments.

Chapter II
Methodology

The present academic contribution does not start from scratch. A European legality principle already exists, albeit a fragmentary one. This principle did not emerge from a vacuum but from the national legal traditions. This research shall therefore follow the methodology with which the ECJ has utilised the principle of legality from national systems and adapted it to the EU context. In particular, the principle of legality in EU law has a twofold status. It is recognised as a general principle of EU law, and more recently, it has been codified as a fundamental right in Article 49 of the Charter. As a general principle of EU law, the principle of legality was developed through ECJ judgements throughout the 1980s.[1] General principles of law exist in most Western legal systems and are sources of law filling gaps of legislation. This can happen through a specific reference to legal texts (such as Article 7 para. 2 ECHR which refers to the general principles of law recognised in civilised nations) or spontaneously by courts.[2] Here one should be careful with terminology and distinguish 'general principles of EU law' from the 'general principles of law' in a specific legal system or international law (as in Article 7 para. 2 ECHR). The former represent specific documented principles developed by the ECJ. General principles of EU law have a tripartite function: they are an aid to the interpretation of EU law, grounds for review of European and national implementing legal instruments, and their breach can establish a claim for damages.[3]

The status of the legality principle as a general principle of EU law is essential for the methodological approach of this research. The general principles of EU law have a dual origin: they stem from common constitutional traditions of the Member States and international conventions, the primary influence being the ECHR. The ECJ usually performs a comparative analysis in order to identify whether a principle is accepted within Member States' national legal orders and examines the ECHR as well. However, when these principles are recognised at the EU level and are adopted as part of EU law, they are instilled with a uniform and autonomous interpretation that may differ from that used in national legal orders;[4] hence the principles are adapted and integrated into the EU's legal system.

1 E.g. Case 80/86 criminal proceedings against Kolpinghuis Nijmegen BV, 8 October 1987.

2 T. Tridimas, 'The General Principles of EU law', Oxford University Press, 2006, p. 17.

3 Ibid., pp. 29–35.

4 For example, the *ne bis in idem* principle, see C–187/01 and C–385/01 criminal proceedings against Gözütok and Brügge, 11 February 2003.

1. Legal transplants, cross-fertilisation and Europeanisation of legal doctrines

How can the practice of the ECJ be approached methodologically? The development of a general principle of EU law involves researching national legal systems shaped by ECHR standards in a comparative and representative manner and adapting the candidate principle to the European legal order. From a methodological point of view, this adaptation of principles from one legal order to another is known as a legal transplant. Legal transplants have been defined: *'as the moving of a rule or a system of law from one country to another, of from one people to another'*.[5] These are, essentially, rules, principles or institutions taken from one legal system and transplanted to another. In comparative law and methodology the main focus has been on horizontal legal transplants (between national systems). However, vertical legal transplants (from national to supranational/international order) have been receiving increased attention.[6]

The concept of legal transplants is abstract and controversial. There are some questions as to whether they are viable and whether they imply a rigid copy-paste; this begs the question whether a viable legal transplant – which is not a rigid copy-paste but it is adapted – can be considered as a true legal transplant in the first place.[7] Especially in the context of EU law, it has been pointed out that any transplantation of legal concepts from the national to the European legal order requires adaptation of the legal principles concerned.[8] Other academic contributions on the function of the legality principle at EU level have already pointed out that national conceptions of the legality principle need to be adapted if transplanted to the EU level.[9] Criticism of the viability of legal transplants can be rebutted by the practice of the ECJ; it has long been well-documented that EU law has evolved partly by the ECJ transplanting national legal rules or principles from the domestic to the EU legal order.[10]

---

5 A. Watson, 'Legal Transplants', Scottish Academic Press Ltd., 1974, p. 21.

6 F. Bignami, 'Rethinking the Legal Foundations of the European Constitutional Order: the Lessons of the New Historical Research', American University International Law Review, vol. 28, 2013, p. 1323; J.M. Smits, 'The Harmonisation of Private Law in Europe: Some Insights from Evolutionary Theory', Special Volume in honour of Alan Watson, Georgia Journal of International and Comparative Law, vol. 31, 2002, pp. 79–99.

7 P. Legrand, 'The Impossibility of Legal Transplants', Maastricht Journal of European and Comparative Law, vol. 4, 1997, pp. 117–118.

8 R. Dehousse, 'Comparing National and EC Law: the Problem of the Level Analysis', American Journal of Comparative law, vol. 42, 1994, pp. 777–778.

9 P. Beauvais, 'Le principe de la légalité pénale dans le droit de l'Union européenne', Thèse, Université Paris X Nanterre UFR, 1 December 2006, p. 29.

10 T. Koopmans, 'The Birth of European law at the Crossroads of Legal Traditions', American Journal of Comparative law, vol. 39, 1991, pp. 497–498; G. Anthony, 'The Europeanisation of United Kingdom Public Law', in R. Harmsen, T.M. Vilson (eds), 'Europeanisation: Institutions, Identities and Citizenship', Editions Rodopi B.V., 2000, p. 90.

The dispute regarding whether a legal transplant is a rigid copy-paste has given rise to some reconciling theories. According to these theories, borrowing legal concepts between two systems should be regarded as the less rigid and more flexible concept of legal cross-fertilisation. While legal transplants might entail certain level of rigidity, legal cross-fertilisation is *'a different, more indirect process. It implies that an external stimulus promotes an evolution within the receiving legal system. The evolution involves an internal adaptation by the receiving legal system in its own way. The new development is a distinctive [...] product of that system rather a bolt-on.'*[11] This view on legal transplants implies that full transplantation is not necessary and an internal adaptation of the principle is inherent to this method. Moreover, cross-fertilisation can be viewed as a positive and deliberate, yet fluid process that mutually influences closely interacting legal orders.[12]

Whereas it is not my intention to participate to the scholarly dialogue regarding the true definition of legal transplants and their level of rigidity, I shall adopt the method of legal cross-fertilisation. It entails a more dynamic perspective, which takes into consideration the integration of legal principles transplanted into the European legal order and therefore reflects better the attitude of the ECJ. Often, this process has been described as a form of 'bottom-up' Europeanisation of legal concepts, in the sense that national concepts receive a distinctive European legal meaning.[13] The influence of EU law on national law (top-down Europeanisation) has also been discussed extensively as cross-fertilisation in academic literature.[14]

The view of legal cross-fertilisation as a more dynamic approach implies a bottom-up approach. It indicates the existence of three stages: the identification of the function of the legality principle in national criminal justice systems; the identification of the existing fragments of the legality principle in the EU legal order; and a synthesis which involves an acclimatisation or 'internal adaptation' of the two previous steps to the European legal system.[15]

2. National legal research: the national nucleus of the legality principle

The common constitutional traditions of Member States play a critical role in the development of the principle of legality in EU law. An examination of the history of

---

11 J. Bell, 'Mechanisms of Cross-fertilization of Administrative Law in Europe', in J. Beatson, T. Tridimas (eds), 'New Directions in European Public law', Hart Publishing, 1998, p. 147.

12 E. Smith, 'Give and Take: Cross-fertilisation of Concepts in Constitutional Law', in J. Beatson, T. Tridimas (eds), 'New Directions in European Public Law', Hart Publishing, 1998, p. 102.

13 The concept of Europeanisation has been used in literature in various ways, see L.P. Olsen, 'The Many Faces of Europeanization', Journal of Common Market Studies, vol. 40, 2002, pp. 921–952.

14 J.W.F. Allison, 'Transplantation and Cross-fertilisation', in J. Beatson, T. Tridimas (eds), 'New Directions in European Public Law', Hart Publishing, 1998, pp. 169–182.

15 E. Smith, 'Give and Take: Cross-fertilisation of Concepts in Constitutional Law', in J. Beatson, T. Tridimas (eds), 'New Directions in European Public Law', Hart Publishing, 1998, p. 105.

the ECJ's jurisprudence highlights the importance of aligning the legal order of the EU with the constitutional values of its Member States.[16] A supranational criminal justice system, which has certain law-making competences, cannot ignore principles and values of the Member States. Therefore, the national nucleus of the legality principle in EU law has the particular role of legitimising the EU as a harmonious union of criminal justice systems. Furthermore, inspiration had to come from somewhere.[17] In particular, various current EU principles and norms have been borrowed from legal systems of Member States.[18] In EU law, comparative law has been seen as a method for lacuna filling.[19] Practically speaking, the recognition and development of a general principle of EU law depends on the degree of convergence of national criminal justice systems.[20] In the case of the legality principle, it will be seen that there is a strong convergence amongst legal systems, especially because of the influence of the ECHR on national legal systems. The ECJ follows the 'large majority rule' in developing general principles of EU law and an evaluative approach is used to develop principles reflecting trends amongst national orders.[21] Thus, the ECJ was able to accept for example the *lex mitior* principle[22] and the prohibition of analogy[23] as parts of EU law, based upon the convergence of Member States' criminal justice systems (despite the English system not recognising the *lex mitior* and the Danish system allowing analogical reasoning in criminal law).[24] The impact of the majority rule on the legal systems of these two countries accordingly is yet to be established.[25] Pragmatism and policy objectives might also play a role in the recognition of general principles of EU law.[26]

---

16 K. Lenaerts, J.A. Gutiérrez-Fons, 'The Constitutional Allocation of Powers and General Principles of EU law', Common Market Law Review, vol. 47, 2010, p. 1632.

17 F. Bignami, 'Rethinking the Legal Foundations of the European Constitutional Order: the Lessons of the New Historical Research', American University International Law Review, vol. 28, 2013, p. 1326.

18 M. Kiikeri, 'Comparative legal reasoning and European law', Kluwer, 2001, pp. 105–107.

19 Ibid., p. 104.

20 K. Lenaerts, J.A. Gutiérrez-Fons, 'The Constitutional Allocation of Powers and General Principles of EU law', Common Market Law Review, vol. 47, 2010, p. 1633.

21 Ibid., pp. 1634–1635.

22 Where the Court used the common legal traditions to establish *lex mitior* as a general principle of EU law in absence of any ECtHR case law that would support such view, joined cases C–387/02, C–391/02 and C–403/02 criminal proceedings against Silvio Berlusconi *et al.*, 3 May 2005.

23 Joined cases C–189/02 P, 202/02 P, 208/02 P *et al.* Dansk Rørindustri A/S *et al.*, 28 June 2005; C–105/03 criminal proceedings against Maria Pupino, 16 June 2005.

24 Article 1 of the Danish Criminal Code. For English law see B. Juratowitch, 'Retroactivity and the Common Law', Hart Publishing, 2008, pp. 115–118.

25 Also in other Member States, see on the *lex mitior* in the Dutch system HR 12 July 2011 NJ 2012, 78 annotation by N. Keijzer.

26 In the area of sanctioning for violations of competition law, the ECJ refused to look into the possibility that there is a common principle to the Member States to prescribe a fixed maximum to a penalty. If such a principle would be ever found to be common, the framework of sanctioning

On a practical note, such comparative research is typically conducted by the AGs in their Opinions. The ECJ rarely uses comparative reasoning per se but, rather, refers to 'legal traditions' *in abstracto*.[27] The Court – apart from a few examples – has not formulated much comparative jurisprudence on this principle. The limitations of language, the lack of knowledge of comparative law, the limited competences in criminal law so far and most importantly the topic itself make exploring the function of the legality principle of specific systems a difficult task for the ECJ. In addition, comparative analysis by the ECJ is often done with a preference to specific legal systems and some systems will be examined more thoroughly than others, influencing legal reasoning and the development of jurisprudence.[28] Important questions on the substance of the principle have been answered more as a result of research focused on international law jurisprudence on the legality principle, rather comparative analysis of national systems.

Therefore it is imperative to take a closer look into national criminal justice systems. Ideally, it would be best to conduct a comparative research into all 30 legal systems of the EU. However, this is an impossible task due to linguistic boundaries and time-constraints. A comprehensive and in depth analysis of the legality principle in a national system demands that research be done in the native language of every system, which entails researchers mastering multiple languages, something which is impractical. Moreover, the in-depth study of 30 systems would be an ambitious task, difficult to complete within the time available for this research project.

It has been decided to limit the national comparative research to three European penal systems, namely England and Wales, the Netherlands and Germany. The German and Dutch legal systems belong to the continental tradition, in which the law is code-based. Continental legal traditions favour statutory law and legal theory is concept-driven. The English system is a prominent example of the common law traditions, where case law is traditionally an official source of criminal liability. Criminal liability was developed on a case-by-case basis and the judicial style is less focused on concepts and deductive reasoning. There is a sharp difference between common and continental traditions when it comes to the legality principle. As it will be shown, this principle is indigenous to the continental tradition. In the English system, its incorporation has been greatly facilitated by the ECtHR. Nevertheless, case law still plays an important role in the development of criminal liability. Due the cohabitation of common and continental traditions in Europe, it is imperative that comparative research on this principle includes systems that represent both groups.

Regarding variations of continental traditions, both the Dutch and German systems subscribe to statutory criminal liability and case law is not considered to

by the Commission in competition law would be revolutionalised, see T–279/02 Degussa v Commission, 5 April 2006, para. 47 and 73.

27 K. Lenaerts, 'Interlocking Legal Orders in the European Union and Comparative Law', International and Comparative Law Quarterly, vol. 52, 2003, pp. 874–875.

28 M. Kiikeri, 'Comparative legal reasoning and European law', Kluwer, 2001, p. 148.

be a formal source of law. However, historically, the Dutch criminal code has been based on the Napoleonic *Code Pénal*. It is less dogmatic and concept-based than the German one. Whereas in the German system internal systemic coherency is vital, the Dutch system is more practical and less formalistic.[29] One might say that the Dutch system presents the middle ground between the casuistic English and the formalistic German systems.

Due to the strong theoretical nature of this topic, I have also taken into account important contributions on the current role of the principle of legality by scholars from other national systems, such as the French and the Belgian. However, the use of such material is not meant to introduce more systems into the research. Many of these scholars have contributed immensely in the philosophical trends behind the legality principle and its European perspective. Their contributions can be considered as part of the theoretical dialogue regarding the legitimation of criminal law.

The aim of the national comparative research is to identify a nucleus of the legality principle from these three systems, upon which the construction of the European legality principle shall be based. My goal is to present an integrated view of the principle at the national level. Thus, findings from the research into the national jurisdictions are analysed from a comparative perspective. However, comparative research is a method and not the goal of this research. My purpose is not to present an in-country report on how the legality principle is applied in Germany, the Netherlands or England, but to use these three national systems to inform the theoretical approach and practical application of this principle. Therefore, the findings of the national research shall be presented in an integrated and contextual fashion.

The main sources of this research have been legal texts and literature on the principle of legality and jurisprudence. I have studied different articles, books, case law and commentaries and I have also used different online databases. Because of the great volume of literature regarding the legality principle – especially in the German legal system – I selected research material based on relevance, status of the author and the topics discussed. My intention was to review the most influential and broadly-accepted scholarly literature, which represents the mainstream theoretical approach of the legality principle in every system. Moreover, as the application of the legality principle may vary between literature and legal practice, I attempt a balance between the two. Due to the differences between the jurisdictions under consideration especially with regard to the history of the legality principle, some systems were researched on a deeper level. In England, where the principle of legality was not explicitly used by courts until well into the 20th century, a variety of case law and literature was necessary in order to gain an understanding of its application. In order to ensure that my view of the legality principle in England is accurate, I have also discussed my findings with leading English scholars in this field.

---

29 J. Keiler, 'Actus Reus and participation in European criminal law', Intersentia, 2013, p. 16; E. Blankenburg, 'Patterns of legal culture: The Netherlands Compared to Neighboring Germany', The American Journal of Comparative Law, vol. 46, 1998, pp. 39–41.

A final issue to be addressed is the terminology and problems that might occur with the translation of terminology into English. This book is written in English, however, the research was conducted in the original language of each system. This means that there will be challenges with regard to the translation or expression of Dutch or German terminology into English. In these cases, I have made an effort to provide the most appropriate translation and where necessary further explanation will be provided. I may also include the translated term in its original language, within the text.

Clarification is necessary regarding Dutch terms that shall be used extensively. In the absence of an accurate translation of *Recht* into English (usually the English words 'law', 'just', or 'legal' are used, although they do not truly convey the meaning of *Recht*) the translation of terms such as *Rechtshandhaving* and *Rechtskarakter* are not easy. *Rechtshandhaving* is literally translated as 'law enforcement' but a more accurate translation is 'order ruled/enforced by law'. The opposite of *Rechtshandhaving* is *Ordehandhaving,* which means 'enforcement of order' or simply 'order'. As diametrical opposites, the terms *Rechtshandhaving* and *Ordehandhaving* differ in that, the order in the first term is legitimised and exercised under 'conditions of law', while in the second case it is simply a form of order, which is not accountable to any legitimation standards. Consequently, the often used term *Rechtskarakter* can be translated as 'intrinsic character of the law' meaning that it meets a set of criteria that characterises it as *law* and differentiates it from state violence.

3. European research: fragments of the principle of legality

The second methodological step is to identify the fragments of the legality principle at the level of EU law. As mentioned before, the legality principle has been recognised as a general principle of EU law. Yet, there is no comprehensive account of the functions and aspects of this principle. The ECJ has already recognised various aspects, however, due to the limited competence of the Court in criminal law matters, the implications of a European legality principle for the European bodies and national implementation measures have not been thoroughly assessed.

In order to conduct my research and identify the elements of the legality principle in EU law, I have consulted various scholarly and academic contributions in this field. I have also examined a variety of European soft, hard-law, and policy instruments such as Frameworks Decisions, Directives and the Commission Reports on their implementation. The European case law database has been searched with keywords such as, principle of legal certainty, non-retroactivity, *nullum crimen sine lege* (or variations of the maxim). The results were overwhelming in numbers. However, I found that not all cases were actually relevant. This suggests the ECJ may use these terms in a broad or inconsistent manner.[30] As elements of the legality principle might feature in other ECJ cases, where the principle is not necessarily relied upon by the Court, I have researched commentaries on ECJ cases in order to identify further case law where elements of the legality principle might be of relevance. My aim was to gather as many cases as possible. Many cases dealing with the legality principle, especially in competition law, are very similar. I have limited my search to case law that raises issues of criminal law and competition law cases where issues of the legality principle are dealt with. Occasionally, however, I shall refer to other ECJ cases that deal with general obligations of the Member States in implementation. Furthermore, I have also used relevant scholarly contributions on the subjects of European institutional, constitutional and human rights law. Both my research in national and EU law is up to date as of 1 January 2015.

4. Internal adaptation: parameters

The third step of this research is a synthesis of the national nucleus of the principle of legality, together with its European fragments. These will be combined, analysed and adapted, in order to develop a coherent European principle of legality. This internal adaptation requires that the findings from the two previous stages be adapted to the European legal order.

The internal adaptation of the principle of legality to the EU legal order assumes that there are certain particularities of the EU legal system, which need to be taken under consideration. It has been pointed out in literature that any comparison between the national and EU legal systems involves certain challenges, which may not arise when comparing national legal systems. It is important to anticipate the problem of compatibility: European and national public policies have different regulatory functions, so they are not always functionally equivalent.[31] There are also inter-dependence problems: the EU and national levels are neither dependent nor independent, but inter-dependent. Therefore emphasis is placed on the interaction between European and national levels.[32] Thirdly, there is the transposition issue, according to which when national principles or structures are transplanted to the EU level, they may serve different needs, as structures and demands differ at the EU level.[33]

Therefore, it is necessary to address certain parameters that should be taken under consideration for the proper adaptation of the legality principle to the EU legal order. These parameters shall influence the result of this research. The aim of working within these parameters is to ensure that this research will remain faithful

30 Similarly J. Raitio, 'The Principle of Legal Certainty in EC Law', Kluwer, 2003, p. 10.

31 R. Dehousse, 'Comparing National and EC Law: the Problem of the Level Analysis', American Journal of Comparative law, vol. 42, 1994, pp. 768–770.

32 Ibid., pp. 771–772.

33 Ibid., pp. 774–778.

to the archetypes of EU law and the principle of legality can be properly adapted. It is also to provide transparency regarding the choices made and the reasons that influence such choices.

The first parameter is that any process of adaptation must respect the EU's legal order. To this extent, this research functions within the legal framework of the Treaties. Another parameter is the supranational character of EU law and what this entails for criminal law. The latter is a law primarily dealing with individuals and not Member States. The EU is no longer simply an international organisation of states, but it is also 'a people's Union', according to Article 1 TEU. On the one hand, the EU is defined as a collection of states and functions through the national authorities as its agents. On the other hand, its supranational character may also entail a direct bond between the EU and citizens. Moreover, the EU also sits above the Member States and supervises their relationship with individuals, when this relationship falls within the scope of EU law. Thus, the EU system has provided protection *vis-à-vis* national practices through principles of justice and fundamental rights found in the Charter, the Treaties, and ECJ case law. For example, the principle of equality and non-discrimination regarding nationality is a protection deriving not from the Member States but from the European legal order.

How does the supranational character of the EU influence the adaptation process? This creates an issue regarding inter-dependence, as there is not only a relationship between individuals and Member States, but also a relationship between individuals and the EU. The supranational character of the EU does not mean that Member States are out of the picture. Member States also have their own relationship with the EU. Criminal law competences are currently shared between the EU and the Member States and therefore respect of national sovereignty is important. While national sovereignty in the field of criminal law has been limited by the Treaties, European criminal law is bound to develop within the context of what is ultimately a 'conflict of sovereignties'. For example, if one would accept that that legal certainty for individuals is better served if Regulations were used for criminal norms rather than Directives, any benefit for individuals would be negated by the violation of national sovereignty.

The specific character of the freedom of movement is another parameter. This is an element of incompatibility between national and European criminal law that needs to be addressed during the adaptation process. Freedom of movement plays an important role in any field of law within the EU, as it is the driving force behind European integration. The European *ius puniendi* is guided by the effort to harmonise criminal legislation in order to facilitate freedom of movement (Article 3 para. 2 TEU). However, this is something not to be found as equivalent at the national level; therefore freedom of movement as a parameter denotes an incompatibility issue with the national level that should be addressed.

The current state of institutional dynamics within the EU and between the EU and the national legal order is also of importance for the adaptation process. It should be taken into consideration that the European legal order's interaction with national legal orders is complicated. Currently, there are two levels of decision-making (EU and national) and two levels of adjudicating (ECJ and national courts). The way in which these interact shall influence the distribution of tasks between each level of criminal legislation and adjudication. The institutional dynamics of the EU might create different demands regarding the legality principle to national law. For example, the legality principle might be called upon to respond to challenges created not only by the definition of criminal law in Directives, but also by their implementation.

5. Conclusion

When researching and writing the legality principle, it is not easy to clearly articulate its historical and cultural roots in a national jurisdiction. The principle can be embedded so deeply – and yet so differently – in legal systems, that its transference to another legal order is often intuitive and not necessarily a mechanical process. Also in national law, this principle is intrinsically connected to various underlying doctrines of modern legal systems, which are themselves a reflection of national culture. It is often difficult to take the legality principle out of context and disassociate it from legal and political cultures, as well as its theoretical basis. For a methodology to be transparent, the process of internal adaptation to the EU legal system requires reasons for certain solutions and how these fit within the European legal order.

A critical view of the current *status quo* of the European legal order is also necessary. If this doctrine is truly to become part of European criminal justice, then the importing legal order will face changes as well. One cannot presume that a coherent doctrine of the legality principle, which guides the construction, interpretation and application of criminal liability, will not bring normative, theoretical or even constitutional changes to the way European criminal law is approached. Thus, whereas the above parameters must be taken into account, it is important to keep in mind that these are not definite barriers to the development of the legality principle in EU law, simply parameters to be evaluated.

Part 2

The legality principle in national criminal law

Chapter III
Theoretical Rationales of the Legality Principle

The principle of legality is a concept that developed during, and in the aftermath of the French Revolution and Enlightenment. Noted philosophers and writers of that era, such as Beccaria, Montesquieu and Feuerbach, adopted this principle into domestic criminal law as a means of rationalising the criminal justice system. The legality principle, alongside other important legal principles, was developed as a means of minimising the potential arbitrariness of criminal law and to prevent abuse by the state. It is now one of the cornerstones of modern criminal justice systems, featuring in criminal codes, national constitutions and international legal instruments. The principle of legality is made up of four sub-principles as explained above.[1]

However, the legality principle is much more than these four prohibitions as it has intrinsic value, adding legitimacy to criminal law. Certain aspects, such as the prohibitions of customary criminal liability and vagueness were also features of legal systems before the French Revolution[2] and also exist in the Chinese and Islamic legal systems.[3] However, there are qualitative differences between the primitive criminal justice systems of the medieval period and the western criminal systems of today. The source of its legitimising function lies in its theoretical rationales.

This Chapter examines the theoretical rationales and core values of the legality principle. Its purpose and relationship to the values of individual autonomy and liberty, democracy, separation of powers and the Rule of Law will be analysed, in addition to the principles of legal certainty and guilt.

The purpose of such analysis is two-fold. First, this Chapter aims at identifying the core values of the legality principle. The principle is approached not only as a set of rules for law making and adjudication, but as a principle that generates legitimacy. Criminal behaviour and the abuse of power are on-going social facts and balancing criminal sanctions with due process and the rights of the individual are core functions of the state. The legality principle is a mechanism for balancing this dual function, enabling the state to maintain legitimacy while imposing penal sanctions.

Secondly, the goal is to delve deeper into the interpretation of these theoretical rationales. Concepts such as liberty, democracy and the Rule of Law are nebulous and do not have a stable or self-evident meaning, having been interpreted differently

---

1 Chapter I para. 1.

2 For example the Constitutio Criminalis Carolina (1532) established certain aspects of the legality principle, see for more V. Krey, 'Keine Strafe ohne Gesetz', Walter de Gruyter, 1983, p. 11.

3 K.S. Gallant, 'The principle of legality in international and comparative criminal law', Cambridge University Press, 2009, pp. 270–271.

by various legal and political philosophers. Different interpretations of these concepts influence the nature and application of the legality principle. Thus, it is important to elucidate and differentiate between the various interpretations. In doing so, this Chapter does not seek to present new theories regarding liberty, or democracy but to outline the various scholarly approaches and, thus, to set the theoretical framework within which this principle operates.

1. The Enlightenment era as the source for the legality principle

The theoretical rationales of the legality principle can be historically traced to the Enlightenment movement, a period of political, sociological and philosophical unrest. However, it would be inaccurate to attribute the modern legality principle solely to the Enlightenment period; certain values, such as collective rule and individual autonomy can be traced as far back as ancient Greece and later to the Christendom of the Middle Ages.[4] Jurists imbue the Enlightenment with contemporary legal principles or values, presuming that the Enlightenment movement was homogenous, and, most importantly, that the scholars of that era enjoy a certain legitimacy and ideological superiority.

However, often disregarded in legal scholarship is the plethora of views on the interpretation of the Enlightenment movement, difficult to summarise comprehensively.[5] The exact nature of the Enlightenment is heavily debated. In particular, the term 'Enlightenment' itself – and the French *Lumières* – are terms used later in the 19th and 20th century.[6] Modern literature suggests that to some extent this term carries an ideological colour, only later imposed upon the movement.[7] Some earlier historical research, which has widely contributed to the approach that classic criminal law scholarship takes on Enlightenment, has suggested that the movement was homogenous and focused on the emancipation of man.[8] This view changed, especially after the 1970s, where scholarship revealed the influence of national and geographical trends in the Enlightenment movement

4 E.g. see for the normative and legal foundations of the person in A. Supiot, 'Homo Juridicus: on the Anthropological Function of the Law', Verso, 2007, pp. 4–40; for a historical account on the influence of ancient Greek philosophy on Christianity see in D. MacCulloch, 'A History of Christianity', Penguin Books, 2010, pp. 19–40.

5 For on overview see D. Outram, 'The Enlightenment', Cambridge University Press, 2013, pp. 1–9.

6 Though the German term *Aufklärung* was already used in the late 18th century, see more on the term and its modern use in J. Schmidt, 'Inventing the Enlightenment: Anti-Jacobins, British Hegelians, and the *Oxford English Dictionary*', Journal of the History of Ideas, vol. 64, 2003, pp. 421–443.

7 Ibid., p. 442.

8 P. Gay, 'The Enlightenment: The Rise of Modern Paganism', W.W. Norton and Company, 1966, pp. 3–10.

and proposed a view on the Enlightenment that cannot be reduced to a single narrative.[9] There is also the opinion that the movement was comprised of different competing streams.[10] Thus, the influence of the Enlightenment on modern criminal law depends on one's own historical interpretation of the era.

In addition, recent scholarship has highlighted the relevance of the Enlightenment movement's social context, emphasising the social dynamics, the emergence of public opinion and the impact of the changing societal culture.[11] Thus, when one refers to 'Enlightenment ideals' in legal research, it is wise to keep in mind that the term does not refer to a historically homogenous set of values.

Furthermore, the main ideals of the Enlightenment, such as the prevalence of science as an authoritative worldview and the triumph of rationality over superstition, were later criticised. In their influential work 'Dialectic of Enlightenment', Horkheimer and Adorno reproached the legacy of the Enlightenment as reflecting a 'disenchantment of the world', which replaced the previous worldview and was pursued with totalitarian force.[12] This interpretation of the Enlightenment legacy prompted other modern influential thinkers, such as Habermas and Foucault, to re-evaluate the Enlightenment in ways that make it still relevant and inspiring.[13] Habermas, for example, argued that the Enlightenment resulted in the creation of the concept of a 'public realm', developed through the exchange of knowledge and culture amongst citizens, and resulted in an increasingly critical attitude towards traditional values; this is an idea that he discusses in his work regarding a modern interpretation of the principle of democracy, discourse theory and communicative action.[14]

In sum, the Enlightenment was not a homogenous movement presenting a package of crystallised ideals. The influence of its ideals has been re-evaluated over time and in essence the Enlightenment is not a closed historical period. Conclusively, an analysis of the Enlightenment views without a critical look at their modern interpretation would be in disharmony with the on-going background philosophical, sociological and historical evolution of these concepts, within which criminal law theory operates and from which it draws knowledge, validity and contemporary relevance.

---

9 J.G.A. Pocock, 'Historiography and Enlightenment: a view of their history', Modern Intellectual History, vol. 5, 2008, pp. 83–96; more on the geographical significance in D. Outram, 'The Enlightenment,' Cambridge University Press, 2013, pp. 1–9.

10 J.I. Israel, 'Radical Enlightenment, Philosophy and the Making of Modernity 1650–1750', Oxford University Press, 2001. The sharp distinction between a radical and moderate Enlightenment and the degree of influence of a 'radical' Enlightenment has been criticised in literature. For example, J. Kent Wright, 'Jonathan Israel, Democratic Enlightenment: Philosophy, Revolution, and Human Rights 1750–1790', H-France Forum, vol. 9, 2014, pp. 1–25.

11 D. Outram, 'The Enlightenment', Cambridge University Press, 2013, pp. 10–25.

12 M. Horkheimer, T.W. Adorno, 'Dialectic of Enlightenment', Stanford University Press, 2002, pp. 1–34.

13 D. Outram, 'The Enlightenment', Cambridge University Press, 2013, pp. 6–7.

14 Ibid.; J. Habermas, 'Between Facts and Norms', Polity Press, 1997.

2. Individual liberty and autonomy

The Enlightenment marked a watershed in terms of the growing view of human beings as born free and endowed with reason.[15] Individuals are perceived as elementary particles of a human society.[16] Western culture emphasises individuality, subjectivity and personality.[17] During the Enlightenment, this Western view of individuals was furthered by revisiting the human beings' origins and reinterpreting the concept of the individual, whose finality is now found within himself, emancipated from the divine.[18] Consequently, there was a shift in the criminal justice system towards a more individualistic approach, as a response to the despotic *Ancien Regime*, where the state employed its *ius puniendi* powers without any external controls.

2.1. Interpretations of individual liberty and autonomy

The promotion of individual liberty does not mean that Enlightenment philosophers supported absolute freedom, anarchy and the abolition of criminal law. On the contrary, the restriction of individual freedom was acknowledged as necessary within society: *'Thus it was necessity that forced men to give up a part of their liberty; it is certain then, that every individual would choose to put into the public stock the smallest portion possible…'.*[19] Although not an absolute notion, liberty became a central value due to the increasingly accepted view of the individual as born free. Liberty should be restricted as little as possible. The state became accountable for protecting liberty: *'…The aggregate of these, the smallest portions possible, forms the right of punishing; all that extends beyond this is abuse, not justice.'*[20]

As liberty is an important notion for modern legal and political systems, its definition is significant. There have been various views on what constitutes liberty. One of the most influential theories on liberty is the distinction between positive and negative liberty by Berlin. Negative liberty means the absence of obstacles or interference to one's personal sphere.[21] State action or other human action can be considered an intervention to the individual's personal sphere according to this interpretation of liberty.

---

15 J.J. Rousseau, 'The Social Contract, or Principles of Political Right', 1762, Book 1, Ch. 1 (republished by Wordsworth Editions, 1998); A. Supiot, 'Homo Juridicus: on the Anthropological Function of the Law', Verso, 2007, pp. 10–13.

16 A. Supiot, 'Homo Juridicus: on the Anthropological Function of the Law', Verso, 2007, p. 14.

17 Ibid., p. 13.

18 Ibid., p. 12.

19 C. Beccaria, 'An essay on Crimes and Punishments', Branden Press Inc, 1983, pp. 2–3 (Chapter 2, Of the right to punish).

20 Ibid.

21 I. Berlin, 'Four Essays on Liberty', Oxford University Press, 1971, pp. 122–131.

Positive liberty requires the presence of something, i.e. self-control or self-mastery. In order to be free, one must be self-determined, namely he is able to determine his own life, choices and destiny. Thus, whilst negative liberty is about individuals' room of action, positive liberty is associated with the source of control.[22] Someone is free in the positive sense if he is the master of his own life.

Positive freedom emphasises individual autonomy. The distinction between a positive freedom and individual autonomy is rather difficult, as, to some extent, these two concepts might concur.[23] There are various theories on individual autonomy. Some focus on the difficult distinction between stimuli that inform the self-governing process and stimuli that undermine it;[24] other theories focus on the actual definition of individual autonomy. Especially with regard to the latter, a basic distinction is between moral autonomy, i.e. the capacity to impose on oneself an individual account of moral obligations (mainly corresponding to Kantian theory), and personal autonomy, a broader concept that does not limit such capacity solely to questions of morality.[25]

One view of individual autonomy is the interpretation of self-ruling as the independence of one's deliberation from others and the capacity to rule oneself; this implies that individuals act competently from their own desires. Thus, there are implications for the desired competency of the agent, such as rational thoughts and self-control or the ability to reflect upon one's desires and values.[26]

One of the most debated questions in scholarship is whether the state should promote positive freedom. The main criticism here is that positive action carries the danger of authoritarianism,[27] with the state assuming that it 'knows better what is best' for individuals. If individuals are viewed as irrational or imprisoned by their own desires, then, state action could indeed be perceived as paternalistic. Having said that, the promotion of positive liberty can take place at more abstract levels as well. Proponents of positive liberty, such as Rousseau, focus on the connection between a positive freedom and democratic rule, with positive freedom enabling individuals to determine their own lives through participation in self-determined societies.[28] According to Berlin, negative liberty can be safeguarded in undemocratic

---

22 Ibid., pp. 131–134.

23 J. Christman, 'Autonomy in Moral and Political Philosophy', The Stanford Encyclopedia of Philosophy (Winter 2014 Edition), E.N. Zalta (ed), URL http://plato.stanford.edu/archives/win2014/entries/autonomy-moral/.

24 S. Buss, 'Personal Autonomy', The Stanford Encyclopedia of Philosophy (Winter 2014 Edition), E.N. Zalta (ed), URL http://plato.stanford.edu/archives/win2014/entries/personal-autonomy/.

25 J. Christman, 'Autonomy in Moral and Political Philosophy', The Stanford Encyclopedia of Philosophy (Winter 2014 Edition), E.N. Zalta (ed), URL http://plato.stanford.edu/archives/win2014/entries/autonomy-moral/.

26 Ibid.

27 I. Berlin, 'Four Essays on Liberty', Oxford University Press, 1971, p. 133.

28 I. Carter, 'Positive and Negative Liberty', The Stanford Encyclopedia of Philosophy (Spring 2012 Edition), E.N. Zalta (ed), URL http://plato.stanford.edu/archives/spr2012/entries/liberty-positive-negative/.

political systems, as absolute monarchies or dictatorships may still respect individual liberty in its negative sense.[29] If one accepts a positive interpretation of liberty, legal norms are therefore seen as a product of the 'general will', with positive liberty being safeguarded, as individuals are the drafters of the norms governing their own actions.

While the distinction between positive and negative liberty is still popular today, a modern approach on liberty suggests that this dichotomy is erroneous and there is only a single concept of freedom. On this view freedom is a triadic notion, which expresses the relation between an agent, certain preventing conditions, and certain doings or becomings of the agent.[30]

2.2. Individual liberty and autonomy in criminal law

In the context of criminal law, an analysis of the notions of liberty and individual autonomy is vital. A distinction should be made here between the vertical relationship of the individual and state and the horizontal relationship between individuals.

Focusing on the vertical relationship between the state and individual, criminal prohibitions and punishment can be seen as obstacles to liberty. Individuals are not free to kill or steal, as these actions are sanctioned.[31] Adopting a negative interpretation of liberty implies that the power of the state to punish is coercion – an obstacle to free action. Criminal norms thus determine the limits of individual sphere and, accordingly, such state interference must be limited.

Criminal norms restrict individual autonomy and self-determination as they prescribe certain behavioural standards to be followed. However, the concept of positive liberty has a major role to play for the legitimacy of criminal law. If individuals are recognised as subjects/agents of the (criminal) law, who are responsible, independent and able to determine their lives, then such criminal law must respect this capacity. It would undermine individual autonomy, for example, if criminal law were to punish those lacking self-control (mental disease for example). Furthermore, a respect of the political concept of individual autonomy requires that criminal norms are a product of participative procedures that allow individuals to determine the common behavioural rules within a society.

In addition, criminal norms must promote conditions in which individuals can exercise self-mastery. A norm that respects individual autonomy safeguards human dignity. Ultimately, the concept of human dignity is behind the claim to individual

29 I. Berlin, 'Four Essays on Liberty', Oxford University Press, 1971, pp. 129–130.

30 G.C.Jr. MacCallum, 'Negative and Positive Freedom', Philosophical Review, vol. 76, 1967, pp. 312–334; I. Carter, 'Positive and Negative Liberty', The Stanford Encyclopedia of Philosophy (Spring 2012 Edition), E.N. Zalta (ed), URL http://plato.stanford.edu/archives/spr2012/entries/liberty-positive-negative/.

31 F.E. Oppenheim, 'Dimensions of Freedom: An Analysis', St. Martin's Press, 1961, pp. 72–81.

autonomy.[32] Human dignity is an abstract concept, encompassing various ideas in relation to normative human attributes. Fostering human dignity in a legal system introduces a moral or ethical dimension to the function of law.[33] Legal norms reflect how individuals are perceived, and individual autonomy is therefore seen as the *'self confident demand for legal recognition as a self determined subject who 'lives, feels, and acts in accordance with his or her own judgement'.*[34]

As far as the criminal law is concerned, the individual is widely regarded as rational agent, the *homo economicus*: the individual who has the ability to make choices, evaluate his behaviour, reflect on his environment, control his impact on the society and eventually choose behaviours that support his needs and goals in life.[35] Individual autonomy is therefore an acknowledgement of human dignity, and *'the capacity of every person to act under minimal conditions of confidence, which comes down to the capacity of every person to discover in the rules of law a minimal regulatory force with regard to her own conduct and those of others.'*[36] Infringing upon personal autonomy deprives individuals of their capacity to act and of confidence in their actions.[37]

Therefore, individual autonomy and human dignity require predictability and legal certainty. Criminal norms do not only determine the limits of individual action (as in negative liberty), but take also the form of behavioural standards that regulate human action. Consequently, criminal law must respect individual autonomy by safeguarding the capacity of individuals to rely on criminal norms. As the ability to choose is an important aspect of the Western perception of individuals, the criminal law system must ensure the exercise of such choice.[38] In fact criminal norms create the possibility of choice for the individuals as they lay down the consequences of specific actions.[39] Criminal law can therefore be seen as a 'choosing system' and the individuals as 'choosing beings'.[40] Legal certainty and the reliability of the law are therefore essential. The idea of law as a 'choosing system' is also reflected in other core principles such as the concept of guilt. Guilt in a criminal context implies deliberate choice to violate societally accepted norms. The 'principle of control' ensures that individuals will only be found culpable when they had some control – as in the ability of choice – on their actions.[41]

---

32 G. Grünwald, 'Bedeutung und Begründung des Satzes nulla poena sine lege', ZStW, vol. 76, 1964, p. 1.

33 J. Habermas, 'The Concept of Human Dignity and the Realistic Utopia of Human Rights', in 'The Crisis of the European Union – A Response', Polity Press, 2012, p. 81.

34 Ibid., p. 86.

35 L. Dupont, 'Beginselen van behoorlijke strafrechtsbedeling', Gouda Quint, 1979, p. 54.

36 E. Claes, 'Criminal Justice, Legality and Human Dignity', in E. Claes, R. Foqué, T. Peters (eds), 'Punishment, Restorative Justice and the Morality of Law', Intersentia, 2005, p. 41.

37 Ibid.

38 H.L.A. Hart, 'Punishment and Responsibility: Essays in the Philosophy of Law', Oxford University Press, 1968, pp. 44–47.

39 Ibid.

40 Ibid., p. 49.

41 A.A. van Dijk, 'Strafrechtelijke aansprakelijkheid heroverwogen. Over opzet, schuld, schulduitsluitingsgronden en straf', Maklu, 2008, p. 162.

Consequently, in light of the vertical relationship between the individuals and the state, individual liberty and autonomy should be protected against state arbitrariness. State-actors must create, apply and interpret norms imposing criminal liability in a limited manner, reflecting respect for individual confidence, rationality and the need for legal certainty.

Bearing in mind the horizontal relationship between individuals, liberty and autonomy are also affected by individuals' acts. The question that various theories on criminal law seek to answer is whether criminal norms should protect liberty from interference by third parties, i.e. other individuals. Do state authorities have a positive duty to create criminal norms to safeguard individual autonomy? Is such protection of individual autonomy and liberty inherent to criminal law?

There are various theoretical rationales for the positive duty of the state to create and apply criminal norms and punishment. Criminal conduct breaches social norms accepted as legitimate by the community;[42] it is punished as such, either because such conduct violates moral standards (*mala in se*) or because the criminal norms are necessary to achieve a further public interest (*mala prohibita*). The distinction between these two rationales is nebulous and controversial.[43] From a moralistic view of criminal law, criminal norms reflect socially accepted moral rules. If one does not accept legal moralism, then criminal norms are mechanisms aimed at promoting an effectively functioning community where disruptive conduct is minimised. On either view, what is evident is that the vast majority of criminal norms reflect rules of social interaction; criminal norms reflect the morals or the priorities and goals of the communities. In this regard, the power of the state to mediate horizontal conflicts between individuals via criminal norms becomes a duty, because it maintains conditions of social life defined by moral values or instrumental goals.

Theories on criminal punishment also contribute to the debate regarding the duty of the state to enforce criminal norms. From a utilitarian perspective, criminal law and punishment is justified by the promotion of social protection.[44] Criminalising certain harmful acts protects the welfare of society and its individuals. Here, the protection of individual liberty and autonomy is collective. The benefits of criminal law are usually found in the concepts of general and special deterrence, rehabilitation and incapacitation.[45] The general deterrence theory is based on the idea that criminalisation and punishment can function as a threat, deterring individuals from engaging in criminal conduct.[46]

---

42 A. Duff, 'Legal Punishment', The Stanford Encyclopedia of Philosophy (Summer 2013 Edition), E.N. Zalta (ed), URL http://plato.stanford.edu/archives/sum2013/entries/legal-punishment/.

43 A. Duff, 'Theories of Criminal Law', The Stanford Encyclopedia of Philosophy (Summer 2013 Edition), E.N. Zalta (ed), URL http://plato.stanford.edu/archives/sum2013/entries/criminal-law/.

44 G.P. Fletcher, 'Basic Concepts of Criminal Law', Oxford University Press, 1998, pp. 30–31.

45 A. Duff, 'Legal Punishment', The Stanford Encyclopedia of Philosophy (Summer 2013 Edition), E.N. Zalta (ed), URL http://plato.stanford.edu/archives/sum2013/entries/legal-punishment/.

46 H.L. Packer, 'The Limits of the Criminal Sanction', Stanford University Press, 1968, p. 39.

This theory is particularly relevant for the legality principle. Beccaria has argued that '*...Crimes will be less frequent in proportion as the code of laws is more universally read and understood: for there is no doubt, but that the eloquence of the passions is greatly assisted by ignorance, and uncertainty of punishments...*'[47] Deterrence is thus connected to legal certainty regarding the rules of individual and societal conduct. Feuerbach, widely considered one of the founding fathers of the legality principle,[48] suggested the *psychologische Zwangstheorie* as the theoretical basis for the legality principle.[49] According to this theory, criminal liability has a psychologically deterrent effect on the individual – stemming from the threat of criminal punishment.[50] Feuerbach's theory as the sole basis for the legality principle has been criticised in scholarship.[51] Deterrence as a justification of punishment has been criticised especially because it is based on the assumption of individuals as self-interested beings, acting after careful consideration of their own interests.[52] Another argument against the theory on deterrence is the lack of statistical support that deterrence works.

While deterrence cannot describe exhaustively human behaviour, it does say something about the reality of human interaction.[53] Scholars who revisit the theory of deterrence, as a partial theoretical support for criminal punishment, interpret it in a broader manner. Packer, for example, has argued that deterrence may have a wider interpretation including both conscious and unconscious behaviour.[54] Individuals are social beings whose behaviour is conditioned by the cultural norms of the societies in which they live. In this regard the horizontal relationship between individuals is governed by learned social practices. Criminal norms reflect rules of behaviour that steer human behaviour towards socially accepted patterns; those rules are learned throughout the socialisation of individuals in their communities and through the threat of punishment. Regardless of whether a criminal act is presented as a conscious or unconscious alternative choice, violating learned and widely accepted social rules of interaction carries a stigma for the individual, which reduces criminal behaviour.

---

47 C. Beccaria, 'An essay on Crimes and Punishments', Branden Press Inc, 1983, pp. 42–43 (Chapter 5: Of the Obscurity of Laws); K. Rozemond, 'Beccaria's Dream on Criminal Law and Nodal Governance', in J. Blad, M. Hildebrandt, K. Rozemond, M. Schuilenburg, P. Van Calster (eds), 'Governing Security under the Rule of Law?', Eleven International Publishing, 2010, pp. 41–46.

48 B. Schünemann, 'Nulla poena sine lege? Rechtstheoretische und verfassungsrechtliche Implikationen der Rechtsgewinnung im Strafrecht', Walter de Gruyter, 1978, p. 2.

49 P.J.A. Feuerbach, 'Lehrbuch des gemeinen in Deutschland gültigen peinlichen Rechts', 1801.

50 H.-L. Schreiber, 'Gesetz und Richter', Alfred Metzner Verlag GmbH, 1976, p. 104.

51 Ibid., pp. 102–112; G. Grünwald, 'Bedeutung und Begründung des Satzes nulla poena sine lege', ZStW, vol. 76, 1964, p. 10.

52 A. Duff, 'Legal Punishment', The Stanford Encyclopedia of Philosophy (Summer 2013 Edition), E.N. Zalta (ed), URL http://plato.stanford.edu/archives/sum2013/entries/legal-punishment/.

53 H.L. Packer, 'The Limits of the Criminal Sanction', Stanford University Press, 1968, p. 41.

54 Ibid., pp. 42–45.

Retributive theories have as a starting point the penal desert: criminal punishment has been earned, either due to the unfair advantage gained by the perpetrator over the law-abiding citizen, or due to an emotional response to crime (revenge/ expiation).[55] Retributive theories focus on the individual per se instead of the social good, and it is often argued that this approach emphasises the role of the offender as a responsible and rational agent.[56] In this regard, criminal norms reflect the moral code of society, and therefore highlight the types of interference to one's personal sphere that merit punishment. The focus on the horizontal aspect of social interaction in the field of criminal law is perhaps more prominent in the theories of restitution or restorative justice. These theories often emphasise on alternatives to traditional criminal punishment, and advocate restoration rather than retribution of harm.[57] Procedural mediation, as an attempt at reconciliation between victim and offender, is regarded as more desirable outcome than traditional criminal proceedings.

Therefore, whichever theory one adopts on criminal punishment, criminal norms are approached as behavioural rules that guide human interaction. The protection of the horizontal individual liberty and autonomy are justified through a variety of scholarly theories and justifications for criminal norms are based on one's own view about where social rules come from and what purpose they serve. The question is not whether there is such a positive duty, but how the state should execute this.

The debate over negative and positive conceptions on liberty is important to consider. Over-zealous protection of individual liberty at a horizontal level can compromise negative liberty: *'Law, including the criminal law, must in a free society be judged ultimately on the basis of its success in promoting human autonomy and the capacity for individual human growth and development'.*[58] Consequently, principles of criminal law, such as *ultima ratio* and proportionality, have been developed in order to balance the two conceptions of liberty, both of which are values to be promoted by criminal law. More libertarian societies will consequently emphasise the negative conception of liberty.

The positive duty to create and enforce criminal norms also has its own internal limits, linked to theories on the moral or instrumental purpose of criminal law. Which moral rules are to receive endorsement of criminal law? Alternatively, which societal goals are of sufficient value to be achieved via criminal law? It has been argued only 'the right kind' of moral rules should be protected through criminal law.[59] Which rules fall into this category involves assessing citizens' societal

---

55 A. Duff, 'Legal Punishment', The Stanford Encyclopedia of Philosophy (Summer 2013 Edition), E.N. Zalta (ed), URL http://plato.stanford.edu/archives/sum2013/entries/legal-punishment/.

56 G.P. Fletcher, 'Basic Concepts of Criminal Law', Oxford University Press, 1998, p. 32; H.L. Packer, 'The Limits of the Criminal Sanction', Stanford University Press, 1968, pp. 37–39.

57 A. Duff, 'Legal Punishment', The Stanford Encyclopedia of Philosophy (Summer 2013 Edition), E.N. Zalta (ed), URL http://plato.stanford.edu/archives/sum2013/entries/legal-punishment/.

58 H.L. Packer, 'The Limits of the Criminal Sanction', Stanford University Press, 1968, p. 65.

59 A. Duff, 'Theories of Criminal Law', The Stanford Encyclopedia of Philosophy (Summer 2013 Edition), E.N. Zalta (ed), URL http://plato.stanford.edu/archives/sum2013/entries/criminal-law/.

bonds, values and cultural norms, and questions of what is considered harm or a public good. Moral values may vary from community to community throughout time. Western political communities have developed a relatively coherent set of moral rules surrounding the concept of human dignity – as inspired by the *Déclaration des droits de l'homme et du citoyen de 1789* – which serves as an ethical/moral minimum.[60] Taking a utilitarian or instrumental perspective on criminal law makes the reasoning for criminalisation more transparent and translates into specific goals: for example the criminalisation of child pornography possession (next to distribution) serves the prevention of child pornography and the protection of children. While transparency is an asset, a utilitarian perspective can lead to opportunism, especially if the goals to be achieved cannot be reconciled with the 'will' and character a community.

3. The principle of democracy

The *Ancien Regime* established a criminal justice system where the *ius puniendi* was in the hands of the monarch and oligarchic elite. The middle and lower social working classes did not participate in the determination of the policies and legislation. The French Revolution did not only lead to a more rational and anthropocentric image of individuals but it also fuelled the reconstruction of society. The Revolution led to the introduction of a political system, which would give voice to the middle-class and safeguard the ideals of individual autonomy and freedom.[61]

3.1. Features of the principle of democracy

While democratic rule goes back to ancient Greece, Enlightenment thinkers such as Rousseau revisited the concept of democracy.[62] The crux of Rousseau's social contract theory is that *'each of us puts his person and all his power in common under the supreme direction of the general will.'*[63] Emphasis on the general will would allow the population an adequate degree of self-governance, according to which *'the addressees of law are simultaneously the authors of their rights'*.[64] The community becomes an autonomous body formed by the union of all individuals, agreeing upon the formation of a society and the rules by which it is governed. The existence, identity, will, and powers of the state can only be derived from the

60 For example E. Claes, 'Legaliteit en rechtsvinding in het strafrecht', Universitaire Pers Leuven, 2003, p. 454; J. Habermas, 'The Concept of Human Dignity and the Realistic Utopia of Human Rights', in 'The Crisis of the European Union – A Response', Polity Press, 2012, pp. 71–100.

61 R. Foqué, A.C. 't Hart, 'Instrumentaliteit en Rechtsbescherming', Gouda Quint, Kluwer, 1990, p. 92.

62 E. Claes, 'Legaliteit en rechtsvinding in het strafrecht', Universitaire Pers Leuven, 2003, p. 93.

63 J. Nottingham (ed), 'Western philosophy, an anthology', Blackwell Publishing, 2008, p. 647.

64 J. Habermas, 'Between Facts and Norms', Polity Press, 1997, p. 104.

members of the community. Individuals do not surrender their individual freedom and autonomy to any person or group but to the majority of the commonwealth, the general will (*la volonté générale*). Although this theory itself is not flawless,[65] it is a basis for construing the concept of representative democracy.

Modern theories of democracy vary. The democratic principle is an open and dynamic doctrine that can take various forms; the distance between theory and practice has prompted political scientists to develop conceptions of democracy which tackle modern challenges.[66] What is more, various other issues, such as the concept of citizenship, political autonomy, equality, civil society, statehood, economic and political theories are key features of democratic theory. Held, for example, has identified a variety of democratic models, such as classical democracy (Athens), republicanism, liberal democracy, competitive elitism, pluralism, and deliberative democracy, with further subdivisions and variants found within these categories.[67] As certain key elements of democracy, such as statehood and sovereignty, are increasingly questioned, further theories of democracy have developed, such as a cosmopolitan democracy.[68]

The concept of democracy as the best political system is also open for debate. The benefits of democratic rule are often thought to be that it allows for the canalisation of interests and rights, which inform decision-making.[69] Others argue that a democratic polity is justified on the concepts of individual/political autonomy and equality.[70]

Individual autonomy and equality are central concepts of democracy.[71] If the state is the product of a collective agreement by autonomous individuals then the powers of the state are derived from the people. Individuals participate in the formation of the general will through procedures, which allow self-determination of the community.[72] Individual autonomy and self-determination are applied in a collective setting.[73] Individuals, as members of the community and keepers of state-power, become citizens of the state with political rights. Equality amongst citizens is a crucial condition of democratic governance as individuals submit themselves to the same conditions they impose on others. The principle of equality is expressed as a tension between the two faces of identity: individuals are alike and hence identical but also different because each is unique.[74]

---

65 Ibid., pp. 102–103 for a critic on Rousseau.

66 For example, the discourse theory see J. Habermas, 'Between Facts and Norms', Polity Press, 1997.

67 D. Held, 'Models of Democracy', Stanford University Press, 2006.

68 Ibid., pp. 304–311.

69 T. Christiano, 'Democracy', The Stanford Encyclopedia of Philosophy (Fall 2008 Edition), E.N. Zalta (ed), URL http://plato.stanford.edu/archives/fall2008/entries/democracy/

70 D. Held, 'Models of Democracy', Stanford University Press, 2006, pp. 262–271.

71 R.A. Dahl, 'Democracy and its Critics', Yale University Press, 1989, pp. 97–105.

72 D. Held, 'Models of Democracy', Stanford University Press, 2006, pp. 262–271.

73 R.A. Dahl, 'Democracy and its Critics', Yale University Press, 1989, p. 100.

74 A. Supiot, 'Homo Juridicus: on the Anthropological Function of the Law', Verso, 2007, p. 14.

Criminal laws produced by democratic procedures find their legitimacy in the fact that they are products of the general will, upon which individuals, as potential victims and perpetrators of criminal conduct, have agreed. Limitations on their freedom are eventually self-imposed. If democracy is to be justified instrumentally (e.g. through its use in promoting better quality decision-making), then democratically determined criminal norms reflect a reliable picture of the community's 'common ground' in terms of competing rights and interests. Criminal norms stand a better chance of being accepted and obeyed by individuals if produced through an inclusive process.

Democracy is important for the legitimacy of criminal law and the theoretical basis of the principle of legality. The role of the latter is to establish a *sine qua non* link between criminal liability and democratic law-making. What should be the link between criminal liability and the democratic principle? In other words, what mandate does the democratic principle generate for the legality principle?

3.2. Procedural and substantive democracy

A controversial issue in scholarship regarding theories of democracy is the debate between procedural and substantive approaches.[75] According to the procedural approach, the democratic legitimacy of criminal law is safeguarded when the law-making body is the outcome of democratic procedures, through elections, public and open discourse and transparent decisions.[76] Laws are produced by public representatives, elected through fair procedures, involving debating and voting on the content and limits of criminal liability. Procedural democracy emphasises the equality of political power; with citizens and their representatives having an equal voice, each opinion enjoys an equal standing. Modern democracies function via majority-rule. The question of what conduct should be criminalised is answered through a consensus of the majority. Majority rule maximises the number of people who can exercise self-determination in collective decision-making, while also increasing the chances of taking decisions that are representative.[77] For the legality principle, this approach means that it suffices that criminal norms are produced by a democratically elected body, working according to the principles of majority-rule. The principle of legality supports an organic criterion for the legitimation of criminal norms, where it is the author and not the content that legitimises criminal law.[78]

What happens, however, when the outcome of an otherwise democratic process violates basic individual rights? In other words, are there any limits to democracy?

75 R.A. Dahl, 'Democracy and its Critics', Yale University Press, 1989, p. 163.

76 Ibid., pp. 108–118.

77 Ibid., pp. 138–144.

78 P. Beauvais, 'Le principe de la légalité pénale dans le droit de l'Union européenne', Thèse, Université Paris X Nanterre UFR, 1 December 2006, p. 131.

Here one can argue that there are certain external limitations to democracy,[79] for example natural rights or an abstract sense of justice. Another way to approach this problem though is by considering that democracy has certain internal limitations. For example, democratic decisions cannot result in the annulment of the democratic procedure itself (by taking away political rights for example), or such decisions cannot compromise other foundational principles of democracy. Locke suggests that such internal limitations occur when decisions may violate fundamental human rights, for example when the individual is forced to comply with a decision that violates the very essence of human dignity, upon which political and individual autonomy is based.[80]

The substantive approach to democracy is founded on this idea, namely that decisions are not only democratic when arrived at via a democratic process, but also when they respect human dignity. It is important to highlight that the theory of substantive democracy *does not* undermine the importance of democratic procedures, or majority rule. A substantive democracy that focuses only on the 'right decision' rather than the process of decision-making would be closer to a dictatorship. The conflict between procedural and substantive version of democracy is actually a conflict between strict procedural democracy and a procedural democracy where there are some internal and substantive limitations imposed upon the process in order to ensure that gross substantive injustice shall not occur.[81] This conflict is more about the balance between procedural and substantive values.

Substantive democracy challenges the idea that political autonomy is respected solely on a statistical understanding of democratic principles.[82] Political autonomy is understood as the individual right to be governed by representatives of the society of which the individual identifies himself as a member. The idea of the social contract is based on the existence of a collective consciousness, with decisions taken by the people for the people. This concept of political freedom and autonomy presupposes an element of collectivism in every society, according to which individuals can identify themselves with the separate collective entity and its decisions, even if their individual autonomy is limited by those decisions.[83] The representativeness of democratic decisions cannot be understood only as a procedural reflection of the various political dynamics, but also as a safeguard that the content of democratic decisions will indeed represent the collective consciousness. While not every individual may agree with the decisions taken, the individual should be able to accept the decisions, and in that way continue being a part of the democratic process without his human dignity being compromised.[84]

---

79 T. Christiano, 'Democracy', The Stanford Encyclopedia of Philosophy (Fall 2008 Edition), E.N. Zalta (ed), URL http://plato.stanford.edu/archives/fall2008/entries/democracy/.

80 Ibid.

81 R.A. Dahl, 'Democracy and its Critics', Yale University Press, 1989, p. 163.

82 E. Claes, 'Legaliteit en rechtsvinding in het strafrecht', Universitaire Pers Leuven, 2003, p. 427.

83 Ibid., p. 426.

84 Ibid., p. 428.

Any social contract cannot continue if the decisions taken nullify completely very basic rights of some of its groups; with such decisions, the people affected cannot take collective responsibility, and neither can they continue to be equal participants of the social contract.

Ultimately, decisions taken through democratic procedures do not suffice; a respect of such notion of democracy would be also to bind the legislator to certain legal principles and rights that lay in the heart of the legal order.[85] The legality principle, accordingly, does not only mean that criminal liability is a product of equal, representative and transparent public discourse, but that these decisions correspond to certain legal principles that protect individual autonomy, human dignity and equality, for example, the requirements of clarity and non-retroactivity in criminal law.

In comparing the two approaches of democracy, a proper balance exists somewhere in the middle. Criticisms of the procedural concept of democracy are: that it promotes a quantification of democratic procedures and political autonomy;[86] the sacrifice of substantial justice for the benefit of procedural justice;[87] the danger of a majority supressing minority rights;[88] and, the improper technocratic and opportunistic function of political parties and democratic procedures in modern times.[89] Arguments supporting a strictly procedural approach are: that democratic procedure is not a mere formal procedure but it is in itself a form of distributive justice and it represents the fundamental right to self-governance;[90] the inevitability of compromising the interests of minority groups, as no approach to democracy can guarantee that all groups will see their interests served;[91] individuals with differentiated views subject themselves to the majority-will under the condition that their views enjoyed equal standing in the deliberations;[92]and, no process can be perfect in modern society, however, the procedural concept of democracy can be improved.[93]

However, even for the supporters of the procedural concept of democracy, it is clear that the right to self-governance (as expressed through the complex democratic procedures) can conflict with substantive rights and certain mechanisms or alternative models to deal with this must be devised. Dahl for example suggests as solutions: the expansion or reduction of the *demos*; the improvement or adjustment of procedures; the evolution of public opinion acting as a guarantee; and/or, a 'quasi guardianship', such as a judicial court which can ensure that gross violations of substantive rights

---

85 Ibid., p. 429.
86 A. Supiot, 'Homo Juridicus: on the Anthropological Function of the Law', Verso, 2007, p. 15.
87 R.A. Dahl, 'Democracy and its Critics', Yale University Press, 1989, p. 164.
88 Ibid., p. 168.
89 E. Claes, 'Legaliteit en rechtsvinding in het strafrecht', Universitaire Pers Leuven, 2003, p. 426.
90 R.A. Dahl, 'Democracy and its Critics', Yale University Press, 1989, p. 164.
91 Ibid., p. 166.
92 J. Habermas, 'Between Facts and Norms', Polity Press, 1997, p. 179.
93 R.A. Dahl, 'Democracy and its Critics', Yale University Press, 1989, p. 167.

shall not occur.[94] The latter solution is used in many modern democracies, either in the form of judicial constitutional review, or in the form of a generally active judiciary, together with bills of rights, which limit the democratic decision-making.

There are numerous examples of strict procedural approaches to democracy throughout history. Perhaps the most prominent example is the period of the Third Reich, during which Hitler and his National Socialist German Workers' Party came to power through democratic elections. Yet the laws passed by that parliament cannot be seen as democratic, not only because Hitler severely compromised the democratic process by silencing his opposition, but also because the content of these laws violated fundamental human rights and basic levels of human dignity.[95] A more dynamic balance between the procedural and substantive approach has been promoted by the ECtHR.[96] In the aftermath of the Second World War's atrocities, the ECtHR's jurisprudence has made clear that the democratic principle operates in context, and that democratic decisions must respect fundamental rights, pluralism and equality.[97]

4. Separation of powers

One common element of both the procedural and substantive approaches to democracy is the paramount position of an elected, representative body for the legitimacy of criminal norms. Separating the roles of the legislature, judiciary and executive and ensuring they have specific and well-defined functions are vital to the effective functioning of the democratic and criminal legal process. The doctrine of separation of powers, as promoted by Montesquieu, aims to structure and balance the *trias politica* by taking a critical look at the relationship between the actors of the state.[98] Its purpose is to decentralise the power of the state, canalise its spontaneity and distribute it amongst the state-actors.[99]

4.1. Montesquieu's theory

Montesquieu outlined a variety of arguments in support of what he considered to be a rational distribution of roles between state-actors, however, his scholarly work on

94 Ibid., pp. 184–191.

95 G. Radbruch, 'Statutory Lawlessness and *Supra*-Statutory Law (1946)' (translated in English by B. Litschewski Paulson and S.L. Paulson), Oxford Journal of Legal Studies, vol. 26, 2006, pp. 5 and 8.

96 Chapter IV para. 9.1.

97 ECtHR Handyside v United Kingdom, App. 5493/72, 7 December 1976, para. 49; P. Beauvais, 'Le principe de la légalité pénale dans le droit de l'Union européenne', Thèse, Université Paris X Nanterre UFR, 1 December 2006, p. 134.

98 R. Foqué, A.C. 't Hart, 'Instrumentaliteit en Rechtsbescherming', Gouda Quint, Kluwer, 1990, p. 73.

99 Montesquieu, 'De l'esprit des lois', 1748, Livre XI Chapitre VI.

this issue is open to interpretation. In one view, Montesquieu emphasised limiting the freedom of courts, something considered vital during the *Ancien Regime.* During the Enlightenment era it was believed that there was a particular need to limit the freedom of courts, to protect the individual from judicial arbitrariness and ensure the power to criminalise conduct remained with the legislature. The existence of an independent judiciary, with a clear mandate to guarantee individual protection from arbitrariness is an important first step in the separation of powers.[100] Most importantly limiting the powers of courts safeguards protection against judicial arbitrariness: *'les juges de la nation ne sont que la bouche qui prononce les paroles de la loi'.*[101] The judges must not deliver judgements based on their personal beliefs, but only in accordance to the general will as expressed by the legislature: *'The laws only can determine the punishment of crimes; and the authority of making penal laws can only reside with the legislator, who represents the whole society united by the social compact.'*[102]

On the other hand, a more holistic appreciation of Montesquieu's work shows that limiting judicial discretion was merely one element of a broader idea underlying his work: a system of 'checks and balances', promoting a 'balanced constitution'.[103] In this view, Montesquieu's desired outcome was balanced cooperation of the arms of government rather than their separation.[104] In particular, Montesquieu's theory on separation of powers had less to do with the technical allocation of tasks – which can be adjusted based on the circumstances of every system – but with the creation of safeguards against the abuse of power of one of *trias politica.* The theory of 'checks and balances' functions with the idea that *'le pouvoir arrête le pouvoir'.*[105] In order to avoid tyranny – and the tyranny of the majority – the *trias politica* must keep each other in check.[106]

Furthermore, it has been highlighted in scholarship that the well-known *'la bouche qui prononce les paroles de la loi'* did not actually mean that courts must be automatic appliers of the law.[107] It seems that this phrase was misinterpreted by Maillia-Garat, a spokesman of the Napoleonic assembly, in order to accentuate the position of the French parliament.[108] The position of this phrase in the chapter about English law in Montesquieu's work, and other historical evidence, point to the

100 Also the parliament cannot have judicial functions, see J. Habermas, 'Between Facts and Norms', Polity Press, 1997, p. 172.

101 Montesquieu, 'De l'esprit des lois', 1748, Livre XI Chapitre VI.

102 C. Beccaria, 'An essay on Crimes and Punishments', Branden Press Inc, 1983, p. 5 (Chapter 3, Of Crimes and Punishments).

103 R. Bellamy, 'The Political Form of the Constitution: the Separation of Powers, Rights and Representative Democracy', Political Studies, vol. 44, 1996, pp. 443–444; D. Held, 'Models of Democracy', Stanford University Press, 2006, p. 66.

104 W.J. Witteveen, 'Evenwicht van machten', W.E.J. Tjeenk Willink, 1991, pp. 34–35.

105 Ibid., p. 70.

106 Montesquieu, 'De l'esprit des lois', 1748, Livre XI Chapitre VI.

107 K.M. Schönfeld, 'Montesquieu en 'la bouche de la loi'', New Rhine Publishers, 1979, p. 43.

108 K.M. Schönfeld, 'Rex, Lex et Judex: Montesquieu and la bouche de la loi revisited', European Constitutional Law Review, vol. 4, 2008, pp. 274–301.

conclusion that Montesquieu was actually referring to judge-made law, or the *judex est lex loquens* (the judge is the speaking law).[109] This reading of Montesquieu's work entails that giving a controlled minimum of decision-making powers to the executive, or allowing courts to interpret legislation does not compromise the separation of powers. There would only be danger if judicial interpretation, or legislative or executive action, remained unlimited by the other powers, and became imbalanced.

4.2. Montesquieu's three models of state

Montesquieu described three models of state in his work: the despotic state, where one may find no laws at all and the judges arbitrarily impose penalties on a case-by-case basis; the monarchic state, where legislation is in place to bind courts, however, on occasion, such legislation can be imprecise and the role of courts in hard cases is to search for the will of the legislator; and, finally, the republican state, where the legislation is so precise that judicial interpretation is automatic.[110] Here, the judges merely apply criminal norms, while the legislature is the sole body entitled to create criminal norms.

Whilst these are theoretical models, they reflect different views on the separation of powers, and therefore different mandates for the legality principle. Should the legality principle allow room for judicial discretion or should it oblige courts to mechanistically apply statutes? The discussion here can be conducted at two levels: first, the desirable political role of the courts within the governmental framework and second, the quality of prescribed criminal conduct and the interpretation of criminal norms.

In relation to the position of courts, Montesquieu's models present roughly three different possibilities. In the despotic state, the courts maintain a hierarchically superior position in terms of determining criminal liability. The decision on how to balance conflicting rights and which criminal norms are necessary resides with judicial bodies. Here, one can imagine a state where there are no parliamentary statutes, only a few abstract norms, or even, a state where there are relatively precise parliamentary statutes, but with no binding force for the courts. Examples of such a state can be found in political systems of Middle Ages and more recently in the historical development of the English common law system.[111] In the common law system, English judges enjoyed wide discretion in the development of new

---

109 Ibid.

110 W.J. Witteveen, 'Evenwicht van machten', W.E.J. Tjeenk Willink, 1991, p. 31.

111 In fact Montesquieu regarded the English system to be a representative of the republican model and in particular of aristocracy. However, it has been pointed out that Montesquieu may have based this conclusions on procedural elements of the common law system, namely the decisive role that jury played. He seems to have neglected that the law was developed following common law principles of judicial adjudication. Montesquieu's portrayal of the English system has received numerous criticisms in scholarship. See W.J. Witteveen, 'Evenwicht van machten',

criminal liability offences until well into the 20th century.[112] The lack of interest by the parliament to take action on criminal law and the well-embedded practice of common law adjudication created a monotonous picture of institutional dynamics.[113] When courts considered that conduct must be prohibited, they simply declared it a criminal offence.[114] A modern adjustment of this model would be a 'jurisdictional state',[115] namely a state where no matter what the parliament has decided, courts may replace those political decisions with their own, something that would entail a *de facto 'juridification of political power'*.[116] The most paramount objection to the political dynamics of this model is its irreconcilable nature with the democratic process, both procedural and substantive. Democracy requires that laws created by elected representatives must be binding and cannot be mere guidelines.

Diametrically opposed to this model is Montesquieu's third model, the republican state. Here, the political power for determining criminal public policy and liability is solely entrusted to the parliament. In this case, however, the allocation of tasks between the courts and the legislator is a rather strict one; courts have a passive role and merely apply the law. This model gained significant popularity as it offered what was most needed at that time, namely a strict control of judicial discretion. It focuses on the assumption that in democratic systems, the vertical relationship between citizens and the state requires protection from abuse.[117] Furthermore, this model indicated a fear of courts. At the time of Montesquieu's writing, a lack of trust in the courts was justified. However, in modern democracies where judges are well-educated, there is usually a demanding and well-controlled admittance procedure to the judiciary and a wide variety of measures to ensure accountability. These measures and the sophistication of modern justice systems do not entail that courts are free from limitations to their discretion, as this would be contrary to democracy. However, they do reveal the desire of a modern democracy to trust her courts and recognise their role in protecting citizens from abuses by the state.

Courts are also recognised as having an important role in the compatibility of criminal law with civil liberties and human rights. In many jurisdictions throughout Europe, courts are responsible for the constitutional review of parliamentary

---

W.E.J. Tjeenk Willink, 1991, pp. 32–33; D. Held, 'Models of Democracy', Stanford University Press, 2006, p. 67.

112 J.R. Spencer, 'Nulla poena sine lege in English Criminal Law', The Cambridge-Tilburg Law Lectures, Kluwer, 1980, pp. 38–39.

113 A. Samuels, 'Comment: Why do we not have a Criminal Code', The Journal of Criminal Law, vol. 67, 2003, pp. 214–219, where the reasons identified are the unwillingness of the legislator, the lack of interest of the public opinion, the complexity and controversies and the attitude of the judges.

114 For example, R v Manley [1933] 1 KB 529.

115 J. Habermas, 'Between Facts and Norms', Polity Press, 1997, p. 249.

116 Ibid., p. 251.

117 Ibid., p. 249.

Ibid., p. 245.

statutes and governmental acts.[118] In jurisdictions such as the Netherlands, where constitutional review is not permitted, courts are still able to review the compatibility of legislation with international treaties, which grants them limited powers of judicial review.[119] In the EU, the ECJ is not entrusted with the mere application of the Treaties but to *'ensure that in the application and interpretation of the Treaties the law is observed'*[120] and hence having jurisdiction to review the legality of European legislation and the interpretation of primary and secondary European legislation inter alia.[121] Similarly, the ECtHR has been a significant authority on the protection of individual liberties within Europe. Whether this development is positive or negative is certainly a debated issue. There is frequent criticism of the overwhelming power of the German Constitutional Court and its interference with the political choices of the parliament.[122] Similarly, in the Netherlands, the debate on whether or not it would be acceptable to introduce constitutional review is on-going.[123] While jurisdictions may struggle with the power entrusted to the judiciary in terms of constitutional review, the development of judicial review highlights the need to provide an external counterbalancing mechanism to the acts of the legislature, thus, departing to some extent from the strict republican model of passive courts.

This departure is also reflected in the growing shift in the concept of democracy, from procedural to substantive. The concept of a legislature truly representing the will of people is largely considered out-dated as history has taught that democratically elected bodies may violate individual rights. The current bureaucratic nature of parliamentary work, policy oriented law-making, and increased legislative functions of the executive create a difficult environment for the legislature to ensure that individual rights and legal principles might not get lost along the way.[124] Thus, while the need to limit judicial powers to respect the will of the legislature is important, the idea that courts must passively apply statutes is out-dated.

The second model, the monarchic state, is a less strict approach to the separation of powers and stands somewhere between the two previous models. Its starting point is the binding effect of legislation on courts and, in this respect, it shares this important feature with the republican state model. However, in this model, the courts enjoy a flexibility of interpretation whenever the wording of the text is

118 Perhaps the most prominent court in this respect is the German Constitutional Court (see Article 93 of the German Constitution).

119 M. Adams, G. van der Schyff, 'Constitutional Review by the Judiciary in the Netherlands', ZaöRV, vol. 66, 2006, pp. 399–413.

120 Article 19 TEU.

121 Articles 263 and 267 TFEU.

122 J. Habermas, 'Between Facts and Norms', Polity Press, 1997, pp. 253–266.

123 M. Adams, G. van der Schyff, 'Constitutional Review by the Judiciary in the Netherlands', ZaöRV, vol. 66, 2006, p. 400.

124 Ibid., p. 410.

imprecise.[125] Here, the political framework is not characterised by a separation but by a balancing of powers.[126] In addition, this model, despite its less attractive name, is in line with both the procedural and substantial aspects of democracy. It preserves the parliamentary statute as the basis of criminal liability, yet simultaneously welcomes the idea that courts may have some room for interpretation and alignment of the statute with the fundamental principles and human rights, whenever the statute is ambiguous. In this model, courts are not entitled in principle to intervene in criminal public policy and the choices of which rights should be protected. They do, however, have the responsibility to ensure that the complex decision-making process – which may involve opportunistic political agendas and the heavy influence of the executive – maintains the balance within the legal order.

As far as the quality of the statute and the nature of judicial interpretation are concerned, the three models vary in their demands. In the despotic model, the statutes, if existent at all, need not have any particular level of clarity or non-retroactivity. This is because in this model, it is the courts that make political choices and in essence the legislative work. While statutory criminal liability may act as a guideline or a starting point, it is the jurisprudence that defines criminal liability. Here, judicial interpretation and jurisprudence are autonomous, namely they develop independently from a stable definition in a legal text.[127]

The demands of statutory quality change dramatically in the republican model. Here, the statute must be precise so that judicial interpretation amounts to a mechanical application of the statute. This model therefore has high expectations from the legislator, which may be criticised as unrealistic. Language has an inherent indeterminacy and vagueness, which hampers clear limits of criminal liability in some cases. At the same time, the speedy progression of social dynamics and technology might overwhelm the legislator. In this model, jurisprudence is rather heteronomous as it develops only with reference to the scope of statutes.[128]

The natural barriers posed by language and the fast pace of developments in modern systems can be less of a problem in the monarchic state model. While the legislator is obliged to be as precise as possible, vagueness of statutes can be counterbalanced through interpretation. In this model, jurisprudence presents a mixture of a heteronomous and autonomous system.[129]

These three variations are only artificial and abstract models that highlight the different positions of institutions. However, the underlying principles of the monarchic state model may be more in tune with the holistic understanding of Montesquieu's view of checks and balances used in modern society, as it combines a strong democratic basis for criminal law, realistic expectations of statutory drafting, and the role of judicial interpretation. This model can be developed further

125 G.J. Wiarda, '3 typen van rechtsvinding', W.E.J. Tjeenk Willink, 1988, p. 14.
126 E. Claes, 'Legaliteit en rechtsvinding in het strafrecht', Universitaire Pers Leuven, 2003, p. 461.
127 G.J. Wiarda, '3 typen van rechtsvinding', W.E.J. Tjeenk Willink, 1988, p. 14.
128 Ibid.
129 Ibid.

so that it highlights the paramount role of the parliamentary statute, by safeguarding the role of the legislature regarding criminal law policy, but also attributing to courts the role of safeguarding the rights of the individual. In other words, this model allows some minimum control of the legislature by courts without allowing courts to engage in judicial activism.

In the context of this model, the legality principle would have to function at four levels. Firstly, it should oblige the legislator to be as precise as possible in drafting criminal norms. Secondly, it should require that courts base criminal liability only on existing legislation, which means that the criminal statute is the source of criminal law. Thirdly, when the wording of criminal norms is unclear, the principle of legality obliges courts to examine the quality of the statute and the will of the legislator by means of interpretation. Should judicial interpretation point to a clear result with regard to the wording of the text, the courts are entitled to apply it. However, should the statute be so imprecise that it lacks any regulatory content, courts should refuse to apply this statute, or in some jurisdictions even determine the statute to be void. Fourthly, and independently from the judicial interpretation of the wording of the statute, the legality principle should also instruct the courts on which norms to apply in case of a conflict of norms over time. In other words, requiring them to determine which parliamentary statute is chronologically legitimate bearing in mind the principles of legal certainty and democratic legitimacy.

5. *Rechtsstaat* and Rule of Law

Another theoretical rationale that should be discussed are the two sister notions of the *Rechtsstaat* and the Rule of Law, though these are complex concepts. However, some general elements and tensions in legal theory should be mentioned.

The Rule of Law and its German counterpart, the *Rechtsstaat,* are not entirely identical as they have different histories[130] albeit their ideas are similar, i.e. the rule of the law as opposed to the rule of men.[131] The law for legal systems, governed by the Rule of Law, is found in legal rules.[132] Roughly speaking, theories regarding the Rule of Law can be grouped into two categories: formal and substantive theories. Formal theories focus on the formal and organic requirements of a proper legal order; substantive theories include requirements of substance, such as certain rights or moral standards.[133]

130 B.Z. Tamanaha, 'On the Rule of Law: History, Politics, Theory', Cambridge University Press, 2004, p. 108.
131 C. Sampford, 'Retrospectivity and the Rule of Law', Oxford University Press, 2006, pp. 39–40.
132 N. MacCormick, 'Rhetoric and the Rule of Law', Oxford University Press, 2005, pp. 14–16.
133 B.Z. Tamanaha, 'On the Rule of Law: History, Politics, Theory', Cambridge University Press, 2004, p. 92.

The formal theories of the Rule of Law include definitions such as those by Dicey,[134] Hayek,[135] Fuller[136] and Raz.[137] For example Hayek's definition of the Rule of Law reads:

> [S]tripped of all technicalities this means that government in all its actions is bound by rules fixed and announced beforehand – rules which make it possible to foresee with fair certainty how the authority will use its coercive powers in given circumstances, and to plan one's individual affairs on the basis of this knowledge.[138]

The aim of the Rule of Law is to limit the arbitrariness of the state-actors by defining in rules their powers.[139] Most definitions for the Rule of Law highlight requirements such as general, clear, prospective and publicly promulgated laws, which bind the government and state-actors. Legal certainty is a central element.[140] For example Raz enumerated certain minimum standards for legal rules such as: non-retroactivity, clarity, adequate publication, and stability.[141] Fuller also enumerates eight elements of the Rule of Law: the statutes have to be general, promulgated, prospective, clear, non-contradictory, not ask the impossible, constant, and there must be a congruence between the laws and the way the officials enforce them.[142]

A characteristic of the formal Rule of Law is its emptiness as far as the content of the law is concerned. As Raz put it:

> A non-democratic legal system, based on the denial of human rights, on extensive poverty, on racial segregation, sexual inequalities, and religious persecution may, in principle, conform to the requirements of the rule of law better than any of the legal systems of the more enlightened Western democracies. This does not mean that it will be better than those Western democracies. It will be an immeasurably worse legal system, but it will excel in one respect: in its conformity to the rule of law.[143]

The substantive theories include all requirements of the formal Rule of Law, but also add features of political morality such as democracy and individual rights. An important contributor is Dworkin with his 'rights thesis' according to which, the Rule of Law has a substantive meaning relating to moral rights and duties that the

---

134 A.V. Dicey, 'Introduction to the study of the law of the constitution', Macmillan, 1959, pp. 202–203.

135 F.A. Hayek, 'The Road to Serfdom', Routledge, 1976.

136 L.L. Fuller, 'The Morality of Law', Yale University Press, 1969.

137 J. Raz, 'The Authority of Law', Oxford University Press, 2009.

138 F.A. Hayek, 'The Road to Serfdom', Routledge, 1976, p. 54.

139 Ibid., p. 61.

140 N. MacCormick, 'Rhetoric and the Rule of Law', Oxford University Press, 2005, p. 16.

141 J. Raz, 'The Authority of Law', Oxford University Press, 2009, pp. 214–219.

142 C. Murphy, 'Lon Fuller and the Moral Value of the Rule of Law', Law and Philosophy, vol. 24, 2005, p. 247.

143 J. Raz, 'The Rule of Law and its Virtue', Law Quarterly Review, vol. 93, 1977, p. 195.

citizens and the state share. This substantive Rule of Law does not distinguish between substantive justice and the formal Rule of Law, but it requires that the norms capture and enforce moral rights.[144] In this version, there is a strong presence of individual rights.[145] The aforementioned procedural and substantive versions of democracy are of relevance, because this version of the Rule of Law is based upon a more substantive version of democracy.[146] Principles such as democracy and the separation of powers are encompassed by a substantive notion of the Rule of Law. This is in contrast to the formal Rule of Law, where these concepts are defined independently.[147] Another characteristic is that courts may have a significant role, and therefore this would result in a 'judicialisation' of politics, as many political questions become constitutional and judicial concerns.[148] As explained above this is an on-going debate when the separation of powers was discussed.[149]

The debate between formal and substantive conceptions of the Rule of Law is long standing. Even strict formal definitions are often criticised for having covertly substantive components.[150] Hence, more pragmatic scholars tend to identify both formal and substantive requirements.[151] For example Allan defines the Rule of Law as follows:

> The rule of law, under this communitarian perception, is not the faithful application of whatever rules emerge from the political battle, regardless of content, but rather the subjection of government (and other significant sources of power) to principles of justice and fairness which express the community's enduring commitment to fundamental ideas of human freedom and human dignity. Allegiance to the rule of law, by citizens and judges, consists not merely in unquestioning obedience to the legislative command, or administrative order, oblivious of its moral quality, but in a more discriminating response, respectful of the constitution as a source of moral constraints on those in powers.[152]

The *Rechtsstaat* represents the narrative of the Rule of Law as developed in Germany: first influenced by Kant's liberalism, it aimed at protecting individual

144 R. Dworkin, 'A Matter of Principle', Harvard University Press, 1985, pp. 11–18.
145 B.Z. Tamanaha, 'On the Rule of Law: History, Politics, Theory', Cambridge University Press, 2004, pp. 102–104.
146 Ibid., pp. 104–108.
147 C. Sampford, 'Retrospectivity and the Rule of Law', Oxford University Press, 2006, p. 49.
148 B.Z. Tamanaha, 'On the Rule of Law: History, Politics, Theory', Cambridge University Press, 2004, pp. 108–110.
149 See for a critic J. Habermas, 'Between Facts and Norms', Polity Press, 1997, pp. 253–266.
150 L. Pech, 'The Rule of Law as a Constitutional Principle of the European Union', Jean Monnet Working Paper 04/2009, p. 28 (available at http://ssrn.com/abstract=1463242).
151 E.g. Lord Bingham, 'The Rule of Law', Cambridge Law Journal, vol. 66, 2007, pp. 75–76.
152 T.R.S. Allan, 'Fairness, Equality, Rationality: Constitutional Theory and Judicial Review', in C.F. Forsyth and I. Hare (eds), 'The Golden Metwand and the Crooked Cord', Oxford University Press, 1998, pp. 16–17.

liberty from state arbitrariness.[153] The German *Rechtsstaat* had a strong formal content – Rule *by* Law – and prescribed organic requirements to limit the state action, until the mid-20th century, where there was a sharp change in attitude.[154] As legal positivism was partly to blame for the participation of courts in the totalitarian regime of the Third Reich, the notion of *Rechtsstaat* received also substantive connotations.[155] The majority of German scholars and judges consider the substantive and formal aspects as co-existent.[156] The different views on the Rule of Law shall be revisited again when common law and civil law traditions are compared.[157]

For criminal law, allegiance to the Rule of Law produces both procedural and substantive requirements that are indissociable. On the one hand, legal certainty is vital (via clear and prospective laws which bind the state-actors), and on the other hand the content of criminal norms must also respect certain basic individual rights, which underpin the legal community. While the legality principle may be considered a formal requirement *prima facie*, its application – especially in judicial interpretation – may also encompass a 'rights' narrative; this is especially because in determining the wording of the text and the scope of criminal liability, the individual rights that are protected or interfered with by criminal provisions must also be interpreted in accordance with the Rule of Law.[158]

A final feature of the Rule of Law is the principle of neutrality, which is important for Western liberal systems. If the Rule of Law is infused with libertarian political theory, individual autonomy becomes a key element. Individual wellbeing is prioritised above the wellbeing of the community. While the restriction of individual autonomy via criminal law is considered a necessity for society to function, such restriction should be as limited as possible. Individuals should retain the liberty to decide for themselves the life they want to pursue.[159] The state in this *Rechtsstaat* is neutral in that it should not impose any particular version of 'good life'. This neutrality can be seen as *'the priority of justice over the good, and hence the fact that questions of the good life recede behind questions of justice.'*[160] Equality is essential in this regard as all individuals should be given the chance to act or at least be able to express their choices. The state becomes a *Rechtsstaat*

153 C. Roxin, 'Strafrecht: Allgemeiner Teil Band I', Verlag C.H. Beck, 2006, para. 5, Mn 19.

154 B.Z. Tamanaha, 'On the Rule of Law: History, Politics, Theory', Cambridge University Press, 2004, pp. 108–110.

155 G. Radbruch, 'Statutory Lawlessness and *Supra*-Statutory Law (1946)' (translated in English by B. Litschewski Paulson and S. L. Paulson), Oxford Journal of Legal Studies, vol. 26, 2006, pp. 5 and 8.

156 R. Grote, 'Rule of Law, Rechtsstaat and 'Etat de droit'', in C. Starck (ed), 'Constitutionalism, Universalism and Democracy – Comparative Analysis', Nomos Verlagsgesellschaft, 1999, p. 286; L. Pech, 'The Rule of Law as a Constitutional Principle of the European Union', Jean Monnet Working Paper 04/2009, p. 34 (available at http://ssrn.com/abstract=1463242).

157 Chapter IV para. 2.

158 N. MacCormick, 'Rhetoric and the Rule of Law', Oxford University Press, 2005, pp. 23–31.

159 E. Claes, 'Legaliteit en rechtsvinding in het strafrecht', Universitaire Pers Leuven, 2003, p. 100.

160 J. Habermas, 'Between Facts and Norms', Polity Press, 1997, p. 309.

when it safeguards the self-determination of every individual in a climate of neutrality and equality.

Under this spirit of individualism and liberty, criminal law can only be legitimate when it gives priority to individual autonomy, as opposed to the public order and security. The neutrality of the liberal *Rechtsstaat,* or Rule of Law, is a product of political liberalism resulting from the Enlightenment, where there was a significant shift towards the value of the individual as a distinct and unique being.[161] In previous societies, such as the Christian Medieval Europe, the state promoted Christian values, while in ancient Greece the state and law promoted certain values and a community life based around the warrior ideal.[162] The libertarian *Rechtsstaat* differs from a communitarian or utilitarian *Rechtsstaat,* where criminal law finds its moral standing in the community, or public interests to be safeguarded through criminal law. As opposed to the liberal *Rechtsstaat*, the starting point of communitarianism is the community, not the individual.[163] In a communitarian state, the law is meant to maintain the community attachments, as individuals are presumed to thrive better within a successful community.[164]

6. Other principles

The legality principle is linked to other legal principles or concepts. Some examples are the principle of guilt, the presumption of innocence, and a generalised concept of legal certainty. Most of these principles can be interpreted from the aforementioned theoretical rationales.

6.1. Principle of legal certainty

One cannot neglect the enormous influence that the principle of legal certainty has had on legal systems. Certainty and predictability are necessary for citizens to understand and plan their conduct. From a sociological, anthropological and psychological perspective, it is the human instinct to battle the uncertainty created by nature and by other individuals that led humans to form ordered and regulated societies and to seek a scientific and rationalised understanding of the natural world surrounding them.[165]

Valuing legal certainty in the criminal justice system forms a part of the ideals of the Rule of Law and individual autonomy. It safeguards the ability of individuals

161 See above para. 2.

162 B.Z. Tamanaha, 'On the Rule of Law: History, Politics, Theory', Cambridge University Press, 2004, p. 42.

163 Ibid.

164 A. Etzioni, 'The New Golden Rule', Basic Books, 1996, pp. 23–24.

165 R. Kolb, 'Réflexions de philosophie du droit international', Editions Bruylant, 2003, pp. 280–282.

to rely upon the law and, therefore, to trust the actions of the state as legitimate, and eventually form their own choices and actions.[166] The obligation to maintain a climate of legal certainty limits state action, but it also safeguards trust in the institutions.

Legal systems should function in predictable manner. Legal certainty is ironically a nebulous concept. It can be expressed as positive and negative obligations on state-actors, such as precision of statutes, expectations regarding acts by the executive, the anticipation of statutory interpretation or of the use of evidence, the stability and non-questionability of norms and their binding effect, the avoidance of confusing multi-layered or chaotic legislation and of over-precise legislation.

As the principle of legal certainty is a rather general concept, clarification of different types of legal certainty is necessary, in particular, objective and subjective legal certainty.[167] Objective legal certainty concerns the legal order in its totality and is expressed as a demand for accessibility, clarity and precision *erga omnes*. Subjective legal certainty is applicable to civil relationships regulated by law (such as contract law) and relies on the protection of good faith. Moreover, one may also distinguish between normative legal certainty, which concerns the certainty of the content of norms, and executive legal certainty, which relates to the predictable mode of applying norms by the executive. Normative legal certainty can be further categorised into synchronic legal certainty and diachronic legal certainty.[168]

Synchronic legal certainty expresses the need for clarity, simplicity and order of legal norms. Individuals must understand at a given, static moment the content of the law, their obligations and rights, the do's and don'ts.[169] It relates to the quality of the statute and ultimately the precision of the norm. Using unclear words, or open-textured terms can be a source for vagueness, however, the precision of a norm is not the same as clarity of words.[170] There can be different types of indeterminacy, such as vagueness, imprecision, incompleteness, incommensurability, immensurability, and ambiguity.[171] Precision of a provision relates as to whether there are 'borderline cases' – the so-called problems of the penumbra –[172] namely cases where one does not know whether or not facts fall within the scope of criminal liability.[173] As natural language is itself indeterminate, legal certainty cannot be easily measured; it is difficult to assert whether a definition is precise or vague, or to set a linguistic threshold. Solidifying a term can be therefore an issue for judicial interpretation. While linguistic clarity cannot be guaranteed, the aim is

166 E. Claes, 'Legaliteit en rechtsvinding in het strafrecht', Universitaire Pers Leuven, 2003, p. 78.
167 R. Kolb, 'Réflexions de philosophie du droit international', Editions Bruylant, 2003, pp. 282–283.
168 Ibid., pp. 283–287.
169 Ibid.
170 R. Geitmann, 'Bundesverfassungsgericht und "offene" Normen', Duncker & Humblot, 1971, p. 28.
171 T. Endicott, 'Vagueness in Law', Oxford University Press, 2000, pp. 31–55.
172 G. Williams, 'Law and Language – III', Law Quarterly Review, vol. 61, 1945, p. 302.
173 T. Endicott, 'Vagueness in Law', Oxford University Press, 2000, p. 31.

to guarantee the ability of individuals to rely on the law. Thus, what is of essence is that norms – and the way they are interpreted – should retain their function of regulating and guiding behaviour.

In order for individuals to understand the law at a given moment, legal instruments must be promulgated or published, and written in a language generally understood.[174] Thus, it is synchronic legal certainty that enriches the legality principle with the requirements of accessibility and comprehensibility. Accessibility means that the norms should be accessible to the general public. Comprehensibility refers to the obligation of the legislation to use a language that is understood by individuals, which is not too technical, excessively detailed or turgid. What is more, in cases of interrelated and layered statutes, criminal liability should be able to be clearly identified. A good systematisation of sources is therefore necessary to avoid conflicting norms on what constitutes criminal conduct, or a labyrinth of provisions that results in ambiguity.[175]

Diachronic legal certainty addresses the necessity for certainty regarding the content of the norms, not at a specific given moment, but through time. Individuals should be able to assume that the criminal legal order has stability.[176] Diachronic legal certainty enriches the legality principle with a general prohibition of extremely frequent changes in the law. While the legislator may amend legislation when it is necessary, such amendments should not be so rapid that the legal order loses its stability and individuals their capacity to regulate their lives. One well-known element of stability is the prohibition of retroactive application of criminal law. Individuals are entitled to anticipate that their actions shall be judged in accordance with current legislation. Retroactive criminal legislation violates the principle of legal certainty, as it takes away the capacity of individuals to rely on such legislation.

Furthermore, legal certainty does not only imply predictability but also acceptability.[177] This requirement is more relevant for judicial interpretation and it requires that the law is not only precise but is also interpreted in a manner that can be 'accepted' as legitimate. The idea of acceptability is that provisions receive meaning in a particular context that contributes to what is foreseeable. To put it differently, one foresees criminalisation that can be expected as legitimate in a legal order. Unlike predictability, which implies that the law is stable and clear, acceptability refers to the fluidity of the law, its flexibility and context-sensitivity.[178] If legal certainty operates within a Rule of Law, a democratic framework and individual rights, then individuals anticipate and trust that courts interpret norms with respect to the underlying principles of the legal order. In other words, individuals foresee the interpretation that they would also accept as plausible in the

---

174 R. Kolb, 'Réflexions de philosophie du droit international', Editions Bruylant, 2003, pp. 283–287.

175 Ibid.

176 Ibid., p. 285.

177 J. Raitio, 'The Principle of Legal Certainty in EC Law', Kluwer, 2003, pp. 347–387.

178 E. Paunio, 'Beyond Predictability – Reflections on Legal Certainty and the Discourse Theory of Law in the EU Legal Order', German Law Journal, vol. 10, 2009, p. 1469.

context of a particular legal order. To some extent one can categorise acceptability also as diachronic legal certainty due to the element of fluidity. Reconciling stability with acceptability and the legitimacy of judicial interpretation is a daunting task, which scholarship has undertaken quite vigorously.[179]

While the principle of legal certainty supports and enriches the principle of legality, one cannot help but wonder whether the two principles are actually one and the same in criminal law. After all, any aspect of the legality principle, such as prohibition of analogy and precision, can be traced back to the need for certainty.

There is definitely overlap between the two concepts, which explains why the principle of legal certainty can be considered a rationale for the principle of legality. One could argue that the legality principle articulates more accurately how legal certainty can be achieved in substantive criminal law and it therefore makes it more specific. It can also be said that the legality principle is much more than simply a plea for legal certainty, as the latter is a value that systems should have, not only for the protection of individuals but also for the administration of justice. It should be pointed out that legal certainty does not only protect individual autonomy but it is also an asset for the proper and successful enforcement of criminal legislation.[180] For example, it is easier for prosecutors to do their job when there is certainty on whether legal norms concerning rape should be used as a basis for prosecution for a forced French kiss, or whether the prosecutor should rely on provisions for sexual assault.

Nevertheless, the principle of legal certainty has replaced some functions of the legality principle in non-continental systems. In the English common law system, a concrete concept of a 'legality principle' as it is understood in continental systems, was unknown.[181] This may be because the continental version of the 'legality principle' was strongly linked to the prevalence of the legislature in criminal matters, something that was not the practice in England until well into the 20th century, as common law had been developing for centuries via judicial decision-making.[182] In common law, the principle of legal certainty may have been more central in the absence of a 'legality principle'. This also seems to be the case in EU law. There, the principle of legal certainty has been closely connected with the principle of legality. As will be seen, in the EU system, the principle of legal certainty has been considered an umbrella concept for the principle of legality.[183]

6.2. Principle of guilt

This principle is also a by-product of a strong emphasis on individual autonomy and liberty. The principle of guilt can be defined as an obligation to recognise criminal

179 J. Habermas, 'Between Facts and Norms', Polity Press, 1997, pp. 194–237.

180 Kamerstukken II 1990/91, 22 008, nr 2, p. 28.

181 A. Ashworth, J. Horder, 'Principles of Criminal Law', Oxford University Press, 2013, pp. 62–65.

182 Chapter IV para. 1, 2 and 3.

183 Joined cases C–74/95 and C–129/95 criminal proceedings against X, 12 December 1996, para. 53.

guilt only when there is a guilty mind. The guilt of the individual is in most cases indispensable for the attribution of criminal liability and therefore one cannot be held liable for an act if he does not have a guilty mind.

The connection between the principle of guilt and the legality principle is interesting.[184] *Prima facie* both principles seem to entail the same thing: the individuals must know the criminal character of their actions in order to be held criminally liable. This connection has led to suggestions that the principle of guilt should be considered not only as one of the rationales of the legality principle, but that the latter is merely the application of the principle of guilt.[185] Whether or not the principle of guilt can be considered a foundation for the legality principle is debated. There is the view that the principle of guilt is an element of the legality principle, as the criteria of guilt cannot be fulfilled unless the individual was aware, or could have been aware, at the time of the commission of the act, of the precise conduct prohibited by legislation.[186] This view has been criticised in German literature. First of all, it is argued that there is a distinction between unlawfulness (*Unrecht*) and criminalisation (*Strafbarkeit*), which is depicted in Article 17 GCC.[187] The principle of guilt is understood as the *Erkennbarkeit des Unrechts*, i.e. the knowledge that the behaviour is unlawful.[188] The legality principle is concerned with the *Strafbarkeit*, that is to say the knowledge that this act has also been criminalised, with certain elements making up the criminal liability and a sanction.[189] This distinction may perhaps be clearer if one focuses on foreseeability per se. Legality demands the general foreseeability of criminal liability, while the principle of guilt ensures the concrete foreseeability of a particular person. For example, Van Dijk argues that the 'principle of control' – on which the principle of guilt is based – and the principle of legality are actually complimentary: while the principle of guilt takes care of the concrete foreseeability of criminalisation by an identified individual, the principle of legality is about a more general foreseeability, which is of concern to any individual.[190]

Secondly, there is a general tendency in German theory to detach the principle of legality from Feuerbach's *psychologische Zwangstheorie*, which supports the deterrent effect of criminal prohibitions on individuals.[191] This theory is closely

184 H.-L. Schreiber, 'Gesetz und Richter', Alfred Metzner Verlag GmbH, 1976, pp. 209–211.

185 P. Westen, 'Two Rules of Legality in Criminal Law', Law and Philosophy, vol. 26, 2007, pp. 229–305.

186 J. de Hullu, 'Materieel strafrecht', Kluwer, 2012, p. 81; M.S. Groenhuijsen, 'Straf en Wet', Gouda Quint, 1987, p. 26.

187 C. Roxin, 'Strafrecht: Allgemeiner Teil Band I', Verlag C.H. Beck, 2006, para. 5, Mn 25.

188 H.-L. Schreiber, 'Gesetz und Richter', Alfred Metzner Verlag GmbH, 1976, p. 211.

189 Ibid., p. 211; G. Grünwald, 'Bedeutung und Begründung des Satzes nulla poena sine lege', ZStW, vol. 76, 1964, p. 12.

190 A.A. van Dijk, 'Strafrechtelijke aansprakelijkheid heroverwogen. Over opzet, schuld, schulduitsluitingsgronden en straf', Maklu, 2008, p. 162.

191 See above, para. 2.2; H.-L. Schreiber, 'Gesetz und Richter', Alfred Metzner Verlag GmbH, 1976, p. 213; G. Grünwald, 'Bedeutung und Begründung des Satzes nulla poena sine lege', ZStW, vol. 76, 1964, p. 10.

linked with the view that the two principles are strongly connected, because it rests on the presumption that individuals would change their actions had they known their criminal nature. The theory has been criticised for approaching individuals as potential offenders and as not being applicable in practice. If the application of criminal law were dependent on whether individuals knew the elements of all criminal provisions (which is not the case), then criminal law would basically apply only to legal professionals.[192] To this end, there is the presumption that everyone should be aware of the law (*Ignorantia juris non excusat*).

The conceptual relationship between the principle of guilt and legality is useful if one approaches them as complimentary principles.[193] The defence of mistake of law can be a useful concept for the legality principle, something that should be kept in mind.[194] Cases where the mistake of law has been accepted are for example when the individual relied on a wrong legal advice, when he exhausted all reasonable efforts to inform himself or when the legislation was not accessible.[195] These modes of application for the mistake of law in national jurisprudence are very similar to the mainstream jurisprudence of the ECtHR, which focuses on the foreseeability of criminalisation, based on the norm and the available case law, the ability of the individual to rely on legal advice and the accessibility of the criminal rule.[196] This similarity reflects the close dogmatic interrelation between the two concepts.

An interesting approach would be to try to view the two concepts' interrelation in the light of individual autonomy (which is essentially the common basis for both principles). It has been proposed for example in literature that the close dogmatic relation between the principles of guilt and legality can be a useful tool in managing the protection of individual autonomy whenever one of the two principles fails.[197] In particular, it has been argued that vagueness in the determination of *actus reus* elements can be absorbed by the principle of guilt, through an application of the mistake of law.[198] This might also be used, for example, in a canalisation of problems of accessibility, or foreseeability of criminal legislation, which cannot be safeguarded by the legality principle, through the acceptance of a mistake of law.[199] This will be discussed later in Chapter VIII, but it is important to keep in mind that the close connection between these two doctrines may open up the road for more creative possibilities, which support the holistic nature of a justice system.[200]

---

192 H.-L. Schreiber, 'Gesetz und Richter', Alfred Metzner Verlag GmbH, 1976, p. 104.

193 A.A. van Dijk, 'Strafrechtelijke aansprakelijkheid heroverwogen. Over opzet, schuld, schulduitsluitingsgronden en straf', Maklu, 2008, p. 162.

194 Chapter VIII para. 3.3.1.

195 J. Blomsma, 'Mens rea and defences in European criminal law', Intersentia, 2012, pp. 464–476.

196 ECtHR Sunday Times v United Kingdom, App. 6538/74, 26 April 1979.

197 W. Naucke, 'Über Generalklauseln und Rechtsanwendung im Strafrecht', JCB Mohr, 1973, pp. 21–25.

198 Ibid., p. 24.

199 Ibid.

200 Chapter VIII para. 3.3.1.

7. Conclusion

In this Chapter, the theoretical rationales for the legality principle were presented. As identified in the beginning, this Chapter had two aims, first to trace the rationales of the legality principle and second, to explain their different interpretations.

The principle of legality is not a doctrine that simply helps the system to function better. It carries an ethical account of how individuals and communities are perceived within legal systems. It is based on certain assumptions, namely that individuals are rational beings and should be treated as such, and that communities reflect certain common shared values protected by criminal law.

As far as individual liberty and autonomy is concerned, criminal law simultaneously limits those concepts but also reinforces them. Criminal norms are a limitation to individual liberty and autonomy, but they also reinforce them by protecting their violation by third parties. This implies that a legality principle must function within a context where criminal law finds a concurrent legitimacy on two antithetical tendencies.

Democracy and the Rule of Law are doctrines that are constantly being developed. There are various models for these concepts developed through reflection and learned experience. The most relevant development within the concept of democracy, which is also reflected in the different interpretations of the Rule of Law, is the growing infusion of a strictly procedural concept with substantive elements. If the legality principle were to be truly based on these concepts, then there would be a tension between formal requirements of criminal norms and substantive ones.

The analysis on the separation of powers shows that the focus of the legality principle should be to ensure that none of the powers shall be left unchecked and become a potential source of arbitrariness in criminal matters. This implies that the legality principle must function in a manner that limits courts' freedom of interpretation (thus negatively restricting it) but, also, in a manner that instructs it (thus positively informing it).[201]

Finally, the variety of interpretations of the theoretical rationales shows that it is possible to construct different versions of the principle of legality. For example, if one assumes that the Rule of Law has only formal requirements then the legality principle should focus on procedures and formal elements, such as the source of law and its precision. If one accepts the concept of a substantive Rule of Law, then, especially in matters of judicial interpretation, the principle of legality should also generate requirements regarding the compatibility of interpretation with basic human rights. Therefore, the legality principle is an open doctrine that can be shaped depending on what it represents.

---

201 Chapter V para. 4.3. and 6.4.

Chapter IV
The Application of the Principle in three National Systems

As explained, the purpose of Part 2 is to identify the national nucleus of the principle of legality, i.e. an approximation of this principle that could inspire the construction of a European legality principle.[1] Therefore, after analysing the theoretical justifications of the legality principle, an analysis of the legality principle's national application in three national systems (German, English and Dutch) shall be presented.

This Chapter shall focus on the *modus operandi* of the principle in national law. It shall observe how this principle is understood in national law both in theory and practice and the challenges faced by domestic legal systems. The aim is to provide the features of this principle in national systems and the problems that exist. The goal is not to devise solutions or a complete theoretical narrative of the legality principle; this will be the focus of the next Chapter (Chapter V).

The present Chapter starts with comparing the ways national systems interpret legal theory and the nature of the legality principle. As will be shown there is a clear difference between the common and continental systems, as the legality principle is the result of each jurisdiction's unique historical development and legal culture. The Chapter continues with an analysis of the ECtHR approach on this principle and its influence on the national legal systems. This Chapter ends with a shift from the 'law in the books' to the 'law in practice' and a problem-based illustration of the current application of the doctrine in national law shall be presented. What will be shown is that the application of this principle presents common problems to all three jurisdictions, despite their doctrinal and historical differences. While common and continental law systems have had diametrically opposed starting points, the traditions are converging and increasingly similar challenges exist.

Before starting with the illustration of the *modus operandi* of this principle in a comparative manner, certain rules and disclaimers are required. First of all, it should be kept in mind that the legality principle is a difficult concept to compare as it is influenced by variables distinctive to each jurisdiction. Such variables can include: legal and non-legal historical developments, social culture, idiosyncrasies of the political framework and internal political dynamics, philosophical trends, even isolated events and court decisions. For example, the participation of courts in the Third Reich contributed to the change of the strongly positivistic nature of the legality principle in Germany;[2] the English conception of the principle of legality

---

1 Chapter I para. 4.3.

2 G. Radbruch, 'Statutory Lawlessness and *Supra*-Statutory Law (1946)' (translated in English by B. Litschewski Paulson and S. L. Paulson), Oxford Journal of Legal Studies, vol. 26, 2006, pp. 5 and 8; T. Mertens, 'Nazism, Legal Positivism and Radbruch's Thesis on Statutory Injustice', Law and Critique, vol. 14, 2003, pp. 277–295.

was developed incrementally over decades, through a series of high profile and disparate cases concerning issues as varied as prostitution and marital rape;[3] the cultural diversity and liberal attitude of the Dutch society has greatly influenced this doctrine in the Netherlands.[4] While there are clear differences and similarities, these are neither static nor definite. The legality principle develops hand in hand with the development of national culture and criminal law. Secondly, practical examples of the legality principle in national jurisdictions in this publication are not exhaustive. As explained, the national comparative research in this book does not aim to present detailed in-country reports.[5] For example, it would be interesting to cover meticulously all aspects of the relationship between statutory and common law offences in English law, but this is an issue relevant only as a peculiarity of the English legal system.[6]

1. Preliminary remarks

When one initially thinks of the legality principle, what springs to mind is the classic phrase: 'there is no crime without law', which, in a nutshell, delineates the primary aim of the principle of legality: to bind state power to the law. It is a mechanism that defines what *law* is, and thereby, it restricts the existence and application of criminal liability to the particular legal framework.

The modern conception of this principle rests on the hypothesis that law is made, rather than derived from nature, or contingent upon its merits, and is therefore closely linked to the school of thought of legal positivism. The basis of legal positivism is that a law's merit does not influence its existence.[7] In other words, the law's injustice or immorality does not negate its existence. The law is what it has been posited to be in authoritative sources (e.g. legislation or judicial decisions).[8]

Although legal positivism does not necessarily favour parliamentary statutes as opposed to judge-made law, the principle of legality was historically developed in connection with the codification movement after the French Revolution, which concerned primarily continental legal systems, the Netherlands and Germany being the continental jurisdictions analysed in this publication. The codification process – led by Portalis – aimed specifically at limiting judicial powers, in addition to the violence and anarchy of the French Revolution itself.[9]

3 Shaw v DPP [1962] AC 220; R v R [1992] 1 AC 599.

4 F. de Witte, 'Sex, Drugs and EU law: the recognition of moral and ethical diversity in EU law', Common Market Law Review, vol. 50, 2013, pp. 1545–1578.

5 Chapter II para. 2.

6 P.S. Atiyah, 'Common law and Statutory law', Modern Law Review, vol. 48, 1985, pp. 25–26.

7 L. Green, 'Legal Positivism', The Stanford Encyclopedia of Philosophy (Fall 2009 Edition), E.N. Zalta (ed), URL http://plato.stanford.edu/archives/fall2009/entries/legal-positivism/

8 H.L.A. Hart, 'The Concept of Law', Oxford University Press, 2012, pp. 100–110.

9 A.C. 't Hart, 'Recht als schild van Perseus', Gouda Quint, 1991, p. 39.

In English law, criminal offences did not begin to be codified in statutory instruments until relatively recently in comparison to continental systems.[10] The principle of legality as understood in the continental systems was a doctrine alien to the English tradition. However, this does not mean that the common law system did not embrace the necessity to limit state powers in criminal law. What it means is what is called 'legality principle' in continental systems does not – or, more accurately, did not – have an equivalent principle in the common law systems. While as it will be seen, this principle was also finally passed on to the English system, it is important to point out that this comparative analysis is dealing with a legal doctrine that was native only to two out of the three national systems that are investigated.

Therefore, from the methodological point of view, it is important to understand that these are three legal systems in which the legality principle has had an unequal presence through time. What is more, the gradual introduction of legality principle into the English legal system involves a delicate balance with other fundamental values of the common law system, and is an on-going challenge for English judges.

2. Theoretical rationales

As it was shown in the previous Chapter, the theoretical rationales of this principle can be interpreted differently; the mandate and function of the legality principle may change depending on what definition one gives to its *ratio*.[11] The principles that inspire the legality principle have received different interpretations in the three national jurisdictions analysed in this publication, with a clear divergence between common and continental systems.

A basic difference between the continental and common law countries is the concept of the Rule of Law.[12] The concept of *Rechtsstaat* – which is fairly similar in the Netherlands and Germany – reflects, in its basic ideals, the protection of individuals *vis-à-vis* state arbitrariness and the importance of libertarian neutrality.[13] The protection of individual autonomy is of central importance, and thus there is increased attention to the vertical conflict between the state and individual. The concept of *Rechtsstaat* in continental systems has been functioning under the umbrella of positivism, which for continental systems means that the written statute is the primary mechanism for the protection of individuals against state arbitrariness. The attainment of the *Rechtsstaat* is achieved via the establishment of written constitutions that contain written rules on how the state

10 A. Samuels, 'Comment: Why do we not have a Criminal Code', The Journal of Criminal Law, vol. 67, 2003, pp. 214–219; J.R. Spencer, 'Nulla poena sine lege in English Criminal Law', The Cambridge-Tilburg Law Lectures, Kluwer, 1980, p. 36.

11 Chapter III para. 7.

12 Chapter III para. 5.

13 J. Habermas, 'Between Facts and Norms', Polity Press, 1997, p. 309.

should exercise its power, and which codify certain fundamental rights. These constitutions enjoy hierarchical supremacy and – despite different approaches towards constitutional review – all state-actors are expected to base and measure their acts upon these constitutional limits. Thus, the continental concept of *Rechtsstaat* values hierarchy and structure.

Within the continental traditions, there are also different legal cultures regarding the issue of individual autonomy. Under the German *Rechtsstaat*, individuals are seen as rational agents, who require legal certainty to make choices. The mainstream German approach is that the legality principle has a double purpose: to ensure foreseeability and the principles of democracy and separation of powers.[14] Others disagree with this view. For example, there is often a distinction made regarding the interpretation of legal certainty and foreseeability: there is subjective foreseeability, seen as conceptually close to the principle of guilt, concerning the certainty of the individual regarding his legal position;[15] and a objective foreseeability, which is understood as a general climate of legal certainty which individuals should have regarding the actions of the state.[16] The disagreement is about whether the legality principle protects not only the individual autonomous sphere, but also the ability of individuals to rely on the law.[17] Some suggest that while the protection of foreseeability and legal certainty is an important theoretical rationale of the legality principle, it mainly concerns the actions of the state (so the subjective foreseeability) and not as a general trust towards the norms and their reliability.[18] Thus, the principle of legality is sometimes approached in Germany as a principle that guarantees precise rules, not to protect the ability of individuals to rely on the law, but to prevent the state from acting *ultra vires*, limiting therefore, any scope of arbitrariness. It has even been suggested that if the principle of legality were to be based on a concept of legal certainty in the sense of foreseeability or reliability, this could lead to a violation of the rationales of the legality principle. This would occur because the decisive issue is not whether the state went beyond the law, but whether the individual could or should have foreseen such action based on the written statute, which implies a shift of the burden from the state to the individual.[19] One could argue that an additional reason for such interpretation of individual liberty relates to the desire to demarcate the principle of individual guilt and the legality principle.

---

14 A. Schönke, H. Schröder, 'Kommentar zum StGB', Verlag C.H. Beck, 2014, para. 1, Mn 16.

15 Chapter III para. 6.2.

16 H.-L. Schreiber, 'Gesetz und Richter', Alfred Metzner Verlag GmbH, 1976, pp. 215–327; B. Schünemann, 'Nulla poena sine lege? Rechtstheoretische und verfassungsrechtliche Implikationen der Rechtsgewinnung im Strafrecht', Walter de Gruyter, 1978, p. 16.

17 B. Jähnke, 'Zur Erosion des Verfassungssatzes "Keine Strafe ohne Gesetz"', ZIS, vol. 7, 2010, p. 464.

18 G. Grünwald, 'Bedeutung und Begründung des Satzes nulla poena sine lege', ZStW, vol. 76, 1964, pp. 13–14; B. Schünemann, 'Nulla poena sine lege? Rechtstheoretische und verfassungsrechtliche Implikationen der Rechtsgewinnung im Strafrecht', Walter de Gruyter, 1978, p. 16.

19 Ibid.

In Dutch scholarship, there is also a distinction between the reliability to the law and the protection against state arbitrariness. Additionally, the close relationship between the principle of guilt and legality is acknowledged;[20] however, this close relationship does not necessarily result in the view that the legality principle should not support reliability to the law.

The English doctrine of the Rule of Law is also oriented towards the limitation of state power and the respect of certain fundamental rights. However, the lack of codification in England, especially the lack of a written constitution and criminal legislation,[21] denotes a less positivistic approach in the application of the Rule of Law. In particular, prior to the Enlightenment and for a significant time afterwards, the limitation of state power was done in a customary manner. There was a widespread belief and commitment amongst legal practice, the state and the community that England is ruled under the Rule of Law and it was only this attitude that ensured that the Rule of Law was applied.[22] There was no special mechanism, nor a specific written document. Tamanaha points out in this respect, that England solved the puzzle of 'how the law limits itself' by answering that it is the attitude to the law that limits it.[23] Berlin pointed out this 'self-restraining attitude':

> What makes [Great Britain] comparatively free, therefore, is the fact that this theoretically omnipotent entity is restrained by custom or opinion from behaving as such. It is clear that what matters is not the form of restraints on power – whether they are legal, or moral, or constitutional – but their effectiveness.[24]

The reliance on custom and a self-restrained state has resulted in less-structured protective mechanisms. The Enlightenment also influenced England, as the doctrine of parliamentary sovereignty was well-established and there was a shift towards parliamentary intervention.[25] The widespread view up until then was that the law reflected certain unwritten, aspirational and unaltered values, which reflected societal culture.[26] This view has subsequently changed. However, the less structured, less hierarchical and less positivistic notion of the Rule of Law can still be seen in the lack of any unified criminal code and in the absence of any written constitution. It also explains the lack of a well-formed doctrine of the principle of legality, at least in comparison with continental traditions.

---

20 J. de Hullu, 'Materieel strafrecht', Kluwer, 2012, p. 81; M.S. Groenhuijsen, 'Straf en Wet', Gouda Quint, 1987, p. 26.

21 An exception is the Magna Carta.

22 B.Z. Tamanaha, 'On the Rule of Law: History, Politics, Theory', Cambridge University Press, 2004, p. 58.

23 Ibid.

24 I. Berlin, 'Four Essays on Liberty', Oxford University Press, 1971, p. 166.

25 B.Z. Tamanaha, 'On the Rule of Law: History, Politics, Theory', Cambridge University Press, 2004, p. 57.

26 Ibid.

With regard to the democratic principle there is also a rather different starting point between continental and common law traditions. In Germany and the Netherlands, the democratic principle has been embraced early on as the main source of legitimation for criminal liability. The parliamentary statute has been the sole source for legitimate criminal liability and any other state powers (executive and courts) are restricted to the statute's limits. On the other hand, the English system had a delayed start regarding the establishment of criminal liability by parliamentary statutes, as it was not the role of the English parliament to develop criminal legislation but it was widely seen as a matter for the judiciary enforcing the common law.[27] Criminal statutes were increasingly used in England during the 19th century, and the legislative movement peaked during the large codification process in the second half of the previous century.[28]

The English legal system also takes a different approach to the separation of powers. In continental systems, already during and after the French Revolution, there was mistrust of the courts. During the *Ancien Regime* courts were seen as the main culprits of arbitrariness. The separation of powers aimed at restraining judicial power as much as possible. Judicial interpretation was to operate within clear limits and the scope of courts to interpret parliamentary statutes was minimal. This meant that the mandate of the legality principle was to ensure clear delineation of the will of parliament and limit judicial interpretation.

In England, there was no such antipathy towards courts. On the contrary, they were perceived as the protectors from sovereign law-makers for many centuries.[29] English courts enjoyed a virtual monopoly in criminal law-making up until the end of the 19th century. The change in approach is reflected in the quote by Bentham:

> When a man has a dog to teach, he falls upon him and beats him: the animal takes note in his own mind of the circumstances in which he has been beaten, and the intimation thus received becomes, in the mind of the dog, a rule of common law... Men are treated like dogs – they are beaten without respite, and without mercy; and out of one man's beating, another man is left to derive instruction as he can.[30]

The concept of parliamentary sovereignty and the role of parliament in legislating criminal law statutes became gradually entrenched, despite tension with the judiciary. The 19th and 20th centuries were peppered with landmark cases such as

---

27 J.R. Spencer, 'Nulla poena sine lege in English Criminal Law', The Cambridge-Tilburg Law Lectures, Kluwer, 1980, pp. 38–39.

28 Mrs Justice Arden, 'Criminal Law at the Crossroads: the Impact of Human Rights from the Law Commissions' Perspective and the Need for a Code', Criminal Law Review, 1999, p. 439; Lord Bingham, 'A Criminal Code: Must we wait for ever?', Criminal Law Review, 1998, p. 694; G. de Búrca, G. Gardner, 'The Codification of the Criminal Law', Oxford Journal of Legal Studies, vol. 10, 1990, pp. 559–571.

29 For a historical account on the matter see C.H. McIlwain, 'The English Common Law, Barrier against Absolutism', American Historical Review, vol. 49, 1943, pp. 23–31.

30 J. Bentham, 'Rationale of Judicial Evidences', 1843, vol. VI, p. 519.

the *Price* judgement in 1884, where the English court declared that its powers should be limited by parliamentary statutes in the area of criminal law.[31] The overview of the English jurisprudence of the 20th century is characterised by cases where courts created or extended criminal offences and others where they renounced explicitly their powers to do so.[32]

These institutional dynamics explain why the English system has been lacking a concrete legality principle, as it is known to continental systems. They also highlight a different basis for the legitimacy of criminal law. Common law, being judicially-made, was legitimate as long as courts were considered a barrier between state arbitrariness (the government/parliament) and the individual, and based itself on common and shared values of the population. Judicial decisions were presumed to be based on the rational judgement of the judges, who applied the learned aspirational principles developed through custom, in a manner that reflected the values of the society.[33]

One wonders at this point whether the early common law system was indeed lacking a legality principle, not in its modern, continental sense, but as a functional equivalent. The continental legality principle has been accepted in the English system in the latter part of the 20th century. The tense institutional dynamics between courts and the parliament on sensitive legal issues remain nevertheless a clear feature of the English system.[34]

3. The normative role of the legality principle

The legality principle being indigenous to the continental tradition has a normative function. It supports a positivistic, hierarchical and structured system for criminal liability. Seen as a mechanism, it generates a set of preconditions under which criminal law is created, applied and interpreted. The normative role of the legality principle is that it defines what *law* is, in other words, it identifies the legitimate sources of criminal liability.

3.1. Sources of criminal liability

The parliamentary statute in continental systems has a central position. As seen in Article 8 of the French Declaration of the Rights of Men: *'The law shall provide for such punishments only as are strictly and obviously necessary, and no one shall suffer punishment except it be legally inflicted in virtue of a law passed and*

---

31 Queen v Price [1884] 12 QBD 247; see below para. 5, for more on this issue.

32 For example Shaw v DPP [1962] AC 220; R v Rimmington and R v Goldstein (joined cases) [2005] UKHL 63.

33 B.Z. Tamanaha, 'On the Rule of Law: History, Politics, Theory', Cambridge University Press, 2004, p. 56.

34 See below, para. 5 and 9.2.

promulgated before the commission of the offense.' The principle of legality rests on the hypothesis that the parliamentary statute, due to its origin from a democratically elected body, is the legitimate basis of criminal law. The principle is entrusted with the task of maintaining the superiority and central position of the parliamentary statute as the sole source of criminal liability. In Germany, where the doctrine is more concept-based, this has been termed the 'statute-reservation' *(Gesetzesvorbehalt)*;[35] the concept means that defining criminal liability is a function reserved only for the statute.

Parliamentary statutes present additional advantages for ensuring legal certainty and protection against judicial arbitrariness. They apply *erga omnes* and guarantee that criminal liability is objective, namely the same for everyone regardless of the individual's position in the society (equality principle). Statutes safeguard the stability of criminal law and they have a continuous effect. Moreover, as binding written norms, they clearly delineate criminal liability and are, thus, a good point of reference for reviewing the legitimate basis of the actions of courts and executive.

On the contrary, in England criminal law was not made but 'found'. English courts were considered to be the *bouche de la loi* – the *custos morum* of the King's subjects,[36] who applied norms regarding criminal liability based on the shared values and norms of English society. Common law was based on the declaratory theory, according to which common law courts never actually create new rules; they rather declare rules that have always pre-existed but were previously undeclared.[37] For example courts have declared many offences such as defamatory libel (1606), perjury (1613), public indecency (1663), blasphemy (1676), disinterring bodies from graves (1788), the incitement of another to commit a criminal offence (1801).[38] While English courts have renounced their powers to declare new criminal offences, the declaratory theory still has some influence in the English system.[39] There are still important common law offences, such as murder, manslaughter and conspiracy to defraud.[40] What is more, the large bulk of criminal law jurisprudence, which defines elements of criminal liability (elements of *actus reus* and *mens rea),* still remains an important part of English criminal law.

This difference between common and continental traditions can be also depicted in the classical distinction between *loi* and *droit.* In continental systems, the legality principle supports the concept of *loi,* according to which law is the parliamentary

---

35 BVerfG 2 BvR 15/62, 3 July 1962.

36 See for example the well-known R v Sidley [1663] 82 ER 1036, cited via B. Juratowitch, 'Retroactivity and the Common Law', Hart Publishing, 2008, p. 119.

37 B. Juratowitch, 'Retroactivity and the Common Law', Hart Publishing, 2008, pp. 119–121.

38 See respectively Case de Libellis Famosis [1606] 77 ER 250; Rowland ap Eliza [1613] 3 Coke Inst. 164; R v Sidley [1663] 82 ER 1036; R v Taylor [1676] 1 Vent 293; Lynn [1784] 100 ER 394; R v Higgins [1801] ER 269, all case law cited via B. Juratowitch, 'Retroactivity and the Common Law', Hart Publishing, 2008, pp. 119–121.

39 B. Juratowitch, 'Retroactivity and the Common Law', Hart Publishing, 2008, p. 120.

40 D. Ormerod, 'Smith and Hogan's Criminal law', Oxford University Press, 2011, pp. 16–17.

statute. *Droit* on the other hand is broader and it includes not only parliamentary written statutes but also case law and forms of customary and unwritten obligations as sources of criminal liability. The latter is closer to what common law recognised as a source of criminal liability.

3.2. Statutes and court judgements

Statutes and jurisprudence are also perceived differently in the two traditions. The hypothesis that the parliamentary statute is the sole source of legitimate criminal liability in the continental systems implies that the statute and jurisprudence are sources with a different value. Statutes and jurisprudence have different purposes in the continental tradition. The statute presents the scope of criminalisation, while jurisprudence applies norms in *ad hoc* situations, clarifying them within the margins set by the statute. Therefore, there is a structural hierarchy between statutes and jurisprudence where the statute has superiority, an element reflected in the normative role of the principle of legality itself.[41]

The principle of legality generates different aspects, which protect the superior value of the statute, the construction of criminal legislation and its interpretation. The principle of strict interpretation and the prohibition of analogy *(lex stricta)*, the prohibition of retroactive application of criminal provisions *(lex praevia)* and the prohibition of customary criminal liability *(lex scripta)* are meant to support the prevalent position of the statute.

The legislator is also bound by the legality principle in order to ensure that statutory liability can provide for a sufficiently accurate scope that will contain judicial interpretation: there is the prohibition of retroactive force of statutes *(lex praevia)* and the prohibition of vague criminal liability *(lex certa)*. Each of the different aspects of the legality principle has a distinct function and they are conceptually independent. Each aspect ensures the supremacy of the statute in different ways. In the most cases, problems regarding foreseeability can be identified as a violation of a specific aspect of the legality principle.

In continental traditions, jurisprudence and judicial interpretation occurs within the context of statutory superiority. Jurisprudence has a different purpose, namely to reflect the application of existing criminal norms to concrete facts but without extending or creating new forms of criminalised behaviour. The court's task is not to create substantive justice in the form of balancing conflicting individual interests, but simply to carry out the application of previously balanced individual interests (as mirrored in the wording of the statute) to a particular situation.

Moreover, the methodology of judicial interpretation is also influenced by a focus on the statute. Interpretation involves establishing a relationship between

41 P. Beauvais, 'Le principe de la légalité pénale dans le droit de l'Union européenne', Thèse, Université Paris X Nanterre UFR, 1 December 2006, p. 73.

facts and norms.[42] Criminal statutes are presumed to have a stable, objective meaning and scope, which determine the criminality of individual acts. Interpretation is a one-sided flowing process where norms determine facts and not vice-versa. Therefore, it is not the circumstances of an act that would give a particular meaning to the norm, but the precise and stable wording of the text that gives a particular meaning to the facts. After interpretation, the norm does not change and the scope of criminal liability remains the same for other similar cases in the future (the same as with past judgements). Therefore, norms are considered isolated from facts. This relationship between facts and norms is called by van Klink *legisme,* because the norms affect the facts by giving them judicial qualification and not vice versa.[43]

Accordingly, the preferred methods of interpretation are those that put forward the wording of the text as the sole factor for interpretation. The legality principle prohibits any interpretational reasoning that inhibits the isolation of facts and norms, such as methods with which courts may incorporate into the statute behaviours that seem 'worthy' of criminalising.

The structural hierarchy between statutes and jurisprudence is an issue that has only been resolved in English law comparatively recently. Increasing legislative intervention in criminal matters has created new challenges for the English judiciary.

First, there is the obvious question of how statutes should be interpreted. English courts were not accustomed to dealing with criminal statutes, which limited their discretion. Various principles regarding statutory interpretation have been developed, however, there is no coherent view of which principle to follow or when.[44] One rule for statutory interpretation is the principle of strict construction of penal statutes. Once considered a part of the old-fashioned 'presumption against unclear changes of law',[45] it is not clear what influence this rule currently has, or how widely accepted it is.[46]

Secondly, there is the issue of the relationship between common law offences and parliamentary statutes. Statutes have only gradually begun to replace common law rules. The question is whether a newly created parliamentary statute is supposed to be the only source of criminal liability on that matter. That would mean that the relevant common law offences should immediately be considered off the map or, alternatively, replaced as much as possible. However, it is not always clear whether the English legislator intends to abolish certain common law offences or he

---

42 See B.M.J. van Klink, 'Bedreigt rechtsvinding de rechtszekerheid? Een kritisch-hermeneutische visie op de rol van de rechter in het materiële strafrecht', Delikt en Delinkwent, vol. 31, 2001, pp. 688–691.

43 Ibid., p. 688.

44 A. Ashworth, 'Interpreting Criminal Statutes: a Crisis of Legality?', Law Quarterly Review, vol. 107, 1991, pp. 425–426.

45 J. Bell, G. Engle, 'Cross on Statutory Interpretation', Butterworths, 1995, p. 167.

46 A. Ashworth, 'Interpreting Criminal Statutes: a Crisis of Legality?', Law Quarterly Review, vol. 107, 1991, p. 431.

intends to simply alter the criminal liability elements of existing common law offences.

English courts approached this situation in an intuitive manner and within the institutional dynamics of the English constitutional framework. Statutory law was considered to be an invasion to the common law:

> There is a presumption that can be stated in various ways. One is that in the absence of any clear indication to the contrary, Parliament can be presumed not to have altered the common law further than was necessary to remedy the mischief. Of course it may and quite often does go further. But the principle is that if the enactment is ambiguous, that meaning which relates the scope of the act to the mischief should be taken rather than a different or wider meaning which the contemporary situation did not call for.[47]

Thus, there have been cases where courts considered that just because an act is not criminalised under the statute, it does not necessarily escape the scope of common law;[48] what is more there have also been occasions where the English court deliberately circumvented the parliamentary statute.[49] Nowadays, it is accepted that where parliament has statutorily created an offence, prosecution should be based on the statute, rather than the common law.[50] Yet difficulties remain which are solved on a case-by-case basis. For example, the parliament usually clarifies the situation by stating explicitly which common law offences are to be replaced.[51] On occasion this may result in ambiguity. An example of a particularly confusing relationship between common law and statutory offences relates to conspiracy to defraud.[52] In this context, additional measures were taken such as the issuing of guidelines to prosecutors.[53] Contradictions between common law and statutory versions of offences have attracted criticism and it has been proposed that when the parliament has not criminalised an act, it should be presumed that this behaviour should be considered legal.[54]

To return to the relationship between statutes and jurisprudence, the continental legality principle has a further characteristic, which is that judicial judgements are not subjected to the same restrictions or requirements as statutory liability. In Germany and the Netherlands, jurisprudence has less value in generating criminal liability. Case law is not meant to elucidate definitions of criminal liability or

---

47 Black Clawson International Ltd v Papierwerke Waldhof-Aschaffenburg [1975] AC 591.

48 DPP v Bhagwan [1972] AC 60.

49 R v Ireland [1998] AC 147.

50 D. Ormerod, 'Smith and Hogan's Criminal law', Oxford University Press, 2011, pp. 16–17.

51 For example, Criminal Law Act 1977 section 5(1), (2).

52 For example see R v Evans [2014] EWHC 3803 (QBD).

53 Attorney General's guidelines for prosecutors on the use of the common law offence of conspiracy to defraud. First published 2007, amended 2012 available at www.gov.uk/use-of-the-common-law-offence-of-conspiracy-to-defraud—6 (accessed 1 December 2014).

54 J.F. Stephen, 'A History of the Criminal Law of England', Routledge/Thoemmes, 1996, p. 360.

constitute a source of law itself; case law is in fact not even addressed to other individuals apart from those involved in the case. Thus, although in most continental systems a significant amount of jurisprudence is accessible to the public and court decisions are considered public documents, the legality principle does not oblige the publication of every case in widely accessible sources.

This is somewhat different in common law systems where case law is regularly published, as it is in itself a binding source of law. In England, the Incorporating Council of Law Reporting publishes reports of cases and judgements are also published in the Weekly Law Reports, both online and via printed copies.[55] Internet and on-line sources have made the publication of case law in all systems much easier and today one may find most cases published on-line.

The continental legality principle also does not encourage the systemic and controlled development of jurisprudence. Jurisprudence is not considered an organism of law where decisions are related to each other, forming in itself a body and source of law. In most systems Supreme Court decisions bind decisions of lower courts and they may review judgements by lower courts as a matter of review and appeal. However, because courts are not supposed to create or expand offences, there is no reason for them to be formally bound by their prior decisions. Therefore, the legality principle does not demand a consistent jurisprudence.

This is very different in common law systems, where: *'the law is a living organism, constantly growing, expanding, adapting itself, like a tree, which maintains its identity all the time, though in its full growth it look very different from what it was when a sapling'.*[56] England is dominated by the concept of precedent, a *stare decisis*. Because for the larger part of 20th century, court decisions could expand or establish new offences, the English jurisdiction developed a system to maintain stable development of law in order to ensure a level of control over casuistry. *Stare decisis* means that lower courts are bound by the decisions of the higher courts but also that England's highest court (formerly known as the House of Lords, currently the Supreme Court) could not deviate from its previous jurisprudence. This has been relaxed by the Practice Statement (1966), according to which, the English Supreme Court, although it continues to bind the lower courts, is not bound by its prior jurisprudence.[57] However, deviations from prior jurisprudence are subjected to scrutiny by the English Supreme Court itself, especially due to *'the especial need for certainty as to the criminal law'.*[58]

Despite the relaxing of *stare decisis*, it still remains a fact that judgements are a source of law, forming an organism, which is dynamic and should remain consistent

---

55 http://iclr.co.uk/ (accessed 2 December 2014).

56 Lord Wright, 'The Study of Law', Law Quarterly Review, vol. 54, 1938, p. 194.

57 Practice Statement [1966] 3 All ER 77 (House of Lords).

58 Ibid.; see for example a series of case law about the retroactive effect of the Human Rights Act, where the departure from prior jurisprudence is scrutinised: R v Lambert [2001] 3 WLR 206; R v Kansas [2001] 3 WLR 1532; D. Beyleveld, R. Kirkham, D. Towend, 'Which presumption? A critique of the House of Lords' reasoning on retrospectivity and the Human Rights Act', Legal Studies, vol. 22, 2002, p. 202.

and coherent: *'To promote a desirable degree of consistency and certainty about the present state of 'the law', courts in this country have long adopted the practice of treating decisions on a point of law as precedents for the future.'*[59] Whether, and to what extent, prior case law can be taken under consideration is a matter of discussion in the adjudication process; this may include a debate on whether there is a similarity of facts or issue of principle.

Such analysis can be seen in *Shaw v DPP*, which concerned the publication of a booklet with contact information for prostitutes in London, an act regarded as conspiracy to corrupt public morals.[60] The English court discussed vigorously which prior jurisprudence could be taken under consideration in order to establish that such an offence existed under common law. An index of prior case law can be usually found in the beginning of a judgement where it is stipulated which prior judgements were followed, cited, considered, affirmed or not considered. Additionally, when there is a need to clarify a point of law, English courts may include this in the judgement as a *per curiam*. Some of the *per curiam* can even clarify on the status of common law offences. For example, the court in *DPP v Bhagwan* stated in a *per curiam* that:

> It is not an offence at common law to agree to 'act to the prejudice of the State' unless the means adopted are unlawful or the prejudice likely to be caused falls within one of the established categories of public mischief which have been held by existing decisions of the courts to be so contrary to public policy as to justify the imposition of penal sanctions.[61]

Furthermore, the continental legality principle does not prohibit the retroactivity of judicial interpretation.[62] Again, this flows naturally from the fact that judicial interpretations are supposed to be kept within the margins of the statute. On the contrary, in a system where jurisprudence is an official source of criminal liability, judicial adjudication can result in development of a previously unclear legal issue. Hence, the doctrine of precedent in England aims at avoiding adjudicative retroactivity. According to this doctrine, retroactivity is limited by judicial adherence to existing principle.[63] In other words, the law may be expanded only if this can be grounded on existing principle.[64] In the well-known marital rape case, the abolition of the marital immunity in prior case law could, as an existing principle, support the total abolition of marital immunity.[65] In other common law

---

59 National Westminster Bank plc (Respondents) v Spectrum Plus Limited and others and others (Appellants) [2005] UKHL 41.

60 Shaw v DPP [1962] AC 220.

61 DPP v Bhagwan [1972] AC 60.

62 W. Joecks, K. Miebach, 'Münchener Kommentar zum Strafgesetzbuch', Verlag C.H. Beck, 2011, para. 1, Mn 33.

63 B. Juratowitch, 'Retroactivity and the Common Law', Hart Publishing, 2008, p. 125.

64 Ibid., p. 126.

65 Ibid., p. 135.

systems such as the Unites States' system, judicial decision expanding the scope of criminal liability can be restricted in its temporal effect through the concept of 'prospective overruling'.[66] The practice of prospective overruling is a judicial technique that allows courts to expand criminal liability for the detriment of the accused, but reduce the negative effects of retroactivity for the *ad hoc* case. In particular, courts may pursue an expansive interpretation but, at the same time, this precedent shall have effect *ex ante* thus not capturing the pending case.

Finally, the continental legality principle does not demand that judicial decisions have particular 'qualities' such as precision or communicative value in the same way as statutes. According to the legality principle judicial decisions must be based on an interpretation of the statute that does not exceed the limits of the scope of criminal liability, but there is no obligation regarding the transparency of judicial reasoning. Because jurisprudence is not a source of criminal liability, judicial reasoning is not meant to have any role in the determination of criminal liability apart from interpreting the statute at hand and applying it to the *ad hoc* facts. This is in contrast to statutes; the communicative effect of statutes, their precision and comprehensibility are qualities protected and ensured by the legality principle. There are certain procedural safeguards, which may require that judicial decisions are well-reasoned and a lack of proper reasoning can result in an overruling of the judgement (for example Articles 338 para. 7 and 275 para. 1 German Code of Criminal Procedure). Nevertheless, this is not an obligation that stems from the legality principle, nor does the principle oblige courts to follow a comprehensive and transparent reasoning. While common law does not seem to demand specific qualities regarding judicial reasoning, English judgements are written in a different style to continental judgements. English judgements to the continental eye resemble much more a debate or a discussion amongst judges where they present their individual views on how the case should be resolved. Not only does the language tend to be less legalistic, but also the reasoning allows for more accountability and transparency on how the interests in a case have been weighed. Whilst the influence of political arguments is clearly presented in English judicial argumentation, in continental systems this is masked by formalistic legal reasoning.[67]

4. The aspects of the principle of legality

The legality principle in continental systems is a doctrine with a given structure; it includes four distinct but interrelated aspects. The principle is codified in criminal codes, and it is considered to be one of the cornerstone principles of criminal law.

---

66 National Westminster Bank plc (Respondents) v Spectrum Plus Limited and others and others (Appellants) [2005] UKHL 41, where the concept and application of prospective overruling in different common law jurisdictions is discussed.

67 B. Markezinis, 'Judicial Style and Reasoning in England and Germany', The Cambridge Law Journal, vol. 59, 2000, pp. 304–308.

While the principle of legality as an idea was developed during the Enlightenment, it was the German legal scholar Feuerbach who developed it from an aspirational idea into a concrete legal principle.[68] He constructed a structured legal doctrine with specific functions.[69]

Feuerbach regarded the legality principle as having four main aspects. Thus, the principle of legality comprises of: the prohibition of retroactive application of the criminal norms; the prohibition of vague and inaccessible criminal norms; the prohibition of extensive interpretation of the prescribed criminal liability; and the prohibition of basing criminal liability on customary law. Feuerbach has also been the source for the *nullum crimen sine lege* maxim, which encapsulates the legality principle.[70] The four aspects also have Latin maxims, terminology I will adopt as mentioned.[71] Each of these aspects has its own standards and criteria.

There are functional equivalents of these principles developed in the English system, albeit less comprehensively. These are not a part of a greater principle, as they were developed under the auspices of a less positivistic – and thus structured – concept of the Rule of Law; in other words, the principle of legality is not approached as a unified mechanism. In addition, due to the gradual codification of offences, the functional equivalents were developed in the context of common law, irrespective of the continental legality principle. Towards the end of the 20th century, and especially after the Human Rights Act in 1998 (which incorporated the ECHR into English law),[72] English judges explicitly used the principle of legality. Since then, these functional equivalents have been used in a similar way to the continental legality principle. Even so, continental lawyers may struggle to identify their own conception of the principle of legality as this is adopted by English courts.

5. *Lex scripta* and the English statute-reservation

The best-known aspect of the legality principle is the maxim 'no crime without law,' and is perhaps the core of the legality principle. The Latin maxim *lex scripta* indicates that criminal liability should be written, however, it entails much more than that. In particular, the principle of *lex scripta* has two layers.

The first layer is that it obliges the judge to apply only criminal norms found in a written form. This is the lowest form of the protective function of the *lex scripta*. A written form is important for achieving protection against state arbitrariness. Written words create stability through time and attribute certain legitimacy or

68 P.J.A. Feuerbach, 'Lehrbuch des gemeinen in Deutschland gültigen peinlichen Rechts', 1801; C. Roxin, 'Strafrecht: Allgemeiner Teil Band I', Verlag C.H. Beck, 2006, para. 5 Mn 22.

69 H.-L. Schreiber, 'Gesetz und Richter', Alfred Metzner Verlag GmbH, 1976, p. 102.

70 P.J.A. Feuerbach, 'Lehrbuch des gemeinen in Deutschland gültigen peinlichen Rechts', 1801.

71 Chapter I para. 1.

72 See further below para. 9.2.

evidentiary power to the exact scope of the *ius puniendi*. In other words, written norms, as opposed to unwritten, safeguard the scope of criminal liability in an objective manner. Customary law can be characterised by uncertainty in its content and scope. Criteria include the existence of a common belief that law has prohibited an act for a substantial period of time.[73] The existence of common community beliefs is debatable due to the heterogeneity in communities. Customary law has been prevalent in early criminal justice systems where codification was absent and courts applied their common sense or moral community standards. Certain moral community standards, such as prohibitions against killing and theft, were considered self-evident common standards.

The second layer of *lex scripta* is that the written form should be in a parliamentary statute. Often this is referred to as *lex parliamentaria*. In literature, it is frequent that *lex parliamentaria* is considered to be a fifth and separate aspect of legality or, sometimes, simply a variation of *lex scripta*.[74] It is thus possible to conclude that *lex scripta* prohibits customary law while *lex parliamentaria* may be also of relevance when discussing the powers of the executive for legislating in criminal liability.[75] In any case, *lex scripta* gives the normative definition of what qualifies as criminal *law* and that is the parliamentary statute, which is of course in a written form. Criminal liability that does not stem from the parliament in the form of a statute is therefore precluded.

A functionally equivalent principle for the English common law can be found in *Price*, one of the earliest decisions where English courts renounced their powers to create criminal law offences: *'these, however, are matters for the legislature, and not for me. It may be that it would be well for Parliament to regulate or to forbid the burning of bodies, but the great leading rule of criminal law is that nothing is a crime unless it is plainly forbidden by law.'*[76] While it is difficult to consider this extract as a principle in the continental sense, it can be seen as an English statute-reservation, a *Gesetzesvorbehalt,* since courts declared that criminal law-making is for parliament. A century later, after the Human Rights Act, similar references to this 'leading principle' can still be traced in case law:

> [W]hat has become an important democratic principle in this country: that it is for those representing the people of the country in Parliament, not the executive and not the judges, to decide what conduct should be treated as lying so far outside the bounds of what is acceptable in our society as to attract criminal penalties. One would need very compelling reasons for departing from that principle.[77]

---

73 B. Lepard, 'Customary International Law: A New Theory with Practical Applications', Cambridge University Press, 2010, pp. 3–13.

74 B. Schünemann, 'Nulla poena sine lege? Rechtstheoretische und verfassungsrechtliche Implikationen der Rechtsgewinnung im Strafrecht', Walter de Gruyter, 1978, p. 3.

75 U. Sieber, 'Die Zukunft des Europäischen Strafrechts', ZStW, vol. 121, 2009, p. 50.

76 Queen v Price [1884] 12 QBD 247.

77 R v Jones (Margaret) [2007] 1 AC 136, para. 29; R v Rimmington and R v Goldstein (joined cases) [2005] UKHL 63.

But how did this development take place? In the same year as *Price*, the English court affirmed its law-making powers in *Queen v Stephenson*.[78] Similarly in *Manley* in 1933, where the court convicted the defendant for 'unlawfully effecting a public mischief'.[79] Later on, the English courts embarked in a journey of renouncing or reclaiming their powers to develop criminal norms but in 1961 a milestone case was decided which was widely criticised and greatly influenced the course of common law. *Shaw v DPP* concerned the publication of the Ladies' Directory, a booklet with information on where to locate prostitutes in London (as the Street Offences Act 1959 had prohibited the prostitution on the streets).[80] The defendant was convicted of conspiracy to corrupt public morals and the case subsequently attracted intense criticism.[81] Three later cases came along, *DPP v Bhagwan* in 1970,[82] *Knuller v DPP* in 1973[83] and *DPP v Withers* in 1975,[84] which had a significant impact as the judges renounced explicitly in all three cases any power to create new offences. However, they did retain the power to adapt the existing offences to new facts.

English courts subsequently contradicted themselves in a series of marital rape cases, which deserve special attention. According to the Sexual Offences Act of 1956 rape was defined as unlawful intercourse without consent. 'Unlawful' intercourse was interpreted as intercourse outside marriage and therefore a husband was exempted from raping his wife. The former special arrangement for the husband was mentioned as 'marital exemption'. The marital exemption case is one of the most important and famous cases in the English criminal law history. The problem dates long before *R v R*.[85] The statutory marital exemption was in line with older common law assertions: *'But the husband cannot be guilty of a rape committed by himself upon his lawful wife, for by their mutual matrimonial consent and contract the wife hath given up herself in this kind unto her husband which she cannot retract.'*[86] Case law prior to *R v R* has limited this exemption in cases where the marriage was dissolving. For example, the courts have previously held that the husband's immunity was lost because there was an order dissolving the cohabitation.[87] In other cases, it was ruled that when there is a divorce petition that

---

78 Queen v Stephenson [1884] 13 QBD 331, cited via B. Juratowitch, 'Retroactivity and the Common Law', Hart Publishing, 2008, p. 39.

79 R v Manley [1933] 1 KB 529.

80 Shaw v DPP [1962] AC 220.

81 A.P. Simester, J.R. Spencer, G.R. Sullivan, G.J. Virgo, 'Simester and Sullivan's Criminal Law: Theory and Doctrine', Hart Publishing, 2013, pp. 26–30; A.L. Goodhart, 'The Shaw case: the law and the public morals', Law Quarterly Review, vol. 77, 1961, pp. 560–568; B. Juratowitch, 'Retroactivity and the Common Law', Hart Publishing, 2008, pp. 185–189.

82 DPP v Bhagwan [1972] AC 60, the conspiracy to commit an act injurious to the public and to evade controls of immigration was examined.

83 Knuller v DPP [1973] AC 435.

84 DPP v Withers [1975] AC 842.

85 R v R [1992] 1 AC 599.

86 M. Hale, 'History of the Pleas of the Crown', vol. 1, 1736, p. 629.

87 R v Clarke [1949] 2 All ER 448.

reaches the *decree nisi* the marriage is considered terminated and the consent of the wife withdrawn.[88] In *R v R*, the couple was living apart and there was no divorce petition when the rape took place. The court concluded that the extension of criminal liability to the husband was acceptable under English law; however, based on the precedent, it is doubtful whether the husband could foresee that his act would be considered as rape.[89]

Much later and after the Human Rights Act in 1998, in *R v Goldstein and Rimmington* the House of Lords affirmed the English equivalent of a statute-reservation and refused to convict the defendants of the common law offence of public nuisance.[90] The importance of parliamentary statute in the creation of criminal offences can be found also in *R v Jones*.[91] Finally, with *Norris v Government of the United States*, the English court refused to recognise as a common law offence the act of price fixing; the court stated that even if there would be a change of perspective in society that would conceive such as an act as criminal, a statute would be necessary to stipulate this.[92] Thus, currently English courts cannot create new criminal liability. Statutes have replaced a plethora of common law offences, yet as seen, the parliament must explicitly state whether and to which extent common law offences are replaced. To this extent, the sources of criminal liability in England include also the existing jurisprudence on the remaining common law offences. Thus, it cannot be said that case law in England is not an official source of criminal liability. To conclude, the current situation in England is a mixed approach to *lex scripta,* whereby the parliament has replaced a great number of common law offences. Some common law offences remain, and there are some areas in which there is a cohabitation of common and statutory offences.

6. *Lex praevia,* Presumption of Non-Retroactivity and Precedence

This aspect of the legality principle prohibits the retroactive prescription and application of criminal liability. Retroactive criminalisation has historically been considered unjust and has been codified into national law: for example Article 1 DCC, Article 16 of the Dutch Constitution, Article 103 para. 2 of the German Constitution and Article 1 GCC. The early acknowledgment of the detrimental effects of retroactivity in criminal law led to the prohibition of retroactivity in early criminal law instruments such as Article 12 of the Dutch Criminal Code of 1809.

Lex praevia is addressed both to the legislator and the judge. As far as the legislator goes, statutory criminal liability should not be given retroactive effect. In

88 R v O'Brien (Edward) [1974] 3 All ER 663.

89 B. Juratowitch, 'Retroactivity and the Common Law', Hart Publishing, 2008, pp. 127–130.

90 R v Rimmington and R v Goldstein (joined cases) [2005] UKHL 63.

91 R v Jones (Margaret) [2007] 1 AC 136.

92 Norris v Government of the United States of America [2008] UKHL 16.

principle, the scope of criminal liability in time is a concern of the legislator. Because the legislator is the one responsible for the formulation and determination of the scope of criminal liability, it is his responsibility not to attach retroactive force to criminal liability. This means that criminal statutes should not contain any clause or provision that extends its application to facts prior to its enforcement. The principle of *lex praevia* is from this perspective a principle guiding the construction of criminal liability.[93] The prohibition of retroactivity is very much a straightforward obligation and not difficult to grasp and apply. Thus, it has not been of particular difficulty to accept that even when criminal liability is determined via reference to norms of tax law for example, any retroactive clause in those norms cannot have effect on criminal liability.[94]

As far as the judge is concerned, *lex praevia* functions as an interpretative tool.[95] Courts use it when there is a change in the criminal status of an act due to new legislation creating, abolishing or amending it.[96] For its application it is important that the *tempus delicti,* the time of the legislative enactments and, also, the nature of the amendment in the criminal liability status are determined.[97] An important feature of *lex praevia* is that it applies only when the retroactive force of the new legislative act would function to the detriment of the accused. This means that more lenient amendments can be applied retroactively. This does not apply only to the *lex praevia* aspect of legality but to all aspects.[98] Therefore, if more lenient customary law exists, or if there is new and more lenient statute, this may be applied.

Similarly in English law, retroactivity in criminal law was frowned upon from the earliest days of the common law.[99] As addressed to the English parliament, the Rule of Law did not lead to the creation of any specific principles that would bind parliament itself. Indeed the parliament in England cannot be bound by any doctrine, since parliamentary sovereignty is a basic constitutional principle, which co-exists with the Rule of Law.[100] In earlier days, according to the old English doctrine of relation, a statute was considered to be in force from the beginning of the parliamentary session during which it was enacted, not when it received the final royal assent.[101] This came to an end when George III (1793) declared that an Act of parliament would be considered enforceable after the royal approval. The

93 Chapter I para. 1.

94 W. Joecks, K. Miebach, 'Münchener Kommentar zum Strafgesetzbuch', Verlag C.H. Beck, 2011, para. 1, Mn 36.

95 Chapter I para. 1.

96 J. de Hullu, 'Materieel strafrecht', Kluwer, 2012, pp. 83–84.

97 Ibid., p. 86.

98 H. Satzger, B. Schmitt, G. Widmaier, 'StGB – Strafgesetzbuch: Kommentar', Heymanns, 2009, p. 10.

99 B. Juratowitch, 'Retroactivity and the Common Law', Hart Publishing, 2008, pp. 28–35.

100 G. Williams, 'Criminal law – the General Part', Stevens and Sons Limited, 1953, p. 439.

101 B. Juratowitch, 'Retroactivity and the Common Law', Hart Publishing, 2008, pp. 28–35.

parliament then enacted 'An Act to Prevent Acts of Parliament from Taking Effect from a Time Prior to the Passing Thereof'.[102]

As the doctrines of parliamentary sovereignty and the Rule of Law coexist, parliament was and is expected to follow the Rule of Law: *'Parliament must be presumed not to legislate contrary to the rule of law. And the rule of law enforces minimum standards of fairness, both substantive and procedural.'*[103] Although there is no equivalent obligation arising from English criminal law,[104] the English parliament was presumed to comply with the Rule of Law. Nowadays, the Human Rights Act provides for more formal mechanisms for holding parliament to account.[105]

This is further reinforced by the second functional equivalent of *lex praevia,* which is the presumption against the retroactivity of criminal statutes, addressed to English courts. Based on the Rule of Law, English theory and practice has developed a presumption that the parliament cannot enact retrospectively criminal legislation. This presumption is addressed to courts and it is a common law principle with which statutes are construed.[106] The presumption applies to the interpretation of statutes when there is no explicit retroactive effect in the wording. A frequently cited case regarding the presumption against retroactivity in criminal law is *R v Miah* where the court construed the statutory liability on illegal immigration as precluding a retroactive effect and revival of prosecution.[107] A much more clear application of the presumption can be seen in *R v Reah.*[108] It is generally accepted that this presumption has a strong force and courts apply it liberally.[109]

A third functional equivalent to *lex praevia* is the rules on precedent and judicial attachment to existing principles.[110] This is again addressed to English courts but it concerns adjudicative retroactivity. As explained, the rules on precedence require courts not to depart from previous authority and, if they do so, to at least ensure that the new rule shall be based on existing principle. More about this will be discussed below as the rules on precedent are of concern mainly to the judicial interpretation.[111] However, it should be mentioned that the rules on precedence are also employed as a mechanism to prevent a retroactive application in adjudication.[112]

---

102 R v Thurston [1663] 83 ER 312 cited via B. Juratowitch, 'Retroactivity and the Common Law', Hart Publishing, 2008, p. 32.

103 Pierson v Secretary of State for the Home Department [1997] 3 All ER 577.

104 B. Juratowitch, 'Retroactivity and the Common Law', Hart Publishing, 2008, p. 68.

105 See further below para. 9.2.

106 B. Juratowitch, 'Retroactivity and the Common Law', Hart Publishing, 2008, pp. 68–71.

107 R v Miah [1997] 2 Cr App R 12.

108 R v Reah [1968] 3 All ER 269.

109 B. Juratowitch, 'Retroactivity and the Common Law', Hart Publishing, 2008, pp. 74–75.

110 Ibid., p. 125.

111 See para. 8.

112 B. Juratowitch, 'Retroactivity and the Common Law', Hart Publishing, 2008, pp. 184–195.

Before concluding the discussion regarding non-retroactivity, it is interesting to point out that the prohibition of retroactivity within continental systems has a different theoretical basis. Despite the common features of the legality principle in the continental systems, there are different legal cultures among jurisdictions.

In particular, in the Netherlands, *lex praevia* is based on a desire to uphold legal certainty, the reliability of the law and prevent state arbitrariness.[113] In Germany, some scholars attempt to keep the principle of guilt and legality demarcated, as stated above.[114] If reliability and foreseeability are not supported by the legality principle, then how can one justify the prohibition of retroactivity?

It is not self-evident how non-retroactivity can be based on democracy and separation of powers. If one accepts the superiority of parliament, a retroactive statute is an exercise of its discretion; also, there is no obvious connection with the separation of powers, as a retroactive statute does not result in judicial arbitrariness. There is the view that the basis of non-retroactivity is the result of a general concept of justice as the detrimental effects of the individual are severe, which can be seen as comparable to the concept of legal certainty.[115] Others suggest that a retroactive statute would imply that the legislator is reacting to individual cases (in the sense that the legislator decides to pass a new amendment with retroactive effect in order to react to a specific action that was not criminalised when it occurred), which entails a violation of the separation of powers;[116] the latter is understood as a violation of the separation of powers by the legislator, who assumes a judicial function through the reaction to an *ad hoc* situation.

7. *LEX CERTA* AND MAXIMUM LEGAL CERTAINTY

This aspect of the legality principle obliges criminal provisions to be constructed by the legislator with precision, so that judicial interpretation is restricted. *Lex certa* is addressed to the legislator and sets certain qualitative requirements regarding the criminal statute. In England, a functional equivalent that binds the legislator can only be considered within the concept of the Rule of Law: *'For if the trumpet give an uncertain sound, who shall prepare himself to battle? So if the law give an uncertain sound, who shall prepare to obey it? It ought therefore to warn before it strikes'*.[117] In traditional common law there is no specific tool to actually bind the legislator apart from the general belief that he shall construct criminal liability in a

---

113 J. de Hullu, 'Materieel strafrecht', Kluwer, 2012, p. 84.

114 Para. 2 and Chapter III para. 6.2.

115 G. Grünwald, 'Bedeutung und Begründung des Satzes nulla poena sine lege', ZStW, vol. 76, 1964, p. 16.

116 Ibid., p. 17; B. Schünemann, 'Nulla poena sine lege? Rechtstheoretische und verfassungsrechtliche Implikationen der Rechtsgewinnung im Strafrecht', Walter de Gruyter, 1978, p. 24.

117 Famous quote by Lord Bacon (Aphorism 8, Treatise on Universal Justice), cited in various judgements, e.g. R v Rimmington and R v Goldstein (joined cases) [2005] UKHL 63, para. 33.

precise manner. This attitude can be seen as the English principle of maximum legal certainty.[118]

Firstly, *lex certa* generates a formal requirement for publication. This is a precondition for parliamentary statutes requiring courts to follow only official criminal norms applicable *erga omnes*. For example, publication in the Netherlands takes place in the *Staatsblad*. Secondly, it demands that criminal liability be defined by the legislator with precision; the wording of the text should allow for the ability of distinction between legal and illegal acts. This is of absolute importance in order to safeguard individual autonomy from state arbitrariness and judicial interpretation. Courts should be able to determine from the wording of the statute the scope of criminalisation. Distinguishing legal from illegal behaviour presupposes that certainty is safeguarded to the maximum amount possible. Such a distinction can only be made through a use of language that is precise. However, as explained above, maximum legal certainty is not the same as absolute precision; precision is a feature of language but it is not a value per se.[119] Maximum legal certainty means that the language of the statute will enable the distinction between legal and illegal acts. The obligation of the legislator to prescribe criminal liability in accordance with *lex certa* operates in two ways.

Firstly, it influences the attitude of the legislator. The legislator should focus only on specific acts of behaviour. The legislature must come to a consensus on specific acts or behavioural patterns to be criminalised. Criminalising all harmful situations endangering a legal interest can violate *lex certa*. Here, this aspect of legality also hides an indirect link to proportionality and the prohibition of excessive criminalisation. For example, a provision that criminalises all disturbances of public order and security not only over-criminalises, but also violates *lex certa*.[120] The legislator may wish to protect public order to its fullest. Over-criminalisation however undermines *lex certa* as it becomes more difficult to distinguish between legal and illegal acts. The *lex certa* principle obliges the legislator to prescribe criminal liability at the level of human conduct, not at the level of harm.

In order to avoid over-criminalisation and vague norms prone to arbitrary interpretation, the way the legislator cognitively approaches codification is crucial. The codification of criminal liability ought to be input-oriented as opposed to output-oriented.[121]

An output-oriented legislator is more concerned with the practical and empirical results of codification. Such an approach encourages more abstract prescriptions. A codification at the level of harm is a typical example of an output-oriented codification. The legislator, after considering the practicality of prohibiting specific conduct as opposed to a general prohibition of a particular harm, prefers the latter

118 A. Ashworth, J. Horder, 'Principles of Criminal Law', Oxford University Press, 2013, pp. 62–65.
119 Chapter III para. 6.1.
120 Beck'scher Onlinekommentar zum StGB, von Heintschel-Heinegg, 2011, para. 1, Mn 23.
121 W. Hassemer, 'Einführung in die Grundlagen des Strafrechts', Verlag C.H. Beck, 1990, p. 255.

in order to effectively protect against that harm to its fullest. The output-oriented model approaches liability as a means for obtaining optimum results or a specific agenda.[122] The more the legislator focuses on empirical results, the less he is concerned with legal certainty, as he aims to be comprehensive, rather than specific.[123]

Lex certa requires a more input-oriented legislator. In an input-oriented codification, the system functions primarily by careful recording and processing of information combined with a relative indifference to the consequences that it causes.[124] An input-oriented model does not mean that the legislator ignores what the scope of criminal liability would be in practice, or whether a particular wording would include or exclude certain conduct, but that the legislator is not motivated by the intention of criminalising acts instrumentally. Thus, *lex certa* entails the 'early cognitive commitment' of the legislator as to what behaviour should be criminalised.[125] This is reflected in the normative boundaries of language, which are decisive for determining the scope of the norm.

Secondly, the *lex certa* obliges the legislator to delineate accurately the behaviour to be criminalised in the statute. Although the legislator may have a very specific criminal conduct in mind, the words chosen may fail to be explicit. A balance must be kept between too detailed and too vague descriptions. On the one hand, provisions have to allow for a variety of human actions to fall within their scope, but in the same time, there must be a clear line. For example, the Dutch provision on murder, which reads *'he who intentionally takes the life of another...'* (Article 287 DCC), does not describe exactly physical acts to be criminalised as there are many ways to take a life, but it does prohibit a particular behavioural pattern. The provision would be more vague if it prohibited harm to the life of another person, as that would perhaps also include comparatively minor injuries or mental harm. While the precision of the words per se is not the goal, the role of language is important. This is because certain terms or words may influence the overall meaning of the norm in ways that other terms do not.

For the description of criminal acts, different types of terms are employed such as every-day language, judicial terms and numbers. Examples found in German literature include numerical terms, e.g. the age of the victim for sexual abuse crimes, which are consequently precise and objective. Descriptive terms refer to terms that have a relatively uniform and objective meaning as they can be conceptualised with the senses, e.g. a tree, human being, weapon, vehicle. Normative terms (also referred to as evaluative terms in English scholarship)[126] are

122 N. Luhmann, 'Rechtssystem und Rechtsdogmatik', Verlag W. Kohlhammer GmbH, 1974, p. 26.
123 W. Hassemer, 'Einführung in die Grundlagen des Strafrechts', Verlag C.H. Beck, 1990, p. 255.
124 N. Luhmann, 'Rechtssystem und Rechtsdogmatik', Verlag W. Kohlhammer GmbH, 1974, p. 26.
125 Ibid.; W. Hassemer, 'Einführung in die Grundlagen des Strafrechts', Verlag C.H. Beck, 1990, p. 255.
126 A.P. Simester, J.R. Spencer, G.R. Sullivan, G.J. Virgo, 'Simester and Sullivan's Criminal Law: Theory and Doctrine', Hart Publishing, 2013, pp. 29–30.

those that cannot be understood with the senses but take their meaning from their function in the judicial world, such as negligence, unlawful, omission and duty of care. Finally, there are general clauses, which are terms without a stable, determined content but gain meaning from the certain social or moral values at any given moment/place such as the term 'public morals'.[127]

Methodology of codification is also relevant. There are many ways to formulate definitions of criminal offences.[128] For example, the legislator can describe the undesirable conduct per se, such as Article 11 para. 1 of the Sexual Offences Act 2003 in England: *'A person aged 18 or over (A) commits an offence if: (a) for the purpose of obtaining sexual gratification, he intentionally causes another person (B) to watch a third person engaging in an activity...'.* Such description can also be omitted and replaced with an axiomatic term, such as Article 300 DCC about assault: *'Assault shall be punished with...'.* What conduct qualifies as assault is not described but this axiomatic judicial term takes content from how it is understood in law. The legislator may also use examples of the most characteristic behavioural patterns in order to clarify the message or to indicate the scope of liability, usually found in criminal liability norms with aggravated circumstances.[129]

The *lex certa* principle does not generate any specific guidelines or preferred methods and neither does the English principle of maximum legal certainty.[130] As explained, what is at stake is not the clarity of a word.[131] The principle of *lex certa* is not about words per se – but about what conduct is prohibited, and to what extent. The legislator is only self-restrained by *lex certa* to make sure that all the elements of the criminal liability are adequately defined. Therefore the principle of *lex certa* does not require any substantial methodological or tangible obligation of the legislator apart from the guideline that criminal liability should be prescribed in such a way that leaves courts with a limited interpretational margin.

However, certain methodologies or terms may have a substantial impact on the precision of a provision. Whatever words or methods the legislator uses, all elements of criminal liability should be included in the provision and the words or context should not allow for diverse interpretations. Hence, general clauses pose the greatest threat to legal certainty, because they allow for various interpretations and

---

127 B. Schünemann, 'Nulla poena sine lege? Rechtstheoretische und verfassungsrechtliche Implikationen der Rechtsgewinnung im Strafrecht', Walter de Gruyter, 1978, pp. 29–30; somewhat similar K. Engisch, 'Einführung in das juristische Denken', W. Kohlhammer GmbH, 2005, p. 33; H.-P. Lemmel, 'Unbestimmte Strafbarkeitsvoraussetzungen im Besonderen Teil des Strafrechts und der Grundsatz nullum crimen sine lege', Duncker & Humblot, 1970, pp. 44–49; R. Geitmann, 'Bundesverfassungsgericht und "offene" Normen', Duncker & Humblot, 1971, p. 108.

128 C. Kelk, 'Studieboek materieel strafrecht', Kluwer, 2010, pp. 91–94.

129 See for example Article 243I GCC on aggravated forms of theft. For more see W. Hassemer, 'Einführung in die Grundlagen des Strafrechts', Verlag C.H. Beck, 1990, p. 258.

130 A.P. Simester, J.R. Spencer, G.R. Sullivan, G.J. Virgo, 'Simester and Sullivan's Criminal Law: Theory and Doctrine', Hart Publishing, 2013, pp. 29–30.

131 R. Geitmann, 'Bundesverfassungsgericht und "offene" Normen', Duncker & Humblot, 1971, p. 28.

definitions, depending on the moral standing of each individual. Defining criminal liability with reference to 'public morals' or the 'nuisance of the public order' may allow courts to incorporate their own view into the interpretation.[132] To some extent, certain problems might also be created with normative terms, as their context in the absence of definitions in the legislation may be in the hands of courts.[133] Hence, one may find certain normative terms defined in statutes (such as 'negligence', 'duty of care', 'aiding') in continental systems; the absence of a statutory definition of these concepts in common law has been criticised in this regard.[134]

In general, the features of language itself influence compliance with *lex certa*. Language retains a certain element of objectivity, as it is the means of communication amongst people. At the same time, it can be fairly subjective, with conceptual shortcomings and instability over time. In daily-spoken language, the same word may have different meanings, while it is also notable by any foreign languages student that dictionary definitions of words can be significantly different from the way the word is understood and used in practice.[135] In comparison to formal and precise language (as used in mathematics), the language of the legislator is not artificial and therefore should remain close to everyday language.[136] With the help of the science of linguistics and the theory of semiotics,[137] one may see that language is dependent upon reality and experience.[138] For example, the word 'weapon' may be understood not only as a pistol or a knife but also as a vehicle or acid when thrown at someone.[139]

Courts must be able to decide whether a behaviour falls under the meaning of the wording of a provision, hence whether this is a good or bad candidate of a norm's meaning. For the term 'document' in Article 267 I GCC (falsification of documents), a driving license or a marriage licence is a good candidate of what the word illustrates, but a page of a book, for example, is a bad candidate.[140] The provision should be defined in such a way that there are always either 'good' or 'bad candidates' in interpretation, but never 'neutral' ones.[141]

---

132 B. Schünemann, 'Nulla poena sine lege? Rechtstheoretische und verfassungsrechtliche Implikationen der Rechtsgewinnung im Strafrecht', Walter de Gruyter, 1978, pp. 30–31.

133 A.P. Simester, J.R. Spencer, G.R. Sullivan, G.J. Virgo, 'Simester and Sullivan's Criminal Law: Theory and Doctrine', Hart Publishing, 2013, pp. 29–30.

134 Ibid.

135 W. Hassemer, 'Einführung in die Grundlagen des Strafrechts', Verlag C.H. Beck, 1990, p. 179.

136 B. Schünemann, 'Nulla poena sine lege? Rechtstheoretische und verfassungsrechtliche Implikationen der Rechtsgewinnung im Strafrecht', Walter de Gruyter, 1978, p. 19.

137 W. Hassemer, 'Einführung in die Grundlagen des Strafrechts', Verlag C.H. Beck, 1990, p. 178.

138 Ibid.

139 H.-P. Lemmel, 'Unbestimmte Strafbarkeitsvoraussetzungen im Besonderen Teil des Strafrechts und der Grundsatz nullum crimen sine lege', Duncker & Humblot, 1970, p. 57.

140 W. Hassemer, 'Einführung in die Grundlagen des Strafrechts', Verlag C.H. Beck, 1990, p. 181.

141 The *lex certa* also applies to legislative delegations to the executive. In Germany for example, legislative delegations should prescribe already all elements of criminal liability and punishment and the executive regulation should only concretise the behaviour explained in the referring

Therefore, it can be concluded that *lex certa* functions as a guide for the legislator in order to safeguard democratic legitimacy, the separation of powers, and individual protection against arbitrary judicial interpretation. What is more, there are no specific criteria regarding what constitutes precision, however, the wording of the text should be prescribed in such a way that courts are able to decide whether behaviour falls within the scope of a norm.

Regarding the English jurisdiction, there is the additional matter of certainty in common law adjudication. Common law development of criminal liability is bound to create a level of uncertainty. One may consider this to be part of judicial interpretation, however, a few examples of vague common law offences should be mentioned. There is a cluster of common law offences dealing with morality such as 'corrupting public morals',[142] 'unlawfully effecting public mischief'[143] and 'outraging public decency,[144] which have been all criticised heavily due to vagueness in their formulation.[145] Some have been abolished due to their indeterminacy.[146] It is argued that these types of vague terms would not normally survive a codification by the English parliament, although some, such as the conspiracy to defraud, have been preserved within the statute.[147] A noted reaction to allegations of uncertainty in common law offences is the one by Lord Morris, in Knuller: *'those who skate on thin ice can hardly expect to find a sign which will denote the precise spot where he [sic] will fall in'.*[148] The 'thin ice' approach is very much different from what the continental legality demands, which is the ability of individuals to distinguish between illegal and legal acts.

8. *Lex stricta*, precedence and strict interpretation

The principle of *lex stricta* is of paramount importance as it restricts judicial arbitrariness. Criminal norms should be interpreted within the margins of the wording of the text. The purpose of this is to bind judicial interpretation to the wording of the statute.[149] This is meant to subject the courts to the superiority of the

---

norm, BVerfG 2 BvR 15/62, 3 July 1962. See also W. Joecks, K. Miebach, 'Münchener Kommentar zum Strafgesetzbuch', Verlag C.H. Beck, 2011, para. 1, Mn 50.

142 Shaw v DPP [1962] AC 220; R v Hamilton [2007] EWCA Crim 2026; Smith v Hughes [1960] 2 All ER 859.

143 R v Manley [1933] 1 KB 529; R v Newland [1954] 1 QB 158.

144 Knuller v DPP [1973] AC 435.

145 A.P. Simester, J.R. Spencer, G.R. Sullivan, G.J. Virgo, 'Simester and Sullivan's Criminal Law: Theory and Doctrine', Hart Publishing, 2013, pp. 54–55; B. Juratowitch, 'Retroactivity and the Common Law', Hart Publishing, 2008, pp. 185–188.

146 DPP v Withers [1975] AC 842.

147 A.P. Simester, J.R. Spencer, G.R. Sullivan, G.J. Virgo, 'Simester and Sullivan's Criminal Law: Theory and Doctrine', Hart Publishing, 2013, pp. 54–55.

148 Knuller v DPP [1973] AC 435; A. Ashworth, J. Horder, 'Principles of Criminal Law', Oxford University Press, 2013, p. 62.

149 BVerfG 1 BvR 718/89, 10 January 1995.

legislature: the legislature – and not the courts – is the one that expresses through its statutes the values to be protected and the scope of their protection.

Naturally, the principle is addressed solely to the courts and obliges them to deduce the scope of criminalisation solely from the wording of the text, which marks the limits of criminalisation.[150] As explained before, the relationship between facts and rules is based on the isolation between them (*legisme*).[151] An example is the case of theft of electricity. If theft is defined as appropriating an object then the question is whether electricity can be considered an object even though an object has the meaning of something tangible. Electricity is not an object per se; it is a force of nature. Should the court consider that electricity somehow falls within the meaning of this term, this term would get a different concept and lose its previous objective and stable meaning.[152]

In continental systems, interpretation is focused on the interrelation between the wording of the statute and the facts. To use Sax's analysis,[153] one can identify five steps in interpretation: (i) the determination of the interpretation criteria (*juristische Hermeneutik*); (ii) the abstract interpretation of the relevant criminal liability norms with these criteria (*Sinndeutung*); (iii) the determination of the relevant and proven facts (*Tatsachenfeststellung*); (iv) the subjection of these facts to the abstractly interpreted norms (*Subsumption*); (iv) finally, the conclusion which can be inferred (*Entscheidung*).

In practice, these steps are not always followed explicitly (consciously or unconsciously). While this approach is rather too elaborate, and in practice courts may follow a simplified version of these steps, it is clear that the determination of the meaning of a norm should take place *in abstracto*, namely in disassociation with the facts. The isolation between facts and norms is important in order to limit the relativity of the language. In order to avoid this, presuming that norms have a stable, objective meaning and isolating the meaning and scope of norms from the *ad hoc* facts ensures that norms will not be construed arbitrarily. As the examination of the wording of a statute is very important, the *lex stricta* principle aims at safeguarding a strict interpretation, through the prohibition of certain methodologies that allow courts to import their own views.

Similarly in common law, the presumption of strict construction applies only after all other methods are used and the statute still remains unclear.[154] A strict construction means that where there is ambiguity, the most favourable – for the accused – interpretation should be adopted. Its application in English law has been

---

150 Ibid.

151 See above para. 3.2; B.M.J. van Klink, 'Bedreigt rechtsvinding de rechtszekerheid? Een kritisch-hermeneutische visie op de rol van de rechter in het materiële strafrecht', Delikt en Delinkwent, vol. 31, 2001, p. 688.

152 RG Rep. 739/99, 01 May 1899 (RGSt 32, 165).

153 W. Sax, 'Das Strafrechtliche "Analogieverbot"', Vandenhoeck & Ruprecht, 1953, p. 47.

154 A.P. Simester, J.R. Spencer, G.R. Sullivan, G.J. Virgo, 'Simester and Sullivan's Criminal Law: Theory and Doctrine', Hart Publishing, 2013, pp. 49–52.

inconsistent and its usefulness often doubted.[155] Others, however, argue that as an auxiliary method it should be maintained. The application of this principle is only granted when other methods of interpretation fail to produce a result.[156]

Generally speaking, all systems have similar methods on statutory interpretation. The first and most appropriate rule for statutory interpretation is grammatical interpretation, or as it is called in English law the 'ordinary meaning of the language'.[157] The focus of this technique is the grammatical context of the statute. Its usefulness rests on the hypothesis that the statute is precise. For example, are magic mushrooms plants? Grammatical interpretation would be easy in this case, as the term 'plant' is sufficiently precise.[158] This method is often prioritised, as interpretation can remain faithful to the wording of the statute.[159] An example could be the 'stepchild' case. Aggravated sexual abuse of family members in Dutch law includes stepchildren. With the use of grammatical interpretation, criminal liability is strictly defined as precluding the conviction of a man who abused his girlfriend's (and not wife's) child.[160]

Owing to the inherent indeterminism of language, teleological interpretation is also employed, according to which the court seeks the *telos* of the provision. Here one must make a distinction between the historical and teleological interpretation.

Both methods share in common that the court attempts to identify the *telos* of the legislator, so in other words, what the legislator intended to cover by the use of the term. However, there is a substantial difference between the two methods, which is discussed more by German literature, albeit also in the Netherlands. In particular, historical interpretation entails that courts attempt to understand the wording of the statute by looking at the *travaux préparatoires* (in the Netherlands mainly) or by trying to identify the intention of the legislator at the time of the construing of the norm (in Germany). Arguably, however, teleological interpretation aims at identifying the *telos* of the provision as it should be currently.[161] One can therefore make the distinction, following the German theory, between an objective (teleological – what the legislative intention *should* be) and subjective (historical – what the legislative intention *actually was*) interpretation.

This distinction is not frequently made in the Netherlands, which may partly explain why there are difficulties in demarcating the historical and teleological interpretation.[162] Also, it should be pointed out that the historical interpretation is used very frequently in the Netherlands owing to the fact that the Dutch

155 Law Com, no 177, para. 3.17.

156 A.P. Simester, J.R. Spencer, G.R. Sullivan, G.J. Virgo, 'Simester and Sullivan's Criminal Law: Theory and Doctrine', Hart Publishing, 2013, pp. 49–52.

157 Ibid., pp. 45–46.

158 BGH NJW 2007, 524, 25 October 2006.

159 J. de Hullu, 'Materieel strafrecht', Kluwer, 2012, p. 98.

160 HR 7 January 1997 NJ 1997, 361.

161 W. Joecks, K. Miebach, 'Münchener Kommentar zum Strafgesetzbuch', Verlag C.H. Beck, 2011, para. 1, Mn 76–77.

162 J. de Hullu, 'Materieel strafrecht', Kluwer, 2012, pp. 99–100.

parliamentary bodies are keen on scrutinising legislation and there are a substantial number of publications relating to debates around legislation.

The English version of this interpretation is the purposive/teleological interpretation, however, this corresponds to the objective – and more dynamic – teleological interpretation.[163] Regarding historical interpretation in England, the general view is that the *travaux préparatoires* may not be used in criminal matters especially when interpretation may broaden the scope of criminal liability;[164] however, this has been applied inconsistently.[165] *A contrario,* it seems that should the parliamentary discussions benefit the defendant their use in interpretation is not frowned upon.[166] Thus, while in Germany the use of objective teleological interpretation is generally criticised,[167] in the Netherlands and England it is generally followed, albeit with care.[168]

Another method that can be employed is the one of systematic interpretation.[169] According to this, the courts try to relate the existing scope of criminalisation to other relevant provisions. However, this technique can only be used with care as it is underlined by an intention for the criminal code to be coherent, which does not necessarily relate to protection from arbitrariness. For example in the 'stepchild' case, one argument of the Dutch court was that the sexual abuse by the partner of the victim's mother could fall under simple sexual abuse as opposed to the aggravated form of the offence.[170]

Finally, perhaps the most important feature of *lex stricta* is the prohibition of analogous interpretation. Analogy, as a way of inductive reasoning in logic, can be defined as *'a parallel drawn between two (or more) entities by indicating one or more respects in which they are similar'*.[171] Analogy usually implies that the compared behaviours or entities are neither identical nor different.[172]

The method of analogy has its roots in the science of logic and simple reasoning inferences found in mathematics:

if A = D
A is similar to B,
then B = D

---

163 A. Ashworth, J. Horder, 'Principles of Criminal Law', Oxford University Press, 2013, pp. 69–71.

164 Thet v Director of Public Prosecutions [2006] EWHC Admin 2701.

165 R v JTB [2009] UKHL 20; A.P. Simester, J.R. Spencer, G.R. Sullivan, G.J. Virgo, 'Simester and Sullivan's Criminal Law: Theory and Doctrine', Hart Publishing, 2013, pp. 46–47.

166 D. Ormerod, 'Smith and Hogan's Criminal law', Oxford University Press, 2011, p. 18.

167 H. Satzger, B. Schmitt, G. Widmaier, 'StGB-Strafgesetzbuch: Kommentar', Heymanns, 2009, para. 1, Mn 45.

168 Haughton v Smith [1975] AC 476; J. de Hullu, 'Materieel strafrecht', Kluwer, 2012, pp. 101–106; A.T.H. Smith, 'Judicial Law Making in the Criminal Law', Law Quarterly Review, vol. 100, 1984, pp. 54–55.

169 BGH NJW 1998, 833, 3 December 1997; J. de Hullu, 'Materieel strafrecht', Kluwer, 2012, p. 100.

170 HR 7 January 1997 NJ 1997, 361.

171 I. Copi, C. Cohen, K. McMahon, 'Introduction to Logic', Pearson, 2011, p. 447; W. Sax, 'Das Strafrechtliche "Analogieverbot"', Vandenhoeck & Ruprecht, 1953, pp. 97–98.

172 A. Kaufmann, 'Analogie und "Natur der Sache"', R. v. Decker & C. F. Mueller, 1982, p. 19.

Analogy results in the criminalisation of behaviour not on a basis of a prescribed rule but on the basis of the similarities or analogies to a prescribed rule. Generally speaking, analogy is a form of the interpretation of a statute. Its prohibition is due to both historical and judicial reasons. The method of analogy was used widely in undemocratic polities such as dictatorships and polities lacking democratic values (Nazi Germany and USSR).[173] There, one can find general provisions establishing analogy as a principle of the criminal system.[174] Prohibiting analogy has therefore become the main focus of *lex stricta* as analogy allows courts to include within the criminal rule behaviours that were not criminalised by the wording of the text.

An example is the interpretation of the term 'weapon' in German law. Is a vehicle a weapon? Prior judgements have accepted that this term should be understood also in non-technical terms, which means that not only armour and knives but also objects or substances that are employed by the perpetrator to exercise violence.[175] An interpretation of the term 'weapon' as including also vehicles would be due to analogy: a car is not a weapon but it may be used in a similar manner as a weapon. Thus, the German Constitutional Court argued that interpreting the term 'weapon' in a non-technical sense is contrary to the principle of *lex stricta*.[176]

With analogy, there is a sharp difference between continental and common law traditions. Analogy in common law has been the main tool with which common law offences were developed through time.[177] Common law emerged following the principle *a similibus ad similia* ('likes cure like').[178] Common law developed the law *'from case to case, like the ancient Mediterranean mariners, hugging the coast from point to point'*.[179] Arbitrariness is controlled through the application of the rules of precedent, which by binding courts to previous authority limits arbitrary judgements.[180] In traditional common law, instead of the statute limiting English courts, English judges limit each other through the rules of precedent.

As explained, precedent is based on judgements that bind courts in future cases. However, unlike statutes, court judgements are already coloured by the facts of the decided case. In other words, what the Dutch call *legisme* – which is the isolation of facts and rules that ensures law retains a stable content –[181] is not to be found in the English precedent rules. Thus, rules on precedent can often favour analogical reasoning, as courts are motivated to focus on the facts of every case and compare

---

173 See B.M.J. van Klink, L.M.M. Royakkers, 'Analogie en rechtszekerheid in het strafrecht', Delikt en Delinkwent, vol. 29, 1999, p. 978.

174 Ibid.

175 E.g. BGH NJW 1975, 1934, 24 July 1975; OLG Düsseldorf NJW 1982, 1111, 9 November 1981.

176 BVerfG 2 BvR 2238/07, 1 September 2008.

177 B. Juratowitch, 'Retroactivity and the Common Law', Hart Publishing, 2008, p. 125.

178 Ibid., pp. 119–124.

179 Lord Wright, 'The Study of Law', Law Quarterly Review, vol. 54, 1938, p. 186.

180 B. Juratowitch, 'Retroactivity and the Common Law', Hart Publishing, 2008, p. 126.

181 See above para. 3.2.

those with the facts of previous cases.[182] Even more, they result in casuistry and complication.[183] Thus a prohibition of analogy at least in its technical sense did not really make sense in traditional common law. This feature explains why, when it comes to statutory interpretation, a prohibition of analogy is not a well-known concept in English law. In the English system, any limits on judicial interpretation of statutes are covered by previously mentioned methods.

Regarding common law adjudication, judicial limits on interpretation are set by the rules on precedent, which are functional equivalent to *lex stricta*. While this may favour analogy in some cases, the rules on precedence can be an effective protection against arbitrary decision-making, as they are hard to deviate from,[184] especially in criminal law.[185] In particular, if one investigates the grounds on which departure from precedent may take place, it becomes clear that such departure only occurs in the handful of hard cases, which make their way up to the English Supreme Court.

Juratowitch, for example, made an inventory of the grounds and reasoning of English courts in dealing with deviations from precedence in criminal law matters.[186] He identifies the following grounds: (i) there is a particular need to adapt the law to new circumstances;[187] (ii) cases where morality may be of importance;[188] (iii) cases where the prior authority is seriously in error;[189] (iv) and cases where the court overrules a prior judicial interpretation of a statute.[190] Generally speaking, the need for foreseeability and the ability to rely on the law plays an important role in the decision-making of English courts.[191]

Having said that, two points should be made here. Firstly, the English system, being as different as it is from continental systems, has provided an alternative to the continental *lex stricta,* and secondly, that this functional equivalent introduces a more substantial view on the limits of interpretation which are to be found not in technical methodologies, but in a certain appreciation of the fact of every case.

9. The principle of legality and the ECHR

Having identified the main characteristics of the legality principle in national systems, I shall turn now to the ECtHR. Its jurisprudence contributed to the principle's different characteristics, the main being the element of foreseeability.

---

182 C. Sampford, 'Retrospectivity and the Rule of Law', Oxford University Press, 2006, p. 176.
183 Ibid.
184 Ibid., p. 177.
185 B. Juratowitch, 'Retroactivity and the Common Law', Hart Publishing, 2008, p. 196.
186 Ibid., pp. 183–197.
187 Joyce v DPP [1946] AC 347 (HL).
188 Shaw v DPP [1962] AC 220.
189 For example DPP for Norhtern Ireland v Lynch [1975] AC 653 (HL).
190 For example R v Shivpuri [1987] AC 1 (HL).
191 C. Sampford, 'Retrospectivity and the Rule of Law', Oxford University Press, 2006, p. 177.

Such an approach has been very influential in national systems. Indeed, as a source of inspiration, the ECtHR's approach has infiltrated national law – and EU law –[192] and changed the nature and function of the legality principle. In this section I shall deal firstly with the conceptualisation of this principle by the ECtHR and secondly, with its impact on national law.

9.1. The ECtHR approach

The jurisprudence of the ECtHR has had a tremendous impact on the development of the legality principle within Europe. The ECtHR, being without affiliation to a particular jurisdiction, has interpreted the legality principle independently from specific national doctrinal contexts and thus takes a fresh look at the principle. In addition, the nature of this court and its mandate to deal with the legality principle as a human right has resulted in a different approach on legality.

One characteristic of the ECtHR's approach is that the principle is not concerned with the origins of the sources of criminal liability. This is evident from the Nuremberg exemption of Article 7 para. 2 ECHR. This derogation has been mainly applied in relation to war crimes.[193] Regarding the concept of *law* in Article 7 para. 1 ECHR – and other provisions of the ECHR – it is understood as *droit* and not *loi*. This may have been due to the combination of common and continental law systems in the Council of Europe.[194] For the ECtHR's approach, qualitative (or historical/universal) elements of the principle of legality, such as accessibility, predictability and foreseeability of criminalisation, are more prevalent than the historical or formal elements, namely those about the source of criminal liability (*lex parliamentaria* and *lex scripta*).[195]

In *X Ltd and Y v UK* for example, the EComHR acknowledged common law as a source of law and, therefore, jurisprudence should also comply with the requirements of foreseeability.[196] The supplementary role of jurisprudence in complementing the scope of criminal liability in the statute was also recognised.[197] While the broader concept of *droit* could be explained as a combination of different traditions, the ECtHR has not accepted this proposition. According to the court, to overlook the important role of case law in continental systems would undermine the character of continental systems almost as much as of common law systems.[198]

192 Chapter VI para. 1.
193 ECtHR Kononov v Latvia, App. 36376/04, 24 July 2008.
194 P. Beauvais, 'Le principe de la légalité pénale dans le droit de l'Union européenne', Thèse, Université Paris X Nanterre UFR, 1 December 2006, p. 122.
195 A. Bernardi, 'Nullum crimen, nulla poena sine lege between European law and national law', in M.C. Bassiouni, V. Militello, H. Satzger (eds), 'European cooperation in penal matters: issues and perspectives', Cedam, 2008, pp. 101–102.
196 EComHR X Ltd Y v United Kingdom, App. 8710/79, 7 May 1982.
197 ECtHR Cantoni v France, App. 178662/91, 15 November 1996.
198 ECtHR Kruslin v France, App. 11801/85, 24 April 1990, para. 29.

This is a rather bold assessment of continental systems, albeit not far from the truth as will be shown.[199]

A second element is that a qualitative view of legality results in the prominent position of the element of foreseeability. The foreseeability of criminal liability includes elements of accessibility, comprehensibility and interpretation in a foreseeable manner by courts:

> Firstly, the law must be adequately accessible: the citizen must be able to have an indication that is adequate in the circumstances of the legal rules applicable to a given case. Secondly, a norm cannot be regarded as a 'law' unless it is formulated with sufficient precision to enable the citizen to regulate his conduct: he must be able – if need be with appropriate advice – to foresee, to a degree that is reasonable in the circumstances, the consequences which a given action may entail.[200]

For the ECtHR, foreseeability is not absolute. It varies depending on the character of the offence and the addressees of norms.[201] This entails that *lex certa* may require different standards of precision depending on the nature of the offences. Courts on the other hand may take under consideration the particular conditions of the addressee of the statute in determining the limits of criminal liability. Thus in *Cantoni*, the ECtHR accepted that within the professional sphere, a certain knowledge of what the law would entail is to be expected, and a criminal provision that would seem vague to the every day citizen is not necessarily vague for the professional to which the provision is addressed:

> This is particularly true in relation to persons carrying on a professional activity, who are used to having to proceed with a high degree of caution when pursuing their occupation. They can on this account be expected to take special care in assessing the risks that such activity entails.[202]

In addition, foreseeability cannot require maximum or absolute legal certainty with regard to statutes, and a level of uncertainty is accepted:

> Those consequences need not be foreseeable with absolute certainty: experience shows this to be unattainable. Again, whilst certainty is highly desirable, it may bring in its train excessive rigidity and the law must be able to keep pace with changing circumstances. Accordingly, many laws are inevitably couched in terms which, to a greater or lesser extent, are vague and whose interpretation and application are question of practice.[203]

---

199 See below para. 10.3.1.
200 ECtHR Sunday Times v United Kingdom, App. 6538/74, 26 April 1979.
201 ECtHR Cantoni v France, App. 178662/91, 15 November 1996.
202 Ibid., para. 35.
203 ECtHR Sunday Times v United Kingdom, App. 6538/74, 26 April 1979, para. 49.

As far as judicial interpretation goes, an obligation for a strict construction and the prohibition of analogy is acknowledged: *'the criminal law must not be excessively construed to an accused's detriment, for instance by analogy.'*[204] But the application of such a prohibition has not been explicitly outlined by the ECtHR. It is the 'foreseeable interpretation' of the law that the ECtHR emphasises. For the ECtHR, an unforeseeable judicial interpretation would be arbitrary.

Foreseeability is not understood as subjective (as in the German doctrine as explained above);[205] whether the actual defendants had foreseen such a result is not of interest (as discussed under the principle of guilt in most countries). What is important is whether the interpretation could be objectively (by a common person) foreseeable.[206] Thus, it is not actual foresight and reliance on the law that is required, but the ability to foresee and rely on criminal norms.[207]

Foreseeability need not be absolute but exists *'to a degree that is reasonable in the circumstances, the consequences which a given action may entail.'*[208] In the marital rape case, the English court found the gradual dismantling of the immunity in previous cases was a sufficient indication of the risk of criminalisation.[209]

In answering the question of whether an interpretation is foreseeable, the wording of a text is decisive, but not necessarily the absolute limit of judicial interpretation. A substantive instead of procedural interpretation of the democratic principle is followed.[210] Courts are co-determinants of criminal liability (with the different balances depending on the common or continental law nature of each jurisdiction).[211] Courts do not create a new order of things, but are preoccupied with the extension of a spontaneous and evolutionary order.[212] But what constitutes a foreseeable interpretation according to the ECtHR? The following guidelines from jurisprudence can be identified:

- Interpretation must generally preserve the communicative value of the statute: *'This condition is satisfied where the individual can know from the wording of the relevant provision...'.*[213] The wording is the starting point and a teleological

204 ECtHR Kokkinakis v Greece, App. 14307/ 88, 25 May 1993, para. 52.

205 See para. 2.

206 B. Juratowitch, 'Retroactivity and the Common Law', Hart Publishing, 2008, p. 130.

207 Ibid.

208 ECtHR Sunday Times v United Kingdom, App. 6538/74, 26 April 1979, para. 49.

209 ECtHR S.W. v United Kingdom, App. 20166/92, 22 November 1995, para. 43.

210 P. Beauvais, 'Le principe de la légalité pénale dans le droit de l'Union européenne', Thèse, Université Paris X Nanterre UFR, 1 December 2006, p. 134.

211 Ibid., p. 135.

212 *'l'attitude du juge est valorisée, car elle est à rebours de la démarche du législateur constructiviste, puisqu'elle ne vise pas la création d'un ordre nouveau mais la prolongation d' un ordre spontané et évolutif, de surcroît sur un mode expérimental',* V. Valentin, 'Les conceptions néo-libérales du droit', Economica, Corpus Essais, 2002, p. 88 cited via P. Beauvais, 'Le principe de la légalité pénale dans le droit de l'Union européenne', Thèse, Université Paris X Nanterre UFR, 1 December 2006, p. 135.

213 ECtHR Kokkinakis v Greece, App. 14307/ 88, 25 May 1993, para. 52.

or historical interpretation is implied, as courts must apply the will of the legislator.

- The statutory meaning may be supported by a perceptive line of jurisprudence[214] and clarified by the interpretation of courts in the current case: *'and, if need be, with the assistance of the courts' interpretation of it, what acts and omissions will make him liable.'*[215] Jurisprudence represents a narration of the evolution of criminal liability.
- Foreseeability of interpretation can also be facilitated by legal advice: *'...he must be able – if need be with appropriate advice – to foresee, to a degree that is reasonable in the circumstances, the consequences which a given action may entail.'*[216] The guideline from the ECtHR is not to be taken literally.[217] It would be absurd to regard behavioural choices as entirely dependent on legal advice, at least outside the professional sphere. One could perhaps re-read this as a general obligation to consider whether, based on the current status quo (and jurisprudence), such an interpretation would be expected in the legal world.
- An additional element, implicit in the ECtHR's jurisprudence, is the horizontal weight of other human rights. This is more concerned with the *'degree that is reasonable in the circumstances'*. In particular, when the right to foreseeability conflicts with other human rights in the ECHR, then the ECtHR aligns the degree of foreseeability with the expected protection of the violated human right. This element is especially visible in the English marital rape case. There the court, after assessing the line of case law which pointed out a gradual dismantling of the marital immunity added: *'The essentially debasing character of rape is so manifest that the result of the decisions of the Court of Appeal and the House of Lords [...] cannot be said to be at variance with the object and purpose of Article 7 (art. 7) of the Convention [...]'*.[218] The rights, which the offence touched, such as equality, intimacy of marriage and sexual integrity, indicated that such immunity would not be in conformity *'not only with a civilised concept of marriage but also, and above all, with the fundamental objectives of the Convention, the very essence of which is respect for human dignity and human freedom.'*[219]

How could one assess the view of the ECtHR in relation to the legality principle? The ECtHR takes a 'rights-conception' to the legality principle.[220] Regarding this

214 ECtHR S.W. v United Kingdom, App. 20166/92, 22 November 1995, para. 43.

215 ECtHR Kokkinakis v Greece, App. 14307/ 88, 25 May 1993, para. 52.

216 ECtHR Sunday Times v United Kingdom, App. 6538/74, 26 April 1979, para. 49.

217 C. Gearty, 'Principles of Human Rights Adjudication', Oxford University Press, 2004, pp. 80–81.

218 ECtHR C.R. v United Kingdom, App 20190/92, 22 November 1995, para. 42.

219 Ibid.

220 The ECtHR approach to this principle evidently echoes Dworkin's 'rights conception' of the Rule of Law (the rights thesis) see R. Dworkin, 'A Matter of Principle', Harvard University Press, 1985, pp. 11–18.

principle as a human right, a right to foreseeable criminalisation, implies a different view of the principle.[221] Human rights are undetermined and their interpretation requires that they be conceptualised in *ad hoc* cases.[222] They are subjected to a balancing exercise and they can be respected or violated to varying degrees. In *Kokkinakis* for example, the individual was criminalised for proselytism, a provision that was formulated ambiguously in Greek law. In this case, the right to clear norms carried more weight if considered in the light of the Greek society, where there was religious intolerance.

Human rights interpretation is also characterised by a tendency towards generalisation.[223] Because fundamental rights underpin the whole system, their interpretation and application in concrete cases must be such, that it can be applied in other cases as well. In addition, human rights are understood as claims against the legal system/state, which have priority over other obligations. These claims may result in certain duties for the state, but only if these claims are acknowledged.[224] Such a conclusion cannot be drawn in the marital rape case(s), as the applicant could not successfully claim that his interest in maintaining stable case law be extended to other similar cases in the past and future, in line with the integrity of the legal order.

Finally, there is also a relational dimension to human rights; their interpretation is influenced by their interconnections. For the legality principle, this means that the right to foreseeable criminalisation is interpreted in the context of other rights involved (violated or interfered with) *in casu.* As a criminal law principle, legality is concerned with the vertical relationship between the state and the individual; but as a human right, its interpretation also includes a horizontal dimension, i.e. interpersonal relationships.[225] To explain this, if one reads the application of the legality in the context of the individual rights protected by a criminal provision (e.g. for the marital rape case, sexual integrity, equality, human dignity), it is inevitable that foreseeable criminalisation depends on whether individuals can draw from rules reasonable expectations with regard to each other.[226] In other words, the relational dimension of the legality principle presumes that criminal norms are not only a barrier to state arbitrariness, but also protect individual autonomy in its positive sense, i.e. they enforce standards of interpersonal activity.

---

221 For a definition of rights and their relationship to principles see R. Dworkin, 'Taking Rights Seriously', Duckworth, 1977, pp. 90–94.

222 E. Claes, 'Criminal Justice, Legality and Human Dignity', in E. Claes, R. Foqué, T. Peters (eds), 'Punishment, Restorative Justice and the Morality of Law', Intersentia, 2005, p. 33.

223 Ibid., p. 34.

224 Ibid., p. 35.

225 Chapter III para. 2.

226 E. Claes, 'Criminal Justice, Legality and Human Dignity', in E. Claes, R. Foqué, T. Peters (eds), 'Punishment, Restorative Justice and the Morality of Law', Intersentia, 2005, p. 35.

9.2. The influence of the ECtHR jurisprudence on national law

ECtHR jurisprudence has greatly influenced national systems, albeit in different ways. For continental systems, the ECtHR promoted a shift of the legality principle from a formal to a more substantive approach. This shift has been also noticed in other systems, such as the French one, where it is referred to as the shift from a material to substantive interpretation of the legality principle.[227]

It should be noted that the continental systems do not implement the ECtHR's approach on sources of criminal liability, especially as far as the Nuremberg exemption is concerned.[228] However, the concepts of foreseeability and foreseeable interpretation have been incorporated into national doctrine, especially by national courts, which use extensively the ECtHR jurisprudence.[229] An example is the case of child pornography in the Netherlands, where the Dutch Supreme Court held that the possession of child pornography is included in the scope of criminal liability that criminalised the possession in stock.[230] The defendant could not claim that such interpretation is not foreseeable especially in relation to the rights protected by the statute, i.e. sexual integrity and dignity of children.[231]

More generally, the ECtHR's influence also accompanied an existing general shift from a procedural concept of democracy to a more substantive one, which has been especially facilitated by the human rights narrative in national constitutions. Particularly after the Third Reich, German constitutionalism incorporates the formal theory of *Rechtsstaat* with substantive elements via the constitutional protection of human rights and the strong position of the German Constitutional Court.

What the ECtHR's conception of legality mainly brought into continental systems was a 'way out' theory for the increasingly problematic application of the legality principle.[232] The focus on foreseeability, more optimum expectations of legal certainty, acceptance of the dynamic role of courts, and the balancing of rights that often occurs during judicial interpretation was very quickly absorbed, reproduced and applied by continental systems.

In England, the ECtHR jurisprudence had a paramount influence as it brought the holistic doctrine of the principle of legality into the English legal order and, in

---

227 P. Beauvais, 'Le principe de la légalité pénale dans le droit de l'Union européenne', Thèse, Université Paris X Nanterre UFR, 1 December 2006, p. 110; see more generally D. Zerouki, 'La légalité criminelle: enrichissement de la conception formelle par une conception matérielle', Jean-Moulin Lyon 3, 2001.

228 See the annotation by G. Knigge in ECtHR C.R. v United Kingdom, 22 November 1995, NJ 1997, 1; an example for the Dutch system is HR 18 September 2001 NJ 2002, 559; see also for English law, R v Bow Street Metropolitan Stipendiary Magistrate Ex p. Pinochet Ugarte (No.3) [1999] 2 WLR 827.

229 BVerfG 1 BvR 718/89, 10 January 1995.

230 HR 21 April 1998 NJ 1998, 782.

231 K. Rozemond, 'Legaliteit in het materiële strafrecht', RM Themis, 1999, p. 125.

232 See further below para. 10.

addition, explicitly created the 'principle of legality'. By reference to the ECtHR jurisprudence, English courts now had access to a single legal doctrine that prohibited retroactivity, vagueness and the development of common law offences in a manner that made criminal prosecutions unforeseeable, instead of the previous functional equivalents. For example, it has been suggested in scholarship that the 'presumption against retroactivity' should be re-interpreted from a presumption to the – stronger – 'prohibition of retroactivity'.[233] English courts have increasingly referred to the principle of legality when dealing with common law offences and have reproduced ECtHR jurisprudence.[234] The ECtHR has dealt with unforeseeable criminal prosecutions in some well-documented cases, such as the marital rape case. It also found some common law offences to be in violation of the legality principle, such as the offence of conduct *contra bonos mores* in *Hashman and Harrup v UK*.[235]

Such influence peaked with the introduction of the Human Rights Act in 1998. The Act received much criticism, especially because it was perceived to be an external intervention to the national system, which would subject English law and institutions to unsolicited review, thus violating the sovereignty of the UK.[236] The Human Rights Act differs from the ECHR in that it incorporates and adapts certain Convention rights and allows derogations.[237] With the Human Rights Act, the principle of legality receives its first official statutory legal basis in the English system.

The Act brought some important changes relevant for the legality principle. Articles 3 and 4 of the Act allow English courts to declare legislation to be in violation of those rights, although this declaration has no effect on the validity on the legislation concerned.[238] This means that English courts can now declare statutes as being in violation of the principle of legality.[239] Giving such a power to courts has changed the institutional dynamics yet again in England, as it has altered the English view of parliamentary sovereignty *vis-à-vis* the Rule of Law.[240] The increasingly positivistic approach to law-making in the UK continued with the Constitutional Reform Act 2005, which provided the first reference to the 'Rule of Law' in a parliamentary text.[241]

These recent constitutional developments, together with the more substantive view of the legality principle introduced via the ECtHR, fuelled a dialogue in English constitutional theory regarding the interpretation of the Rule of Law,

---

233 B. Juratowitch, 'Retroactivity and the Common Law', Hart Publishing, 2008, p. 197.
234 R v Rimmington and R v Goldstein (joined cases) [2005] UKHL 63.
235 ECtHR Hashman and Harrup v United Kingdom, App. 25594/94, 25 November 1999.
236 C. Gearty, 'Principles of Human Rights Adjudication', Oxford University Press, 2004, pp. 1–7.
237 Ibid., pp. 9–13.
238 Ibid., p. 12.
239 For example, R v Sadique and another [2011] EWCA Crim 2872; R v Misra and Srivastava [2004] EWCA Crim 2375, para. 37 (for further case law).
240 Lord Hope, obiter, in Jackson v Her Majesty's Attorney General [2005] UKHL 56, para. 107.
241 Constitutional Reform Act 2005.

similar to that found in continental countries. The question in English constitutional law is therefore whether the Rule of Law follows a majoritarian view of democracy and legitimacy of criminal norms, where parliament should enjoy supremacy, or whether a more substantive view is preferable (such as the 'rights-conception' Rule of Law by Dworkin or the communitarian model by Allan),[242] granting English courts powers to review the compatibility of parliamentary legislation with human rights standards.[243]

Ultimately, a human rights based approach towards the legality principle brings substantial changes to it as a doctrine, which has influenced national law. Such influence will be discussed further below, where the current application of the legality principle will be analysed. It will be seen that there are substantial discrepancies between the theory of legality and its practice. What will be also shown is that ECtHR's 'rights-conception' has not necessarily caused the erosion of the legality principle, as the source of its problems are the result of inherent deficiencies in the doctrine; on the contrary it can be the starting point for solutions.

10. The erosion of the legality principle

Having analysed how the principle of legality is conceived in the legal systems and how the ECtHR has interpreted this principle, one should investigate how the principle is actually applied in practice. In this section, the focus shall shift from the 'law in the books' to the 'law in practice'.

It will be shown that the current application of the legality principle is rather dogmatically inconsistent, as the way the legality principle is supposed to function in theory is not mirrored in practice. The mismatch between the 'law in books' and 'law in practice' has been often referred to as an erosion of the principle of legality.[244]

Judicial and legislative practice shows that the current doctrine is anachronistic and fails to adequately shield individuals from arbitrariness. Additionally, some aspects of the legality principle do not function properly. Continental traditions have developed certain *de facto* common law elements themselves. In light of the current dialogue regarding the definition of *Rechtsstaat* and the separation of powers, the problem of judicial arbitrariness is not limited to the restriction of their powers, but also includes the legitimacy of their reasoning. If one recalls the analysis of the separation of powers, a modern 'checks and balances' approach

242 T.R.S. Allan, 'The Rule of Law as the Rule of Reason: Consent and Constitutionalism', Law Quarterly Review, vol. 115, 1999, p. 221.

243 C. Gearty, 'Principles of Human Rights Adjudication', Oxford University Press, 2004, pp. 61–68.

244 B. Jähnke, 'Zur Erosion des Verfassungssatzes "Keine Strafe ohne Gesetz"', ZIS, vol. 7, 2010, pp. 463–470; B. Schünemann, 'Nulla poena sine lege? Rechtstheoretische und verfassungsrechtliche Implikationen der Rechtsgewinnung im Strafrecht', Walter de Gruyter, 1978, p. 8; E. Claes, 'Legaliteit en rechtsvinding in het strafrecht', Universitaire Pers Leuven, 2003, p. 16.

requires that courts keep legislatures in check, and thus protect individuals from arbitrary legislative decisions. What is more, judicial arbitrariness is not only defined in association with the scope for interpretation, but also in the substance of the decision. As it was mentioned in Chapter III, a modern view of the separation of powers requires that the legality principle limits judicial functions, but also informs decision-making.[245]

I will first analyse the elements of *lex stricta* and *lex certa,* which will better illustrate the deficiencies of the legality principle. I will then continue with the impact of these deficiencies on *lex scripta;* if courts have an increased judicial role in practice, then the question of the sources of criminal liability is to be raised. I will conclude with my analysis of the *lex praevia.*

10.1. *Lex stricta*

As explained, the principle of *lex stricta* restricts judicial interpretation through the binding of courts to the wording of a statute. This results in the prohibition of analogy, which is the main protective guarantee from judicial arbitrariness. The justification of prohibiting analogy has been primarily for historical reasons, as it has been associated with totalitarian regimes (such as the Nazi regime);[246] in addition, technically, it can potentially lead to the extension of criminal liability. In practice however, analogy in this context is difficult to define, often employed and is ultimately insufficient to protect against judicial arbitrariness. This leads to the questions: can judicial arbitrariness be prevented by a prohibition of analogy? Does such a prohibition curtail but also inform judicial interpretation?

10.1.1. Can analogical reasoning be distinguished from interpretation?

The first problem of prohibiting analogy is its indeterminacy as a method. The attribution of criminal liability in analogy is based on a pair of preconditions: first, the behaviour under discussion does not or cannot fall under any prescribed criminal liability; and second, this behaviour presents analogies or similarities, to another prescribed criminal liability.[247] I explained analogy previously by referring to techniques of logic.[248] When a court says that new facts A are like old facts B, a new category of facts is created, category C, which includes both A and B facts.

245 Chapter III para. 4.

246 N. Jörg, C. Kelk, A. Klip, 'Strafrecht met mate', Kluwer, 2012, pp. 32–33; C. Kelk, 'Studieboek materieel strafrecht', Kluwer, 2010, p. 109.

247 B.M.J. van Klink, L.M.M. Royakkers, 'Analogie en rechtszekerheid in het strafrecht', Delikt en Delinkwent, vol. 29, 1999, p. 979.

248 A. Tversky, 'Features of similarity', Psychological Review, vol. 84, 1977, pp. 327–352, cited via B.M.J. van Klink, L.M.M. Royakkers, 'Analogie en rechtszekerheid in het strafrecht', Delikt en Delinkwent, vol. 29, 1999, p. 979.

However, within this category C, facts B are the prototype while facts A are just a variation.[249]

As analogy in language is not as clear as analogy in mathematics, indeterminacy in language makes it difficult to identify analogical interpretation. As seen in the example with the term 'weapon,' it is not always clear whether a term may include the facts under discussion. The first requirement for analogy – that behaviour does not fall under the scope of any prescribed liability – can be difficult to pin down. If the word 'weapon' is understood in a technical sense, then vehicles, acid or aggressive dogs are not weapons; they can have a similar use to weapons though, which would be analogical reasoning. However, if weapon is understood more abstractly these items can be considered as weapons without considering this as analogical reasoning. The German Constitutional Court preferred the latter option when qualifying acid as weapon.[250]

One may argue that any analogy in this case was indirect, or hidden within the interpretation of the term 'weapon,' but it is not self-evident that the term 'weapon' cannot include vehicles. A certain level of analogy is often present within judicial interpretation, especially when courts attempt to subject facts to norms. If the individual had attacked the victim with a heavy brick, or a baseball bat, there would be little objection to considering those instruments weapons. But in order to reach this conclusion, a background analogical comparison between other instruments that are considered weapons and the instruments under consideration would be necessary to decide that they are all, ultimately, weapons.

If one looks at analogy and interpretation from the perspective of legal methodology, every interpretation bears some analogy: *'Every interpretation is analogical'*.[251] An advantage of the common law system is that analogy is an accepted aspect of judicial interpretation. Because criminal liability is always generalised to encompass a variety of different behaviours, courts must always compare facts with norms to decide whether the facts at hand reflect the normative and typical definition of a crime. One could represent the norms with the *Sollen* (what one ought to do), and the facts with the *Sein* (what has taken place). Norms (*Sollen*) and facts (*Sein*) are neither identical nor different and their meeting point constitutes interpretation. Analogy is the exact meeting point between identical and different elements, between *Sollen* and *Sein*; it is defined as the cohabitation between identity and difference.[252] Interpretation of the law is inherently analogical.[253] As analogical reasoning is inherent to interpretation, identifying the point at which

249 Ibid.; see above para. 8.

250 BVerfG 2 BvR 2238/07, 1 September 2008, para. 2b and c.

251 (translated from German by the author) W. Hassemer, 'Tatbestand und Typus', Carl Heymanns Verlag, 1968, p. 164; similarly in A. Kaufmann, 'Analogie und "Natur der Sache"', R. v. Decker & C. F. Mueller, 1982, p. 19.

252 M. Heidegger, 'Identität und Differenz', Pfullingen, 1957, p. 10, cited via A. Kaufmann, 'Analogie und "Natur der Sache"', R. v. Decker & C. F. Mueller, 1982, p. 19.

253 Ibid.

analogy becomes problematic is not easy. Thus, the first problem with the prohibition of analogy is that it is not clear what it is prohibited, when and why.

10.1.2. Is analogical reasoning used in practice?

Apart from the difficulty of defining analogy, there are various cases where seemingly straightforward analogical reasoning is employed by courts. In cases concerning narcotics, courts employ analogical reasoning when statutes fail to list all the procedures and substances that qualify as narcotics. An example is the 'opium case', where the Dutch Supreme Court held that the term 'hashish' includes not only products from the top part of the plant, as stated in the statute, but also products from other parts of the plant.[254] In a similar case, mixing acacia leaves with passion fruit in special tubes qualifies as preparation of narcotic substances, even though the statute does not list specifically those plants as narcotics, but it does list chemicals that they contain. According to the Dutch Supreme Court, should this interpretation be against the legality principle, the purpose of the statute would be defeated.[255]

Similar attitudes in cases involving narcotics can be found in Germany. In one case, the defendant had traded magic mushrooms in perfume and potpourri pillows. At the time of the commission of the act, the law prohibited narcotic substances from plants, but not from organisms (fungi). After the act occurred, an amendment was introduced including substances from organisms. It is self-evident that mushrooms are not plants but organisms. The German Federal Court argued that interpreting the term 'plants' as including mushrooms is not against the legality principle as the every-day use of the term includes mushrooms.[256] However, this reasoning is actually analogical ('mushrooms are similar to plants'). This is also evident from the subsequent amendment. Clearly, the legislator did not use the term 'plants' in its every-day sense, but as a technical term; otherwise, the amendment would not have been necessary.

The analogical reasoning inherent to any interpretative task can be better illustrated in the case of electricity theft in the Netherlands.[257] The question was whether electrical energy was a 'good' under Article 310 DCC, which could be removed from a person's possession. The Dutch Supreme Court followed three conceptual steps of interpretation that do not seem overtly analogical: it interpreted the norm by deducing the characteristics that constitute the prescribed criminal conduct; the selected characteristics were interpreted in the context of the new

254 HR 7 March 1972 NJ 1972, 348.
255 HR 23 October 2012 NJ 2012, 616.
256 BGH NJW 2007, 524, 25 October 2006.
257 HR 23 May 1921 NJ 1921, 564, annotation by Taverne.

facts; the coherency and the judicial context of the findings regarding criminal liability was finally tested.[258]

As first step, the court identified the characteristics of the general rule behind the wording of Article 310 DCC, by construing the norm abstractly.[259] In this way the court takes some distance from the rule, as it was laid down, in order to reconstrue the norm by bringing it closer to the facts and by clarifying it. The Dutch Supreme Court created the following criteria, regarding the term 'good': autonomous existence, capability to be moved, availability and economic value.[260] The second step was to interpret those results in the light of the new facts. It was argued that as long as electrical energy can be accumulated, be available for use, has an economic value and independent existence, then it can be considered a 'good'. For the third step, the court considered its decision in the light of the purpose of criminal norms regarding theft in the judicial system. The term 'good' cannot be understood any longer as capturing only material but also immaterial goods; due to technological developments, individuals can own also immaterial goods and these can be removed from their possession. The case has been severely criticised by many authors including Taverne, who argued in his annotation to the case that this was a classic case of analogy: *'be honest and acknowledge analogy!'*.[261] It is interesting that a similar case in England had the completely opposite result. The English court found that electrical energy was not property that could be appropriated. However, it is argued that this interpretation was justified on grounds of consistency, as there was a separate provision for abstracting electricity, which was not used by the prosecutor in this case.[262]

A similar problem can be found in cases regarding computer data.[263] The facts concerned an employee in a computer data company who copied a disk with data and programs without permission. The Dutch court followed the reasoning in the electricity case. The computer data was 'just like electricity': the data met the criteria of autonomous existence, capability to be moved, availability and economic value.[264] The court in addition brought the criteria closer to the facts by redefining the availability criterion as the ability of the good to be reproduced. This was a crucial readjustment because computer data is available through reproduction.[265] The Dutch

258 A. Tversky, 'Features of similarity', Psychological Review, vol. 84, 1977, pp. 327–352 cited via B.M.J. van Klink, L.M.M. Royakkers, 'Analogie en rechtszekerheid in het strafrecht', Delikt en Delinkwent, vol. 29, 1999, pp. 981–988.

259 C. Kelk, 'Studieboek materieel strafrecht', Kluwer, 2010, p. 105.

260 M.S. Groenhuijsen, F.P.E. Wiemans, 'Van electriciteit naar computercriminaliteit', Gouda Quint, 1989, p. 84; B.M.J. van Klink, L.M.M. Royakkers, 'Analogie en rechtszekerheid in het strafrecht', Delikt en Delinkwent, vol. 29, 1999, p. 984.

261 'Wees eerlijk en erken analogie!' annotation by Taverne in HR 23 May 1921 NJ 1921, 564.

262 Low v Blease [1975] Criminal Law Review 513.

263 Hof Arnhem 27 October 1983 NJ 1983, 80; M.S. Groenhuijsen, F.P.E. Wiemans, 'Van electriciteit naar computercriminaliteit', Gouda Quint, 1989, p. 82.

264 Ibid., p. 84.

265 Ibid.

court however, encountered difficulties with the *actus reus* element of appropriation. Copying of data did not result in appropriation because the company was still the owner of the original disc.[266] Although in this case, the court did not convict the employee, the interpretative technique generated criticism. Many writers criticised the 'analogy' between energy and computer data, while others stated that the case would have been decided better under intellectual property law.[267] The acquittal, on the other hand, highlighted a legal lacuna in relation to cyber crime.

Although both the electricity and computer data cases received criticism in scholarly literature, a significant difference is that two years after the computer data case, the Dutch Minister of Justice established a commission to examine whether the Dutch legislation needs adjustments to combat computer crime. That resulted in a 1987 report proposing that provisions penalising computer crime should be included in the criminal code.[268] The underlying criticism of the commission was that computer data cannot be subjected to ordinary provisions, such as theft, because they do not fall under the term 'good', in contrast to the Dutch court's interpretation. Later case law held that back-up copies of electronic data could not be appropriated in the legal sense.[269]

Generally speaking when it comes to technological developments, analogy is often employed. For example, the Dutch court convicted boys who stole the virtual mask of their friend's avatar in a virtual reality video game. The virtual good had an economic value, since it was purchased in the game.[270]

10.1.3. Will courts update norms to new circumstances?

As explained, many cases where analogical reasoning is seemingly used involve an adaptation of the norm to new circumstances. In other words, the court's reasoning is not only analogical but also teleological and considers the question: if the legislator legislated today, would theft of electricity or processing of magic mushrooms be criminalised? Ultimately, it is difficult to demarcate analogical reasoning from objective teleological reasoning, as both methods can be used with the aim or the result of updating anachronistic provisions to new circumstances.

When it comes to technological advancement, the German and Dutch courts are not always reluctant to apply analogical reasoning and objective teleological interpretation.[271] For example, the German Federal Court held that committing timber theft (theft of wood from a private forest) with the use of a motor vehicle falls under the relevant German provision of timber theft, which at that time

---

266 Ibid.

267 Ibid., pp. 85–96.

268 Commissie Franken, 'Informatietechniek en strafrecht', Rapport van de Commissie computer-criminaliteit, Staatsuitgeverij, 1987.

269 See HR 3 December 1996 NJ 1997, 574.

270 Rechtbank Leeuwarden 21 October 2008 LJN BG0939.

271 J. de Hullu, 'Materieel strafrecht', Kluwer, 2012, pp. 101–106.

criminalised this act only if an animal-hauled carriage was used.[272] The court explained that although this interpretation cannot be based on the wording of the norm, it could be based on its purpose as the norm was anachronistic.

Similarly, the Dutch 'kidnapping case' is an illustration in this regard.[273] The defendant had illegally adopted children from Brazil and brought them to the Netherlands. Article 278 DCC criminalised only those who take illegally Dutch citizens outside the Netherlands. The Dutch Supreme Court extended the scope of the provision to cover the facts of the case. It considered the act of kidnapping from another country to the Netherlands to be the same as kidnapping from the Netherlands to another country. This is a very interesting example of judicial analogy because the court encompasses within the provision precisely the opposite behaviour to that which was criminalised.[274] This case is also an example of an objective teleological interpretation.[275] There are various cases reported where norms are adapted to modern times with the use of objective teleological interpretation.[276]

These cases represent a deviation from the traditional understanding of the legality principle, which does not allow courts to take over the role of the legislator. Although it cannot be said that it is appropriate on all occasions, they do show that analogy and the objective teleological reasoning are not forbidden fruit, especially when it comes to anachronistic provisions.

For example, in German law, it is argued that the objective teleological interpretation should be applied when interpreting anachronistic statutes and the will of the legislator has lost its meaning.[277] In such cases, courts do not replace the will of the legislator with their own, but they retain the dynamism of the law. Retaining dynamism of the law, according to this view, is also one of the intentions of the legislator. The will of the legislator includes not only substantive choices regarding protected legal interests, but also that these choices can be relevant in the future.[278] Therefore, the legitimacy of the objective teleological interpretation in those cases is based on the dynamism of criminal provisions, a value inherent to the law. This is strikingly different to the traditional doctrine of the legality principle.

10.1.4. Does the prohibition of analogy protect from judicial arbitrariness?

Even if one accepts that prohibiting analogy may not always be possible, the questions that remain are: how can the legality principle protect individuals from judicial arbitrariness? Can the prohibition of analogy offer protection against it?

---

272 BGH NJW 1957, 1642, 12 September 1957.

273 HR 20 November 2001 NJ 2003, 632.

274 B.M.J. van Klink, L.M.M. Royakkers, 'Analogie en rechtszekerheid in het strafrecht', Delikt en Delinkwent, vol. 29, 1999, p. 993.

275 See annotation by R. de Lange in HR 7 March 2004 NJ 2004, 675.

276 See annotation by 't Hart in HR 11 May 1982 NJ 1982, 583; HR 28 February 1989 NJ 1989, 658.

277 A. Schönke, H. Schröder, 'Kommentar zum StGB', Verlag C.H. Beck, 2014, para. 1, Mn 44.

278 Ibid.

The prohibition of analogy curtails judicial arbitrariness by preventing courts from taking over legislative functions. As mentioned, it is not always possible to define analogy and to prevent courts from incorporating new developments to the scope of liability. On occasion, it may be said that is not even desirable to restrict judicial interpretation extensively, as criminal provisions must remain contemporary and relevant. These are the main problems of the prohibition of analogy discussed so far.

However, there is an additional, and perhaps more significant, problem of this prohibition. In practice the *lex stricta* principle does not function so much as a prohibition of analogical reasoning. The focus on methodologies to prevent judicial arbitrariness is inadequate and in some cases, not helpful. Thus, if one considers *lex stricta* as only a prohibition of a methodology, the principle of legality fails to adequately protect against judicial arbitrariness. This is because judicial arbitrariness can take different forms. Certainly, one form is taking over the legislative functions. Another form, though, may be found in the judicial reasoning per se, namely the arguments that courts use for interpreting criminal liability. To illustrate this, a case will be presented where a judicial interpretation was declared to be in violation of *lex stricta*. This case is a landmark German judgement on the principle of legality.

The *Sitzblockaden* case was about the interpretation of Article 240 GCC, which criminalises coercion and it includes the term 'force' (*Gewalt*).[279] The question was whether 'force' referred to psychological as well as physical force. Participants in a sit-in demonstration were regarded as exercising psychological force over the driver of the truck who supplied a nuclear plant. Here the grammatical interpretation would suggest that also psychological force falls within the scope of criminalisation, as the provision only mentions the term 'force' without any further distinction. Yet the German Constitutional Court concluded that interpreting psychological force as coercion would be an arbitrary interpretation and, thus, against the principle of legality. What is interesting about this case is that the German Constitutional Court did not come to this conclusion by using the prohibition of analogy. It rather argued that the interpretation of the conflicting rights followed by the lower court was irreconcilable with the will of the legislator and the German legal order in general.

In particular, the German Constitutional Court did not deal with the grammatical meaning of 'force' in light of the *telos* of the norm by a mere application of methodologies. On the contrary, it considered which rights were protected and inflicted by this norm and whether an interpretation of psychological force as coercion could be generalised and applied in similar cases:

> The legislator did not want to penalise in Article 240 GCC every compulsion on the free volition of someone else. Otherwise other behavioural patterns – which are in social life, for instance in the educational system, the working world or the traffic area partly necessary, partly inevitable – would have come under threat of

---

279 BVerfG 1 BvR 718/89, 10 January 1995.

> punishment. [...] It is no longer foreseeable with sufficient certainty which forms of physical behaviour, which prevent others psychologically to enforce their will, shall be prohibited and which not. In situations in which force merely consists of bodily presence and the compulsion on the constrained person is merely psychological in nature, criminal liability is no longer determined previous to the deed by the legislator but by the judge in the case at hand; thus after the offence is committed and based on the judge's conviction of whether or not an act is worthy of punishment. That opens up a significant leeway for the criminal prosecution of coercion. The varying treatment of cases of blockades during demonstration in jurisprudence – on the one hand to protest against the use of nuclear power and on the other hand in cases of protests against closing down factories, increases of tuitions, subsidy reductions or traffic planning – proves this.[280]

The problem here was the lower court's interpretation and weighing of interests involved in coercion. The balancing followed by the lower court could not be reproduced in future cases, as it would lead to an excessive restriction of individual autonomy. This case demonstrates that judicial arbitrariness is not only understood as exceeding the wording of the text but also as appreciating individual interests protected by criminal law in a manner that inflicts excessively on individual rights. In other words, judicial arbitrariness is also such an interpretation that does not correspond with the protection of rights as these are envisioned in the legal order.

With subtlety, the German Constitutional Court adopted a 'rights-conception' to the legality principle similar to the ECtHR by focusing on the concept of foreseeability and how this would be influenced by judicial interpretation. It explored possible interpretations in the light of the specific situation at hand and weighed the right to foreseeable criminalisation of passive acts of intimidation during demonstrations against the purpose of the criminal provision. It found that the right to foreseeability outweighs the obligation to protect individuals from emotional coercion in the specific context of the German society. The claim to foreseeability in this case was successful because criminalisation of psychological force would create chaos in future cases. The norm would become so broad that it would be impossible to predict what intimidating act would be coercive for the purpose of criminalisation. It would create confusion regarding permissibility of acts during demonstrations and also other situations, involving intimidation at work or school.

What is clear is that *lex stricta* is not limited to a prohibition of analogy but involves other considerations such as foreseeability (can individuals foresee criminalisation?), the danger of arbitrary state action in similar cases (does this interpretation of the norm allow for arbitrary prosecutions and judicial interpretations?) and the determination of the *telos* of criminalisation, which is aligned with the balancing of rights within the legal order (the legislator could not have wished to criminalise simple peer pressure). This approach echoes what has

280 Ibid. (translation by the author).

been discussed regarding the interpretation of legal certainty not only as predictability but also as acceptability:[281] it could not be an acceptable interpretation within the context of the German society to read in that provision a criminalisation of psychological pressure. Therefore, the current application of *lex stricta* involves revisiting legislative choices and considering an interpretation that can best represent the purpose of the provision within a specific legal order. In *Sitzblockaden*, it considered that it would be unacceptable to interpret coercion as including psychological pressure. That would be excessive not because the wording of the text excluded such possibility, but because the criminal provision would excessively restrict and limit individual autonomy in daily life.

Ultimately, limiting judicial arbitrariness is not necessarily about prohibiting analogy, but considering whether criminal liability would excessively infringe on the individual rights at hand. What is more, the German Constitutional Court has explicitly accepted that the prohibition of analogy means more than its technical sense and it should be understood as a general limitation of arbitrary and unforeseeable interpretation of criminal liability, beyond the wording of the legislation as this is interpreted.[282]

Therefore, especially in difficult cases, courts seem to use the *lex stricta* differently than a mere prohibition of analogy, as judicial arbitrariness may take the form of an unacceptable balancing and interpretation of legal interests. It has become increasingly necessary to curtail the arbitrary interpretation of individual rights.

To illustrate such a problematic interpretation, I shall analyse the French kiss case in the Netherlands. In this case, a man was indicted for rape (Article 242 DCC) when he forced his tongue into the mouth of another man.[283] The question was whether the statutory definition of rape as sexual penetration of the human body could be applied in the case of a French kiss. This term covers a great deal of sexual acts from a purely grammatical aspect; a French kiss is indeed a sexual penetration of the human body. Grammatically speaking there would be no problem for the Dutch Supreme Court for interpreting this as rape. It would not constitute analogical reasoning to do so based on the wording of the provision. In this sense, the case is similar to the German *Sitzblockaden* where grammatical interpretation would in principle allow a conviction.

However, here the Dutch Supreme Court followed a different path. In fact, in previous case law the term 'penetration of the body' was extended to sexual acts that involved penetration of the body using tools.[284] The Dutch Supreme Court used three main arguments: (i) via a historical interpretation (and not grammatical), it is possible to extend rape to a French kiss because it is indeed a sexual penetration of the body; (ii) the *ratio* of the provision is to protect sexual integrity and the act

---

281 Chapter III para. 6.1.

282 Ibid., a view repeated in other cases, e.g. BVerfG 2 BvR 1907/97, 9 February 1998.

283 HR 21 April 1998 NJ 1998, 781.

284 Ibid.

violated this right; (iii) it would be problematic for legal certainty to differentiate between all the other criminalised sexual penetrations and this one.[285]

Fifteen years later, in 2013, the Dutch Supreme Court changed its view.[286] According to the court's new reasoning, a French kiss cannot be regarded as rape, as this type of intrusion to the body is not as equal in terms of gravity to acts previously considered as rape. Due to the difference in severity of these two situations legal certainty was not a problem, in contrast to the previous case. The primary view of the court seems to have been that it is unreasonable to qualify a French kiss as rape.

In both cases equality and legal certainty are interrelated, but the court accords different weight to those concepts.[287] The criticism resulting from both cases is that the Dutch Supreme Court failed to acknowledge how these two concepts are interrelated in the particular circumstances of every case. In the first case, legal certainty was prioritised as individuals could not foresee the limits of criminalisation if a French kiss would fall outside the scope of rape. If this is so, then any other acts of intrusion to the body (the classic example is the pencil in the ear) could therefore qualify as rape. In the second case, the court emphasised the difference in the gravity of the intrusion, by arguing that a forced French kiss is not as severe as forced sex. Yet, in both cases the court does not really take under consideration how legal certainty and equality interrelate. Sexual offences are unique due to their invasiveness and the type of harm caused. The harm caused depends on factors such as the age of the victim, the type of the violation of sexual autonomy and the duration of the act. A French kiss particularly in the context of a prolonged abuse can potentially be as traumatic to the victim as other forms of sexual penetration.

Therefore, there is a growing need to understand judicial arbitrariness at the level of the reasoning used and the prioritisation of the interests involved. In the previously mentioned 'kidnapping case', the Dutch Supreme Court maintained that the legitimacy of its interpretation was to be found in aligning the scope of criminal liability with the Dutch legal order: '*...the conclusion to be drawn is that the Article, in accordance with the current legal and social realities, both in national and in international perspective, must be interpreted as including also the same act conducted from abroad to the Netherlands*'.[288]

As judicial interpretation involves revisiting legislative choices and assessing them in the light of the circumstances of a case, the danger is that courts may be influenced by policy. This is a form of judicial arbitrariness that the prohibition of analogy cannot prevent. The prohibition of analogy prevents from exceeding the

285 Ibid.

286 HR 26 November 2013 NJ 2014, 62, annotation by N. Keijzer; K. Rozemond, 'Nogmaals de tongzoen', Ars Aequi, 2014, pp. 291–296.

287 K. Rozemond, 'Nogmaals de tongzoen', Ars Aequi, 2014, pp. 294–295.

288 HR 20 November 2001, NJ 2003, 632, para. 4.12 (translated by the author).

wording of a provision but it tells the court little about how to understand the provision.

In the Netherlands for example, sexual liberalism has been replaced by a more conservative approach, something identifiable in judicial reasoning. The Dutch Supreme Court, in a recent child pornography case, has held that the interpretation of the phrase 'depiction of sexual act' in Article 240b DCC includes photos that may cause sexual arousal.[289] For the court, this meant that abuse or harm was not a necessary element of the offence. The reasoning was based on the changed *ratio legis* in the statutory amendment, from protecting children from sexual exploitation and abuse to protecting the sexual integrity of children in a more abstract manner (so of all children). However, this decision is flawed. In particular, the *ratio legis* – as formed by international treaties – did not aim at criminalising any depiction of a naked body but only those with a primarily sexual purpose, or explicit sexual conduct, something pointed out by AG Knigge.[290] The criterion of sexual arousal is problematic as it is subjectively defined.

What undermined the legitimacy of this interpretation were two points. First, the Dutch Supreme Court interpreted the *ratio legis* in a manner inconsistent with the optimum balancing of interests the norm should achieve. If the purpose of prohibiting child pornography is to prevent sexual arousal of paedophiles, then the only possible measure would be to cover children with burqas, as AG Knigge rightly pointed out.[291] Second, in interpreting the *ratio legis*, the court failed to consider the right to foreseeability in the specific context of this criminal provision. How could one demarcate illegal from legal photographs if the criterion is something as subjective as sexual arousal? Will Dutch parents be prohibited from taking photographs of their children at the beach?

In order to prevent judicial arbitrariness, it is not enough that the principle of legality prohibits analogy, or that it obliges a strict interpretation, but that it also provides for substantive guidelines on how public policy and individual rights should be balanced.[292] In other words, the principle of legality should *inform* judicial interpretation, next to restricting it.

To be clear, I do not argue that the prohibition of analogy is of no use, as there are some cases where analogical reasoning can be detected and prevented. Neither is it argued that an obligation of strict interpretation is of no use. What is stated here is that the prohibition of analogy cannot in itself adequately protect from judicial arbitrariness because judicial arbitrariness can be the result of an illegitimate substantive interpretation of a provision. From this analysis it is evident that the legitimacy of judicial interpretation must also be found in the quality of its

---

289 HR 7 December 2010 NJ 2011, 81 annotation by Schalken.

290 Conclusie, Hoge Raad (Advocaat-Generaal), 12 January 2010, ECLI:NL:PHR:2010:BO6446, para. 51 and 111.

291 Ibid., para. 86.

292 M.J. Borgers, 'De communicatieve strafrechter', in W.J.M. Voermans, M.J. Borgers, C.H. Sieburgh, 'Controverses rondom legaliteit en legitimatie', Kluwer, 2011, p. 160.

reasoning. However, the current doctrine of *lex stricta* cannot cope with this demand to an adequate degree. This is why the approach of the ECtHR has been prevalent in national case law, as demonstrated above; it provides more adequate safeguards for determining the foreseeability of criminalisation.

10.2. *Lex certa*

It has been explained that *lex certa* entails that the legislator ought to construct criminal liability with precision.[293] It is addressed to the legislator and it functions as a principle that should guide parliamentary discussions and choices regarding the chosen wording and the commitment of the legislator regarding conduct to be criminalised. The aim of *lex certa* is to retain the communicative value and legal certainty of statutes and for courts to have as limited scope as possible to prevent arbitrary interpretations. Yet, the problems involved are numerous. First of all, the control of compliance with the *lex certa* has been passed over to courts; as a consequence courts may try to fix vagueness. Secondly, criteria for precision are difficult to create. Those that already exist are relative themselves or heavily rely on judicial interpretation: e.g. the more severe the offence the higher the level of precision,[294] or a norm violates *lex certa* if courts, after exhausting all interpretative techniques, have failed to clarify its context.[295] Thirdly, maximum legal certainty is in practice unattainable, something that lessens the influence of the application of *lex certa.*

10.2.1. Who checks the compliance with lex certa?

The first and most profound problem is that while in principle it is supposed to be a addressed to the legislator, in the end it rests upon courts to decide whether a criminal provision is precise or not. Certainly the legislator is bound by this obligation and it is taken under consideration as is evident not only by the quality of criminal provisions, but also from parliamentary discussions (such as the discussion in the Dutch parliament regarding the vague construction of money laundering provision).[296] In some systems, such as the Dutch one, the bicameral system allows for more scrutiny in this respect.

However, the question of whether the legislator did a good job or not is left to courts. In the Netherlands, constitutional review of legislation cannot be carried out by courts, which means that courts may not be in a position to declare legislation void. However, there is competence to review the compatibility of legislation with Article 1 of the DCC (the legality principle) and Article 7 ECHR (as an international

293 See above para. 7.
294 BVerfG 2 BvL 4/62, 25 July 1962.
295 BVerfG 2 BvR 1980/07, 10 March 2009.
296 Kamerstukken II 2000/01, 27 159, nr. 5, p. 10.

treaty, see Article 94 Dutch Constitution). In Germany, the review of the constitutionality of statutes is allowed and courts may therefore review the compatibility of statutes with *lex certa.* In England courts may, since the Human Rights Act, check the compatibility of statutes with the legality principle although they cannot strike down legislation.[297] There is case law from all three systems in this regard.[298] In all three systems, the determination of whether the legislative provision is adequately precise is to be decided by courts. This seems to be rather paradoxical: if one of the aims of *lex certa* is to protect the separation of powers and individuals from judicial arbitrariness, how can courts be entrusted with the task to enforce this obligation? Doesn't this defeat the purpose of *lex certa*? In this respect one can accept this oxymoron only if courts are approached also as institutions guaranteeing the proper separation of powers themselves and the preservation of the legal order in general.

Having said that, the legislator has its part to play in the determination of criminal liability. Different methods and terms may be used and courts will be called upon to evaluate these efforts. However, it is a difficult task to separate the function of *lex certa* and *lex stricta.* In particular, courts, in order to decide on whether a term is vague, must first make an attempt at interpretation. Thus the German Constitutional Court when faced with the compatibility of the term 'disadvantage' in Article 266 I GCC (*Untreue* – breach of trust) first attempted to exhaust the interpretational methods available.[299] It followed first a grammatical interpretation to determine the linguistic meaning; it continued with a systematic interpretation comparing other provisions such as Article 263 I GCC, which contained the same term; then it used a teleological interpretation, and concluded its analysis with a reference to the existing jurisprudence. The court held that when a norm can be concretised to certain core-patterns of behaviour through interpretation, the *lex certa* has not been violated.[300] A provision violates *lex certa* when it is impossible to locate a core of behavioural pattern through interpretation.[301] While, according to *lex certa,* provisions that are too vague and allow room for discretion should violate the legality principle, the compatibility of statutes with *lex certa* depends upon judicial interpretation.

In the field of traffic law for example, German legislation (Article 316 GCC) is abstract and does not precisely indicate the level of alcohol prohibited in the body for dangerous driving offences, an issue left to the discretion of courts. Here, the courts have an almost legislative function. The German Federal Court initially set the limit for the amount of alcohol in a person's blood (in German BAK) at 1,5‰ in

297 See above para. 9.2.

298 For example HR 2 April 1985 NJ 1985, 796; BGH NJW 2004, 2990, 22 July 2004; R v Sadique and another [2011] EWCA Crim 2872; R v Misra and Srivastava [2004] EWCA Crim 2375 and para. 37(for further case law).

299 BVerfG 2 BvR 1980/07, 10 March 2009.

300 C. Roxin, 'Strafrecht: Allgemeiner Teil Band I', Verlag C.H. Beck, 2006, para. 5, Mn 77.

301 BVerfG 2 BvR 1980/07, 10 March 2009.

1953,[302] which was later sank to 1,3‰ in 1966[303] and again after some decades to 1,1‰ in 1990.[304] It has been suggested in literature that these limits constituted customary law, which violated *lex certa*.[305] Yet the German Constitutional Court has held that the jurisprudential adjustment of alcohol percentages does not violate the principle of legality.[306]

Therefore the line between *lex certa* and *lex stricta* is blurred but more importantly the compatibility of the legislation with the *lex certa* depends upon the ability and discretion of courts to 'save' legislation. This perhaps explains why there are so few cases in which legislation is found to be incompatible with *lex certa*.[307] This may be seen as a foreseeable consequence of the legislator abdicating responsibility to be precise and it can provide an incentive to the legislator to prescribe more abstract forms of criminal liability, secure in the knowledge that the courts will deal with the norm in one way or the other.

10.2.2. Are there any specific criteria to determine precision?

A second problem is that there is no specific definition of precision, or benchmark to measure the precision of a norm. As precision is a rather indeterminate concept, it is rather difficult to formulate criteria.

A quantitative way of determining the equilibrium of *lex certa* has been suggested in scholarship. In particular, Schünemann proposes a 50% threshold for the determination of the *lex certa*.[308] If the majority of cases that fall under the norm are cases that the legislator did not intend to criminalise, then the wording of the provision fails to express what the legislator wanted, and therefore, the norm is too vague. This theory has been considered too difficult to apply, as even 49% of unanticipated cases would be unacceptable.[309] It is evident that Schünemann's formula does not require a statistical evaluation of case law, but that courts should assess the application of the norm to investigate whether, in the majority of cases, the norm applies to conduct the legislator intended to criminalise. This is a good approach, yet it requires determination of what the legislator intended to cover with

302 BGH NJW 1954, 159, 5 November 1953.

303 BGH NJW 1967, 116, 9 December 1966.

304 BGH NJW 1990, 2393, 28 June 1990.

305 W. Joecks, K. Miebach, 'Münchener Kommentar zum Strafgesetzbuch', Verlag C.H. Beck, 2011, para. 1, Mn 34; Beck'scher Onlinekommentar zum StGB, von Heintschel-Heinegg, 2011, para. 1, Mn 8.

306 BVerfG 2 BvR 752/90, 23 June 1990.

307 A few in Germany for example BGH NJW 2004, 2990, 22 Jully 2004 and BVerfG 2 BvR 234/87, 22 June 1988, yet to my knowledge, none in the Netherlands. For English law see for a collection of case law on this matter in R v Misra and Srivastava [2004] EWCA Crim 2375, para. 37.

308 B. Schünemann, 'Nulla poena sine lege? Rechtstheoretische und verfassungsrechtliche Implikationen der Rechtsgewinnung im Strafrecht', Walter de Gruyter, 1978, pp. 35–37.

309 C. Roxin, 'Strafrecht: Allgemeiner Teil Band I', Verlag C.H. Beck, 2006, para. 5, Mn 74.

the provision, and involves certain judicial choices on the scope of criminalisation, which does not limit judicial arbitrariness.

The courts have generated certain criteria. For example the German Constitutional Court has held that the level of precision should be dependent on the gravity of criminal liability.[310] In other words, the more grave the criminal conduct, the more precise the provision. This is a type of proportionality criterion, balancing the precision of a norm and the character of the offence.[311] Thus, the German Federal Court declared Article 370a of the German Fiscal Code in violation of the principle of *lex certa*.[312] It should be mentioned that this provision has been problematic for many years. In its very first version, the provision criminalised cases of serious tax evasion, committed by a group; the crime was considered a felony, as opposed to the non-aggravated form of tax evasion, which is a misdemeanour. However, because of the way the provision was defined, even minor cases of tax evasion committed, e.g. by family members who filed their tax declarations together, would fall in the scope of the offence.

Consequently, the legislator amended this provision by adding the requirement of 'to a great extent' as an additional element of the offence. The German Federal Court dealt with the compatibility of this later term with the *lex certa*. The court explained that this requirement lacks precision as it leaves significant room for courts to apply their own knowledge and judgement of the appropriate amount of money; different courts have determined the threshold for it to be set at € 50.000, € 250.000 and € 500.000.[313] The court held that this level of vagueness cannot be tolerated for a felony and the German legislator has changed this offence to a misdemeanour.[314]

The court's underlying reasoning is that for crimes that have a more severe character of social condemnation and punishment, the uncertainty of the norm undermines the theoretical rationale of the principle of legality. With felonies, there is a higher intrusion of the *ius puniendi* to individual autonomy.

Foreseeability, once again, plays an important role. All three national systems make use of the requirement of foreseeability as analysed by the ECtHR. Abstract notions and uncertain general clauses are in line with *lex certa,* if, with the help of the available interpretative methods, an individual can foresee criminalisation.[315]

In line with the ECtHR's jurisprudence, individuals are considered norm-addressees. The national courts have accepted that the level of precision demanded by the legislation varies depending on the qualification of individuals as norm-

---

310 BVerfG 2 BvL 4/62, 25 July 1962.

311 BVerfG 2 BvR 794/95, 20 March 2002; H. Satzger, B. Schmitt, G. Widmaier, 'StGB-Strafgesetzbuch: Kommentar', Heymanns, 2009, para. 1, Mn 20.

312 BGH NJW 2004, 2990, 22 July 2004.

313 Ibid., for a further list with case law.

314 F.K. Peter, 'Streichung des §370a AO', Steuer und Studium, 2008, pp. 428–430.

315 BVerfG 2 BvR 1980/07, 10 March 2009, para. 21; BVerfG 1 BvR 1476/91, 10 October 1995; HR 31 October 2000 NJ 2001, 14; HR 5 December 2000 NJ 2001, 98; R v Perrin [2002] EWCA Crim 747.

addressees. Norms that are addressed to professionals, for example, may sustain a lesser level of precision as it is expected that individuals will be able to understand the norm within the context of their profession, and also that they shall inform themselves accordingly. The Dutch Supreme Court has held, for example, that when it comes to criminal liability addressed to professionals, such as food-safety norms, the foreseeability of the criminalisation is determined by taking into consideration the responsibility of professionals to be familiar with legislation affecting their field.[316] The court has also added that there is a certain duty to be informed about the law for those carrying out professional activities relating to food market.[317] Similarly, the German and English courts have held the same position regarding professionals.[318]

Although courts usually define foreseeable criminal liability from the point of view of laymen,[319] for professionals, there is an obligation to be informed regarding criminal legislation that governs someone's field of work. This affects how foreseeability is determined.[320] Therefore, it is clear that when it comes to *lex certa* the influence of the ECtHR approach is profound.

10.2.3. Is maximum certainty attainable?

It was explained that *lex certa* is not really about the precision of the language but about the precision of the scope of criminal liability. Yet, the third and final problem of *lex certa* is the increasingly vague formulations of criminal liability. The legislator is often confronted with situations where an 'early cognitive commitment' regarding the exact behavioural pattern to be criminalised is not possible.[321] The courts have accepted that precision regarding the scope of criminal liability does not have to be maximum, but rather optimum and certain unavoidable vagueness is accepted. This gives some leeway to the legislator to legislate *in abstracto.*

An example is the term 'good morals' in Article 228 GCC, about consent to bodily harm, which does not violate the *lex certa* as the individual can at least be

---

316 See HR 31 October 2000, NJ 2001, 14.

317 Ibid., also see HR 25 February 2003 NJ 2003, 572.

318 R v Ideal Waste Paper [2011] EWCA Crim 3237, para. 42; BVerfG 2 BvR 871/04, 29 April 2010.

319 BVerfG 1 BvR 1053/82, 23 October 1985; also see H. Satzger, 'Die Internationalisierung des Strafrechts als Herausforderung für den strafrechtlichen Bestimmtheitsgrundsatz', JuS, 2004, p. 943; Beck'scher Onlinekommentar zum StGB, von Heintschel-Heinegg, 2011, para. 1, Mn 10. There seems to be a difference between the approach of German Constitutional Court and German Federal Court which is about the 'foreseeability of the norm' (*Voraussehbarkeit*) and 'the calculability of the norm' (*Berechenbarkeit*); the former is a subjective approach while the second is objective in the sense that the margin of application of a norm flows from the norm logically without difficulty; see for more H.-P. Lemmel, 'Unbestimmte Strafbarkeitsvoraussetzungen im Besonderen Teil des Strafrechts und der Grundsatz nullum crimen sine lege', Duncker & Humblot, 1970, p. 54.

320 W. Joecks, K. Miebach, 'Münchener Kommentar zum Strafgesetzbuch', Verlag C.H. Beck, 2011, para. 1, Mn 49.

321 See above para. 7.

guided regarding the risk of criminalisation.[322] The term 'disadvantage' in Article 266 I GCC (breach of trust) has survived the test of *lex certa* as well.[323] In a case concerning inappropriate behaviour in public, the Dutch Supreme Court accepted the compatibility of the provision with the *lex certa* principle.[324] The case concerned a provision regarding appropriate behaviour on trains and at train stations. The defendant had placed her feet on a chair and had used offensive vocabulary towards the station staff. The provision described some behaviour that would fall under the scope of the provision. The use of a general clause in this provision was interpreted as inevitable and therefore acceptable in terms of the *lex certa* principle. According to the court, inevitable vagueness is limited by the restriction of locations where the behaviour can take place (trains and train stations).[325] The second argument was that this kind of prohibited behaviour is *'inevitably couched in terms which, [...] are vague and whose interpretation and application are questions of practice'*.[326] The Dutch Supreme Court, citing the ECtHR, explained that in this case a more precise formulation would not be possible.[327]

There are also provisions where vagueness is avoidable, but deliberate and necessary. A broader formulation is preferred for general terms such as 'participation', 'preparatory acts' and 'omissions'. This is to be expected because the provisions of the general part apply to various provisions of the special part and therefore by their nature they must remain relatively abstract. However, this also means that these provisions are altered during judicial application, which may require that the legislator intervenes and gives further directions to courts. Certain examples include the provisions regarding inchoate offences and omissions where courts are left with the task of determining more concrete criteria for the scope of liability in those cases.[328]

One could conclude that this aspect of *lex certa* does not generate much guidance apart from a general attitude of self-restrain for the legislator to be precise in law-making. This is an approach towards the Rule of Law similar to English

322 BGH NJW 1953, 473, 29 January 1953; Beck'scher Onlinekommentar zum StGB, von Heintschel-Heinegg, 2011, para. 1, Mn 23.

323 BVerfG 2 BvR 1980/07, 10 March 2009.

324 HR 2 April 1985 NJ 1985, 796.

325 The first argument reads that the vagueness of the prescribed behavior is limited by other elements of the criminal liability (for example that the behavior must take place only in trains and stations or another example would be outside bars). For example, in HR 1 September 1998 NJ 1999, 61, the Dutch Supreme Court used the same approach in a case relating to the use of public places or services for other than the usual goals – usage of telephone booths, parking places.

326 HR 2 April 1985, NJ 1985, 796, thus the Dutch Supreme Court cites directly the ECtHR, see ECtHR Sunday Times v United Kingdom, Appl. 6538/74, 26 April 1979.

327 HR 31 October 2000, NJ 2001, 14.

328 HR 12 December 2000 NJ 2002, 516 annotation by Knigge, also K. Rozemond, 'De casuïstische grenzen van het materiële strafrecht', Delikt en Delinkwent, vol. 36, 2007, p. 465; A.A. Franken, 'Casuïstiek en legaliteit in het materieel strafrecht', Delikt en Delinkwent, vol. 67, 2006, p. 949.

law.[329] While courts solve these problems by applying the criterion of foreseeability, most cases of vague prescription are solved within the auspices of judicial interpretation. In the end, the decisive criterion is not that the wording of the norm provides clear-cut limits to distinguish between legal and illegal acts (what was termed before 'the ability of distinction')[330] but whether individuals can draw from norms sufficient guidance regarding their acts. Such guidance, however, is informed by a variety of factors: judicial interpretation, the offence itself, the general context in which the offence operates (whether an abstract formulation is inevitable, the field of law and the severity of the offence) and the individuals to which the norm is addressed.

10.3. *Lex scripta*

Lex scripta means that criminal liability takes a written form (thereby excluding customary law) and that only the statutes can be a legitimate source for criminal liability. Having said that, the current application of the *lex certa* and *stricta* show that judicial interpretation and jurisprudence have a communicative value, namely they do determine the scope of criminal liability – at least to some extent – and individuals are expected to draw guidelines from a variety of sources. This challenges the existing presumption that case law is not a legitimate source of criminal liability. What is more, jurisprudence develops the context of criminal liability through time. The problem with this aspect of the legality principle is that it does not generate any particular protection against casuistry. This is particularly the case with continental systems; as mentioned in the common law tradition, there is a system in place that provides for control over the development of jurisprudence.[331]

10.3.1. Is case law a source of criminal liability?

As seen in the application of *lex certa* and *lex stricta,* courts do determine the scope of criminal liability. While that statute is the basis upon which courts operate, which mean that new criminal offences are not created by courts, the concretisation of the scope of criminal liability is found in case law. An illustrative example is that German courts concretise the scope of criminal liability regarding blood alcohol levels in traffic offences.[332] Whenever there are general clauses or indeterminate terms in legislation, courts will attempt to define behaviour into more specific patterns; their decisions therefore help to define criminal liability, complementing the statute.

---

329 See above para. 2.
330 See above para. 7.
331 See above para. 5 and 8.
332 See above para. 8.

In *Sitzblockaden*, it was the court that finally determined the scope of criminal liability. Similarly, in a case of narcotics the German Federal Court concretised the term 'not of a small amount' found in the statute, concerning the import of large quantities of narcotics as an aggravated form, to a specific numeric threshold.[333] Furthermore, in the latter case it applied to its judgement the same criterion of *lex certa* applied to statutes: the graver the crime, the more precision is required.[334]

From the cases presented earlier, it is evident that legislator and courts share the responsibility for determining the scope of criminal liability. Courts develop criteria for the concretisation of legal provisions, which affect the scope of criminal liability. It is further expected that individuals will draw guidance from the wording of the statute as interpreted by jurisprudence (also seen in the ECtHR approach to legality).[335] Courts interpret the will of the legislator and contribute to the evolution of the scope of criminal liability. This entails that the classical understanding of the legislator, as having the monopoly in determining the scope of criminal liability, is inaccurate. This is self-evident in English law but not in continental systems. In fact, judicial interpretation is not a task isolated from the rest of the legal order, the development of society, language, technology and morals. Interpretation is not static but is a dynamic process. While it is not the case that courts can create new forms of criminal liability to fill recently developed legal lacunae, judicial interpretation is influenced by a range of factors, which means that the scope of criminal liability might change through time.

This means that case law takes the form of a source of criminal liability (although unofficial) in addition to the statute in continental systems. The problem with the legality principle is that there is no normative guidance on the communicative value of case law, the transparency of reasoning or the retroactivity of interpretation. This paradox has been noted by the German Constitutional Court. It has held that jurisprudence does not have the binding nature of statutes and, therefore, a change in the interpretation of a criminal norm would not – in principle – be a violation of the legality principle. However, the court also stated that such a change in interpretation should nevertheless satisfy minimum requirements of continuity in the law and of legitimate expectations.[336] From this analysis it is noticeable that while statutes are, in principle, the sole source of criminal liability in continental systems, in practice, judicial interpretation has a dynamic character. This development has prompted a discussion in Dutch literature about whether features of common law, such as *stare decisis*, should also be adopted by continental systems.[337]

333 BGH NJW 1984, 675, 7 November 1983.
334 Ibid.
335 See above para. 9.1.
336 BVerfG 2 BvR 1230/10, 16 May 2011.
337 D.H. de Jong, 'Naar een common law-conceptie van legaliteit?', Delikt en Delinkwent, vol. 29, 1999, pp. 687–690; B.M.J. van Klink, 'Bedreigt rechtsvinding de rechtszekerheid? Een kritisch-hermeneutische visie op de rol van de rechter in het materiële strafrecht', Delikt en Delinkwent,

10.3.2. Is jurisprudence an organism of law?

In continental systems, jurisprudence, as a collection of case law interpreting and applying specific provisions, is not considered a live organism of law as in common law systems. Only statutes determine the scope of criminal liability and prior case law has no role to play. Yet this is not actually the case in practice. In many of the aforementioned cases, courts do take into consideration how prior case law has interpreted a provision, what criteria have been used, and what impact the chosen interpretational path would have for future cases. Examples include the French kiss cases, where the Dutch Supreme Court took into consideration the prior case law,[338] the *Sitzblockaden* case,[339] and virtually any case where there was an interpretational problem regarding a specific term.

Often courts approach case law as an informal source of criminal liability, and prior jurisprudence as the narrative of the evolution of criminal liability concepts over time.[340] Examination of case law may give rise to the need for more limited interpretation, such as in the case of *Sitzblockaden,* where the German Constitutional Court considered the problematic casuistry of prior jurisprudence on the interpretation 'coercion:'

> The ambiguity of the broadened term 'force' has also not diminished in the course of time due to a consolidated understanding of its meaning, especially when taking note that the Federal Court of Justice has in other cases such as rape defined the term 'force' much more narrowly. (see for example BGH, NJW 1981, S. 2204). As the aforementioned examples show, the criminality of sitting demonstrations under the heading of coercion remained highly uncertain. Also the continuing disagreement in case law and literature regarding the criminal nature of sitting demonstrations (cf. Schäfer, LK, a.a.O., Rdnr. 21 bis 27; Otto, NStZ 1992, S. 568) show that a consolidated legal interpretation has not yet arisen. The required precision does also not arise from the fact that due to the pertinent jurisprudence of the higher courts, at least the risk of criminal punishment is recognisable (to the public).[341]

The issue of casuistry prompted courts and academics to investigate mechanisms by which this could be diminished, often echoing English conventions regarding precedence.[342] The problem here is how to prevent casuistry, i.e. how to control judicial development and ensure that jurisprudence develops in a consistent manner. The continental perception of the legality principle concerns primarily legal

---

vol. 31, 2001, pp. 688–691; K. Rozemond, 'De casuïstische grenzen van het materiële strafrecht', Delikt en Delinkwent, vol. 36, 2007, p. 465.

338 HR 21 April 1998 NJ 1998, 781.

339 BVerfG 1 BvR 718/89, 10 January 1995.

340 BVerfG 2 BvR 1980/07, 10 March 2009.

341 BVerfG 1 BvR 718/89, 10 January 1995.

342 D.H. de Jong, 'Naar een common law-conceptie van legaliteit?', Delikt en Delinkwent, vol. 29, 1999, pp. 687–690.

certainty and foreseeability – principles that could be applicable in the context of jurisprudence. However, the view that interpretation should be consistent with prior cases is something that does not flow from the doctrine of the legality principle itself, but is the natural response of continental systems to growing problems of casuistry. The common law system is certainly more equipped to deal with casuistry through the rules of precedent.

10.4. *Lex praevia*

Lex praevia has created the least problems regarding its application. Generally speaking, the prohibition of retroactivity is well embedded in legal systems, and it is rare to find criminal legislation that derogates from the principle of non-retroactivity. Retroactivity in a criminal law statute is widely considered unjust, though there are a few challenges.

One challenge is the distinction between continuous and continuing criminal acts and determining the *tempus delicti* for each category. Continuous offences are acts committed instantly and repeated many times, over a longer period of time. An example is the repetitive molestation of a minor during childhood. Considering every act under the chapeau of a continuous offence allows these repetitive acts to be indicted together. Continuing offences are acts that, by their nature, have duration, for example abduction or unlawful imprisonment. In continuing offences, the protected legal good is brought to a continuing state of violation. The *tempus delicti* and rules on statute limitation for each category may vary. In general for a continuous offence, an amendment of legislation would require that the indictment be split between the acts that were committed before and after the amendment. For continuing acts though, the *tempus delicti* is crystallised the moment the violation of the legal good ceased. Thus, the legislation applied is the one in force when the violation of the legal good ceases.[343]

Moreover, there are questions regarding the scope of application of the legality principle. Thus, there is disagreement as to whether statutory limitations and jurisdictional rules may be altered retroactively. Regarding retroactivity of statutory limitation rules, a revival of prosecutions is not accepted in the Netherlands.[344] However, retroactive extension of statutory limitations may be granted if still running and considered reasonable.[345] Although the term 'reasonable' may be

343 For English law see the guidelines for indictment about the different treatment of continuous and continuing offences www.cps.gov.uk/legal/d_to_g/drafting_the_indictment/ (assessed on 20/12/2014). For Dutch law, see J. de Hullu, 'Materieel strafrecht', Kluwer, 2012, p. 134.

344 HR 17 December 1996 NJ 1997, 26; G. Knigge, 'Verandering van wetgeving', Gouda Quint, 1984, pp. 223–264; M.S. Groenhuijsen, 'Verlenging of afschaffing van verjaringstermijnen in het strafrecht', Delikt en Delinkwent, 2002, pp. 813–822.

345 HR 18 September 2001, NJ 2002, 559. The ECtHR has accepted that such a retroactivity does not infringe Article 7 ECHR in ECtHR Coëme v Belgium, App. 32492/96, 22 June 2000.

difficult to define – and is thus criticised –[346] a retroactive extension was found to be reasonable in legislation of war crimes,[347] indecent[348] and grave/heinous offences[349] and felonies.[350] In Germany, retroactive extension of statute of limitation does not violate the legality principle.[351] When it comes to jurisdictional rules, there is consensus that they are of procedural nature and therefore the legality principle does not apply[352] (although courts may be reluctant to grant retroactive application of jurisdictional rules that activate prosecutions).[353] This is nevertheless a flexible rule.[354] At the same time, there is criticism as to whether the exclusion of rules relating to the right of prosecution (such as jurisdiction), should be excluded from the scope of the legality principle.[355] This might be of interest for EU law, as it will be seen later on.[356]

Furthermore, there seem to be challenges as to what constitutes a change of legislation. Thus in the Netherlands, there is a distinction between 'changes of circumstances' and 'changed perception of criminal liability', however, this is usually relevant for the application of *lex mitior*.[357]

In England, retroactivity of statutes is rare due to the Human Rights Act. Of greater interest is the retroactive application of jurisprudence. For example, English courts have applied retroactively the marital rape jurisprudence to facts that took place in 1970s.[358] Arguably, it cannot be said that in 1970, case law and the socio-cultural context indicated that an individual could foresee criminalisation in this context. Although English courts have rejected the idea of prospective overruling, in the Dutch system it has been employed, though on rare occasions and it is debated in scholarship.[359] Having said that, it is difficult to reconcile prospective

346 J. de Hullu, 'Materieel strafrecht', Kluwer, 2012, p. 86; for further issues see M.S. Groenhuijsen, 'Enkele aspecten van rechterlijk 'prospective overruling' in het straf(proces)recht', in M.S. Groenhuijsen, J.B.H.M. Simmelink (eds), 'Glijdende schalen' (Liber amicorum J. de Hullu), Wolf Legal Publishers, 2003, pp. 188–191.

347 Act of 8 April 1971 Stb. 1971 210.

348 Act of 7 July 1994, Stb. 1994, 529.

349 Act of 16 November 2005, Stb. 2005, 595.

350 Act of 5 July 2006, Stb. 2006, 310.

351 BVerfG 2 BvL 15 and 23/68, 26 February 1969, see W. Joecks, K. Miebach, 'Münchener Kommentar zum Strafgesetzbuch', Verlag C.H. Beck, 2011, para. 1, Mn 17.

352 W. Joecks, K. Miebach, 'Münchener Kommentar zum Strafgesetzbuch', Verlag C.H. Beck, 2011, para. 1, Mn 17.

353 See HR 21 October 2008 NJ 2009, 108.

354 This can be seen in HR 18 September 2001 NJ 2002, 559.

355 W. Joecks, K. Miebach, 'Münchener Kommentar zum Strafgesetzbuch', Verlag C.H. Beck, 2011, para. 1, Mn 17.

356 Chapter VII para. 6.2. and Chapter VIII para. 3.3.

357 HR 15 Januari 1952 NJ 1952, 242; see more in G. Knigge, 'Verandering van wetgeving', Gouda Quint, 1984, pp. 459–463.

358 R v C [2004] EWCA Crim 292.

359 HR 6 January 1998, NJ 1998, 367; M.S. Groenhuijsen, 'Enkele aspecten van rechterlijk 'prospective overruling' in het straf(proces)recht', in M.S. Groenhuijsen, J.B.H.M. Simmelink (eds), 'Glijdende schalen' (Liber amicorum J. de Hullu), Wolf Legal Publishers, 2003, pp. 197–198.

overruling with the legality principle: if an interpretation must be foreseeable, why would prospective overruling be necessary?

11. Conclusion

The aim of this Chapter was to observe the *modus operandi* of the legality principle in three national systems. The goal was to understand how this principle is defined, approached and applied, as well as the questions it raises. The experience gained from this Chapter will be of use in identifying the features of the legality principle, which can inform the European legality principle. This is because by observing national application, one can identify where national systems converge, the impact of the ECtHR and the problems faced by this principle. In the next Chapter, the problems and features of the legality principle shall be analysed in the context of current theories of legitimation, so that a coherent theory of the legality principle can emerge.

Despite their diametrically opposed starting points, common and continental systems have been converging under the umbrella of the ECtHR. Both traditions recognise the statute as the supreme source of criminal liability and in both traditions case law cannot create criminal liability. However, in the English system, case law is recognised as an official source of criminal liability for the remaining common law offences. The legality principle enjoys respect and application in all three national systems, with relatively distinct aspects and obligations of the legislator and courts. Most importantly, in all three systems the legality principle faces similar challenges.

However, the systems are not in harmony. In English law, the combination of common and statutory offences and, traditionally, the more dynamic position of courts denote a more flexible application of the legality principle than in continental systems. One cannot expect that the legality principle will be applied the same way in both traditions. The principle of legality in England remains still highly similar to the ECtHR approach, as the latter is the main source of inspiration. The continental version of this principle, which prohibits criminal liability based on case law, has not been adapted fully into the common law system as there are still common law offences and the parliament may only replace common law as far as this is explicitly stated in the statute. In addition other aspects of the legality principle such as precision of statutes are still in development, especially after the Human Rights Act.

The Dutch and German systems are undergoing a cultural legal shift, as the principle of legality applied in practice is not in line with the doctrinal theory. This principle is indigenous to these systems and has been rooted deeply in legal doctrine. A cumbersome principle to some extent, it faces problems as the doctrine cannot be reconciled with the practice.

It is evident that the theory, nature and application of the principle of legality present some serious challenges. First, the so-called erosion of the legality principle cannot be attributed to lack of obedience by state-actors or external influences, such as the ECtHR. It is clear that the principle has internal deficiencies that do not allow it to serve its purpose, namely to prevent arbitrariness. It was explained that the prohibition of analogy is inadequate to curtail judicial activism to a sufficient degree. Preventing judicial arbitrariness further requires that courts give transparent and adequate reasons that explain how and why a norm is interpreted in a particular manner and how foreseeability can be achieved in the context of a particular case. It is important to prevent courts from interpreting rights protected or interfered with by a criminal norm in a manner that does not respect the character of a legal order. Furthermore, demanding absolute precision from the law is unrealistic. Jurisprudence is not static but is an evolving organism whose development determines the boundaries of criminal prosecution. Controls on its development are necessary. However, the legality principle as conceived by national systems (especially the continental ones) does not provide for adequate controls.

Second, the principle of legality is highly influenced by the perception regarding its theoretical basis. As explained in Chapter III, its basis is subject to different interpretations, which are not static. The current doctrinal view of the legality principle, especially in continental systems, is based on an anachronistic interpretation of separation of powers, parliamentary democracy and the Rule of Law. Courts do not mechanically apply the law and a democratic Rule of Law necessitates that certain rights are also protected. The principle of legality disregards the reality that criminal norms aim to protect the individual not only from the state, but also from other individuals. Thus, the main tension seems to be between the need to tackle crime – and adapt the law to new situations – while maintaining foreseeability. This is specifically seen in the tendency of judicial decisions to revisit legislative choices and read within the wording of the text different ways in which the right to foreseeable criminalisation can be reconciled with the purpose of criminalisation.

The ECtHR approach seems to have dominated in all three systems. Its influence however, was different. For the continental systems it offered a less rigid doctrine instead of a strictly positivistic form of legality; for English law, it offered a doctrine with some positivistic elements, which complemented existing principles.

To this extent, the ECtHR approach to legality introduced not only a shift in its *modus operandi*, but suggested a different approach to how criminal law should be legitimised, how the courts and legislator could balance their relationship, and what constitutes a legitimate court decision. The 'rights-conception' to the legality principle was quickly absorbed by national courts because it gave them another basis for decision-making.

However, the ECtHR did not propose a complete theory on the legality principle that would function in national law without further theoretical analysis, adaptation or concretisation. What is more the ECtHR itself is a court that strikes a balance between different systems and its role is supervisory. A foreseeability requirement, which gives courts leeway to align the legal order with existing individual rights, can pose the danger that policy concerns motivate court decisions. In a world where information is available as never before, it would be difficult to argue that broad interpretations of criminal norms are not foreseeable. In addition, national courts are not the ECtHR, which focuses only on issues of human rights. National courts function within the political and societal context of their jurisdiction and operate within their own political *zeitgeist.* As policies can mask themselves behind individual rights, there is no guarantee flowing from the legality principle that illegitimate motivations shall not occur. The fact that interpretation X is foreseeable because the norm's wording was vague and open to interpretation does not mean that this interpretation is necessarily legitimate. Thus what are needed, are guidelines or principles where policy and individual rights can be transparently assessed in order to limit judicial arbitrariness.

In order to find out how the legality principle could be reformed in order to truly protect against arbitrariness, one must investigate different theories available for the legitimacy of criminal law. Since the role of the legality principle is to legitimise *ius puniendi,* one must understand what constitutes true legitimacy.

CHAPTER V
THREE MODELS OF CRIMINAL JUSTICE

This Chapter examines existing legal theories regarding the legitimation of criminal justice. As explained in Chapter I, legitimacy in criminal law relates to the definition of permissible use of coercive power. This Chapter analyses three different standards of criminal law legitimacy. In particular, the challenges and features of the legality principle as identified in the previous Chapter and the various interpretations of its theoretical bases (Chapter III) will be analysed in the context of three theoretical models of criminal justice.

One of the conclusions drawn in the previous Chapter regarding the practical operation of the legality principle is that there is tension between the two conceptions of the character of criminal liability. On one hand, criminal norms should be stable and relatively slow to change; the law is a fixed body of rules with a specific content. Conversely, it is important for criminal liability to retain an open texture, as it is a means to bring about social change, and must adapt in line with societal developments. This antithetical account of the legitimate nature of criminal liability highlights a deeper conflict regarding the purpose of law.

There is an on-going dialogue within legal philosophy regarding the nature and purpose of law. Over the years, there have been two influential, yet conflicting schools of thought: formalism and realism. Formalism involves a conventional understanding of the law; law is a convention, with an independent structure and nature, static and unchanging. Realism, on the other hand, rejects a static concept of law and builds upon the idea that law should reflect social change and the common good; by definition law derives its content from its factual circumstances and social need.

Various theories have been developed in legal philosophy, outlining and extolling the virtues of formalism and realism, and, on occasion, providing for a third way. Examples are Hart's discussion on formalism and rule-scepticism, Dworkin's models of conventionalism, pragmatism and theory of integrity and Habermas' discourse theory. In criminal law, various theories have also been formulated, for example, Damaška's activist and reactive state models, Claes' conventionalism, pragmatic and ethical models of criminal law, and 't Hart and Foqué's relational theory of (criminal) law.

In this Chapter, the legality principle shall be revisited through three different criminal justice models, which represent roughly legal formalism, realism and a relational model, i.e. an attempt to reconcile – but not combine – formalism and realism. It should be stated that the models of criminal justice presented are merely theoretical models – they do not represent any existing jurisdictions. They merely identify the different theories available for legitimising criminal law, in other words what makes a criminal *law*. They provide a critical theoretical framework within which the *ius puniendi* operates, helping to understand the development of the legality principle, but also to remedy its deficiencies. I will start with a brief explanation of each of the theoretical frameworks and how they influence criminal law. Afterwards I will present a critical analysis of three different models of criminal justice.

1. Formalism, Realism and Relational Theory

There are three different theories that seek to explain the legitimacy of law. These theories derive from the historical evolution of legal systems and changes of attitude towards the nature and function of law.

Formalism (or conventionalism) is the idea that legal rules and principles have a predetermined content and interrelations forming a coherent structure.[1] Norms are verbally formulated and their meaning is static and applies the same way to cases.[2] Rule formalism requires that courts apply the law mechanically: *'The law is the law. It is not what the judges think it is, but what it really is. Their job is to apply it, not to change it to fit their own ethics or politics'*.[3] There is an obvious relationship between positivism and formalism, as they are both based on the idea that law is made.[4] For formalism, law is a convention and represents a common agreement among individuals, which once agreed upon, informs all future state action. Formalism therefore bases the legitimacy of all legal rules and consequent coercion on past political decisions. Hence, law in formalist theory cannot be comprehensive in a modern sense; it cannot cover newly emerging challenges, as there are always issues arising, which could not have been anticipated.[5] Legal formalism obliges courts to respect established law, their decisions only retaining legitimacy if based on it. It also asserts that there is no other law apart from the one stemming from past political decisions. For legal formalism, legal certainty is of great importance, because fair warning is guaranteed by the law's creation in the past.[6]

Realism (or pragmatism) represents a more sceptical attitude towards the law.[7] Prior political decisions do not provide a sufficient legitimation for coercive power. Legitimacy is based upon efficiency, justice or other contemporary advantages of the coercive measure itself. The *ratio* of such legitimacy is that it promotes the good of the community;[8] legal certainty and consistency with past decisions are virtues that do not, in themselves, justify coercion. For realism, legitimacy of coercion is a

1 B.Z. Tamanaha, 'Law as a Means to an End', Cambridge University Press, 2006, p. 66.
2 H.L.A. Hart, 'The Concept of Law', Oxford University Press, 2012, p. 129.
3 R. Dworkin, 'Law's Empire', Hart Publishing, 2006, p. 114.
4 Ibid., p. 116 (for some differences as well).
5 Ibid., p. 115.
6 Ibid., p. 117–120; H.L.A. Hart, 'The Concept of Law', Oxford University Press, 2012, pp. 129–130.
7 H.L.A. Hart, 'The Concept of Law', Oxford University Press, 2012, pp. 136–141.
8 R. Dworkin, 'Law's Empire', Hart Publishing, 2006, p. 149.

contemporaneous issue, and/or future oriented. Realism also rejects the existence of individual rights unless these improve the common wellbeing.[9] It should be noted that realism does not devalue completely the concepts of legal certainty, justice or individual rights as sources of legitimacy. However, these mechanisms retain value only if they somehow improve society or bring about a desired result. Rights are *'the servants of the best future'*.[10] Legal principles, just like rights, have no independent legitimacy or value. Due to the instrumental use of the law to achieve a desired result in society, this theory is often called instrumentalism.[11]

Relational theories were developed with the aim of offering a third alternative to the previous antithetical theories of law.[12] Relational theories of law contain features of the previous theories; yet, they do not form a middle ground between conventionalism and pragmatism. Relational theory is an entirely new theory, which contrasts with formalism and realism. It rejects the idea that law has either a backward or a forward-looking approach.[13] This theory takes a more meta-approach on the nature of the law; it encompasses the need to acknowledge law as a coherent and independent system, but at the same time retain its openness to adaptation, and the need for law to be contemporarily relevant. In this regard, one could say that relational theory does not function at the same level as formalism and realism but at a level above them.[14] For relational theory, the law is an autonomous and but also open system;[15] its role is to mediate between the equally inherent and legitimate aims of stability and dynamism.[16] However, as this theory focuses on how these relate to each other, it accepts law's autonomous nature. In particular, the autonomy and independence of law is found in the concept of human dignity,[17] from which principles and rights emerge and have an independent force.[18] Human dignity refers to the right of every person to be recognised by the law as unique, but also recognises the legal system itself as a legitimate context within which individuals can cooperate and interact upon the basis of shared values.[19] For

9 Ibid., p. 160.
10 Ibid.
11 B.Z. Tamanaha, 'Law as a Means to an End', Cambridge University Press, 2006, p. 62.
12 More generally about the characteristics of relationism see G.A.G. Gottlieb, 'Relationism: Legal Theory for a Relational Society', University of Chicago Law Review, vol. 50, 1983, pp. 567–612.
13 R. Dworkin, 'Law's Empire', Hart Publishing, 2006, p. 225.
14 Ibid., p. 226, where he states that while conventionalism and pragmatism are *themselves* interpretations of the nature of the law, the theory on integrity is a program *of* interpretation.
15 S. Gutwirth, 'Waarheidsaanspraken in recht en wetenschap', Maklu, 1993, p. 330.
16 C.P.M. Cleiren, 'Evolueren naar meer horizontale en multi-dimensionale verhoudingen in het strafrecht', Kluwer, 2010, p. 25.
17 R. Foqué, 'Criminal Justice in a Democracy: Towards a Relational Conception of Criminal Law and Punishment', Criminal Law and Philosophy, vol. 2, 2008, p. 223.
18 R. Dworkin, 'Law's Empire', Hart Publishing, 2006, p. 243.
19 R. Foqué, 'Criminal Justice in a Democracy: Towards a Relational Conception of Criminal Law and Punishment', Criminal Law and Philosophy, vol. 2, 2008, p. 223.

relational theory, individual rights have primary importance.[20] It accepts that courts and the legislature have different roles, but rejects the idea that the law should be at the interpretative mercy of courts. However, it also denies that laws have a static content, indifferent to contemporary realities. Judicial interpretation finds legitimacy on points of principle and rights, and not public policies.[21]

Formalism, realism and relational theories can be traced back to the Enlightenment.[22] The Enlightenment is usually the period credited with the development of concepts such as human rights, and principles of justice and fairness. The Enlightenment promoted also an instrumental view of the law.[23] Ideas of fairness, democracy and the protection of individual autonomy from the state were pursued instrumentally, so that a new model for both society and law could be established. The French Revolution and subsequent law reform movement, including the codification process during the 18th and 19th centuries, also aimed to create a more rational society, as well as control over natural and societal uncertainties.[24] While non-instrumental views until the Enlightenment considered law as an immanent ordering, the growing influence of science at this time meant that, for the Enlightenment era, law became a source of social order. In other words, from a concept of 'law is order' there was a shift towards 'law maintains order'.[25] This shift opened the door for questions about the utility and efficiency of the law in maintaining order. Ultimately, the Enlightenment movement helped develop ideas regarding the instrumental and protective value of the law.[26]

2. Sword and Shield: Two Finalities of Criminal Law

How do these general theories relate to criminal law? Arguably, criminal law has both instrumental and protective finalities.[27] The two aims seem antithetical: the instrumental finality strives to defend societal interests by limiting individual autonomy, while the protective finality aims to safeguard individual autonomy by limiting the societal intrusion into the private sphere. Thus, the instrumental finality can be seen as a sword, while the protective as a shield. These finalities reflect the

20 See more generally, B. Archibald, 'Restorative Justice and the Rule of Law: Rethinking Due Process through a Relational Theory of Rights', 2013, available at http://ssrn.com/abstract=2395224.
21 R. Dworkin, 'Law's Empire', Hart Publishing, 2006, p. 244.
22 For a more general account and debate see S.M. Quevedo, 'Formalist and Instrumentalist Legal Reasoning and Legal Theory', California Law Review, vol. 73, 1985, pp. 119–157.
23 K. Rozemond, 'Beccaria's Dream on Criminal Law and Nodal Governance', in J. Blad, M. Hildebrandt, K. Rozemond, M. Schuilenburg, P. Van Calster (eds), 'Governing Security under the Rule of Law?', Eleven International Publishing, 2010, p. 44.
24 R. Foqué, A.C. 't Hart, 'Instrumentaliteit en Rechtsbescherming', Gouda Quint, Kluwer, 1990, p. 305.
25 B.Z. Tamanaha, 'Law as a Means to an End', Cambridge University Press, 2006, p. 21.
26 S. Gutwirth, 'Waarheidsaanspraken in recht en wetenschap', Maklu, 1993, pp. 340–343.
27 E. Claes, 'Legaliteit en rechtsvinding in het strafrecht', Universitaire Pers Leuven, 2003, p. 77.

different interpretations of individual liberty and autonomy, namely the negative and positive protection of liberty as explained in Chapter III.[28]

According to the instrumental finality, the sword, criminal law is a tool to effectively battle crime, maintain order and ensure that certain behavioural standards are set that reflect the values of the legal order.[29] One can identify two elements of the instrumental finality of criminal law.

Firstly, criminal law is considered an instrument to combat crime and create a climate of safety for the citizens (the crime-control element).[30] Individuals cannot thrive within society unless their individual autonomy is protected from intrusion by other individuals. Criminal law therefore finds its legitimacy in the fact that it protects the positive expression of individual autonomy in a horizontal manner. Imprisonment as a criminal punishment represents the harshest and most restrictive individual sanction.

Secondly, this finality has a more abstract aim. In particular, criminal law becomes the instrument by which societies are shaped. By criminalising certain behaviours the state articulates certain common ethical standards and moral values (the society-shaping element). Criminal law aims to encourage certain behavioural tendencies (such as the obligation to stop at the site of an accident) or stabilise existing ones, therefore canalising interpersonal relationships.[31] For example, a criminal justice system where adultery is criminalised constitutes a society where the sanctity of marriage is considered vital and needs to be protected. The choice to protect certain interests via criminal law highlights the character of each society and its underlying shared cultural and moral values. Therefore, criminal law becomes the primary code governing horizontal interpersonal relationships, publically identifying the behavioural patterns that are unacceptable within that society, and accommodating interpersonal conflicts of rights.

Criminal law is not only a tool to shape society and enforce public policy interests, it has also a protective finality; criminal law is a shield. I have already mentioned that the instrumental element of criminal law aims to protect the invasion of individual autonomy by other individuals. The protective finality is about the protection of individual autonomy (including potential perpetrators) from excessive or arbitrary use of the punitive powers by the state.

Criminal law is also legitimised through its role in safeguarding a climate of certainty and trust for the individuals.[32] This aim highlights the vertical relationship between individuals and the state.[33] In particular, criminal law safeguards and guarantees individual autonomy from interference by the state. The

---

28 Chapter III para. 2.1 and 2.2.

29 H.L. Packer, 'The Limits of the Criminal Sanction', Stanford University Press, 1968, p. 158.

30 Ibid.

31 B. Schünemann, 'Nulla poena sine lege? Rechtstheoretische und verfassungsrechtliche Implikationen der Rechtsgewinnung im Strafrecht', Walter de Gruyter, 1978, p. 13.

32 E. Claes, 'Legaliteit en rechtsvinding in het strafrecht', Universitaire Pers Leuven, 2003, p. 78.

33 C.P.M. Cleiren, 'Evolueren naar meer horizontale en multi-dimensionale verhoudingen in het strafrecht', Kluwer, 2010, p. 4.

protective aim of criminal law seeks to restrict state power.[34] Criminal law defines, articulates and prescribes the oppressive powers of the state so that individuals can live their lives with in a climate of certainty. Arguably, this might initially seem difficult to reconcile with the nature of criminal justice as punitive and restrictive. However, in modern societies, criminal law is not purely about the punitive power of the state, or the protection of citizens *vis-à-vis* potential perpetrators. A criminal justice system where the state punishes individuals for any act considered harmful or immoral at the time, without its being prohibited by law, is not enforcing criminal law but abusing its powers. The protective aim therefore attaches to criminal law a different meaning than mere 'order,' as it also guarantees that individuals can enjoy legal certainty.

The protective finality also has two elements, which are interconnected. On the one hand, criminal law limits the oppressive powers of the state by creating a platform of legitimate enforcement (protection against arbitrariness). Criminalisation that is not based on legally binding rules is not legitimate, and therefore state authorities must exercise their powers within the limits set by law.

On the other hand, criminal laws are also a platform that allows individuals to plan their lives with knowledge of the consequences of their actions. In particular, individuals rely on criminal law as a means of knowing which of their choices will carry criminal punishment and which not. The protective finality therefore allows for individuals to positively exercise autonomy with a level of legal certainty (protection against uncertainty). Both elements of the protective finality are interrelated: excessively vague legislation, for example, does not only leave too much room for judicial interpretation, which may be used in an arbitrary manner, but also fails to allow individuals to foresee what conduct may or may not be legal.

It is possible to discern a conceptual relationship between the instrumental and protective elements of criminal law. The crime-control element (instrumental finality) involves a desire to bring order to society, and protect individual autonomy against criminal conduct by other individuals. This is, however, conditional upon protection against arbitrariness (protective finality), which aims to limit the arbitrary exercise of the crime-control powers. The society-shaping element (instrumental finality) aims to encourage commonly accepted behavioural standards within a community, something also conditional on protection against uncertainty in criminal law (protective finality), which ultimately means that an individual should be able to rely on criminal norms.

3. Three models of criminal justice

The nature of criminal law depends heavily upon one's view as to what primarily legitimises criminal law; one may distinguish three models of criminal justice in this regard and each model has its own view on the inherent nature of criminal

[34] H.L. Packer, 'The Limits of the Criminal Sanction', Stanford University Press, 1968, p. 163.

law.[35] The models may be described as: the classical, instrumentalist and relational models.

The classical model corresponds to the previously listed formalist theory of law, the instrumentalist model to pragmatism and the relational model to the relational theory, as explained above. I chose the term 'classical' instead of conventionalism or formalism, because in criminal law, this approach presents the classical doctrinal view on how a criminal justice system finds legitimacy in Western democracies; thus, the model is more accessible to readers not entirely familiar with more general theories of formalism. My choice for the term 'instrumentalist', as opposed to pragmatist or realist, is because this term is not only more descriptive of the nature of law in this model, but it is also more symbolic for European criminal law, as it will be shown.[36] I use the term 'relational' instead of 'theory of integrity' or 'ethical model', as the model presented is an amalgamation of different relational theories, instead of a reproduction of just one.

The first criminal justice model – the classical model – approaches the character of criminal law solely in terms of its protective finality: one calls criminal norms *law* because they are an organised attempt to protect the individual/accused from the oppressive power of the state. Criminal law is a legitimate exercise of state-force only when there is protection against the arbitrary use of such power and protection against a climate of uncertainty for individuals. When the punitive power of the state is guided by these two elements, state-power and criminal punishment change in character from abusive *puniendi* into *law*, a *ius puniendi*. The instrumental finality does not play a determining role in the conceptualisation of criminal law as *law*; certain policies against child pornography or intellectual property (crime-control element), or the aim of criminal legislation to create certain common ethical standards on hate speech for example (society-shaping element), are not an inherent part of the legitimacy of criminal law. Whether the state criminalises particular offences does not have a determining role in whether its criminal law is legitimate. The instrumental finality of criminal law is therefore irrelevant and criminal law becomes an autonomous concept, detached from existing policy considerations. The principle of legality is, therefore, autonomous from any policy goals such as crime prevention, security, order and combatting crime.[37]

Thus, the question that the legality principle answers in this model is: how can criminal law protect individuals against arbitrariness (protection against arbitrariness) and against uncertainty (protection against uncertainty)?

The instrumentalist model approaches the legal qualification of criminal law solely from the instrumental finality. A legitimate criminal law is the one that

35 R. Foqué, A.C. 't Hart, 'Instrumentaliteit en Rechtsbescherming', Gouda Quint, Kluwer, 1990, p. 17.

36 Chapter VII para. 3.2.

37 A.A.G. Peters, 'Het rechtskarakter van het strafrecht', Kluwer, 1972, p. 9.

effectively pursues policy goals that improve the wellbeing of the society.[38] The driving force of criminal law involves policies such as prevention and prosecution of crime, security, and protection of sensitive victim-groups. In this model, criminal law is not an autonomous entity, but a tool in the hands of the state to be used for the implementation of societal interests. Any protective function of the individual/accused is considered a policy in itself, which may be of importance or not based on societal *zeitgeist*. Thus, in this model, the legality principle is a policy itself, weighed against other interests. Criminal law has no autonomy as a concept; it does not have an inherent or independent nature, but it is neutral and subordinate to the political values and goals at stake at any given moment.[39] Such a model of justice, which detaches the idea of *law* from its protective finality, is an extreme form of 'instrumentalism' especially when the protection of individuals is approached with opportunism. The instrumental finality of criminal law is different from the instrumentalist model in that this finality is a *'conscious attitude towards law held by legal actors...that law is a tool to be utilised to achieve ends'*,[40] whereas the instrumentalist model of justice is a *'theory or account of the nature of law held by legal actors...that law is purely a means to an end, an empty vessel devoid of any inherent principle or binding content or integrity unto itself.'*[41]

Thus, the question that the legality principle answers in this model is: when is it politically optimum and desirable that the protection of individuals against arbitrariness and uncertainty (protective finality as a policy) takes precedence over the function of criminal law to keep order within the society and shape it (instrumental/both aspects)?

The third model of justice takes a different approach on how the protective and instrumental finalities of criminal law are related, and how criminal law is legitimised. This model accepts that both the protective and instrumental finalities play a role in the legitimacy of criminal law, because they are inherent to the function of the law.[42] In this model, which is often called a relational,[43] ethical,[44] or rights-conception[45] model of justice (though I have adopted the term relational), criminal law gains its legitimacy when it not only protects individual autonomy (both elements of protective finality) but also when it makes individual autonomy possible within the development of society, and protects individual autonomy from

38 H.L. Packer, 'The Limits of the Criminal Sanction', Stanford University Press, 1968, p. 158.

39 R. Foqué, A.C. 't Hart, 'Instrumentaliteit en Rechtsbescherming', Gouda Quint, Kluwer, 1990, p. 116.

40 B.Z. Tamanaha, 'Law as a Means to an End', Cambridge University Press, 2006, p. 7.

41 Ibid.

42 J. Claessen, 'Misdaad en straf: een herbezinning op het strafrecht vanuit mystiek perspectief', Wolf Legal Publishers, 2010, p. 113.

43 R. Foqué, A.C. 't Hart, 'Instrumentaliteit en Rechtsbescherming', Gouda Quint, Kluwer, 1990, p. 116.

44 E. Claes, 'Legaliteit en rechtsvinding in het strafrecht', Universitaire Pers Leuven, 2003, p. 370.

45 R. Dworkin, 'A Matter of Principle', Harvard University Press, 1985, p. 11; K. Rozemond, 'Legaliteit in het materiële strafrecht', RM Themis, 1999, pp. 117–130.

horizontal conflicts (incorporating both elements of the instrumental aim). The relational criminal justice model brings together the instrumental and protective aims of criminal punishment and therefore brings within the character of criminal law the balance between these antithetical goals.

The purpose of the legality principle in this model is to discover how criminal law can combat crime (crime-control element) while not being applied arbitrarily (protection against arbitrariness), and how criminal law can shape the society (society-shaping element) while providing a stable framework for individuals to rely on in terms of their behaviour (protection against uncertainty element). Thus, in this model, legal principles that legitimise criminal law such as the principle of legality, gain more than one dimension because they do not solely focus on either of the two protective or instrumental aims. Legitimacy in this model is achieved via the balancing of the two finalities and thus, principles that aim at legitimising the law must bring about such mediating effect.

4. The classical model of criminal justice

Historically, the classical model was developed to tackle arbitrary and unjust totalitarian criminal justice systems in Europe during the Middle Ages. While the Enlightenment movement offered a rich theoretical basis for a new ideology of criminal justice, the classical model emerged as a response to certain particular problems of that time, as they emerged after the French Revolution.[46] The arbitrary, limitless powers of the state to punish individuals and the theocratic nature of criminal justice was considered arbitrary: disproportional and cruel penal sanctions, a lack of proper legislation, lack of transparency in the criminal justice process and lack of legal certainty regarding criminal conduct created unjust regimes.[47] The need for a new basis legitimising criminal law was based around an understanding of individuals as autonomous subjects of criminal justice and the importance of individuals' wellbeing. The classical model of criminal justice brings to the foreground the conflict between the individual and the state. Legitimacy is established by balancing this vertical relationship, through the empowerment of the individual. Therefore, the legality principle in the classical model focuses on rebalancing the vertical relationship between the individual and the state, by limiting the latter thereby empowering the former.[48] The legality principle imputes legitimacy to criminal norms by emphasising their protective aim. Criminal law becomes legitimate because the legality principle ensures a robust level of protection for

46 E. Claes, 'Legaliteit en rechtsvinding in het strafrecht', Universitaire Pers Leuven, 2003, pp. 87–88.

47 L. Dupont, 'Beginselen van behoorlijke strafrechtsbedeling', Gouda Quint, 1979, p. 42.

48 Franz von Liszt cited via B. Schünemann, 'Nulla poena sine lege? Rechtstheoretische und verfassungsrechtliche Implikationen der Rechtsgewinnung im Strafrecht', Walter de Gruyter, 1978, p. 1.

individuals. This reaction to the *Ancien Regime* stems from the values of individual autonomy, liberty, democracy and separation of powers.[49]

4.1. Characteristics and theoretical rationales

As explained the classical model of criminal justice is inspired by conventionalism/formalism. It is based on the idea that law finds legitimacy in the past: pre-existing values and accepted norms. The criminal justice system is a reactive one: its purpose is restricted to providing a framework within which individuals can lead their lives. It is highly individualistic in nature in that it is not overly concerned with public policy aims.[50] In particular, the basic characteristics of such criminal justice systems are the following.

Firstly, the legitimacy of coercive norms comes only from guaranteeing the protective finality of criminal law.[51] A legitimate criminal justice system is one that maximises the individual sphere of action. The nature of law is to protect individuals from state arbitrariness.[52] There is a difference between 'order' and criminal *law* and the purpose of the latter is not 'policing society' but 'policing police'.[53] To ensure societal order, a state needs only *de facto* power, which is a different concept to a legitimate *de jure* power. The term *law* may replace the term 'order' only when certain principles, such as the legality principle, legitimise the use of state-power.

Secondly, this approach to the nature of criminal law means that the instrumental finality does not fall within the definition of criminal *law* but within the definition of 'order.' It is not the substance of a judicial decision or a criminal norm that is important, but how this decision was made or applied.[54] To give an example: it is not the protection of children's sexual integrity that makes the criminal norms regarding child pornography legitimate, or legitimises a conviction. What legitimises it is how the criminal norm was adopted, written and applied. The legitimacy of criminal norms is therefore autonomous and independent from instrumental goals or policies. The same goes for legal principles. Principles, and the principle of legality in particular, have an autonomous and independent character as they do not depend on the different instrumental policies of the state, and are not constructed as policies themselves. In the end, what imputes legitimacy to *ius puniendi* is that it is governed by autonomous principles.[55]

---

49 E. Claes, 'Legaliteit en rechtsvinding in het strafrecht', Universitaire Pers Leuven, 2003, pp. 87–88.

50 M.R. Damaška, 'The Faces of Justice and State Authority', Yale University Press, 1986, p. 73.

51 H.L. Packer, 'The Limits of the Criminal Sanction', Stanford University Press, 1968, p. 158.

52 L. Dupont, 'Beginselen van behoorlijke strafrechtsbedeling', Gouda Quint, 1979, p. 49.

53 A.A.G. Peters, 'Het rechtskarakter van het strafrecht', Kluwer, 1972, pp. 6–7.

54 Ibid., p. 9.

55 Ibid.

The sole purpose and autonomous role of the legality principle is to govern the vertical relationship between individuals and the state and set limits to the latter. This also entails that criminal law has an autonomous character: policies come and go and what was previously considered to be criminal is subsequently accepted. In the classical model, there should be also a maximum protection of individuals against the instrumental goals of the state; this entails that the *ius puniendi* of the state should be limited as much as possible.[56] In this sense, the powers of the state to dictate to its citizens what constitutes 'the good life' are to be limited as much as possible, as what has priority is the freedom of individuals to determine for themselves their own pursuit of happiness.[57]

Thirdly, principles are considered open-ended and multi-interpretational, with their own criteria of application. Those, three elements aim at securing the independent nature of legal principles (and criminal law) from policy goals. Principles are open-ended in that they are more abstract than criminal rules.[58] A distinction between rules and principles is important in this model, not only because principles are inherently more abstract, but also because rules are often coloured by policy goals. In contrast, principles should remain independent. Principles are also multi-interpretational, which means that there are various ways for them to be interpreted in order to bring about their protective function. For example, the principle of legality can generate guidelines regarding different state-actors, such as judicial interpretation and legislation-making. Principles also have their own criteria of application, which means that they enjoy hierarchically superior position over rules and cannot be set aside by changes in the law.[59]

These being the basic characteristics of the classical model, the theoretical basis of the legality principle must be adjusted accordingly. Criminal justice must guarantee so that individual autonomy is protected against state arbitrariness. Individual liberty and autonomy are cornerstone values in the classical model. Both negative and positive aspects of individual liberty are to be protected from the arbitrariness of the state, thus sheltering individuals' personal sphere (minimum state interference) and their ability to rely on the law (legal certainty).[60]

Consequently, this model adopts a formal theory of the Rule of Law.[61] In the classical model, the Rule of Law generates only formal and organic requirements. As individual liberty and autonomy are considered cornerstones values, it is important that individual autonomy is protected by the imposition of different views of the good life by the state. Thus, the Rule of Law here protects individuals from

---

56 E. Claes, 'Legaliteit en rechtsvinding in het strafrecht', Universitaire Pers Leuven, 2003, pp. 84–85.

57 I.–S. Kim, 'Der Gesetzlichkeitsgrundsatz im Lichte der Rechtsidee', in B. Schünemann, H. Achenbach (eds), 'Festschrift für Claus Roxin zum 70. Geburtstag am 15. Mai 2001', De Gruyter, 2001, p. 121.

58 A.A.G. Peters, 'Het rechtskarakter van het strafrecht', Kluwer, 1972, pp. 13–14.

59 Ibid.

60 R. Dworkin, 'Law's Empire', Hart Publishing, 2006, p. 117.

61 Chapter III para. 5.

any form of intrusion in their personal sphere and the principle of neutrality is of paramount importance in the formal concept of the Rule of Law. As mentioned above, a classical criminal justice system is reactive.

The legality principle in the classical model adopts the principle of democracy as its cornerstone: the legislature is the only legitimate body that can create, amend or otherwise determine criminal norms.[62] This emphasis on democratic processes echoes the theory of law as a convention. However, as explained before, this model focuses on the how and not what the law is. Similarly, it is the procedural concept of democracy that is at stake.[63] This means that, ultimately, the procedural nature of the principle of democracy is emphasised, in other words, the legality principle supports the democratic process (criminal liability thereby being produced by democratic procedures).[64] This is a consequence of the detachment of the content of criminal law from its instrumental aim: the substance of norms (so what they criminalise and what they do not) is part of the political priorities debated in the legislature. Important is the outward appearance, but not the substance of the law.

In this model, the separation of powers is also relatively strict.[65] The legislator decides what behaviour should be criminalised, and to what degree, whereas the courts are to apply criminal norms on an *ad hoc* basis.[66] Courts may only base their decisions on pre-existing statutory laws, rather than their own morality or current political aims. However, it is not the case that in the classical model judicial interpretation is seen as a mechanistic process; this would be naive.[67] The separation of powers aims to legitimise the actions of courts by subjecting their discretion to the limits set out in the parliamentary statute.[68] Even within conventionalism, there are different trends regarding the strictness of the separation of powers.[69] In a strict classical model, courts decisions must only take place within the strict limits of statutory criminal liability; interpretation here is closer to the literal interpretation of the law (*Buchstabieren*). In a soft classical model, courts may interpret statutory criminal liability more freely, that is to say, they may interpret a provision with some flexibility as long as it would be permitted by its wording.[70]

---

62 G. Grünwald, 'Bedeutung und Begründung des Satzes nulla poena sine lege', ZStW, vol. 76, 1964, pp. 13–14.

63 Chapter III para. 3.2.

64 E. Claes, 'Legaliteit en rechtsvinding in het strafrecht', Universitaire Pers Leuven, 2003, pp. 426–427.

65 Chapter III para. 4.

66 R. Dworkin, 'Law's Empire', Hart Publishing, 2006, p. 118.

67 B. Schünemann, 'Nulla poena sine lege? Rechtstheoretische und verfassungsrechtliche Implikationen der Rechtsgewinnung im Strafrecht', Walter de Gruyter, 1978, p. 10.

68 Ibid., p. 11.

69 R. Dworkin, 'Law's Empire', Hart Publishing, 2006, pp. 124–130.

70 Ibid., pp. 124–125.

4.2. Characteristics of the legality principle

The legality principle in this model is more formalistic. It is an autonomous principle separated from rules (thereby open-ended), multi-facial (generating different protective guarantees that affect the construction, interpretation and application of law), and it has its own criteria for application (hierarchy).

Its main function is to safeguard the superiority of the statute as the sole source of criminal liability. The principle follows a strict separation of powers between courts and legislature, which entails that judicial interpretation should adhere strictly to the wording of the statute as much as possible. In principle, courts are not allowed to revisit the choices of the legislator. They mainly ensure that the law is applied in specific cases. By this, it is not meant that courts have no interpretive function of criminal statutes, but they do not have a guaranteeing function within the legal system.

Foreseeability in this model is understood as the ability of individuals to foresee the intervention of the state in their personal sphere and thus to retain control of their lives. Such foreseeability is achieved through the existence of accessible, clear and non-retroactive rules applied by courts in a manner consistent with the wording of the statute. As the protection of individual autonomy is an inherent part of criminal law, foreseeability in this context is rather passive: individuals are neither obliged nor expected to look for the provision in the darkest corners of a library, nor ponder the possible grey zones of criminal law. This model of justice is coloured by a strong liberal ideology. The main purpose of criminal law here is to create obstacles for the state not the individual.[71]

The legality principle thus generates requirements that guarantee the communicative and superior value of the statute and binds courts to its wording. The legality principle:

- Invalidates any source of criminal liability that has no parliamentary approval. This means that every aspect of prohibited behaviour must be outlined in a statute.
- Restricts judicial interpretation to the wording of the statute. Its meaning must remain stable and unchanged by judicial interpretation and statutory interpretation should remain as strict as possible. Different methods of interpretation can be employed to discover the content of the norm, with the grammatical method of interpretation preferred. Depending on whether one is operating under a softer classical model, a historical (subjective teleological) or systemic method can be used. The objective teleological method (the *telos* as it would be termed today) is not accepted as the idea behind the classical model is that past decisions of the legislature give legitimacy to criminal norms. As seen, conventionalism is backward-oriented. As individual autonomy is the main

[71] H.L. Packer, 'The Limits of the Criminal Sanction', Stanford University Press, 1968, p. 163.

basis for this model, analogy, or any other interpretation that extends criminal liability beyond the statute, is not tolerated. This is because analogical interpretation extends the scope of the statute, in effect creating new law, something that is unacceptable.[72] Analogical reasoning, because it naturally produces the evolution of legal concepts, is against a core value of the classical model – the contextual stability of norms –.[73]

- Prevents courts from inserting their personal views regarding the definitions in criminal norms by obliging the legislature to ensure statutes are as precise as possible.
- Ensures that criminal liability does not operate in a manner that compromises foreseeability, prohibiting retroactive criminalisation by both the legislator and the courts, and ensuring the clarity of statutes. As legal certainty and foreseeability are key concepts in this model, it is important that statutes must be as precise as possible in this respect.

4.3. Criticism

After explaining the main premise of this model and how the principle of legality is conceived, one should provide a critical assessment. In this section some advantages and disadvantages of this model shall be presented.

An important advantage of the classical model of criminal justice is that it preserves the autonomous nature of criminal law. Defining legitimacy as protection against arbitrariness and uncertainty retains the autonomous character of criminal law *vis-à-vis* political manipulation. This is achieved not only by emphasising individual autonomy and political liberalism but also via the construction of a principle of legality that is distinguished from rules and policies. Focusing on the vertical relationship between the individual and the state means that criminal law is detached from context-related concerns. No matter how societies may change and how legal interests and morals may vary, the legitimacy of criminal law remains independent. Binding judicial interpretation to the wording of the text means that courts cannot incorporate into their judgements their political views. In this model, certainty and foreseeability are highly achieved and safeguarded.

Furthermore, this model promotes a well-structured judicial system by supporting well-defined distribution of tasks between legislator and courts and a strong preference for hierarchical statutory sources of criminal liability. In addition, the principle of legality has a seemingly more ordered and clear-cut image. The interpretation of its aspects shows in advance when the principle would be violated: e.g. if courts extent the scope of criminal liability, the principle of legality is violated. One knows what the principle stands for and how it should be applied.

---

72 R. Dworkin, 'Law's Empire', Hart Publishing, 2006, p. 116.

73 S.M. Quevedo, 'Formalist and Instrumentalist Legal Reasoning and Legal Theory', California Law Review, vol. 73, 1985, pp. 142–143.

Having said that, the classical model has also some important disadvantages. It does not help explain the principle of legality as it is applied in national law. It is based on anachronistic accounts of the *ratio* of the legality principle. It also fails to protect the individual against arbitrariness in all its expressions, as it neglects – and thus does not limit – the instrumental finality of criminal law.

Firstly, this model of justice does not fit within current constitutional dialogues in national jurisdictions, which strive to reconcile two antithetical views regarding the Rule of Law.[74] As explained, the Rule of Law inhabits a twilight zone between a formal and substantive approach to criminal law.[75] Although there is no defined middle ground, the principle of legality as understood in current national jurisdictions is not consistent with a purely classical model. Thus, it would be inconsistent to accept a criminal model of justice bound to a formal conception of the Rule of Law. The same can be said regarding the procedural conception of democracy; national systems favour a mixed approach to democracy, combining procedural and substantive elements – in other words, a procedural democracy limited by basic standards of fundamental rights.[76]

The legality principle, in this context, is based on a strict view of the separation of powers. The classical model focuses on the manner in which state powers can be separated, rather than how each arm of government may keep the others in check. In a more holistic account of Montesquieu's theory, the separation of powers is a balancing mechanism where the arms of government keep each other in check, thereby avoiding excessive centralisation of powers in one of the *trias politica*. In addition, courts are approached as potentially dangerous institutions. While this is indeed a legitimate concern, arbitrariness can also stem from the executive and legislature. Courts, in modern times, have a safeguarding function as well; for example, they review legislation or ensure its compatibility with human rights either directly or via judicial interpretation of statutes. To a certain extent, the classical model brings about the opposite effects of those intended. The idea of binding courts to the parliamentary statute via *lex certa* and *lex stricta* aims to ensure that courts may not engage in judicial activism. However, if the positive duty of courts to keep the legislature 'in check' is not envisaged as part of the legal system's theoretical model, the danger is that this task will be performed arbitrarily. In essence, in this model law and its interpretation of the principle of legality loses its argumentative character.[77] The proper role of courts is therefore not fully addressed by the legality principle within a classical model of justice.

74 For example, see T.R.S. Allan, 'Fairness, Equality, Rationality: Constitutional Theory and Judicial Review', in C.F. Forsyth and I. Hare (eds), 'The Golden Metwand and the Crooked Cord', Oxford University Press, 1998, pp. 16–17; R. Dworkin, 'A Matter of Principle', Harvard University Press, 1985, pp. 11–18; Lord Bingham, 'The Rule of Law', Cambridge Law Journal, vol. 66, 2007, pp. 75–76.

75 Chapter III para. 5.

76 E. Claes, 'Legaliteit en rechtsvinding in het strafrecht', Universitaire Pers Leuven, 2003, p. 462.

77 Ibid., pp. 174–176.

Secondly, the legality principle provides less adequate protection against judicial arbitrariness. A lack of proper understanding of the powers of courts created a risk of the type of arbitrariness that the classical model failed to foresee.[78] As explained, in the practical application of the legality principle, systems face genuine problems regarding judicial activism and arbitrariness, especially with regards to the issue of casuistry. There is little room to rebuild a normative tool by which the legality principle may curtail casuistry via jurisprudence. Consistency in jurisprudence requires consistency with past decisions.[79]

One idea to solve this issue within the classical model is to defend a form of precedent similar to the English *stare decisis.* This would be impeded by the fact that in this model the principle of legality does not accept judicial interpretation's role in defining criminal liability. If jurisprudence can never help to define criminal liability, there is no point in attempting to control it. The only way to provide some protection against casuistry and fragmentation in jurisprudence would be to reconstruct the model as a judicially-based system. This is not inconsistent with a classical model of criminal justice necessarily. Prior judicial decisions can constitute, after all, conventions. Therefore, it is not impossible to reconstruct this model in order to limit certain of its deficiencies. However, it would require a thorough reconsideration of the principle of democracy and separation of powers, which is not in line with current practice.

In addition, the legality principle on this view does not adequately ensure that the reasoning of judgements shall not be arbitrary. It was argued for example that the prohibition of analogy alone cannot adequately protect against arbitrariness.[80] One of the problems of the prohibition of analogy was that it is difficult to distinguish from other purposive methods of interpretation and in the end it is not clear what is prohibited. Perhaps there are ways to battle this problem. One of the main premises of this model is to stop courts from replacing the legislator's will with their own. That will ensure democracy but also consistency and stability. As it was also explained, analogical reasoning is frequently used in cases with anachronistic provisions.[81] A way to rationalise the problem with analogy is to investigate the source of norm ageing.[82] If a norm contains a word that does not encapsulate all features of the concept as is understood in the modern social context, then analogical reasoning is not necessarily illegitimate. Examples are the terms 'document' and 'object', which nowadays include also virtual reality features. An analogical interpretation here would not mean that judicial decisions replace the will of the legislator. If, however, it is the values or the policy assumptions behind

78 M.J. Borgers, 'De communicatieve strafrechter', in W.J.M. Voermans, M.J. Borgers, C.H. Sieburgh, 'Controverses rondom legaliteit en legitimatie', Kluwer, 2011, p. 120.

79 R. Dworkin, 'Law's Empire', Hart Publishing, 2006, p. 130.

80 Chapter IV para. 10.1.4.

81 Chapter IV para. 10.1.3.

82 S.M. Quevedo, 'Formalist and Instrumentalist Legal Reasoning and Legal Theory', California Law Review, vol. 73, 1985, pp. 144–145.

the norm that need updating, then such an aged provision could not be changed without violating the principle of legality (and democracy) in this model. Arguably, this is not a clear-cut distinction either. But it helps to repair some problems of this principle, because it traces the permissibility of analogical reasoning to the protection of the theoretical rationales of the principle.

An important impediment of the legality principle in this model is its primary focus on respecting the wording of the statute without informing further judicial interpretation. It does not generate tools to ensure that the interpretation of the wording of the text will reflect the proper balancing of rights, as intended by the legislator. One of the key challenges in the current application of the principle is to control the way courts weigh individual rights and fill legal lacunae. The legality principle in the classical model would be of little use in the *Sitzblockaden* case for example; clearly, the case primarily concerned the individual rights rather than analogical reasoning.

If one understands courts as mere appliers of the law and neglects their proper role in the *trias politica*, the legality principle cannot address possible arbitrariness that may occur when courts give priority to instrumental goals. In *Sitzblockaden*, 'psychological force' would have been covered grammatically by the provision, and the German Constitutional Court pointed out that prior jurisprudence had accepted this interpretation of coercion before. The court did not respect the wording of the statute simply because it was laid down as such, but because its chosen interpretation of such wording ensured the integrity of the German legal order, as reflected in the conflicting rights in this case. Was this a legitimate decision? According to the classical model, the answer is yes, as the result was to restrict criminal liability, and the court's interpretation fell within the wording of the provision. But would the answer be the same if the case involved psychological coercion in the form of school bullying? One can choose to ignore the court's role in safeguarding individual rights and due process within the criminal justice system, but if ignored, one runs the risk that it will take place arbitrarily.

Thus, the principle of legality within a classical model of justice does not offer sufficient protection to individuals, as it does not generate guidelines on how courts may distinguish policy objectives from individual rights and how to prioritise them. Judicial arbitrariness is not only caused by excessively broad interpretation of statutory wording, but by arbitrary reasoning. Policy considerations, such as combatting crime or encouraging societal change are instrumentalist arguments. Yet not every instrumentalist objective is legitimate. It makes a difference if a court bases its interpretation of a norm on the need to prevent sexual gratification and not the protection of sexual/bodily integrity of children. In the first instance, the instrumental goals of the norm's interpretation result in an excessive limitation of individual action. However, excluding the instrumental finality of criminal law from this model means that the legality principle does not influence or restrict use of instrumental reasoning.

Crime-control and societal development are not significant for the legitimacy of the *ius puniendi*. The horizontal dimension, which includes interpersonal relationships, does not have a determining formative effect on the legitimacy of criminal law.[83] As explained, the instrumental finality of *ius puniendi* is an institutionalised channelling of inter-personal conflicts between individuals. In exercising *ius puniendi* the state is protecting individual autonomy albeit in a different way: it ensures that the necessary limitation of the accused's individual autonomy is legitimate while also seeking to protect or reinstate the violated autonomy of the alleged victim. In this regard, the need for individuals to be protected from state action is not necessarily more legitimate, moral or ethical than the claim of individuals to be protected against other individuals.[84] Both claims are an expression of the value of individual autonomy, which after all is supposed to be in the heart of criminal systems. In the marital rape case, why would the right of the husband to be free from state arbitrariness be a legitimate aspect of individual autonomy, but not the wife's right to freedom from rape? In that sense, the right of individuals to exist in a society where their individual autonomy is protected from third parties stems from the same concept of individual autonomy, which shields individuals from state arbitrariness.[85]

Therefore, in the end both instrumental and protective aims of criminal law offer a more *in abstracto* protection of individuals: a legitimate criminal norm protects both victims and accused from violation of their individual autonomy albeit, in different ways.[86] The classical model, by excluding protection of individual autonomy from third persons (the horizontal dimension) from the legitimacy of criminal law, denies an inherent function of criminal law.[87]

As explained, the consequence of this limited view is not that the instrumental finality of criminal law does not exist, but that it is not recognised or controlled by legal principles. That is of concern as the instrumental finality remains in the hands of state-actors without any acknowledgement. The danger is that:

> [O]ur judges actually pay more attention to so-called conventional sources of law like statutes and precedents than conventionalism allows them to do. A self-consciously strict conventionalist judge would lose interest in legislation and precedent at just the point when it became clear that the explicit extension of these supposed conventions had run out. He would then acknowledge that there was no law, and he would have no further concern for consistency with the past; he would proceed to make new law by asking what law the present legislature would make or

83 J. Habermas, 'Between Facts and Norms', Polity Press, 1997, pp. 245–246.

84 C.P.M. Cleiren, 'Evolueren naar meer horizontale en multi-dimensionale verhoudingen in het strafrecht', Kluwer, 2010, pp. 7–8; see also Chapter III para. 2.2.

85 Chapter III para. 2.2.

86 J. Claessen, 'Misdaad en straf: een herbezinning op het strafrecht vanuit mystiek perspectief', Wolf Legal Publishers, 2010, p. 114.

87 L. Dupont, 'Beginselen van behoorlijke strafrechtsbedeling', Gouda Quint, 1979, pp. 48–77.

what the people want or what would be in the community's best interests for the future.[88]

Maximum legal certainty in criminal law is impossible not only because language is inherently indeterminate, but also because criminal norms aim to protect individual autonomy in both vertical and horizontal conflicts; the latter entails that on occasion, an element of generality is necessary and desirable.[89] In order to assess the legitimacy of more abstract norms, courts assess foreseeability not only with respect to individual autonomy in its vertical dimension but also the horizontal dimension. Whether or not a provision is legitimately vague depends on whether the statute generates sufficient guidance to individuals, by taking under consideration the character of the offence and how it would inform interpersonal relationships. In other words, the expectations created for individuals by criminal norms with regard to their interpersonal relationships are of importance.

In conclusion, excluding the instrumental finality from the legitimacy of criminal law means that the legality principle is doctrinally impaired from adequately supervising how protective and instrumental goals are weighed and prioritised. Ultimately, the legality principle in this model is not a method of interpretation (i.e. a principle supervising and guiding the process of interpretation); it only addresses one function of interpretation, namely the closeness to the wording of the text.

5. The instrumentalist model of criminal justice

Legitimising criminal law within the instrumentalist model is different from the classical model. Here criminal law becomes a tool to enforce certain policies and goals. The instrumentalist model constitutes an on-going reaction to the lacunae of the classical model, and therefore is not an archetypical construction for the legality principle independent of the classical model. On the contrary, its starting points are certain failures of the classical model.[90]

The instrumentalist model represents a certain tendency in the last few decades, to use criminal law as an instrument to achieve certain policy goals. The so-called 'instrumentalisation' of criminal law refers to the increasing tendency in legislative and judicial practice to emphasise protection of society and ways that criminal law can contribute to that end.[91] It is important to reiterate the definition of the instrumentalist model: *'a theory or account of the nature of law held by legal*

88 R. Dworkin, 'Law's Empire', Hart Publishing, 2006, p. 130.

89 E. Claes, 'Legaliteit en rechtsvinding in het strafrecht', Universitaire Pers Leuven, 2003, p. 204.

90 Ibid., p. 221.

91 A.A.G. Peters, 'Het rechtskarakter van het strafrecht', Kluwer, 1972, p. 5.

actors...that law is purely a means to an end, an empty vessel devoid of any inherent principle or binding content or integrity unto itself.'[92]

Instrumentalism and legal realism is a prevalent philosophical movement since the 20th century. As explained the basic premise of realism is that justification of norms is found in their contemporary value and purpose. Instrumentalist thinking introduces a more critical perception to the legitimacy of law. A frequent criticism of instrumentalists towards the formalists (classical model of criminal law) is that legal formalism does not take under adequate consideration of the social context within which legal rules operate.[93] Although instrumentalism oozes the pragmatic approach towards the world usually associated with modern times, its roots can be found in the Enlightenment. As explained above realism, or instrumentalist thinking, was promoted by the Enlightenment legacy.[94] This can be noticed at different levels.

First, an instrumentalist approach stems from the very same Enlightenment ideals. Individual autonomy, rational individuals, a rationalised society as opposed to theocracy and superstition, and a scientific explanation of the world gave rise to a more pragmatic and calculative understanding of the world (and the law). If certain structures or features are not God-given, then their effectiveness, usefulness or desirability can be challenged and evaluated. This allowed for a more critical evaluation of the purpose and utility of societal, political and legal structures. The instrumentalist ideology of the Enlightenment is further reflected in more specific theories regarding individual autonomy and criminal punishment. Deterrence for example is a theory with roots in instrumentalism and the same can be said about the utilitarian justification of legal punishment. Important philosophers for the legality principle, such as Beccaria and Feuerbach, had partly justified the principle of legality on instrumentalist ideology, a topic that I will address later on in more detail. Bentham was also an important contributor to instrumental thinking. He supported that legitimacy of criminal law is to be found in its utilitarian goals, so legitimate laws are the ones promoting happiness of citizens.[95]

A second level where instrumentalist ideology can be seen depicted in the Enlightenment is the political movement itself. Next to the theoretical renaissance of certain concepts such as individual autonomy, it was the goal of promoting the interests of the middle economic class that motivated the battle against state arbitrariness. The necessity for anticipated criminalisation and for democratic ruling mirrored the antipathy towards the feudal elite.[96] Therefore, the movement

---

92 B.Z. Tamanaha, 'Law as a Means to an End', Cambridge University Press, 2006, p. 7.

93 S.M. Quevedo, 'Formalist and Instrumentalist Legal Reasoning and Legal Theory', California Law Review, vol. 73, 1985, p. 122.

94 See above para. 1.

95 J. Driver, 'The History of Utilitarianism', The Stanford Encyclopedia of Philosophy (Winter 2014 Edition), E.N. Zalta (ed), URL http://plato.stanford.edu/archives/win2014/entries/utilitarianism-history/

96 L. Dupont, 'Beginselen van behoorlijke strafrechtsbedeling', Gouda Quint, 1979, p. 51.

itself was driven by the instrumentalist ideology of replacing the existing system with a structure (and respective principles) that was considered better for the people.

5.1. Main characteristics and theoretical rationales

This model rests upon the hypothesis that criminal law has no particular inherent nature, but it is a tool to achieve specific ends, such as political aims and objectives.[97] Legitimate criminal law has no autonomous or independent purpose, as its purpose is a result of policy priorities at any given moment.[98]

The instrumental finality, particularly the crime-control element,[99] is the primary explanation for the legitimacy and function of criminal law.[100] In particular, in this model: *'law is the instrument to serve the social good'*,[101] which in criminal law translates to the concept of crime-control, in other words, ensuring a safe and secure society.[102] Certainly there are different views of the concept of 'order'. From a criminological perspective, it has been often considered that society is similar to a living organism and crime a disease to be treated. Though such a metaphorical understanding of 'order' may be too extreme, and therefore may lead to a radical or absolute perception of instrumentalism,[103] this model does not distinguish between the concepts of 'order' and 'order ruled by law' (*ordehandhaving* and *rechtshandhaving*).[104]

The way 'order' is conceived depends on whether one takes a utilitarian or communitarian perspective. Within the utilitarian perspective, criminal law and judicial decisions are legitimised not based on how and to what extent they protect individuals against state arbitrariness, but on how efficiently they enforce the policy goals that aim to improve society, the wellbeing of individuals, and the preservation, creation or increase of welfare goods.[105] Therefore the rationale behind the utilitarian perspective is setting goals that improve public welfare, and effectively enforcing those goals. From the communitarian perspective, criminal law and judicial decisions are legitimised when they enforce society's moral values. This differs from the utilitarian perspective in the sense that the legitimacy of criminal law follows a certain symbolic rationale.[106] In either perspective, the state in the

---

97 B.Z. Tamanaha, 'Law as a Means to an End', Cambridge University Press, 2006, p. 7.

98 R. Foqué, A.C. 't Hart, 'Instrumentaliteit en Rechtsbescherming', Gouda Quint, Kluwer, 1990, p. 116.

99 H.L. Packer, 'The Limits of the Criminal Sanction', Stanford University Press, 1968, p. 158.

100 J. Claessen, 'Misdaad en straf: een herbezinning op het strafrecht vanuit mystiek perspectief', Wolf Legal Publishers, 2010, p. 114.

101 B.Z. Tamanaha, 'Law as a Means to an End', Cambridge University Press, 2006, p. 4.

102 E. Claes, 'Legaliteit en rechtsvinding in het strafrecht', Universitaire Pers Leuven, 2003, p. 221.

103 Ibid., p. 224.

104 Chapter II para. 2.

105 H.L. Packer, 'The Limits of the Criminal Sanction', Stanford University Press, 1968, p. 158.

106 E. Claes, 'Legaliteit en rechtsvinding in het strafrecht', Universitaire Pers Leuven, 2003, pp. 230–235.

instrumentalist model is active, striving to promote a coherent perception of the 'good life' or increase the common good.[107]

Individual autonomy in this model is not as highly prioritised as in the classical model, as individuals need not be reliable judges of their own interests.[108] Individual autonomy can be interpreted differently in this model. One idea is that it is a tool for maintaining personal wellbeing of individuals, or, from a communitarian perspective as a socially constructed concept where individual autonomy is enhanced through social attachments and the social fabric.[109] Other concepts such as democracy, equality, separation of powers, legal certainty and the Rule of Law are approached from utilitarian or communitarian perspectives.[110] As explained, democracy may also acquire instrumental justifications, such as the argument that it safeguards the quality of decisions.[111]

There is, however, the possibility to maintain a more traditional definition of individual autonomy within this model (understood as the ability to rely to the law). One could argue that foreseeing criminalisation is an effective way to prevent individuals from committing offences. In fact, such instrumentalist interpretation of the legality principle can be supported by the Enlightenment legacy, where criminal law was also instrumentally justified. Indeed, an important point in Beccaria's theory was that a criminal system with clear and known laws is more effective.[112] A similar instrumentalist account can be found in Feuerbach's theory of deterrence. The main assumption of the *psychologische Zwangstheorie* entails that individuals shall be deterred by punishment. Such a result can occur only if laws are clear and known to the public.[113] A prevalent view in the Enlightenment thinking was that maintaining foreseeability and trust of individuals towards state action would also ensure prevention of crime.[114]

The powers of the state are used for maximising the common welfare, which means that courts are expected to have increased discretion. In this model, courts are literally the *bouche de la loi* in the sense that they concretise and evaluate the *telos* of legislation, based on what is currently best for the social order. As this model is based on pragmatism, it rejects the idea that statutes created in the past may be legitimate, without adaptation to modern circumstances. Contemporary virtues and their efficiency are what justify coercion.[115]

---

107 M.R. Damaška, 'The Faces of Justice and State Authority', Yale University Press, 1986, p. 80.
108 Ibid., p. 81.
109 A. Etzioni, 'The New Golden Rule', Basic Books, 1996, pp. 23–28.
110 E. Claes, 'Legaliteit en rechtsvinding in het strafrecht', Universitaire Pers Leuven, 2003, pp. 249–265.
111 Chapter III para. 3.1.
112 K. Rozemond, 'Beccaria's Dream on Criminal Law and Nodal Governance', in J. Blad, M. Hildebrandt, K. Rozemond, M. Schuilenburg, P. Van Calster (eds), 'Governing Security under the Rule of Law?', Eleven International Publishing, 2010, p. 42.
113 Chapter III para. 2.1.
114 L. Dupont, 'Beginselen van behoorlijke strafrechtsbedeling', Gouda Quint, 1979, p. 53.
115 R. Dworkin, 'Law's Empire', Hart Publishing, 2006, p. 151.

As criminal law is a tool to pursue specific societal goals (to enforce certain values or to increase prosperity) criminal norms gain a horizontal dimension.[116] Criminal norms create certain behavioural patterns for individuals that enforce those utilitarian and communitarian ideas, and therefore create certain expectations regarding their application. However, legal certainty here is not interpreted as maximum foreseeability, or expectations regarding state action, but as a harmoniously and efficiently coordinated society. Individuals have the right to be able to concretise their expectations of each other in a situation, and thus the state must protect the ability of individuals to employ criminal norms as a means of mediating their conflicting rights.[117] An alternative account of legal certainty would be foreseeability regarding state action whenever this increases the efficiency of criminal law, via deterrence.

Principles and individual rights are also considered goals or policies without autonomous standing.[118] For instrumentalism, criminal law is a means to an end.[119] The legislator in such a criminal justice system drafts criminal liability with an output-oriented mentality, as the focus is more on the practical and empirical effects of legislation.[120] Whenever courts apply the principle of legality it is to achieve certain policy goals. An instrumentally-oriented court employs legal rules as a tool to reach the desired end.[121] The protection of the individual against arbitrariness is also an aim and criminal law may be protective only because it facilitates certain policy.[122]

Generally speaking, the conflict between the protective and instrumental finality is resolved by prioritising the latter and minimising the former.[123] Additional legitimacy of criminal law through the protective finality is not considered necessary; the instrumentalist model is regarded as enough.[124] A legitimate legal order is one where criminal norms assist the enforcement and protection of social interests.[125] The need to protect individuals against the state may feature in this system as an effective policy to increase compliance with the law, but it will be weighed against other policy interests and it could also be considered a luxury when more pressing needs are present.[126] The result is that if courts can legitimise

116 E. Claes, 'Legaliteit en rechtsvinding in het strafrecht', Universitaire Pers Leuven, 2003, pp. 265–268.

117 Ibid., p. 274.

118 R. Dworkin, 'Law's Empire', Hart Publishing, 2006, p. 160.

119 B.Z. Tamanaha, 'Law as a Means to an End', Cambridge University Press, 2006, p. 4.

120 Chapter IV para. 7.

121 B.Z. Tamanaha, 'Law as a Means to an End', Cambridge University Press, 2006, p. 7.

122 Ibid., p. 5.

123 E. Claes, 'Legaliteit en rechtsvinding in het strafrecht', Universitaire Pers Leuven, 2003, p. 221.

124 Ibid., p. 236.

125 J. Claessen, 'Misdaad en straf: een herbezinning op het strafrecht vanuit mystiek perspectief', Wolf Legal Publishers, 2010, p. 114.

126 Ibid.

statutory interpretation sufficiently on either utilitarian or communitarian grounds, there is no need to look into any consideration of protection of individuals.

A modern version of the instrumentalist model can be seen in the historical development of criminal law, particularly in the second half of the 20th century. There was rapid technological advancement and new forms of criminal behaviour, such as terrorism and cyber-crime. In particular, there was a shift towards the minimisation of the protection of individual autonomy for the benefit of societal order. Examples can be seen in the development of abstract and risk-oriented laws, increasing limitations on privacy, preventive measures, and the interpretation of criminal laws, where courts often prioritise the societal safeguarding at the expense of individual autonomy.[127]

The emergence of the Risk Society has had a particular impact in this regard.[128] The shift from the Welfare State, which distributed 'goods,' to a risk management state, which distributes 'bads', illustrates the problems that criminal law currently faces.[129] The rise of the Risk Society means that the state must promote security and certainty in an increasingly uncertain environment, brought out by rapid technological advancements and more complex forms of social interaction. Technology creates a world that cannot be fully comprehended with our senses, and the risks created therefore need to be managed and in some cases restricted by the state. The increasing need for safety and security of citizens provokes a reaction, which is the need to control these risks.[130] A culture of control has been developed in modern society, influencing criminal justice systems.[131]

5.2. The legality principle within this model

Unlike the classical model, the legality principle in the instrumentalist model is approached from a pragmatic point of view, as it is a necessary element in enforcing different policies and community morals. It is not an autonomous, independent and hierarchically superior principle, but a policy, which serves communitarian or instrumental goals. Moreover, whenever its application cannot serve these goals, it is set aside, as crime-control takes precedence as a legitimate basis for coercion.[132]

The starting point is that some uncertainty in criminal laws is unavoidable.[133] Individuals should expect to find 'thin ice' along the way. To be clear, uncertainty is

---

127 C.P.M. Cleiren, 'Evolueren naar meer horizontale en multi-dimensionale verhoudingen in het strafrecht', Kluwer, 2010, pp. 4–7.

128 U. Beck, 'Risk Society – Towards a New Modernity', Sage, 1992, pp. 19–84.

129 D. Roef, 'Strafrechtelijke verantwoordelijkheid in de risicomaatschappij', in E. Vos, G. van Calster (eds), 'Risico en voorzorg in de risicomaatschappij', Intersentia, 2004, p. 203.

130 C.P.M. Cleiren, 'Evolueren naar meer horizontale en multi-dimensionale verhoudingen in het strafrecht', Kluwer, 2010, p. 6.

131 D. Garland, 'The Culture of Control – Crime and Social Order in Contemporary Society', Oxford University, Press, 2001, pp. 1–53.

132 M.R. Damaška, 'The Faces of Justice and State Authority', Yale University Press, 1986, p. 82.

133 M.S. Groenhuijsen, 'Straf en Wet', Gouda Quint, 1987, p. 17.

not a virtue of the instrumentalist model. If legal certainly serves the right purpose, it shall be promoted. What it is meant is that legal certainty is not an inherent element of this model. As criminal norms draw legitimacy from their contemporary social function, uncertainty becomes frequently desirable. Thus, the issue becomes in what circumstances the legality principle allows the legislator to create abstract criminal norms in order to include possible future developments. The legality principle in this model instructs courts to ensure that individuals can find some minimum behavioural guidance in criminal law. Criminal statutes in most situations must remain abstract in order to retain their contemporary relevance and flexibility.[134]

Judicial interpretation is not rule-bound but purpose-orientated.[135] Courts first decide what result they would consider most appropriate, and norms are manipulated accordingly. While in the previous model, judges are 'rule-conscious', for this model they are 'consciously goal-oriented'.[136] Judicial interpretation is influenced predominantly by communitarian and utilitarian goals, while the limits of interpretation are only restricted to a minimum of foreseeability. Courts are obliged to interpret criminal liability with respect to social goods and interests, as individuals would be otherwise deprived of the certainty and stability society requires. The legality principle is approached here as coordinating individuals' mutual expectations.[137] The courts must choose the interpretation that articulates societal values best. Unlike the classical model where judicial interpretation requires objective interpretation of relevant facts and norms, in the instrumentalist model, it involves a measuring of the consequences of different results.[138] Courts revisit legislative choices and uphold them only if they are still effective.

The wording of the text offers a 'rule of thumb'.[139] It is not the wording of the statute itself that is the limit of criminalisation, but the communitarian and utilitarian goals. Should deviation be deemed necessary for achieving important policies, then it is considered an obligation. It is the optimum pursuit of the common good that justifies criminal norms. The casuistry created by this case-by-case treatment is not a collateral damage but an element of the system.

This type of *ius puniendi* eventually aims to educate citizens regarding the moral and good life.[140] This is because criminal law becomes a tool to enforce certain ways of life and its legitimacy is challenged on this fact. In addition to an educational role, the legality principle has a role in controlling reasoning in judicial interpretation. Individuals expect that their individual claims and expectations will be weighed against communitarian or utilitarian ideals. Courts must employ such

---

134 B.Z. Tamanaha, 'Law as a Means to an End', Cambridge University Press, 2006, p. 228.

135 Ibid., p. 227.

136 Ibid., p. 241.

137 E. Claes, 'Legaliteit en rechtsvinding in het strafrecht', Universitaire Pers Leuven, 2003, p. 280.

138 B.Z. Tamanaha, 'Law as a Means to an End', Cambridge University Press, 2006, p. 229.

139 Ibid., p. 229.

140 E. Claes, 'Legaliteit en rechtsvinding in het strafrecht', Universitaire Pers Leuven, 2003, p. 280.

reasoning as is best for the promotion of societal values or the prosperity of society.[141] Thus the legality principle in this model addresses more the substance of the argumentation than in the classical model.

Jurisprudence is considered an organism of law depicting the development of the scope of criminal liability. The factual circumstances of cases play an important role in the choices made during the interpretative process, as courts look into how the conflict of rights is conceptualised in the specific facts of a case. Therefore, as opposed to *legisme,* this model views judicial interpretation as a hermeneutical process.[142] This means that facts influence the meaning of the provisions, so that the latter do not have a stable, objective meaning. The hermeneutic interpretation implies that the development of jurisprudence may depend too much on the facts of every case, creating a risk of casuistry.

Courts take into consideration existing practice and previous interpretation regarding criminal norms. This is what Claes calls the 'a-theoretical component,' in the sense that courts do not really do an *in abstracto* theoretical assessment of the conflicting rights; they are guided by a specific 'feeling' or 'intuition' regarding the application of a certain norm as it has been considered in practice.[143] An analogy here could be made with the interpretation of the legality principle by the ECtHR, which holds that judicial interpretation should be consistent with the essence of the offence.[144] Without an *in abstracto* theoretical assessment of norms, their meaning is influenced entirely from the facts.[145]

Norms have a fluid and dynamic meaning as they are influenced by different factual circumstances. In the English case of *Hamilton* for example, a barrister was prosecuted for outraging public decency when he placed a camera in a well-hidden case, filming footage up the skirts of women in a super market queue. The constitutive term 'public' has been interpreted in various ways throughout the years in English courts. Initially, common law had developed a criterion for the offence: if the act had been seen by at least two people then the threshold for the definition of 'public' was satisfied; the same was also true if the crime was committed in public or took place in a private place but was capable of being seen by the public. Later on, the definition was expanded, e.g. it was necessary for only one person to see the act.[146] Later case law expanded the definition further and it was sufficient that the act could have been seen by the public, even if no one actually saw it.[147] The English court held in *Hamilton* that the term under the present circumstances

---

141 Ibid., p. 281.

142 Chapter IV para. 3.2; B.M.J. van Klink, 'Bedreigt rechtsvinding de rechtszekerheid? Een kritisch-hermeneutische visie op de rol van de rechter in het materiële strafrecht', Delikt en Delinkwent, vol. 31, 2001, p. 688.

143 E. Claes, 'Legaliteit en rechtsvinding in het strafrecht', Universitaire Pers Leuven, 2003, pp. 296–297.

144 ECtHR C.R. v United Kingdom, App 20190/92, 22 November 1995, para. 34 and 41.

145 E. Claes, 'Legaliteit en rechtsvinding in het strafrecht', Universitaire Pers Leuven, 2003, p. 298.

146 R v Mayling [1963] 2 QB 717.

147 R v May [1990] 91 Cr App R 157.

meant that an act is public if people would have been able to see it, if looking carefully.[148] It is evident how the initial understanding of the norm changed based on the different facts presented to the court. In essence, judicial interpretation is often empirical.[149] Because courts are purpose-oriented in their reasoning, they may consider hypothetically and empirically what would happen if the norm received various interpretations.

5.3. Criticism

Having discussed the basic features of this model, a critical analysis will follow in this section. This model presents certain advantages over the classical model.

First, the instrumentalist model can certainly provide a better explanation for the current status quo, especially when it comes to the role of the *lex certa,* the increased power of the courts, and the purpose-oriented judicial interpretation. What is more, it also shows that foreseeability in this model is also approached instrumentally, as courts define what could have been foreseen based on what they want to achieve. For example the ECtHR in the marital rape case had concerns about out-dated conceptions of marriage, allowing a rapist to escape conviction, and negative publicity within the English society.[150] Foreseeability in this respect can be easily approached with an instrumental intention and construed in a manner that meets the required result; if one walks on thin ice, it can break at any moment.

The instrumentalist model is also more practice-friendly in that it fits better with the reality and how the principle applies in practice.[151] Being practice-friendly might not seem a very convincing argument. Nevertheless, the ability to depict reality into a theoretical construction is not only a descriptive feature but can also have a moral value. Thus, one can argue that dynamism is also a morally defendable virtue of a system, as it maintains the context-sensitivity and responsiveness of law. This is especially the case with judicial interpretation.

The classical model does not adequately acknowledge the character of interpretation as a process of confrontation, mediation, channelling and concretisation of individual rights protected by statute. It acknowledges a few methodologies regarding the interpretation of the statute's wording and not the process by which courts weigh the different rights. The instrumentalist model is able to embrace the actual task of judicial interpretation by obliging courts to be transparent in their choices and policy priorities. It addresses the substance of interpretation itself, making the courts accountable for their policy choices, and explaining, for example, how and why the protection of sexual integrity and gender equality was to be prioritised over an out-dated view of marriage and the role of

148 R v Hamilton [2007] EWCA Crim 2026.
149 E. Claes, 'Legaliteit en rechtsvinding in het strafrecht', Universitaire Pers Leuven, 2003, p. 298.
150 C. Gearty, 'Principles of Human Rights Adjudication', Oxford University Press, 2004, p. 80.
151 E. Claes, 'Legaliteit en rechtsvinding in het strafrecht', Universitaire Pers Leuven, 2003, p. 298.

women. The process of legitimising the marital rape decision involves clarifying why and how far the prioritisation of competing policy choices respects utilitarian or communitarians goals of a society.

A personal judicial view on which societal good to prioritise can be easily hidden underneath grammatical interpretation. For example, in the marital rape case, the English court based its decision on the grammatical interpretation of the statutory term 'unlawful'. There were various possible outcomes. One was to take the literal interpretation of 'unlawful' as meaning outside of marriage, preserving the husband's immunity. Alternatively, the word could have been interpreted so as to leave intact the exceptions to immunity in previous case law and preserve future exceptions. Finally, the court could have openly accepted that the irrelevancy of this term, which would result that the husband's immunity was no longer consistent with the values of modern society. The court ultimately chose this final grammatical interpretation, stating that the term was redundant.[152]

In the instrumentalist model the legality principle would normally oblige English courts to explain why this prioritisation of values was a legitimate choice based on the communitarian or utilitarian policies. Thus, the advantage of the instrumentalist model, in contrast to the classical model, is that the legality principle controls judicial interpretation and the manner in which courts may arbitrarily apply their own views of what should be criminalised. In this context, such principle of legality can also be applied to jurisprudence, as an organism of law.[153]

Another advantage to the instrumentalist model is that it acknowledges a horizontal dimension of individual autonomy.[154] As explained in Chapter III, individual autonomy is also interpreted in a horizontal manner.[155] As criminal norms determine behavioural standards, courts are obliged to look specifically at how these norms function on a practical level. This makes the reasoning of the court transparent and thus accountable.

However, there are also significant problems with the instrumentalist model. First and foremost, the model gives little weight to the protective finality of criminal law in relation to the individual, which means that if the court bases its reasoning on the pursuit of utilitarian and communitarian goals, the individual is in a vulnerable position *vis-à-vis* arbitrary judicial decisions. The main hypothesis of the instrumentalist model, that criminal law is legitimised only through the pursuit of utilitarian and communitarian goals. This is clearly open to criticism, as the question arises of whether such a model can be reconciled with human dignity and individual autonomy.

As explained, there is room in a communitarian theory for individual autonomy. However, individual autonomy is not always sacrosanct within the instrumentalist

152 R v R [1992] 1 AC 599.

153 E. Claes, 'Legaliteit en rechtsvinding in het strafrecht', Universitaire Pers Leuven, 2003, pp. 300–301.

154 Ibid., p. 300.

155 Chapter III para. 2.

model, particularly the negative dimension of individual autonomy (the protection from state arbitrariness). Prioritising instrumental aims does not automatically entail that individual autonomy is also protected. One cannot assume that individual autonomy is always guaranteed when society is safe, secure and more prosperous. Quite the contrary, such a criminal justice system is at the mercy of the utilitarian and communitarian objectives of the state. Moreover, such criminal law does not in itself have any inherent protective value. It becomes neutral and subordinate to those objectives.

These disadvantages are less evident if one gives such an interpretation to this model whereby foreseeability is safeguarded because it promotes effectiveness. As mentioned, it has been argued that foreseeable criminalisation maintains the effectiveness of punishment through deterrence. This model may become more defendable and plausible in this way. Yet, this justification of foreseeability can be always revisited. If the protection of individual autonomy is not an inherent justification to the system, then the link between foreseeability and effectiveness can be challenged. It could be argued for example that in a specific situation (e.g. terrorism or computer crime) vague norms make the system more effective than clear norms. While protection of individual autonomy is not necessarily de-prioritised in this interpretation of the model, it is not assured completely either.

The instrumentalist model can therefore endanger individual autonomy and human dignity. It is not hard to imagine extreme instrumentalism, a topic popular in contemporary art. Popular films and books such as V for Vendetta, Children of Men and the Hunger Games depict fictitious societies in which basic standards of human rights, such as the right to life, privacy, or freedom of expression are set aside for the purpose of combating crime, disease or social control. However, there are equivalent real-world examples, in the fields of economics, crime-prevention and terrorism. Newer legislation for combating tax fraud in Greece, for example, is openly retroactive.[156] Its sole purpose was to increase state-income and to meet international financial obligations. No matter how legitimate these goals may be, criminal norms cannot be truly regarded as legitimate purely as a result of their instrumental aims. They must also seek to preserve individual autonomy and human dignity.

One may argue that individual autonomy is protected horizontally, as the instrumentalist model's central aim in the criminal context is to reduce crime, thus protecting citizens from harm inflicted upon each other. However, prioritising this goal increases state control over society.[157] What is more, the instrumentalist model can be paternalistic, as it seeks to educate individuals about what is best for them.[158] Thus, a model for legitimising criminal law where instrumental goals are central

156 M. Καϊάφα-Γκμπάντι, 'Οι επιλογές του Ν 3943/2011 για την οριοθέτηση του αξιοποίνου των φορολογικών αδικημάτων: Μια ατυχής προσπάθεια αυξημένης προστασίας των περιουσιακών απαιτήσεων του δημοσίου', Ποινική Δικαιοσύνη, vol. 12, 2011, pp. 1307–1320.

157 E. Claes, 'Legaliteit en rechtsvinding in het strafrecht', Universitaire Pers Leuven, 2003, p. 369.

158 Ibid.

and civil order is prioritised over the rights of the individual cannot be defended as legitimate.

The second problem rests with the process of judicial interpretation itself. It was explained that that one of the flaws of the classical model is that it fails to properly appreciate the complexities of judicial interpretation. The classical model approaches interpretation as a *legisme* process, whereas it has a *hermeneutic* character. While the instrumentalist model is closer to the reality of judicial interpretation, it fails to appreciate the value of consistency.[159] Whereas there is value ensuring that legal norms are of practical use rather than simply theoretical constructs, the intuitive, empirical and ultimately casuistic development of jurisprudence in the instrumentalist model is still problematic.[160]

Is there any room for *stare decisis* within the instrumentalist model's legality principle, in order to achieve a greater level of consistency? By consistency in interpretation, one refers to an obligation for courts to interpret a norm by formulating guidance for its application, which can be used as a framework for interpreting prior and future cases. It is interesting to see that there is a form of *stare decisis* even in continental systems, albeit not institutionalised, structured or binding as with common law systems.

In fact, courts in the continent have been trying to formulate guiding theories regarding *in concreto* application of norms to facts in cases concerning conflict of rights. This occurs more frequently in the interpretation of general norms, which are usually more prone to casuistry due to their inherent abstractness and situational approach. Due to their abstract nature, constitutive elements of criminal liability are often victims of casuistry, for example the concept of attempt.[161] Consistency entails that courts consider first, *in abstracto,* which rights are engaged, then the hierarchy of these rights, and finally their application *in concreto*.[162] However, neither the instrumentalist nor the classical model promotes the idea of consistency in jurisprudence. The instrumentalist model focuses more on the situational approach in judicial interpretation, while the classical model does not recognise any need for consistency in judicial interpretation.

To conclude, the instrumentalist model explains the *modus operandi* of the legality principle in current practice, but it is not a satisfactory model for criminal justice. It is difficult to reconcile with the Rule of Law, and the principles of individual autonomy and dignity. Some of the requirements of the legality principle in this model may violate the neutrality inherent in the Rule of Law, for example the educative effect of judicial interpretation. The model may also violate the principle of democracy. While in legal practice statutory limits are regularly tested, the

---

159 C.P.M. Cleiren, 'Evolueren naar meer horizontale en multi-dimensionale verhoudingen in het strafrecht', Kluwer, 2010, pp. 28–29.

160 Ibid., pp. 22–23.

161 K. Rozemond, 'De casuïstische grenzen van het materiële strafrecht', Delikt en Delinkwent, vol. 36, 2007, p. 465.

162 W. Sax, 'Das Strafrechtliche "Analogieverbot"', Vandenhoeck & Ruprecht, 1953, p. 47.

instrumentalist model does not provide clear guidance regarding judicial interpretation of norms. What is more, the instrumentalist model's minimalist approach towards the protection of individual autonomy may leave criminal law an 'empty vessel' devoid of moral substance, a tool for policy aims with no guarantee that human dignity will not be harmed.

6. The relational model of criminal justice

The relational model offers an alternative basis for the legitimacy of criminal law. Contrary to the previous models, it starts from the presumption that both instrumental and protective finalities legitimise criminal law. Legitimate criminal law balances both instrumental and protective aims. This model does not prioritise one goal over and above the other but it incorporates both, focusing on their relationship and interaction.

6.1. Main characteristics and theoretical rationales

Individual autonomy in this model is approached as a moral and ethical element of human dignity. Individual autonomy is an intrinsic part of self-determination: *'self confident demand for legal recognition as a self determined subject who 'lives, feels, and acts in accordance with his or her own judgement'*.[163] While individuals have a right to make choices regarding their own lives, individual autonomy means *'the capacity of every person to act under minimal conditions of confidence, which comes down to the capacity of every person to discover in the rules of law a minimal regulatory force with regard to her own conduct and those of others.'*[164] Individuals are entitled to self-determination within the framework of a well-regulated society. Basing the concept of individual autonomy on the value of human dignity means that the legitimacy of criminal law is based on a distinct and autonomous element: the protection and respect of the human dignity of autonomous citizens.

The pursuit of a private life, respected by the state, is influenced by personal interests; the ability of individuals to take responsibility for their own lives, pursue personal choice and life projects. However, every person is also obliged to respect societal values, which are important for the protection of the individual.[165]

Upon this understanding of individual autonomy and human dignity, it is clear that the relational model regards such autonomy as entailing both positive and negative aspects. Individuals should be protected from interventions into their

163 J. Habermas, 'The Concept of Human Dignity and the Realistic Utopia of Human Rights', in 'The Crisis of the European Union – A Response', Polity Press, 2012, p. 86.

164 E. Claes, 'Criminal Justice, Legality and Human Dignity', in E. Claes, R. Foqué, T. Peters (eds), 'Punishment, Restorative Justice and the Morality of Law', Intersentia, 2005, p. 41.

165 E. Claes, 'Legaliteit en rechtsvinding in het strafrecht', Universitaire Pers Leuven, 2003, p. 371.

individual autonomy (negative liberty), but should also be able to exercise their autonomy within society (positive expression). Moreover, the protection of individual autonomy is understood both in its vertical and horizontal dimension. Individual autonomy conflicts both with the state (vertical) but also with other peoples' individual autonomy (horizontal).[166] Respect of individual autonomy obliges the state to both limit its action and to take action.

Accordingly, the Rule of Law and the democratic principle are neither completely formalistic nor totally substantive.[167] The Rule of Law does not only generate formal requirements regarding the use of the *ius puniendi,* but also requires substantive *'principles of good governance which transcend the supremacy of majority rule'*.[168] Thus, the difference here from the instrumentalist model is that adherence to the Rule of Law does not stem from communitarian or utilitarian goals, but from principles of justice.[169] This model is also different from the classical model, as it embraces some substantive elements of the Rule of Law. Democracy is also approached in a more substantive sense, emphasising not only procedures, but also political autonomy, understood as involving *'the participation of every citizen in decisions which foster and embody a collective sense of justice, founded on open debate and full deliberation'*.[170]

This view of democracy and the Rule of Law differs from a procedural approach, in that it provides some room for substantive elements, which are found on principles of justice and individual rights as envisaged within a constitutional framework. This approach ensures strong protection of individual autonomy, and more objective standards than the instrumentalist model. Thus, it is more in line with the principle of democratic neutrality, so vital in a liberal conception of the Rule of Law. However, in comparison with the classical model, neutrality and liberalism are not absolute in the relational model.

The *trias politica* have distinct functions while keeping each other in check. Thus the concept of separation of powers translates as a system of 'checks and balances,' of 'equilibrium of powers' or of a 'balanced constitution'. Unlike the classical model where a stricter separation of powers is observed, the relational model is more consistent with Montesquieu's normative framework and current constitutional reality, as it assumes that legislatures might disregard basic rights.[171] Preventing a centralisation of power in one of the three arms of government is vital to avoid the creation of a totalitarian regime. Courts are not only potential culprits of arbitrariness, but also guarantors against it within the legal order.

---

166 Chapter III para. 2.2.

167 Chapter III para. 5.

168 T.R.S. Allan, 'Fairness, Equality, Rationality: Constitutional Theory and Judicial Review', in C.F. Forsyth and I. Hare (eds), 'The Golden Metwand and the Crooked Cord', Oxford University Press, 1998, p. 15.

169 Ibid., pp. 16–17.

170 Ibid., p. 19.

171 Chapter III para. 4.

Thus, in the relational model, the legislator remains the most appropriate body for the creation of criminal norms. Because of the mixed approach towards the democratic principle, democratic legitimacy emphasises fair process and procedure, but also for decisions to respect constitutional rights. To this extent, the legislator is not free to pursue any political goals – as in the instrumentalist model – but he is obliged to ensure that policy aims adhere to existing individual rights, as political choices are integral elements of the legal order, becoming internalised through the legislative process.[172] Such consideration of substantive evaluation of the legislative work is not prevalent in the classical model, where legitimation is derived mainly from proper procedures.

On the other hand, courts are entitled, indeed obliged, to balance policies with individual rights in *ad hoc* cases when provisions are not clear or ambiguous.[173] This is the practical reality of modern courts. In fact, in the jurisdictions examined in Chapter IV courts have the power to observe the compatibility of statutes with human rights standards enshrined in domestic, regional and international legal instruments.

This equilibrium, as opposed to an absolute separation of powers, is a more appropriate way to respect the *ratio* of the separation of powers;[174] it is also a more accurate representation of the distinctive roles of the legislator and the courts.[175] Both the legislator and the court's distinctive tasks are sufficiently recognised, as the legislator is the acknowledged arm of the *trias politica* with a democratic mandate for creating criminal norms, while the courts concretise and apply those rules.

It is important to acknowledge that this model is a more realistic view of current institutional dynamics in all three national systems under discussion, as one of the flaws of the legality principle in the classical model is the reluctance to accept and also canalise the interpretive powers of courts, resulting in the risk of judicial arbitrariness.

As a consequence of the theoretical basis for the relational model, the protective and instrumental finalities of criminal law legitimise the *ius puniendi.* At the beginning of this Chapter it was stated that the question the legality principle is supposed to answer in the relational model is: how can criminal law combat crime (crime-control element) while not being applied arbitrarily (protection against arbitrariness) and how can criminal law shape society (society-shaping element) while maintaining stable and clear rules that allow individuals to make choices regarding their conduct (protection against uncertainty element)? Here this question can be refined, by looking at how the relational model interprets the protective and

---

172 E. Claes, 'Legaliteit en rechtsvinding in het strafrecht', Universitaire Pers Leuven, 2003, p. 460.

173 C.P.M. Cleiren, 'Evolueren naar meer horizontale en multi-dimensionale verhoudingen in het strafrecht', Kluwer, 2010, p. 27.

174 M.J. Borgers, 'De communicatieve strafrechter', in W.J.M. Voermans, M.J. Borgers, C.H. Sieburgh, 'Controverses rondom legaliteit en legitimatie', Kluwer, 2011, pp. 162–165.

175 Ibid., pp. 120–121.

instrumental finalities, as they are understood differently in comparison with the other two models.

In the classical model, the protective finality is understood as protection of individual from the state (vertical). Criminal law does not have an acknowledged instrumental aim and that does not play a pivotal role in its legitimacy. In the instrumentalist model, the instrumental finality is the main basis for the legitimacy of criminal law, and protection against state arbitrariness is important as a policy whenever deemed necessary in the light of utilitarian or communitarian goals. In the instrumentalist model, the protective finality is again interpreted as a vertical conflict, but it is subordinate to the instrumentalist function of criminal law.[176]

The relational model takes a different view. The instrumental finality is not understood as 'order' (*ordehandhaving*), but as 'order ruled by law' (*rechtshandhaving*), as not every order is an order ruled by *law*. It is important to remember that at the beginning of this Chapter two approaches to the instrumental finality were identified: the crime-control element, which is mainly focused on security and civil order (and therefore here there is an implicit categorisation of individuals into suspects and victims); and the society-shaping element, which relates to the function of criminal law as a means of shaping a specific society and mediating individual rights in horizontal conflicts.

In the relational model, the crime-control and society-shaping elements of the instrumental finality are read together. That does not mean that the desire of the state to maintain safety is not recognised. Conversely, any kind of utilitarian or communitarian goal or crime-prevention policy that might exist cannot be legitimate unless it canalises human interaction and the balancing of rights between individuals, maintaining the integrity of the legal order, legal values, and principles. In other words, the safety or security of the population is analogous to the concept of a 'social contract': individuals should be able to identify in criminal norms a mutual limitation of their individual autonomy reflecting basic principles and values of the legal order.[177] By interpreting the instrumental aim in this way, the relational model obliges the state to legitimise its policies by adhering to the social values and integrity of the legal order. Thus, the instrumental finality is controlled by *law*. This is why not every order is an order ruled by *law*.

Furthermore, while in the instrumentalist model the protective finality was subordinate to the instrumental finality; in the relational model the opposite is true: the instrumental finality is subordinate to the protective finality of criminal law.[178] Thus the protective finality in this model is superior.

In particular the protective finality entails: first, the protection of every individual from the state (vertical protection); second, the protection of every

176 E. Claes, 'Legaliteit en rechtsvinding in het strafrecht', Universitaire Pers Leuven, 2003, p. 421.
177 Ibid., pp. 422–425.
178 Ibid., p. 421.

individual from third parties (horizontal protection).[179] The protective finality in this model has a safeguarding function for individuals: individual autonomy is guaranteed by *law*. Such safeguards can only properly protect the individual if one recognises every limit upon individual autonomy as a 'legal relationship', which needs to governed and legitimised through *law*. Thus, criminal law finds its legitimacy in the protection of individual autonomy, both in its legal interaction with the state, and with third parties. The horizontal protection of individual autonomy is particularly important in the context of foreseeability.

In Chapter III, it was stated that a consequence of accepting individual autonomy and human dignity as the basis of criminal law is that legal certainty and foreseeability in the context of criminal justice are essential.[180] It was also explained that the classical model's requirement of maximum legal certainty was impossible to apply. In the instrumentalist model, legal certainty was interpreted as the efficient coordination of the legal order, which was also too limited.

Any approach to legal certainty within the relational model must have regard to the separation of powers and the democratic process. In the relational model, legal certainty is defined, not as maximum certainty or precision, but as a trust that the conditions under which individuals are brought together into a society shall be respected by the state.[181] This means that both the legislator and courts should enable individuals to rely on criminal norms. In criminal norms, individuals should find behavioural standards that will enable them to function with self-confidence and self-respect to their own choices. Furthermore, courts should ensure that such clarity is present in statutes, and is not diminished through judicial interpretation, endangering human dignity.

Within the concept of legal certainty, courts must balance the rights of the individual as outlined in the statute and interpret and apply the statute with reference to human dignity and the integrity of the legal order.[182] As seen Chapter III, legal certainty can also take the form of acceptability.[183] This entails an additional obligation for courts to make their reasoning transparent: individuals should trust that courts will explain how, in an *ad hoc* case, criminal statutes are applied and concretised, particularly with respect to their own individual rights as these are understood in horizontal relationships.

Acceptability requires some room for interpretation regarding the statute so that interpretation can be context-sensitive. This is different from the classical model, where the legitimacy of law does not depend to contextual elements. This means that in the relational model – and contrary to the classical model – maximum

179 J. Claessen, 'Misdaad en straf: een herbezinning op het strafrecht vanuit mystiek perspectief', Wolf Legal Publishers, 2010, p. 114.

180 Chapter III para. 2.2.

181 E. Claes, 'Legaliteit en rechtsvinding in het strafrecht', Universitaire Pers Leuven, 2003, p. 465.

182 Ibid.

183 Chapter III para. 6.1; E. Paunio, 'Beyond Predictability – Reflections on Legal Certainty and the Discourse Theory of Law in the EU Legal Order', German Law Journal, vol. 10, 2009, p. 1469.

predictability is not possible or desirable. Legal certainty must balance predictability and acceptability of criminal law. The nature of judicial adjudication involves inherent uncertainty. What is important is that judicial interpretation does not limit individuals from using the norms to guide their own behaviour and preserves their trust in the courts' ability to base their decisions on a proper balancing of rights. This interpretation of legal certainty entails the requirement of the reliability of legislation but also requires transparency in legal reasoning.

6.2. The legality principle is a 'principle'

As with the classical model, within the relational model there is room to make a distinction between principles, rules and policies. Such distinction is important in order to achieve legitimacy. Whereas for the classical model this distinction aims at safeguarding the independent role of principles, in the relational model there is an additional value. In particular, a distinction between these concepts allows for more transparent reasoning (by the legislator and courts).

Rules and principles may differ. Principles are usually more abstract in their formulation than rules, in that principles do not denote the legal consequences that follow automatically when the conditions provided are met.[184] This does not mean that rules are always extremely precise. On the contrary, criminal norms have an open texture in the sense that courts should be able to apply the norm in a variety of situations. The term 'object' in the criminal liability of theft has an open texture in that courts can concretise it as including a variety of items and substances. As legal principles tend to be more abstract than rules, they should also have a more open texture than rules.

The open texture of principles differs in that it does not mean that the text must be abstract; openness has nothing to do with regulating a specific situation in a detailed manner.[185] The open texture of principles means that they may be used in any context or situation as long as they are relevant.[186] Thus, the principle of proportionality regarding penal sanctions can be concretised only when one places it in the context of a particular offence. The open texture or indeterminacy of principles entails that, in the relational model, legal principles – and the legality principle – are counterfactual: *'the counterfactual concepts are neither purely factual nor purely idealistic, but a constant mediation between idealism and factuality'*.[187] In other words, it is important that principles are open to interpretation without though losing the substance of their *ratio*.

---

184 R. Dworkin, 'Taking Rights Seriously', Duckworth, 1977, p. 25.

185 Ibid., p. 387.

186 A.A.G. Peters, 'Het rechtskarakter van het strafrecht', Kluwer, 1972, pp. 13–14.

187 A free interpretation of '*de contrafaktische begrippen zijn louter feitelijk noch louter ideëel (en in zoverre dus ook contra-ideëel), maar een constant bemiddeling tussen idealiteit en feitelijkheid*' in A.C. 't Hart, 'Recht als schild van Perseus', Gouda Quint, 1991, p. 51.

This means that there is a further protective dimension of the legality principle: the legality principle must be a counterfactual principle in order to guarantee that criminal law will remain open and responsive to social development.[188]

> Legal concepts and principles are characterised by their counterfactual character. Together they constitute a well systematised basic formal structure. On the one hand, they are always in need of inculturation, interpretation and contextualisation. On the other hand, however, they could never be monopolised by any one of those particular concretisations. Because of their counterfactual character, legal concepts and principles always remain underdetermined. In a vital democracy, this under determinacy is a necessary condition for the mediating role a legal order has to play in facilitating and stabilising public debate.[189]

The legality principle would lose its protective function if it were to be interpreted as prohibiting courts from controlling the legislature, simply because it was interpreted in such a manner in the past.

Rules operate in an all-or-nothing fashion, either the rule is applied or not.[190] Principles, however, are weighed and balanced. Principles may have a more relative application when they clash with other principles or rules.[191] In the relational model, legality is also a steering principle of fundamental importance. It is not just one of the many principles that courts and legislators need to take under consideration when designing or applying criminal liability; this approach would make the principle of legality passive. As a multifunctional principle, it steers decision-making;[192] it *informs* interpretation.[193] It obliges state-actors to make decisions around criminal liability that adhere to the legality principle and values underpinning the legal order. When it is said that the legality principle legitimises the *ius puniendi,* what is meant is that it guides decision-making by the legislature and in courts: it provides the framework within which these decisions are made.

Distinguishing policies from rules and principles is imperative. Policy *'sets out a goal to be reached, generally an improvement in some economic, political or social feature of the community'.*[194] While in the instrumentalist model the principle of legality can be seen as a policy or a means to an end, in the relational model it is seen as a principle. It is a *'standard that is to be observed, not because it will advance or secure an economic, political or social situation deemed desirable, but*

188 J. Claessen, 'Misdaad en straf: een herbezinning op het strafrecht vanuit mystiek perspectief', Wolf Legal Publishers, 2010, p. 114.

189 R. Foqué, 'Criminal Justice in a Democracy: Towards a Relational Conception of Criminal Law and Punishment', Criminal Law and Philosophy, vol. 2, 2008, p. 220; R. Foqué, A.C. 't Hart, 'Instrumentaliteit en Rechtsbescherming', Gouda Quint, Kluwer, 1990, p. 129.

190 R. Dworkin, 'Taking Rights Seriously', Duckworth, 1977, pp. 24–26.

191 Ibid., pp. 26–28.

192 E. Claes, 'Legaliteit en rechtsvinding in het strafrecht', Universitaire Pers Leuven, 2003, pp. 397–398.

193 Chapter IV para. 10.1.4.

194 R. Dworkin, 'Taking Rights Seriously', Duckworth, 1977, pp. 24–26.

because it is a requirement of justice or fairness or some other dimension of morality'.[195] In the relational model, principles represent certain important values or ethical notions of the legal order; they are autonomous in their own right, not subservient to the common good as in the instrumentalist model. If the legality principle is removed, criminal law loses its legitimacy; this feature is shared between the classical and relational models. Both models approach principles as independent values and sources for legitimation. In the instrumentalist model though, policies represent the momentum of political opportunism. It is thus important for the protective function of the relational model that principles and policies remain distinct.

This distinction has two consequences: first the legality principle in the relational model is not a policy or a means to an end; second, as a steering and inclusive principle, one must distinguish between principles and individuals rights which impart internal ethical integrity to the legal order, from policies. It is important to make clear in its application that legality is not *itself* weighed with other principle/policies, but it involves weighing other rights or policies in it is application. Finally, the legality principle gives *priority* to legal principles/human rights, as these underpin the legal order and protect human dignity. This function is not absolute, but it is the starting point (or better a rebuttable presumption) upon which legality operates in the relational model.[196]

6.3. Application of the legality principle

What does the legality entail in a relational model? First of all, courts cannot create criminal liability. The relational model follows a substantive interpretation of the democratic principle, as well as the checks and balances approach of the separation of powers. However, this does not entail, as explained, that criminal law making powers can be attributed to the courts. *Lex parliamentaria* remains as a function of the legality principle in this model.

However, in the light of these two theoretical bases of the legality principle, although courts cannot create criminal liability, they can interpret the statute in specific cases. Thus, jurisprudence has to be acknowledged as a source of law, albeit not in a hierarchically equal position to the statute.[197] The openness and counterfactual characteristics of the legality principle in this model allow for problems of casuistry and foreseeability of jurisprudential interpretation to be addressed.[198]

---

195 Ibid.

196 E. Claes, 'Legaliteit en rechtsvinding in het strafrecht', Universitaire Pers Leuven, 2003, pp. 408–409.

197 M. Delmas-Marty, 'Towards a Truly Common Law: Europe as a Laboratory for Legal Pluralism', Cambridge University Press, 2002, p. 52.

198 M.J. Borgers, 'De communicatieve strafrechter', in W.J.M. Voermans, M.J. Borgers, C.H. Sieburgh, 'Controverses rondom legaliteit en legitimatie', Kluwer, 2011, pp. 132–138.

The second consequence concerns the consistency of jurisprudence or *lex methodologica,* which obliges courts to ensure that the interpretation of a provision shall be consistent in prior and future cases preventing arbitrariness, casuistry and unforeseeable criminalisation. This obligation is fulfilled when courts, during judicial interpretation, are able to balance the interests *in abstracto* before they translate them *in concreto*. This means that the court should first consider how the conflicting rights are balanced within this norm, a part of the reasoning that can be repeated and used in future cases to prevent casuistry.[199] Thus, there is an obligation of the courts to create type of theoretical approach, a *ratio decidendi* to the conflicting interests engaged by a norm, before this is applied to the *ad hoc* facts. Perhaps, one could even understand this as an unofficial form of *stare decisis,* where courts are able to follow prior jurisprudence with consistency and individuals can be informed on the way the norms are theoretically interpreted.

Legal certainty does not entail that the legislator must prescribe criminal liability with maximum precision. What is important is that the norm should outline at least a behavioural standard on which individuals may rely. Foreseeability is interpreted as the ability of individuals to rely on the law and anticipate penal sanctions, and as a mutual trust in institutions to maintain in their decisions the integrity of the legal order (legal certainty as acceptability). This also entails that context-sensitivity must be preserved; precision depends on the norm-addressees, the character of the offence and the circumstances of the case.

As norms guide behaviour, it is important that those norms are accessible. The legislator must also legitimise whatever utilitarian or communitarian policies are being pursued with the legal principles and other rights that underpin the legal order. In order for rules to be foreseeable (and acceptable), precision is not the only virtue, as words are open to interpretation. Language in criminal provisions is aimed at the layman, and individuals tend to give their own interpretation to norms in the context of accepted societal values.[200] Criminal liability reflects the balance of such values, which individuals would expect to read into criminal norms.[201] Foreseeability in the relational model therefore includes a horizontal dimension: individuals should foresee criminal liability based on the wording of the statute, as it would be expected to operate in the current community.[202]

One of the problems of the classical model was that it was difficult to reconcile the judicial control of the compatibility of legislation with the *lex certa*.[203] Here this

---

199 C.P.M. Cleiren, 'Evolueren naar meer horizontale en multi-dimensionale verhoudingen in het strafrecht', Kluwer, 2010, pp. 28–29.

200 H. Satzger, 'Die Internationalisierung des Strafrechts als Herausforderung für den strafrechtlichen Bestimmtheitsgrundsatz', JuS, 2004, p. 943; Beck'scher Onlinekommentar zum StGB, von Heintschel-Heinegg, 2011, para. 1, Mn 10.

201 M.J. Borgers, 'De communicatieve strafrechter', in W.J.M. Voermans, M.J. Borgers, C.H. Sieburgh, 'Controverses rondom legaliteit en legitimatie', Kluwer, 2011, pp. 152–154.

202 K. Rozemond, 'Legaliteit in het materiële strafrecht', RM Themis, 1999, p. 125.

203 M.J. Borgers, 'De communicatieve strafrechter', in W.J.M. Voermans, M.J. Borgers, C.H. Sieburgh, 'Controverses rondom legaliteit en legitimatie', Kluwer, 2011, p. 120.

problem does not exist. The legality principle in the relational model does not oblige the legislator to limit excessively the possibility of interpretation. On the contrary, it obliges courts to take into consideration the reliability of the law.

For the interpretation of criminal norms, the relational model is able to address problems of judicial interpretation in its substance. The main characteristic here is the requirement of transparency, which entails that individuals should be able to observe in the reasoning of the court a balancing of interests, legal principles and policies that correspond to the values of the community.[204] Courts must communicate their reasoning to individuals.[205] Similarly, the element of controllability entails that transparency in court reasoning shall give individuals the opportunity to control whether the courts interpreted the statute correctly, how courts weighed and prioritised the individual rights and legal interests involved – and thus maintain a trust in courts and the state.[206] In other words, courts should ensure that their legal reasoning is open and transparent so that the individual is able to maintain a trust in the legal order and regard the decision as legitimate.

Claes, in this respect, has created certain guidelines for judicial interpretation and adjudication in the relational model. First, the requirement of translation, which entails that the court should translate and reconstruct the wording of a statute into distinct policies, legal values and principles. Second, the court should respect the ethical minimum of the legal order (for example, such ethical minimum would be to give an interpretation to the norm that respects its reliability). Third, courts should attempt to reconcile and balance legal principles and values. Fourth, the courts should attempt to connect these principles with other principles of the legal order. Fifth, if it is necessary courts should balance those rights and values in the best possible theoretical framework. Finally, courts should apply this framework by examining individual concretised rights and in this context the court should give priority to legal principles over the policy goals.[207]

In the relational model, guidelines and methods are different. As seen in the classical model, the legality principle generates only methods of judicial interpretation, which do not, however, help much in limiting judicial arbitrariness. Methods in the relational model are considered 'rules of thumb' which give an idea to courts as to how to approach the statute. Guidelines determine substantive interpretation and reasoning.[208]

Retroactivity is strictly prohibited in the relational model, which raises interesting issues regarding the retroactivity of judicial interpretation. The fact that

---

204 C.P.M. Cleiren, 'Evolueren naar meer horizontale en multi-dimensionale verhoudingen in het strafrecht', Kluwer, 2010, pp. 28–29.

205 M.J. Borgers, 'De communicatieve strafrechter', in W.J.M. Voermans, M.J. Borgers, C.H. Sieburgh, 'Controverses rondom legaliteit en legitimatie', Kluwer, 2011, p. 152.

206 C.P.M. Cleiren, 'Evolueren naar meer horizontale en multi-dimensionale verhoudingen in het strafrecht', Kluwer, 2010, pp. 28–29.

207 E. Claes, 'Legaliteit en rechtsvinding in het strafrecht', Universitaire Pers Leuven, 2003, pp. 471 and 454–457.

208 Ibid., p. 478.

case law, in this model, is acknowledged as a source of criminal liability allows pondering on the application of *lex praevia* regarding case law. Can the legality principle in this model prohibit retroactivity in judicial interpretation?

In theory, if *lex stricta* and *lex scripta* – especially regarding the consistency of jurisprudence – function adequately, there is no need to protect individuals from judicial reasoning. Such reasoning, if foreseeable, would not be truly retroactive. However, one has to consider the possibility of courts giving an *ex ante* effect, an issue which has been addressed by national scholarship.[209] Prospective overruling has the danger of motivating the courts to hijack legislative functions.

If prospective overruling is necessary, the courts have not properly balanced the rights of individuals. If a court feels the need to exclude the current case from its interpretation, this means that the reasoning for such interpretation was purely instrumentalist and it did not assess the rights of individuals *in concreto.* If the court had done so, there would be no need to prevent its decision from applying in the present case. Should the court find that foreseeability was so inhibited by its interpretation that it should not capture the present case, this interpretation would not be legitimate.[210]

Therefore, prospective overruling is not line with the relational model. This is not because *lex praevia* cannot apply to court decisions, but because the judgement to which a prospective overruling effect would be attached would not be a legitimate interpretation in accordance with the *lex stricta.*

6.4. Criticism

After explaining the general features of this model, some critical remarks will be presented, followed by the conclusion to this Chapter. Generally speaking, the relational model presents certain disadvantages, especially with regard to the classical model. By definition the legality principle in this model is less formalistic. If legitimacy depends also on substantive elements (so which rights and how are prioritised), then it is not always possible to discern in advance how the legality principle will be applied. Certainly, this has been promoted as an advantage of this model; however, the legality principle becomes a more complicated and less clear-cut doctrine. It is not always easy to define in advance whether the principle has been observed unless one analyses the case at hand.

The relational theory, as with all theories that incorporate into the legitimacy discourse a critic on substantive rights and morals, values liberalism to a lesser extent than the classical model. While human dignity functions as a safeguard

209 M.S. Groenhuijsen, 'Enkele aspecten van rechterlijk 'prospective overruling' in het straf(proces) recht', in M.S. Groenhuijsen, J.B.H.M. Simmelink (eds), 'Glijdende schalen' (Liber amicorum J. de Hullu), Wolf Legal Publishers, 2003, p. 186.

210 See for another option in M.J. Borgers, 'De communicatieve strafrechter', in W.J.M. Voermans, M.J. Borgers, C.H. Sieburgh, 'Controverses rondom legaliteit en legitimatie', Kluwer, 2011, p. 151 (footnote 176).

against instrumental arguments (and foreseeability is incorporated in the concept of human dignity), a legitimacy of criminal law that stems also from its horizontal dimension may restrict liberal rights. One could argue that the relational model of criminal justice does not bring any noticeable and distinct solutions to the question of how to solve hard cases. However, as explained below, this is counterbalanced by providing at least a legitimate framework for judicial discourse. In addition, any theory that accepts individual rights as a part of the question of legitimacy may meet the criticism of possible instrumentalisation or moralisation of criminal law.[211] It is not always possible to separate judicial interpretation from the political background noise of a society. Furthermore, legal certainty, understood as predictability, is counterbalanced with acceptability in this model. Evidently, one may criticise this feature of the relational model. The fear is that by embracing the increasing role of courts and the occasional abstractness of legislation as a value of the system (under certain conditions as explained), this might pose the threat of abuse and covert instrumentalism. Thus, the crux of the matter is the extent to which the relational model shelters criminal justice from instrumentalism.

Having said that, the relational model seems to generate a legality principle that is not only consistent with current constitutional dialogue, theoretical rationales and tendencies in the practical *modus operandi* of the principle, but also helps to resolve some problems faced by national jurisdictions. In essence, the relational model of criminal justice does relate to practical legal realities, but it could also be a much more desirable and defendable model of justice than the classical and instrumentalist models.

First of all, the legality principle retains the superiority of the statute in line with the democratic principle, but in the same time recognises case law as a source of law, which allows the legality principle to address further the demands of transparency in jurisprudential development. The *lex methodologica* does not necessarily entail that courts create or expand criminal liability, it aims to control the way the law is interpreted by courts through time and ensures that there is a 'perceptive line of case law'. It obliges courts to approach their judgement as a source of law, and thus make sure that their interpretation of the statute remains stable, as part of a body of jurisprudence, avoiding casuistry.

The *lex certa* on the other hand is not burdened with unclear criteria of precision and – while not maximum – courts and legislators must ensure that provisions are constructed so that individuals can obtain guidance from them in terms of their conduct. *Lex stricta* on the other hand offers much needed transparency regarding the reasoning of judgements. Courts take into account various considerations in their interpretation and application of the law, such as the individual rights involved, the will of the legislator, current policies and political agenda. Their decisions could be instrumentally motivated or not

---

211 M. Delmas-Marty, 'Towards a Truly Common Law: Europe as a Laboratory for Legal Pluralism', Cambridge University Press, 2002, pp. 125–128.

depending on whether the judges themselves are 'rule-conscious' or 'purpose-oriented'. Because the inherent character of criminal law is both instrumental and protective, courts are obliged to employ only legitimate instrumental or protective reasoning. Transparency is a significant barrier against arbitrariness because it exposes judicial reasoning – and any influence of underlying constitutional principles – to the public eye. Tamanaha, who has vigorously criticised the increasing influence of instrumentalism on the law, outlines a scenario where two judges decide on the same case and reach the same conclusion: the first judge is a rule-bound judge and convicts the accused on the sole application of the law alone.[212] The second judge is a purpose-oriented judge, who reaches the same conclusion due to the prioritisation of certain policies he values. These two judgements, despite having the same result, are not equally legitimate.[213]

Perhaps, the most important contribution of the relational model in the debate of legitimacy is that it forces state-actors to consider every single principle, policy, value or argument they use in creating or applying criminal liability, within the context of political/individual autonomy, human dignity and the integrity of the legal order. This is an important advantage compared to both the classical and instrumentalist models. The classical model is oblivious to this necessity, while the instrumentalist model lacks guarantees. The relational model therefore obliges the state to abandon opportunism and properly legitimise criminal law.

One may criticise the fact that the protection of individuals translates as protection of potential victims from perpetrators, and therefore the traditional understanding of criminal law as a shield from state arbitrariness is relativised. However, this feature has also an important advantage: the relational model at least controls the conflict between the vertical and horizontal dimensions. In the classical model, every time protective and instrumental aims clash (so with almost every challenging case), the balance and how the courts or the legislator choose to solve the conflict is outside the protective concept of *law*. The classical model does not provide adequate help for legitimising the mediation between those two finalities. The relational model balances both aims, aligning them within the legal order. If arbitrariness is to be restricted, it is important to confront the conflict between the two finalities of criminal law.

Finally, it is important to remember that these models are merely abstract formulations that do not represent reality per se. None of the three models is ideal or practically operational without difficulties. Whereas the relational model is a more defendable option, it also presents challenges as demonstrated above. In the end, the benefit in providing a theoretical framework for a criminal justice system is that one may recognise the value choices made with the legality principle.

---

212 B.Z. Tamanaha, 'Law as a Means to an End', Cambridge University Press, 2006, p. 242.

213 Ibid.

7. Conclusion

In this Chapter, the aim was to find a model of justice that may solve the current problems that the legality principle faces, but that also reflects a legitimacy of criminal law, which is desirable and defendable. Dealing with these models of justice on a macro level was necessary since the current status quo of the legality principle in national law showed that the principle faces significant problems in its application. It was therefore necessary to take a step back and consider the existing choices regarding the role of this principle.

Three models of criminal justice were discussed, all of which are based on broader theories regarding the nature of law. The classical and instrumentalist models are not in line with modern constitutional thought. The classical model does not reflect current practice and cannot protect adequately against all forms of arbitrariness. The instrumentalist model can reflect current practice but it fails to protect against arbitrariness. The main problem with both of these models is that they are based on the assumption that only one of the finalities of criminal law can legitimise it. Criminal justice in the relational model is not legitimised by a choice between either of the two finalities. Rather, they complement each other and, thus, this model controls overt dominance of either finality. In essence, it is in the mediation and dialectic relationship of the two finalities where criminal law finds legitimacy.

A relational model does not only justify current practice, but is also a more constitutionally defendable model. Moreover, this model explains and solves certain problems; in other words, it prevents the legality principle from erosion. Such erosion can now be explained as a lack of counterfacticity, i.e. openness for development while maintaining its theoretical footing.[214]

In conclusion, the legality principle in the relational model is a steering, autonomous, counterfactual and open principle, which is made up of the following elements:

- *Lex parliamentaria:* the statute remains the sole source that can create criminal liability, but case law is recognised as source of law that can clarify and help define concepts of criminal liability.
- *Lex methodologica:* Jurisprudence must develop with consistency and thus courts should first discuss conflicting interests *in abstracto,* so that facts will not taint the statutory interpretation and lead to casuistry.
- *Lex certa:* Statutes should provide a behavioural standard for individuals. Foreseeability is defined as accessibility, the ability of citizens to rely on, be guided by, and accept the law, especially with regard to judicial interpretation.
- *Lex praevia*: retroactivity of the law is prohibited.

---

214 Chapter IV para. 10.

- *Lex stricta*: interpretation of statutes should take place in accordance with specific guidelines, which aim to provide transparency and controllability as to which principles, policies and rights influence the courts and how these are weighed (a *lex transparentia).* Individual rights should always been given priority over public policies.

With this Chapter, Part 2 comes to an end. As explained before, this Part aimed to investigate the common elements of the principle of legality in the national cultures. Part 2 started with an analysis of the *ratio* of the principle and its different possible interpretations; the conclusions indicate that these principles are capable of different interpretations. Deeper analysis also showed that certain concepts, such as the Rule of Law, are constantly evolving and are open to change. It is important to keep in mind the openness of such concepts, as this will play a role in EU law.[215] Theories on the role and definition of state, its proper function and its relationship with individuals, are not closed doctrines.

The national application of the legality principle was observed from a comparative and problem-based point of view. A general conclusion from this analysis is that the principle of legality is also not a closed doctrine. It has been applied in common law and in continental systems, albeit in different ways. The ECtHR's 'rights-conception' has greatly influenced national and international conceptions of the principle. However, the legality principle in national systems seems to be evolving. Various deficiencies and inconsistencies were identified that precluded a national comparative analysis from generating a coherent theory on legality. The problems explained were not so much related to differences between systems, but to deeper deficiencies regarding the theoretical basis for the legitimacy of criminal law.

Finally, the results of the comparative research were put into the perspective of three models of criminal justice. In searching for a criminal justice model, different theories on legitimacy were visited. The conclusion of this analysis was that the model that best reflects modern constitutional thinking (protecting individuals from vertical and horizontal arbitrariness, and acknowledging the courts' role in checking the power of the legislature while remaining democratic) is the relational model, which combines both instrumental and classical aims. It provides a framework that can preserve the *ratio* of the principle and yet provide remedies for its appropriate function.

215 Chapter VII para. 1 and 8.

Part 3

The Principle of Legality in European Criminal Law

Chapter VI
Fragments of the Legality Principle in European Criminal Law

Part 3 is dedicated to the analysis of the application of the legality principle in European criminal law and it is structured as follows. In this Chapter, the status quo of the principle of legality is examined. Its purpose is to identify the features of this principle in European criminal law and the lacunae and problems associated with it. In Chapter VII, the identified problems are examined from the general perspective of the European criminal justice system. The challenges legitimising such a system are analysed and a relational model of European criminal justice is proposed. In Chapter VIII, the principle of legality in European criminal law is revisited and reconstructed.

In this Chapter an inventory of the features of the legality principle in European criminal law is presented. The approach is similar to Chapter IV, as the aim is to observe the problems and lacunae of its application; in other words, the *modus operandi* of the principle of legality in EU law. The fragments of this principle in EU law are collected and mapped with reference to its different aspects in order to gain some perspective in a manner equivalent to the national legality principle. First, with regard to the *lex scripta* element, the sources of European criminal liability will be the focus, especially with respect to statutes and jurisprudence. In investigating *lex praevia* the focus is on its theoretical rationale, its application and specifically in curtailing the retroactivity of criminal liability. For *lex certa* the problem of predictability and accessibility of criminalisation is addressed. Finally, for *lex stricta* the question is whether there are any rules, principles or methods to guide judicial interpretation in European criminal law. Because the European criminal justice system functions at two levels, the application of these aspects is examined on both levels. As described below, the interaction of the European and national legal orders raises further questions regarding the distributive role of the legality principle and the obligation stemming from this principle for national and European authorities.

Furthermore, a problem-based approach is followed for each element in order to identify the problems, inconsistencies and lacunae associated with the legality principle. As explained below, this principle is applied in a fragmented manner. Its various aspects have emerged judicially, incrementally and reflectively. To some extent, the ECJ has developed the legality principle in a common law manner. In particular, the Court identifies the application of its aspects on an *ad hoc* basis, reflecting the problems that arise. Such an approach causes not only fragmentation but also lacunae. Thus, specific competition law cases are also considered. The punitive character of competition law has attracted the application of many substantive and procedural criminal law principles, including the legality principle. The questions raised in this Chapter shall be answered in the last two Chapters.

1. The status of the principle of legality

The principle of legality has been developed mainly as a general principle of EU law. It has been codified in Article 49 of the Charter and Article 7 ECHR and the jurisprudence of the ECtHR have been cited as its source by the ECJ. In particular, as it will be demonstrated in this Chapter, the ECJ has incorporated the ECtHR's approach on the legality principle. This 'rights-conception' approach can be located throughout the ECJ's case law.[1]

As a general principle of EU law, the principle of legality emerged from the ECJ judgements of the 1980s.[2] The Treaties contain codified principles or values related to the principle of legality, such as human dignity, freedom, democracy, equality, the Rule of Law and justice (Article 2 TEU). Obviously, the principle of legality falls under the doctrine of the Rule of Law, because the legal certainty principle is an indispensable requirement of a polity governed by the Rule of Law.[3] As explained in Chapter II, the general principles of EU law emerge from national constitutional traditions, the ECtHR's jurisprudence and other international conventions.[4] Consequently, owning to its character as a general principle of EU law and the pivotal influence that the ECHR has played in the development of general principles, the principle of legality in EU law is bound to be built upon the pattern of the ECtHR's 'rights-conception' approach. As was also stated in Chapter II, general principles of EU law have a tripartite function; they are an aid to interpreting the law, grounds for the review of European and national implementation acts, and breach of these can establish a claim of liability for damages.[5]

When used as an interpretational tool, the legality principle generates specific requirements guiding national and European authorities. This principle may define the obligations of Member States during implementation and guide the interpretation of European and national instruments. For example, in *Fedesa*, a Regulation was drafted with a retroactive implementation period. The ECJ concluded that the Regulation could not be interpreted in a manner requiring Member States to apply it retroactively.[6] As a ground for review, the violation of the principle of legality can theoretically result in the annulment of a European act.[7] Because there is no directly enforceable system in criminal law, its application as a ground for review of European legislation is currently restricted. As a ground for

1 Chapter IV para. 9.1.
2 Case 80/86 criminal proceedings against Kolpinghuis Nijmegen BV, 8 October 1987.
3 W. van Gerven, 'The European Union – A Polity of States and Peoples', Hart Publishing, 2005, pp. 137–153.
4 Chapter II para. 1.
5 T. Tridimas, 'The General Principles of EU law', Oxford University Press, 2006, pp. 29–35.
6 Case 331/88 The Queen v Minister of Agriculture, Fisheries and Food and Secretary of State for Health, ex parte: Fedesa and others, 13 November 1990, para. 44.
7 C–303/05 Advocaten voor de Wereld VZW v Leden van de Ministerraad, 3 May 2007.

review, it may also be used for infringement proceedings, namely the proceedings against a Member State that fails to fulfil its obligations. Although there is no precedent in the criminal law field, the principle of legal certainty has been used as a guiding principle for implementation in other legal areas.[8]

The principle of legality evolved mainly within the category of other general principles of EU law and particularly the principle of legal certainty. The principle of legal certainty expresses the idea that *'rules should be clear and precise, so that individuals may ascertain unequivocally what their rights and obligations are and may take steps accordingly'*.[9] It is applied in all fields of law and its context is rather vague as it rarely generates specific guidelines. Therefore, it should always be specified in *ad hoc* cases.[10] The legal certainty principle in EU law, as in national law, can have antithetical goals. In criminal law, legal certainty can support the rights of the perpetrator and the administration of justice.[11] In EU law, similar conclusions can be drawn. For example, the principle has been used not only to limit the indirect effect of Directives against individuals,[12] but also as a criterion for the effective implementation of EU law. The ECJ has determined that the principle of legality is a special application of the principle of legal certainty in criminal law matters.[13]

Theoretically, all aspects of the principle of legality can be derived from the general notion of legal certainty. However, other theoretical bases of the principle of legality such as individual autonomy, democracy and Rule of Law have rarely been located in ECJ case law. Some exceptions can be found in competition law where the deterrent character of the fines is mentioned, but these are more closely connected to the applicability of a fine.[14] Therefore, the theoretical rationale of the legality principle in European criminal law is underdeveloped. This is a problem, because it is unclear what is protected by this principle in European criminal law.

2. Sources of Criminal Liability

What type of law can bear criminal liability in EU law? Can it only be the notion of *loi,* namely parliamentary statutes or also in the notion of *droit,* namely jurisprudence? In answering that question, this section addresses the *lex scripta*, specifically the statutory criminal liability, the jurisprudence in this field and the Nuremberg exception.

---

8 For example Case 300/81 Commission v Italy, 1 March 1983.

9 C–308/06 The Queen, on the application of International Association of Independent Tanker Owners (Intertanko) and Others v Secretary of State for Transport, 3 June 2008, para. 69.

10 T. Tridimas, 'The General Principles of EU law', Oxford University Press, 2006, pp. 243–244.

11 Chapter III para. 6.1.

12 Case 41/74 Yvonne van Duyn v Home Office, 4 December 1974.

13 Joined cases C–74/95 and C–129/95 criminal proceedings against X, 12 December 1996.

14 C–76/06 P Britannia Alloys & Chemicals Ltd v Commission of the European Communities, 7 June 2007.

Under Article 49 of the Charter, the principle of legality is presented as follows:

> 1. No one shall be held guilty of any criminal offence on account of any act or omission which did not constitute a criminal offence under national law or international law at the time when it was committed. Nor shall a heavier penalty be imposed than the one that was applicable at the time the criminal offence was committed. If, subsequent to the commission of a criminal offence, the law provides for a lighter penalty, that penalty shall be applicable; 2. This Article shall not prejudice the trial and punishment of any person for any act or omission which, at the time when it was committed, was criminal according to the general principles recognised by the community of nations.

The provision is nearly identical to Article 7 ECHR, wherein para. 2 includes the Nuremberg exception that allows for criminal prosecution based on commonly accepted principles. This exemplifies that the sources of criminal liability in EU law are approached in a manner similar to the ECtHR. In this regard, it is difficult to determine whether this is actually the case, because the application of the legality principle has been rather unclear.

2.1. Statutory criminal liability

Despite the Nuremberg exception in Article 49 of the Charter, there is a strong reservation for the European legislator relative to the prescription of criminal liability. This appears at the level of prescription of criminal liability by European bodies and the level of implementation by national authorities.

First, at the European level, Article 83 TFEU prescribes that criminal liability at the EU level can only occur in the form of a Directive issued by the European legislator. Ostensibly, a proper legal basis for European criminal law is based on Article 83 TFEU. However, this is not an undisputed claim. For example, before the Treaty of Lisbon, in *Commission v Council,* a case about the protection of the environment through criminal law, the ECJ declared that criminal liability could be based on Treaty provisions regarding environmental policy.[15] Currently, pursuant to Article 83 para. 2 TFEU, a proper criminal law base exists that allows the European legislator to employ criminal law as a tool to address other important criminal law policies. Despite this, a question emerges as to whether a constitutive element of a European legality should be the strict and legitimate use of European criminal law competences, because these are shared with national law. In other words, would it violate the principle of legality if the EU was to base criminal norms on Treaty provisions that do not prescribe criminal law competences? For constitutional law or European institutional law, that would be a violation of the Treaties. But for criminal law, that would be an illegitimate use of criminal law powers. The principle of legality is supposed to define what the legitimate source of criminal

---

15 C–176/03 Commission of the European Communities v Council of the European Union, 13 September 2005.

liability is and how to properly employ the *ius puniendi*. A further concern is about the manner in which existing competences are exercised. Because the European criminal justice system does not replace national systems and its competences are specific, one may wonder whether the legality principle should also guide the exercise of such competences.[16] Unlike national law, criminal law competences in European criminal law are restricted to specific areas. The question here is whether the exercise of the competences described in Article 83 TFEU should be further justified.

A second issue concerns the definition of the European legislator. In the co-decision procedure, the European legislator actually comprises two bodies – the Council of the EU and the European Parliament. Thus, a second issue involves the definition of the principle of democracy in European criminal law. To define the obligations of European legality, the theoretical rationale it supports must be understood.[17]

A third issue concerns the requirement of *lex scripta* in national implementing law. At the national level, the ECJ has determined that national criminal proceedings cannot be based solely on European rules; there must be a national rule establishing liability.[18] This is particularly the case for the direct effect of unimplemented or wrongly implemented Directives.[19] When the implementation period for a Directive expires and the national parliament fails to act, or does it incorrectly, the provisions of Directives gain direct effect in the national legal order.[20] However, this direct effect is granted only to citizens invoking rights from the Directive. In the criminal law setting, unimplemented Directives may not impose criminal liability to individuals because of the principle of legality. The ECJ in *Kolpinghuis* limited the direct effect in criminal law cases because of the principle of legality.[21] The Court decided that it would violate the principle of legality if the national criminal prosecution were based on a Directive that lacks a legal basis in the national legal order. More generally, the ECJ often refers to this application of the principle of legality as 'the principle that penalties must have a proper legal basis' and the proper legal basis required is a national legal basis.[22]

Such a legal basis is also needed when the national prosecution is based on a Regulation. While Regulations should not be implemented into national law, because they have a direct effect, the ECJ has held that a Regulation cannot form the basis of criminal liability without a national legal basis.[23] This holding should be followed by the national systems, irrespective of the obligations of the national legality principle. One may observe that the *lex scripta* in EU law approaches

---

16 See Chapter VIII para. 2.1.
17 See Chapter VII para. 7.2 and Chapter VIII para. 1.2.
18 C–224/09 criminal proceedings against Martha Nussbaumer, 7 October 2010.
19 A. Klip, 'European Criminal Law: An Integrative Approach', Intersentia, 2012, p. 190.
20 Case 41/74 Yvonne van Duyn v Home Office, 4 December 1974.
21 Case 80/86 criminal proceedings against Kolpinghuis Nijmegen BV, 8 October 1987.
22 C–457/02 criminal proceedings against Antonio Niselli, 11 November 2004.
23 C–60/02 criminal proceedings against X, 7 January 2004, para. 60–62.

criminal law-making as a co-operative process between the European and the national legislator. Within this legislative cooperation, the principle of legality seems to have a distributive role; criminal law-making must satisfy specific requirements at the European and national level. The question here is as follows: What types of requirements should the European legislator satisfy and which requirements should the national legislators satisfy?[24]

Regarding the requirements for the European legislator, one issue concerns whether criminal liability can be drafted into a Regulation via an extensive interpretation of other Treaty provisions such as Articles 86 or 325 TFEU. The answer to this question depends on a previously raised issue regarding European criminal law competences. Would it violate the legality principle if the European legislator were to exercise its competences *ultra vires*? While such a possibility would violate the Treaties, the legitimising function of the principle of legality could also be relevant in this case.

The European legality principle has been underdeveloped with regard to the requirements for the national legislator. In particular, there has been general guidance emerging from the ECJ case law regarding the quality of implementing legislation; however, because of the lack of jurisdiction in infringement proceedings until the end of 2014, the ECJ was unable to make this guidance more concrete in the criminal law context. Current general guidelines have emerged from infringement proceedings in non-criminal law areas. For example, the ECJ has noted that a given practice by the administration or a jurisprudential doctrine does not suffice as an implementation, stating: *'[C]ase-law established by national courts cannot be a substitute for implementing provisions'*.[25] The legality principle cannot be met *'even where the settled case-law of a Member State interprets the provision of national law in a manner deemed to satisfy the requirements of a Directive'*.[26]

Another related issue is why a European legality would intervene in the national implementation process. The immediate answer comes from the status of the principle in EU law. The legality principle, as a general principle of EU law, binds not only European bodies but also national authorities when they implement, apply or enforce European rules. However, this does not suffice as a rationale for the national application of the European legality principle, because it is an answer based on a systemic structure rather than a theoretical rationale. It is analogous to pronouncing that the national *lex stricta* principle applies to national courts, because the principle of legality has a constitutional bearing and constitutional norms bind courts. This is an inadequate justification for why the legality principle functions in a particular manner. The normative function of the principle of legality

---

24 See Chapter VIII para. 2.2.

25 C–233/00 Commission of the European Communities v French Republic, 27 June 2003, para. 44.

26 C–144/99 Commission of the European Communities v Kingdom of the Netherlands, 10 May 2011, para. 21. See for more case law and comments on this issue in F.G.H Kristen, 'Misbruik van voorwetenschap naar Europees recht', Wolf Legal Publishers, 2004, p. 41.

must stem from its theoretical rationales and a theory of legitimacy. Thus, another pivotal issue is the theoretical rationale for applying a European legality principle to national state-actors. This justification could be manifold. For example, one argument could be that this aspect is supported by the desire to oblige national authorities to provide effective national implementation rules for the effective enforcement of EU law. Arguably, it also involves the desire of the European legal system to protect individuals from arbitrary prosecutions on the basis of abstract national laws.[27]

2.2. Jurisprudence and criminal liability

Although the legality principle in EU law seemingly supports the concept of *loi* as the source for criminal liability, this view is not applied consistently in all cases, especially in the case of jurisprudence. The jurisprudence of the ECJ can determine the content of rules to such an extent that it falls short of a 'common law approach'.

This is especially the case in competition law. The liability for competition law infringements is enunciated in Articles 101 and 102 TFEU. These provisions contain the definition of behaviours that disturb competition. Because the prohibited acts are vaguely formulated, there are problems in application. This issue is discussed in detail below. This indeterminacy has resulted in a wider role for the Commission and the ECJ. According to Article 103 TFEU, a Regulation should prescribe appropriate sanctions and divide the tasks between the Commission and ECJ for the enforcement of Articles 101 and 102 TFEU. Regulation 17/62,[28] replaced by Regulation 1/2003,[29] has distributed powers between the Commission and the ECJ. In Article 15 and 23, respectively, the Commission is prescribed the power to impose sanctions. Both Regulations provide very little guidance to the nature of the prohibited conduct. After a complaint has been filed, the role of the ECJ is to review the conduct and rule based on the decisions of the Commission.

In case law, the ECJ has specifically adopted the approach of *droit* instead of *loi* by extensive reference to the ECtHR's approach on the legality principle.[30] In *Treuhand,* the Court based liability for participating in anticompetitive conduct on prior jurisprudence, because Articles 101 and 102 TFEU do not explicitly penalise participation in such conduct. The ECJ held that because of the acceptance of case law as a source of law in addition to statutes, a perceptive line of case law, if foreseeable, can be the basis for an interpretation of the Treaty provisions.[31]

---

27 See Chapter VIII para. 1.1.

28 Regulation 17/62 of 21 February 1962 implementing Articles 85 and 86 of the Treaty OJ 13, 21.02.1962, pp. 204–211.

29 Regulation 1/2003 of 16 December 2002 on the implementation of the rules on competition laid down in Articles 81 and 82 of the Treaty OJ L 1, 4.1.2003, pp. 1–25.

30 T–99/04 AC Treuhand AG v Commission of the European Communities, 8 July 2008, para. 140.

31 Ibid., para. 140–142.

This rationale is also extended to acts of the Commission.[32] In regard to the separation of powers between the Commission and the European legislator, the powers of the Commission to define prohibited conduct garnered serious criticism in numerous cases. The ECJ provided arguments to support the delegation of these powers from the European legislator to the Commission. According to the ECJ, the powers of the Commission are not unlimited because the Regulation, while leaving some discretion to the Commission, restricts these powers by setting a maximum of the penalties (10% of turnover) and setting the gravity and the duration of the offence as criteria. Moreover, the Commission is bound by general principles of law such as the principles of equality and proportionality, and the provisions on the Leniency Notice (which state that a company collaborating with the Commission during an investigation may receive lower fines). Finally, according to the Court, the judicial review of the Commission's decisions serves as a guarantee that the Commission does not function arbitrarily.[33] The Court has affirmed that this situation does not conflict with the Rule of Law and the separation of powers.[34]

This reasoning can be challenged on several grounds. First, the Commission has discretion to define its own criteria regarding the infringements considered more serious and the mitigating factors applicable. For example, in the case of parent companies and subsidiaries, the Commission has created certain indicia to prove the existence of decisive influence by the parent company to the subsidiary, such as the way of representation of the two companies, the simultaneous servitude of the same natural persons in the decision-making bodies of both companies and separate legal personalities.[35] The Commission also developed a rebuttable presumption, namely when the parent company owns 100% of the subsidiary decisive influence is presumed and therefore, there is no reason to use further indicia. This presumption is also supported by the ECJ.[36]

This is an example in which the elements of the prohibited behaviour are not clarified in the legislation, but are, in fact, created by the Commission. The two provisions in the Treaties are so laconic that the Commission and the ECJ must determine which agreements have the object or effect of preventing, restricting, or distorting competition. In principle, all competitive agreements distort competition by slowing it down or boosting it.[37] More will be discussed later about this. For now, it suffices to say that in competition law a specific decision-making power is granted to the Commission. The practice of the Commission and the jurisprudence of the ECJ have provided significant guidance to companies. Hence, an unclear

---

32 For example T–279/02 Degussa v Commission, 5 April 2006.

33 There are various cases where these arguments are presented, see for example joined cases C–189/02 P, 202/02 P, 208/02 P *et al.* Dansk Rørindustri A/S *et al,* 28 June 2005; T–279/02 Degussa v Commission, 5 April 2006; T–299/08 Elf Aquitaine SA v Commission, 17 May 2011.

34 C–501/11 P Schindler Holding Ltd and Others v European Commission, 18 July 2013.

35 T–299/08 Elf Aquitaine SA v Commission, 17 May 2011.

36 Ibid.

37 P. Craig, G. De Búrca, 'EU Law: Texts, Cases and Materials', Oxford University Press, 2011, pp. 972–982.

practice of the Commission can result in the violation of the principle of legitimate expectations.[38]

A Commission practice that has received an official status as *droit* is the Guidelines on sanctioning.[39] In 1998, the first Guidelines were published. They were later amended in 2006, when substantial changes were made to the calculation of fines. The new Guidelines departed from the previous regime of the categories of tariffs based on the severity of the offence and the focus on sentencing was placed on the duration of the offence and recidivism. These Guidelines are supposed to help the Commission develop a consistent methodology and inevitably increase legal certainty and transparency.[40] Nonetheless, the amendment of the Guidelines created several problems of foreseeability for calculating sanctions, because the new calculation can result in higher fines. The subsequent retroactive application of the new tariff system resulted in a plethora of case law. The ECJ was forced to examine the status of these Guidelines. According to the ECJ, the Guidelines, despite being an internal Commission document without legislative status, produced external effects on individuals.[41] They imposed a limit on the exercise of the Commission's discretion. Consequently, the Commission cannot deviate from these without breaching the general principles of EU law.[42] In this regard, the ECJ held the following:

> [I]t follows from that case-law that the concept of 'law' ('droit') for the purposes of Article 7(1) corresponds to 'law' ('loi') used in other provisions of the ECHR and encompasses both law of legislative origin and that deriving from case-law. Although that provision, which enshrines in particular the principle that offences and punishments are to be strictly defined by law (nullum crimen, nulla poena sine lege), cannot be interpreted as prohibiting the gradual clarification of the rules of criminal liability, it may, according to that case-law, preclude the retroactive application of a new interpretation of a rule establishing an offence. That is particularly true, according to that case law, of a judicial interpretation which produces a result which was not reasonably foreseeable at the time when the offence was committed, especially in the light of the interpretation put on the provision in the case-law at the material time. [...] Like that case-law on new developments in case-law, a change in an enforcement policy, in this instance the Commission's general competition policy in the matter of fines, especially where it comes about as a result of the adoption of rules of conduct such as the Guidelines, may have an impact from the aspect of the principle of non-retroactivity. Having particular regard to their legal effects and to their general application, as indicated at paragraph 211 of

---

38 T–299/08 Elf Aquitaine SA v Commission, 17 May 2011, para. 36.

39 Commission Guidelines on the method of setting fines imposed pursuant to Article 23(2)(a) of Regulation No 1/2003 OJ C 210, 1.9.2006, pp. 2–5.

40 Ibid. (Preamble).

41 Joined cases C–189/02 P, 202/02 P, 208/02 P *et al.* Dansk Rørindustri A/S *et al,* 28 June 2005, para. 209.

42 Ibid., para. 210–211.

> this judgement, such rules of conduct come, in principle, within the principle of 'law' for the purposes of Article 7(1) of the ECHR.[43]

By an analogical comparison between case law and administrative practices, the ECJ accepts that the sources of law can be found not only in ordinary legislation but also in practices of the executive body. This means that authorities should ensure that they fulfil the requirements of foreseeability in those acts. However, the instruments or communication documents that are included in the concept of *droit* are unclear. As stated by the ECJ above, the Guidelines are sources of law because they explain generally the practice of the Commission to impose fines; therefore, they inform citizens of the concept of fines and their calculation.

Despite recognition of these Guidelines as a source of law subjected to the requirements of the legality principle, the ECJ does not seem to give full effect to the legality principle. In principle, the Guidelines are subject to the legality principle; however, it seems that the retroactive application of the amended Guidelines, which raises the level of fines, does not violate that principle. The Court held that the defendants could not legitimately expect that the Commission will not increase the fines.[44] This is true even if the Commission has imposed certain fines in the past.[45] Therefore, the Court concluded that the increased level of fines was foreseeable and the principle of non-retroactivity had not been violated.[46]

In EU law, competition and criminal law are different regimes; therefore, the pivotal question is whether the definition of *law* in competition law cases can influence the same in the criminal law context. In principle, the directly enforceable competition law system is unique and not reproducible in European criminal law. However, the issue whether the concept of *droit*, which is prevalent in competition law cases and the ECtHR, can influence the application of the legality principle in European criminal law remains. Perhaps the ECJ would be more inclined to accept an implementation of European criminal law instruments via case law as compatible with the legality principle. Although the Court has previously rejected this line of reasoning, the fact remains that the sufficiency of a statute, as a legal foundation, depends on its interpretation. For example, if Dutch courts consistently interpret the liability on theft as also encompassing credit-card theft, (as a way of implementing provisions of the Framework Decision 2001/413 on non-cash payment means),[47] one has to wonder whether this is an acceptable form of implementation. A similar question could be raised regarding the jurisprudence of the ECJ. Perhaps the case

43 Ibid., para. 215–223.
44 Ibid., para. 228.
45 Ibid., para. 227.
46 Ibid., para. 231–332.
47 Framework Decision 2001/413 of 28 May 2001 combating fraud and counterfeiting of non-cash means of payment OJ L 149, 2.6.2001, pp. 1–4.

law of the Court could be considered as a source of criminal liability to instruct national parliaments and courts.[48]

2.3. Nuremberg exception

It is generally understood that the Nuremberg exception is part of the European legal order. Interestingly, Article 7 para. 2 ECHR and Article 49 para. 2 of the Charter are identical, except that the term 'civilised' does not appear in the Charter. According to background research, there is no explanation why drafters chose to remove this term; there is merely an assumption that all Member States are civilised nations.[49] According to the explanatory document, the Charter's meaning remains the same as its equivalent in the ECHR and Article 49 para. 2 is referring to crimes against humanity in particular.[50] It does not intend to capture jurisprudential development such as those in the marital rape case.[51]

One could inquire as to why the Nuremberg exemption is relevant in European criminal law. The Nuremberg exception was introduced because of the atrocities committed during and after the Second World War, and there is no evidence that it was meant to apply outside of that context. The question remains why European criminal law would be concerned with crimes against humanity whereas neither the Treaties have competence in these fields nor does the ECJ have the authority to deal with those issues. One may assume that drafters merely intended the Charter to comply with the ECHR. However, the relevance of this provision for European criminal law is unclear.[52]

3. Non-retroactivity of criminal liability

The first case that recognised the legality principle as a general principle of EU law was a case involving retroactivity in criminal law matters.[53] This element is perhaps one of the most developed aspects of the legality principle in EU law and presents few difficulties or lacunae.

The retroactive application of rules is a phenomenon met in different areas of law. In EU law, the challenges of retroactive legislation have been encountered also in non-criminal cases. Retroactivity in criminal law must be distinguished from

48 Chapter VIII para. 3.1.1.

49 Draft Charter of Fundamental Rights of the European Union, Brussels, 11 October 2000, CHARTE 4473/00 CONVENT 49.

50 EU Network of Independent Experts on Fundamental Rights, Commentary of the Charter of Fundamental Rights of the European Union, June 2006, p. 383.

51 Ibid.

52 See for a proposal on the application of the Nuremberg exception with regard to *lex mitior* in A. Klip, 'European Criminal Law: An Integrative Approach', Intersentia, 2012, p. 187.

53 Case 63/83 Regina v Kirk, 10 July 1984.

retroactivity in the non-criminal law context. In contrast to criminal law cases, where *lex praevia* has absolute application, retroactivity in non-criminal law measures may be allowed under specific preconditions and is obligatory in only some cases.[54]

The principle of *lex praevia* is viewed as a special application of the principle of legitimate expectations. This is particularly interesting because in national criminal law, the principle of *lex praevia* is not associated with the principle of legitimate expectations, as the latter is part of civil and administrative law.[55] From the usage of the principle, it is generally considered to have a strong application in European criminal law and has been widely developed by the ECJ to resolve varied situations in which retroactivity might occur.

3.1. Theoretical rationales: the principle of legitimate expectations

In EU law, there is not a very clear theoretical basis for the principle of legality as a principle of criminal law. Because there is no coherent general part of criminal law it is very easily associated with similar principles of law. The principle of *lex praevia* is seen as a particular application of the principle of legitimate expectations. The latter is an expression of the principle of legal certainty and is applied when the European legislation or actions of institutions violate legitimate expectations of individuals.[56] Therefore, the application of the principle of legitimate expectations requires the EU to actively create a situation that is subsequently altered. The principle of legitimate expectations is not absolute. In some cases, retroactivity may be allowed, provided that that the expectations of the affected individuals are respected.[57] In reality, the ECJ performs a balancing test, weighing the expectations of the individual affected with the legal interest involved with the retroactive measures.[58]

The principles of legitimate expectations and *lex praevia* share some common features: they both have at their core the protection of the interests of the individual from the arbitrary state, which are inflicted by the sudden change of legislation for *ex post facto* events. Retroactive legislation affects situations that citizens can no longer control or change; this betrays the trust of the citizens in the state and creates an impossible and unjust situation. Moreover, the principle of legitimate expectations is closely linked with the phenomenon of retroactivity, where its application is crucial. However, this does not mean that the legitimate expectations of individuals cannot be affected on other occasions such as by vague norms, a

54 T. Tridimas, 'The General Principles of EU law', Oxford University Press, 2006, pp. 254–265.

55 G. ten Berge, R. Widdershoven, 'The Principle of Legitimate Expectations in Dutch Constitutional and Administrative Law', Netherlands Reports to the Fifteen International Congress of Comparative Law, Bristol, 1998, pp. 421–452.

56 T. Tridimas, 'The General Principles of EU law', Oxford University Press, 2006, pp. 251–252.

57 Ibid., p. 256.

58 Ibid., pp. 254–280.

sudden change of legislation or violation of equality. Thus, this principle can be broader in its application than *lex praevia*.

The conceptual connection between the two principles is easily understood, but in national law, the principle of legitimate expectations is more prevalent in civil and administrative law, where the state creates specific, claimable rights. The proposition that the principle of *lex praevia* stems from the legitimate expectations principle is presumably made because EU law was historically focused on economic and administrative law.[59]

In national criminal law, the concept of legitimate expectations is disparate because criminal liability is not concerned with the creation but with the restriction of individual rights. Therefore, treating the principle of *lex praevia* as a special application of the principle of legitimate expectations may be problematic. Understanding the distinction between the *lex praevia* principle and the legitimate expectations principle is important, because the latter principle is not absolute. The ECJ can weigh the interests of individuals involved with the public interests that support retroactivity. In contrast, *lex praevia* is stronger, not only in national criminal law but also in European criminal law. In *Fedesa*, the ECJ recognised these differences and noted that retroactivity in criminal and non-criminal law measures differs.[60]

In competition law cases, the application of the principle of legitimate expectations is dissimilar to that of *lex praevia*. In analogy to the liberal ideology of criminal law, the economy is governed by the ideology of free market and *laissez-faire* liberalism. Therefore, the prohibition of specific competitive practices is only restrictive and does not provide rights to individuals. Thus, in some cases, the ECJ has treated the principles of legitimate expectations and the *lex praevia* as two different grounds for review.[61] However, the ECJ does not provide substantially different arguments when reviewing these principles. With regard to the legitimate expectations principle, the Court has weighed the individual's interests of legitimate expectations with the necessity to enforce an anti-competitive policy. The Court held that this principle applies when the administration has given clear assurances to individuals.[62] Although the Commission might have given the impression of a consistent method to be followed, it has discretion to amend such practices. Consequently, individuals cannot claim to have legitimate expectations from a situation that can be altered by the Commission. According to the ECJ, the Commission should be able to adjust fines at any time to align the enforcement of competition law with the needs of this policy. For the principle of *lex praevia*, the ECJ employs similar reasoning, which focuses on whether the retroactivity was

59 Ibid., p. 251 and pp. 273–280.

60 Case 331/88 The Queen v Minister of Agriculture, Fisheries and Food and Secretary of State for Health, ex parte: Fedesa and others, 13 November 1990, para. 44–45.

61 T–224/00 Archer Daniels Midland Company and Archer Daniels Midland Ingredients Ltd v Commission of the European Communities, 9 July 2003, para. 39–61 and 62–68.

62 Ibid.

foreseeable and whether individuals should be warned in light of the discretionary powers of the Commission for determining of fines.[63]

It is important to note that, although the principles of legitimate expectations and *lex praevia* are conceptually linked, they should still be distinguished because they deal with different fields of law. The use of the principle of legitimate expectations in criminal law cases could not only confuse but also introduce a broader application of the *lex praevia* principle. In national law, the *lex certa* and *lex stricta* aspects of the legality principle can have relative application. When interpreting the law, the scope of a criminal provision is inevitably adjusted in line with social developments. On the contrary, the principle of *lex praevia* is easier to apply; a provision is either retroactive or it is not. In most cases, there is no room for argument. The prohibition of retroactivity is very strong in its application in criminal law.[64]

Nevertheless, the principle of legitimate expectations may have some importance in issues relating to criminal procedure. It is important to note that the principle of legality does not apply to procedural rules. However, the ECtHR has accepted that Article 6 ECHR also protects the legitimate expectations created by criminal procedural rules when they provide the option of expediency, in which case some procedural rights are waived in exchange for a reduced sentence. It has been held that these procedural rules cannot be retroactively amended, if this invalidates a 'deal', as that would run counter to fair trial rights.[65] Similarly, in competition law, the Leniency Notice is one of the successful strategies in the field of EU competition policy, because it offers reduced fines (and sometimes immunity) to companies that cooperate with the Commission with regard to anticompetitive agreements.[66] The Leniency Notice does not guarantee reduced fines in all cases, but it produces legitimate expectations to the companies that opt for it, which the Commission is bound to respect. Therefore, the amendment to the Leniency Notice was not applied to any pending cases, as opposed to the Guidelines.[67] Perhaps this is because in the context of the Leniency Notice, a deal accompanies the expectations of the individuals who admit their guilt and testify against their fellow traders. The same cannot be said for the Guidelines as far as the principle of legitimate expectations is concerned.

3.2. The application of non-retroactivity

The principle of *lex praevia* is addressed to legislators who are prohibited from prescribing criminal liability retroactively and courts that are proscribed from

63 Ibid.

64 Case 331/88 The Queen v Minister of Agriculture, Fisheries and Food and Secretary of State for Health, ex parte: Fedesa and others, 13 November 1990.

65 ECtHR Scoppola v Italy, App. 10249/03, 17 September 2009.

66 Commission Notice on Immunity from fines and reduction of fines in cartel cases OJ C 298, 8.12.2006, p. 17–22.

67 A. Jones, B. Sufrin, 'EU Competition Law: Texts, Cases and Materials', Oxford University Press, 2011, p. 1122.

interpreting and applying liability rules retroactively. Therefore, this aspect of legality is a rule for drafting criminal legislation as well as a principle of interpretation.

The obligation of European legislator entails two different elements. First, as far as Regulations are concerned, the application of the *lex praevia* principle is a responsibility of the national authorities, because Regulations are not instruments prescribing criminal liability. Thus, a Regulation may be prescribed with a retroactive effect.[68]

Second, Directives may not instruct Member States to attach retroactive effects to criminal liability norms. The European legislator has never prescribed retroactive criminal liability in Directives or Framework Decisions. For Regulations and Directives of non-criminal law nature, the *lex praevia* principle functions as a presumption of non-retroactivity similar to English law.[69]

A question arising in this context is whether the principle of *lex praevia* precludes the European legislator from prescribing an implementation period with a retroactive effect. A retroactive implementation period is used infrequently in EU law and is therefore a rather exceptional situation. It is usually found when an existing Directive is annulled (due to procedural defects) and replaced with a new Directive. In such a rare case, the European legislator may prescribe a retroactive implementation period. This retroactive implementation period is in fact artificial, because the Directive is considered implemented.

An example of retroactive implementation is found in *Fedesa*. Here, the ECJ dealt with a retroactive implementation period of the Directive on livestock, farming and substances with hormones. The Directive replaced a previously annulled Directive with identical content. It was issued on 7 March 1988 with a retroactive implementation going back to 1 January 1988. The Court held that:

> [T]hat provision cannot be interpreted as imposing on Member States the obligation to adopt measures which conflict with Community law, in particular with the principle that penal provisions may not have retroactive effect. Nor may it provide a basis for criminal proceedings instituted under provisions of national law which may have been adopted in implementation of the annulled Directive and whose sole basis is to be found in that Directive.[70]

However, in regard to annulment of criminal law instruments such as the now repealed Framework Decision 2003/08 on the protection of the environment in criminal law,[71] the Directive 2008/99 was not prescribed with a retroactive

68 Case 63/83 Regina v Kirk, 10 July 1984.

69 T. Tridimas, 'The General Principles of EU law', Oxford University Press, 2006, pp. 271–273.

70 Case 331/88 The Queen v Minister of Agriculture, Fisheries and Food and Secretary of State for Health, ex parte: Fedesa and others, 13 November 1990, para. 44.

71 Framework Decision 2003/80 of 27 January 2003 on the protection of the environment through criminal law OJ L 29, 5.2.2003, pp. 55–58.

implementation period.[72] It seems that the European legislator is much more sensitive when it comes to issues of criminal law. To conclude, the retroactive implementation period of Directives does not seem to be contrary to the principle of *lex praevia* when there is a pre-existing national criminal provision that prohibited the committed act at the time it was committed. According to the ECJ, the principle of *lex praevia* in EU law would preclude Member States from implementing a national criminal provision with a retroactive effect.

The principle of *lex praevia* is also addressed to the national legislator. This stems from the character of the legality principle as a general principle of EU law that binds European and national authorities in the implementation or application of EU law. As mentioned, the national legislator is prohibited from retroactively applying a criminal liability rule with a European origin. However, there seems to be a lacuna, especially with regard to the national interpretation of criminal liability. The obligation of conform interpretation cannot result in the aggravation or establishment of new criminal liability. However, what happens if the Directive did not exist when the criminal act was committed? In *Pupino*, the criminal act occurred before the Framework Decision was issued. The ECJ held that any interpretation should respect the principle of legality and Article 6 ECHR.[73] Therefore, this question is addressed to national courts. Especially in *Pupino*, the problem of retroactivity was procedural in nature. However, one may wonder whether it would constitute a violation of *lex praevia* if there were substantive criminal provisions. Hence, a question that arises is whether the *lex praevia* prohibits the interpretation of national law in conformity with a Directive that does not exist at the time the offence was committed. This seems to depend on the foreseeability of the interpretation; however, the issue whether the *lex praevia* should set limits to the obligation of conform interpretation remains open.[74]

An interesting possibility is to apply the principle of *lex praevia* to judicial decisions (prospective overruling). This would restrict the temporal effect of judgements. Such a possibility has not yet been discussed in European criminal law but it has been applied in other areas of law. Thus, the ECJ can limit the temporal effect of its judgements if the financial consequences are severe for a Member State. In *Defrenne*, where the principle of equal pay between men and women was given direct effect, the Court limited the temporal effect of this judgement to apply only to pending cases with 'compelling reasons'.[75] These 'compelling reasons' are mostly defined as financial reasons.[76] It is unclear whether similar circumstances

---

72 Directive 2008/99 of 19 November 2008 on the protection of the environment through criminal law OJ L 328, 6.12.2008, pp. 28–37.

73 C–105/03 criminal proceedings against Maria Pupino, 16 June 2005.

74 See Chapter VIII para. 3.2.

75 Case 43/75 Gabrielle Defrenne v Société anonyme belge de navigation aérienne Sabena, 8 April 1976, para. 69.

76 See for more in C. Waldhoff, 'Recent developments relating to the retroactive effect of decisions of the ECJ', Common Market Law Review, vol. 46, 2009, pp. 173–190.

could arise in criminal law, perhaps in the context of incorrect implementation, the interpretation of financial offences or environmental crimes.

3.2.1. Tempus legis

The application of the *lex praevia* principle involves the determination of three specific elements: the time the legislation was enacted, the time the act was committed and the amendment of the definition of criminal liability. In regard to the first element, the determination of the time of the legislative enactment depends on the institutional rules of every system. In EU law, Directives and Regulations obtain legal effect on the day specified therein or, in the absence of this, on the 20th day following the publication of the document to the Official Journal (Article 297 TFEU).[77] In addition, there is an implementation period for Directives, which is usually two years, unless stated otherwise in the instrument. Note that the date of actual publication is important. If the date stated on the Official Journal does not correspond to the actual publication date, the latter date is decisive.[78] Variations in the dates of availability of the Official Journal in different Member States are not considered, as this would jeopardise the uniform application of EU law.[79] This puts extra pressure on national authorities to ensure that there are no delays.

3.2.2. Tempus delicti

In regard to the second element of the *lex praevia* principle, the *tempus delicti* is the time point at which the criminal act is committed. The exact time of the commission of an act depends not only on evidentiary proof but also on the type of act involved. Because the ECJ is not a criminal court, *tempus delicti* is infrequently discussed. In most cases, it is the national judge who determines the *tempus delicti*.

In competition law cases, problems might occur with the continuing and continuous acts.[80] While concluding an agreement is an instant definable event, the breach of the legal good protected by the agreement is a continuing violation. This status ceases only when the agreement expires. Therefore, anticompetitive behaviour presents the characteristics of a continuing offence. In most competition law cases, the determination of the *tempus delicti* has no effect on the principle of legality, but influences the calculation of fines instead.[81] The ECJ held that anticompetitive behaviour generally has the elements of a 'single and continuous' offence, comprising different agreements and practices.[82] Using of the term

77 C–228/99 Silos e Mangimi Martini SpA v Ministero delle Finanze, 8 November 2001, para. 15.
78 Case 98/78 A. Racke v Hauptzollamt Mainz, 25 January 1979.
79 Ibid., para. 16.
80 See Chapter IV para. 10.4.
81 Joined cases T–101/05 and T–111/05, BASF AG and UCB SA v the Commission, 12 December 2007.
82 Ibid., para. 177–179.

'continuous' instead of the correct 'continuing' could imply that the ECJ is unaware of this distinction. The ECJ also held that the statute of limitation period starts from the last day of the time period of the anticompetitive behaviour.[83] Note that the Treaty provisions on competition law not only criminalise agreements but also similar practices. Therefore, if an agreement has expired but the practices continue, the *tempus delicti* is determined at the end of such practices.[84]

3.3. Amendments of criminal liability

The final and crucial element in the application of the *lex praevia* principle is the amendment of criminal liability. What qualifies an amendment of criminal liability will be examined below.

From a normative viewpoint, the task of defining the amendment of criminal liability coincides with the task of defining criminal liability norms. Theoretically, any norm that can contribute to the definition of criminal liability should be subject to the *lex praevia* principle.

For example, German law criminalises violations of Regulation 2580/2001 on combating terrorism in the Foreign Trade Act (*Außenwirtschaftsgesetz*).[85] In *E and F*, individuals were prosecuted in Germany for financing an organisation that had been included in terrorist lists by virtue of Council Decisions published from 2002 to 2009. During this period, the procedure of listing individuals was considered defective, as it did not respect procedural safeguards. Therefore, the Decisions until 2006 were considered void. Consequently, the Council's Decision in 2007 included an amended procedure maintaining the name of the organisation in the list. The German prosecutor argued that the 2007 Decision retroactively validate the prohibited nature of the defendants' activities. However, the ECJ, in its preliminary ruling, held that the Council Decisions, the Regulation, and national provisions together form the basis of criminal liability. According to the ECJ, if the German court accepted that the 2007 Decision validated the annulled Decisions in an *ex post facto* manner, this would violate the *lex praevia* principle.[86]

A normative distinction that limits that scope of *lex praevia* is the distinction between procedural and substantive criminal rules. According to national and EU law, the legality principle only applies to substantive rules, whereas in procedural law, the norms applied are those in force on the day of the trial. AG Bot has made a distinction between procedural and substantive norms in the application of the *lex praevia* principle.[87] The distinction between procedural and substantive norms is

---

83 Ibid.

84 Ibid., para. 187.

85 Regulation 2580/2001 of 27 December 2001 on specific restrictive measures directed against certain persons and entities with a view to combating terrorism OJ L 344, 28.12.2001, pp. 70–75.

86 C–550/09 criminal proceedings against E and F, 29 June 2010, para. 60–62.

87 Opinion AG Bot of 26 October 2010 in C–352/09P ThyssenKrupp Nirosta GmbH v European Commission, 29 March 2011, para. 88–90.

normative and it meets little difficulty in national law. However, in EU law the absence of a codified criminal code and the multilevel system of norms may cause problems in distinguishing procedural from substantive norms.

From a substantive viewpoint, any amendment that changes the scope of criminal liability (e.g. adding or deleting elements in the definition, or changing norms in the general part, such as definitions of attempt or participation) qualifies as an amendment of criminal liability. The *lex praevia* principle is meant to apply to amendments that expand the scope of liability. Amendments that limit the scope of liability are related to the application of *lex mitior.*

Treaty provisions are also covered by the general principles of EU law. Thus, the ECJ has determined that amendments of Treaty provisions fall under the principle of legality. Detrimental retroactivity of Treaty provisions is not allowed.[88] However, this may not include all types of amendments of Treaty provisions, as explained below.

In competition law, the ECJ held that the succession of the European Steel and Coal Community to the EC does not challenge the powers of the Commission but has an impact on substantive norms. Because of the expiration of the CS Treaty, the legal basis of the Commission's powers was no longer contained in Article 65 CS, but in Articles 81 and 82 EC and Regulation 1/2003. The Court held that because of the necessity of continuity of the European legal order and as the objective and nature of the infringement remained the same (as Article 65 CS and the EC provisions were interpreted similarly by the Court), the principle of legality was unaffected if the Commission's powers are based on the EC regime.[89] Yet, the substantive norm applied in this case would be Article 65 CS.

4. Precision and accessibility of criminal liability

The *lex certa* principle requires criminal liability to be prescribed with precision so that the individual can foresee criminalisation. It has been recognised as a general principle of EU law.[90] The *lex certa* principle is considered a special application of the principle of legal certainty and legality in criminal matters. There are very few cases in criminal law wherein the Court refers to this aspect. On the other hand, the principle of legal certainty has often been applied in other areas of law.

It should be clarified that *lex certa* and the legal certainty principle (as it is used in EU law) are not the same. The principle of legal certainty is much broader in its application.[91] The overuse of the principle of legal certainty as a *passe-partout*

88 C–193/94 criminal proceedings against Sofia Skanavi and Konstantin Chryssanthakopoulos, 19 February 1996, para. 16.

89 T–24/07 ThyssenKrupp Stainless AG v Commission of the European Communities, 1 July 2009, para. 74–88.

90 C–308/06 The Queen, on the application of International Association of Independent Tanker Owners (Intertanko) and Others v Secretary of State for Transport, 3 June 2008, para. 71.

91 J. Raitio, 'The Principle of Legal Certainty in EC Law', Kluwer, 2003, p. 125.

makes this task rather difficult. It has been utilised before the ECJ in various contexts.[92]

4.1. Theoretical rationales: the principles of legitimate expectations and legal certainty

The principle of legitimate expectations, as mentioned previously, is considered to be a special application of the principle of legal certainty. For the *lex praevia* principle, the principle of legitimate expectations is very important, as the non-retroactivity rule is perceived to stem from this principle. However, the principle of legitimate expectations has an even closer conceptual connection with the principle of *lex certa*; both principles deal with foreseeability and what citizens should expect. However, the scarcity in the application of *lex certa* does not give any evidence of their true connection.

There seems to be a particular difference between the legal certainty principle and the legitimate expectations principle in terms of timing. AG Cosmas demarcated these two principles by attributing to the legal certainty principle a static character,[93] whereas the principle of legitimate expectations is perceived with a diachronic character.[94] Tridimas suggests that, although the principle of legitimate expectations can generate claims for individuals, the principle of legal certainty is more general in its context.[95] The principle of *lex certa* presents two basic functions in European criminal law. It deals with the level of precision and foreseeability of legislation and requires that legislation be accessible and open to the public.

4.2. Accessibility of criminal legislation

The *lex certa* principle demands that criminal liability be accessible to the individual. There are a few requirements to assess the accessibility of Directives and Regulations that determine criminal liability.[96]

First, these instruments should be published in an official source, namely the Official Journal of the EU (Article 297 TFEU). This should suffice, as the Official Journal is generally available also electronically. The importance of publication should not be underestimated. According to Article 297 TFEU, the promulgation of instruments is a constitutive requirement of the formal legislative procedure, i.e. an unpublished Directive or Regulation does not exist yet.[97] The accessibility of

92 T. Tridimas, 'The General Principles of EU law', Oxford University Press, 2006, p. 243.
93 Ibid., p. 252.
94 Opinion AG Cosmas of 8 June 1995 in C–63/93 Fintan Duff *et al.* v Minister for Agriculture and Food and Attorney General, 15 February 1996, para. 25.
95 T. Tridimas, 'The General Principles of EU law', Oxford University Press, 2006, p. 252.
96 Regulations are mentioned for cases where they may define acts that are criminalised further in a national criminal provision.
97 Case 98/78 A. Racke v Hauptzollamt Mainz, 25 January 1979.

European documents was reinforced with Regulation 1049/2001, relating to public access.[98] This Regulation includes certain exceptions regarding publication of documents for reasons of public security. However, in criminal law, such exemptions would contradict the *lex certa* principle.

An interesting case is observed in an unpublished Annex to a Regulation.[99] The Annex, which was not published because of public security, listed the items prohibited in an airplane cabin. An Austrian national was carrying tennis rackets in his bag, which were prohibited by the Annex and he was not allowed on board. The Court held that, according to the principle of legal certainty, European rules should enable the parties concerned to know precisely the extent of their obligations.[100] It is obvious that passengers cannot guess what items are prohibited, especially if items such as tennis rackets and manicure tools are included in the list. In this case, the *lex certa* principle was not respected; therefore, individuals cannot be expected to comply with a secret annex.[101]

It should be underscored that in EU law there is generally a tendency towards transparency and openness to the public. Articles 10 para. 3 and 11 para. 2 and 3 TFEU promote openness and transparency of institutions, legislation and procedures for the public and the civil society. There are online databases on case law, legislation and step-by-step legislative procedures and documents in the European Parliament. The EU offers legal information on specific common cross-border issues, while individuals may inquire about a particular legal problem.

Regarding the online version of the Official Journal, the ECJ held in 2007 that an electronic version of European legislation, which predates its official publication in the Official Journal, does not fulfil the accessibility requirements of *lex certa*.[102] However, this issue was resolved in 2013. After 1 July 2013, the electronic publication of the Official Journal is the only authentic version that produces legal effects.[103] A paper version may be found authentic only in exceptional cases. This change improves the accessibility of legislation.

Second, because Europe is a multilingual union, the accessibility of criminal legislation is influenced by the language factor. Thus, the publication of the

---

98 Regulation 1049/2001 of 30 May 2001 regarding public access to European Parliament, Council and Commission documents OJ L 145, 31.5.2001, pp. 43–48.

99 Now amended by Regulation 1448/2006 of 29 September 2006 amending Regulation (EC) No 622/2003 laying down measures for the implementation of the common basic standards on aviation security OJ L 271, 30.9.2006, pp. 31–32.

100 C–345/06 Gottfried Heinrich, 10 March 2009, para. 45.

101 The ECJ also held that unpublished parts of EU legislation cannot give rise to obligations for individuals in civil and criminal law proceedings due to the principle of legal certainty. See C–108/01 Consorzio del Prosciutto di Parma and Salumificio S. Rita SpA v Asda Stores Ltd and Hygrade Foods Ltd, 20 May 2003, para. 95–96.

102 C–161/06 Skoma-Lux sro v Celní ředitelství Olomouc, 11 December 2007, para. 48. The case relates to a custom offence but its ruling can be presumed to apply as well in criminal law matters.

103 Regulation 216/2013 of 7 March 2013 on the electronic publication of the Official Journal of the European Union OJ L 69, 13.3.2013, pp. 1–3.

instruments in the Official Journal does not suffice unless it is in the language of the European citizen in question. The Court has held that if European legislation is not available in the language concerned, obligations cannot be imposed.[104] According to the ECJ, this conforms not only to the principle of legal certainty but also to the principle of equality.[105] This obligation to publish legislation in all official languages of the EU does not seem to apply to non-EU nationals, who do not speak a European language. This obviates the need for translations in a multitude of international languages, something that would be too onerous.[106] Nevertheless, having twenty-four official versions of one instrument could create problems in defining the scope of criminal liability, especially because there can be divergences between the texts. In those situations, usually the ECJ will resort to a contextual or teleological interpretation.[107]

An additional issue raised is whether the same requirements should be applied to national implementing legislation. This issue is complicated by the fact that European citizenship is the basis for the accessibility requirements to European criminal legislation. Perhaps, the national implementing legislation should be translated into all European languages so that residents of the Member States who exercise their right to free movement are aware of their European criminal law obligations. For example, when implementing European criminal legislation, should the Dutch legislator be required to translate it to all European languages so that residents with European citizenship but not fluent in Dutch, are aware of new provisions?[108] Another example would include national legislation that directly refers to European texts that are not yet translated in the defendant's language. At the European level, European citizenship and the plurality of languages could create special circumstances for the application of the *lex certa* principle.[109]

The final consideration on the accessibility of criminal rules relates to the accessibility of criminal jurisprudence. In competition law cases, the ECJ has accepted that its prior jurisprudence can form guidance for individuals because case law is a source of law.[110] Although, a considerable amount of ECJ's case law is published, including the AG Opinions and in most European languages, translations may take time while not all case law is published.

---

104 C–228/99 Silos e Mangimi Martini SpA v Ministero delle Finanze, 8 November 2001, para. 15–16.

105 C–161/06 Skoma-Lux sro v Celní ředitelství Olomouc, 11 December 2007, para. 39.

106 See, however, Directive 2010/64 of 20 October 2010 on the right to interpretation and translation in criminal proceedings OJ L 280, 26.10.2010, pp. 1–7.

107 Case 238/84, criminal proceedings against Hans Röser, 27 February 1986.

108 Chapter VIII para. 3.3.1.

109 T. Schilling, 'Beyond Multilingualism: On Different Approaches to the Handling of Diverging Language Versions of a Community Law', European Law Journal, vol. 16, 2010, pp. 47–66.

110 E.g. T–99/04 AC Treuhand AG v Commission of the European Communities, 8 July 2008.

4.3. Precision of EU criminal legislation

The ECJ has generally followed the ECtHR approach in dealing with the precision of statutes, emphasising foreseeability and reliability.[111] Because the *lex certa* principle is guiding the construction of criminal liability and is a general principle of EU law, it applies to European and national legislators. However, European and national legislators are not governed by the same mandate. They legislate at a different level; the European legislator defines the minimum scope of criminal liability, whereas the national legislators must then concretise it and transform it into national law.

The pivotal question is whether the *lex certa* principle should be applied to Directives. This issue underscores the actual relationship between the European and national legislators in determining criminal liability as well as the value European norms may have for individuals. The first problem with the application of the *lex certa* principle to European instruments is that the principle supports the protection of individuals against an arbitrary state. By definition, Directives require implementation by national law, and that implementation forms the basis of criminal liability. European criminal law instruments are not intended for individuals but for national legislators. How can it be accepted that the *lex certa* principle is relevant to Directives, if these are not meant to be addressed to individuals? In *Intertanko*, the ECJ did not deny that the *lex certa* principle is applicable to Directives, but it held that it is the national legislation that must comply with the principle.[112]

The problem is that although EU law demands that European legislation have a certain degree of precision, the manner in which this could be judged is unclear because implementation is always required.[113] In other areas of law, the principle of legal certainty has been addressed to the European legislator, as it is a ground for reviewing European legislation.[114] Moreover, the Court has never dismissed a complaint of ambiguity in European criminal law instruments, despite the fact that it held in the end that there was no violation.[115] The question that remains open is how the obligation of the European legislator to prescribe criminal liability in Directives with precision could be justified theoretically, if individual autonomy and foreseeability are not interfered with.[116]

---

111 C–308/06 The Queen, on the application of International Association of Independent Tanker Owners (Intertanko) and Others v Secretary of State for Transport, 3 June 2008, para. 71.

112 Ibid.

113 T.A.J.A. Vandamme, 'The invalid Directive: the legal authority of a Union act requiring domestic law making', Europa Law Publishing, 2005, p. 197.

114 T. Tridimas, 'The General Principles of EU law', Oxford University Press, 2006, pp. 244–246.

115 C–303/05 Advocaten voor de Wereld VZW v Leden van de Ministerraad, 3 May 2007; C–308/06 The Queen, on the application of International Association of Independent Tanker Owners (Intertanko) and Others v Secretary of State for Transport, 3 June 2008.

116 See Chapter VIII para. 1.3 and 2.2.

4.4. Problems of ambiguity in EU legislation

There are various examples of criminal norms in European instruments that are potentially vague. Examples include the European instruments on terrorism, child pornography, racism and xenophobia.[117] The core criticism of vague European definitions of crimes is that they prevent the national legislator from respecting the *lex certa* principle. For instance, Article 3(1) (a) of the Framework Decision 2002/475, as replaced with Framework Decision 2008/919, on combatting terrorism reads:

> [P]ublic provocation to commit a terrorist offence shall mean the distribution, or otherwise making available, of a message to the public, with the intent to incite the commission of one of the offences listed in Article 1(1)(a) to (h), where such conduct, whether or not directly advocating terrorist offences, causes a danger that one or more such offences may be committed.[118]

The vague definition provided in this provision presents challenges for defining the minimum scope of criminal liability. Framework Decision 2008/919 does provide some guidance in that it includes, in Article 2, that these offences are not meant to be contrary to freedom of expression; however, there is no indication about the manner in which this apparent conflict can be resolved.

Another example is found in Articles 2 and 3 of the Joint Action 98/742 on corruption in the private sector when it creates the offence of *'such conduct which involves, or could involve, the distortion of competition, as a minimum within the common market, and which results, or might result, in economic damage to others by the improper award or improper execution of a contract'.*[119] Similarly, Framework Decision 2003/568, which replaced this Joint Action, reproduces this definition of liability in Article 2(3) that states: *'A Member State may declare that it will limit the scope of paragraph 1 to such conduct which involves, or could involve, a distortion of competition in relation to the purchase of goods or commercial activities'.*[120] The meaning of the hypothetical element 'could involve distortion' is vague on its face and results in vague national implementation. A similar criticism for vagueness can be directed at the term 'breach of duty' in the same instrument.[121]

---

117 European Criminal Policy Initiative, 'A Manifesto on European Criminal Policy', ZIS, vol. 12, 2009, p. 713.

118 Framework Decision 2002/475 of 13 June 2002 on combating terrorism OJ L 164, 22.6.2002, pp. 3–7; Framework Decision 2008/919 of 28 November 2008 amending Framework Decision 2002/475/JHA on combating terrorism OJ L 330, 9.12.2008, pp. 21–23.

119 Joint Action 98/742/JHA of 22 December 1998 on corruption in the private sector OJ L 358, 31.12.1998, pp. 2–4.

120 Framework Decision 2003/568 of 22 July 2003 on combating corruption in the private sector OJ L 192, 31.7.2003, pp. 54–56.

121 European Criminal Policy Initiative, 'A Manifesto on European Criminal Policy', ZIS, vol. 12, 2009, p. 713.

Other examples of potentially vague definitions can be found in the sphere of competition law. The definition of anti-competitive behaviour states in Article 101 para. 1 TFEU:

> The following shall be prohibited as incompatible with the internal market: all agreements between undertakings, decisions by associations of undertakings and concerted practices which may affect trade between Member States and which have as their object or effect the prevention, restriction or distortion of competition within the internal market, and in particular those which: a) directly or indirectly fix purchase or selling prices or any other trading conditions;(b) limit or control production, markets, technical development, or investment; (c) share markets or sources of supply; (d) apply dissimilar conditions to equivalent transactions with other trading parties, thereby placing them at a competitive disadvantage; (e) make the conclusion of contracts subject to acceptance by the other parties of supplementary obligations which, by their nature or according to commercial usage, have no connection with the subject of such contracts.

Article 101 TFEU is over-inclusive in two ways. First, there is ambiguity in the scope of this definition with regard to anti-competitive contracts. All contracts in the world of trade are by their very nature restrictive. It cannot be that the competition rules prohibit every contract.[122] Second, agreements may have features that both promote and yet restrict competition. Agreements can restrict parties by imposing commitments but they can also boost competition, for instance, by introducing new products.[123] It becomes imperative to determine the agreements that distort competition in a way that is prohibited. The ECJ draws a balance between positive and negative effects of agreements of competition law; however, in essence, it condemns agreements because of their objective and type without any market analysis on their real effects. The other potential problem with application of Article 101 for which the ECJ has been criticised is the lack of market analysis to support its decision.[124] Apart from the interpretational trends discussed below in the *lex stricta* principle section, it is evident that the wording of this definition is vague and, as it is used in a directly enforceable sanctioning system of sanctioning, there are serious concerns for the respect of *lex certa*.

An additional example relates to the definitions of the elements of the general part of criminal law. Framework Decisions and Directives include the obligation to criminalise certain forms of participation, negligence and attempt without providing a definition of those terms. Thus, the Commission in its Annex to the report on the implementation of the Framework Decision on terrorism refers to the problems created by the different interpretations of the term 'incitement' in Italy, Spain,

---

122 P. Craig, G. De Búrca, 'EU Law: Texts, Cases and Materials', Oxford University Press, 2011, pp. 972–982.

123 Ibid., pp. 950–951.

124 Ibid.

France and the UK.[125] The Commission seems to regret that there is the lack of a definition for 'incitement' because this causes discrepancies with the implementation among Member States. However, some cases uphold the lack of unified definitions in European legislation. In *Intertanko*, the ECJ argued that the European legislator does not violate the *lex certa* principle by not defining 'serious negligence', because this term corresponds to different national concepts; therefore, this is a task of the national legislator. Simultaneously though, the ECJ gave its own definition of the term.[126]

The latter is in line with the ECJ's tactic to give autonomous and uniform interpretation to European concepts.[127] However, the question remains why the European legislator could not provide this definition. Obviously, the Court wanted to avoid revoking the Directive. However, the reasoning is contradictory. Ironically, the ECJ provides its own autonomous and uniform definition of 'serious negligence', and it simultaneously states that it would be impossible for the European legislator to define such a concept.[128] It is true that with elements of the general part, it is not possible or desirable to achieve the same level of precision as with definitions of the special part. A valid question remains why the European legislator failed to provide a simple definition as the ECJ managed to do in the end. The lack of definitions of general elements found in European legislation is highly problematic because it inhibits European criminal norms from achieving an autonomous and uniform concept. It is incongruous how a European legislator can prescribe criminal liability without first providing uniform explanations on the manner in which criminal liability is understood and structured in EU law.[129]

A very interesting initiative underway is the drafting of model provisions to guide the Council's negotiations in criminal law matters.[130] The good news is that the Council recognises the necessity of clarity in defining criminal liability. However, the model provisions are not revolutionary. Elements of the general part remain unexplained, whereas the structure of the provisions does not amend the pattern previously used. Therefore, the question of codifying definitions of the general part remains open.

---

125 Commission Staff Working Paper, Annex to the Report from the Commission based on Article 11 of the Council Framework decision of Decision of 13 June 2002 on combating terrorism SEC (2004) 655, 8.6.2004, p. 20.

126 C–308/06 The Queen, on the application of International Association of Independent Tanker Owners (Intertanko) and Others v Secretary of State for Transport, 3 June 2008, para. 77.

127 C–261/09 Gaetano Mantello, 16 November 2010, para. 38.

128 C–308/06 The Queen, on the application of International Association of Independent Tanker Owners (Intertanko) and Others v Secretary of State for Transport, 3 June 2008, para. 73.

129 J. Blomsma, C. Peristeridou, 'The way forward: a general part of European criminal law', in F. Galli, A. Weyembergh, 'Approximation of substantive criminal law in the EU: the way forward', IEE, 2013, pp. 123–124.

130 Draft Council conclusions on model provisions, guiding the Council's criminal law deliberations 16542/2/09 REV 2 JAI 868 DROIPEN 160, 27.11.2009.

The principle of *lex certa* does not only require clear and unambiguous definitions of liability but also the comprehensibility of legislation. The European legislator often produces a series of legislative instruments that refer to each other, or they cover fragments of the same area. In this situation, the problem is to understand the manner in which these Directives interact and the scope of criminal liability that they create. They create difficulty in comprehending criminal liability rules, because coherency and consistency is limited. A particular example is the use of the reference technique in describing criminal liability in European instruments. According to this method, some elements of the definition of liability, or the description of the conduct in its whole, can be found in other European instruments.

For example, in Directive 2005/35 regarding ship-source pollution, as amended by Directive 2009/123, the scope of criminal liability can be understood only though cross-readings of the Marpol Convention and Annexes of existing Regulations (Article 2–5a of the Directive).[131] Similarly, Article 3 of Directive 2008/99 on the protection of the environment through criminal law describes criminal liability as the unlawful commission of certain acts, whereas the term 'unlawful' refers to an Annex with European provisions found in different enlisted instruments.[132] To find the definition of criminal liability, one must locate and consult these provisions. The national legislator, to detect the acts to be criminalised, should therefore relate criminal liability in national law with already implemented provisions of the Directives and Regulations. The use of the reference technique results in incoherency and incomprehensibility; one must employ good legal research skills. On the other hand, the effectiveness and economy of this method cannot be denied. The problematic use of the reference technique was highlighted by the European Parliament: *'the use of many cross references in legal texts as a violation of the lex certa principle: legislation has to be clear-cut and easily understandable so that it becomes predictable for all whether an act amounts to a criminal offence or not'*.[133]

Particular concerns are raised with the practice of dynamic reference, i.e. the automatic and not-explicit replacement of a referred Regulation with its amended version. This is in contrast to the static reference where the referring instruments must be amended to include updated references. EU law seems to follow the dynamic reference. Thus, Article 24 para. 2 of Regulation 1760/2000 on the registration of bovine animals determines that any references to the repealed

131 Directive 2005/35 of 7 September 2005 on ship-source pollution and on the introduction of penalties for infringements OJ L 255, 30.9.2005, pp. 11–21; Directive 2009/123 of 21 October 2009 amending Directive 2005/35/EC on ship-source pollution and on the introduction of penalties for infringements OJ L 280, 27.10.2009, pp. 52–55.

132 Directive 2008/99 of 19 November 2008 on the protection of the environment through criminal law OJ L 328, 6.12.2008, pp. 28–37.

133 European Parliament Resolution of 22 May 2012 on an EU approach to criminal law (2010/2310(INI)), 22.5.2012, p. 8.

Regulation will be considered as reference to the new Regulation.[134] Given the fact that there are national criminal provisions that establish criminal liability for the violation of some of these technical Regulations, the use of dynamic reference in the European instruments is problematic.

In practice, problems of incomprehensibility or vagueness can be observed only in implementation practices. The reports of implementation by the Commission could aid in correcting European legislation. This culture of monitoring implementation is an important element for the improvement of both European and national legislation. Thus, in Directive 89/592 on insider dealing, which was implemented through criminal law, there was a misinterpretation of the intention of the European legislator regarding the definition of the prohibited act.[135] The question was whether the term 'with full knowledge of the facts' is actually a *mens rea* requirement.[136] The ECJ explicitly emphasised that European legislation defined insider dealing objectively, and the intent of the European legislator was to achieve uniform full harmonisation leaving no room to define insider dealing in a stricter manner by adding a *mens rea* requirement.[137]

During implementation, it was evident that national parliaments considered the expression 'with full knowledge of the facts' as an implied *mens rea* element; hence, in the amended Directive, this expression was consequently deleted.[138] Monitoring possible vagueness in European instruments through implementation reports is certainly effective, but it cannot guarantee that the European legislator will follow up. In the case of insider dealing, it took more than a decade before the European legislator introduced the amendment. This is because any legislative change of Directives needs to go through the rather time-consuming drafting and implementation processes. Therefore, the *lex certa* principle at the European level can be rather cumbersome in this regard.

4.5. Precision of national implementing legislation

National legislators should also respect the principle of legal certainty; therefore, a violation of the principle would result in an incorrect or incomplete implementation. However, the European standards of the *lex certa* principle could conflict with the national standards of the principle. Although it is the responsibility of the national

---

134 Regulation 1760/2000 of 17 July 2000 establishing a system for the identification and registration of bovine animals and regarding the labelling of beef and beef products and repealing Regulation 820/97 OJ L 204, 11.8.2000, pp. 1–10.

135 Directive 89/592 of 13 November 1989 coordinating regulations on insider dealing OJ L 334, 18.11.1989, pp. 30–32 and Directive 2003/06 of 28 January 2003 on insider dealing and market manipulation (market abuse) OJ L 96, 12.4.2003, pp. 16–25.

136 C–45/08 Spector Photo Group NV and Chris Van Raemdonck v Commissie voor het Bank–, Financie– en Assurantiewezen (CBFA), 23 December 2009.

137 Ibid., para. 34–37.

138 Directive 2003/06 of 28 January 2003 on insider dealing and market manipulation (market abuse) OJ L 96, 12.4.2003, pp. 16–25.

legislator to ensure an appropriate level of predictability for national criminal liability, the ECJ also provides certain guidelines on this concept. Note that, at the moment, there are still no infringement proceedings for incorrect or absent implementation in European criminal law. Examples can be found, however, in areas other than criminal law. The ECJ has developed guidelines for the evaluation of national implementing legislation.[139] These criteria have been used by the Commission as evaluation criteria in the evaluation reports of European instruments, including criminal law instruments. The four evaluation criteria are the following:

> 1. [T]he form and methods of implementation of the result to be achieved must be chosen in a manner which ensures that the Directive functions effectively with account being taken of its aims; 2. [E]ach Member State is obliged to implement Directives in a manner which satisfies the requirements of clarity and legal certainty and thus to transpose the provisions of the Directive into national provisions having binding force; 3. [T]ransposition need not necessarily require enactment in precisely the same words in an express legal provision; thus a general legal context (such as appropriate pre-existing measures) may be sufficient, as long as the full application of the Directive is assured in a sufficiently clear and precise manner; 4. [D]irectives must be implemented within the period prescribed therein.[140]

Legal certainty is a cornerstone principle for implementation. What are the obligations derived for the national legislator? The most interesting criteria for the *lex certa* principle are the first three. The first guideline seems to refer to the methods and form of implementation and it conveys discretion as long as the implementation is effective. Little guidance can be derived from this. The second and third guidelines refer to the requirement of legal certainty. The Commission limits the application of the legal certainty principle to the binding force of the instrument. This is self-evident, as criminal liability cannot be established by soft-law instruments.

The Commission continues by explaining whether and to what extent existing norms can be used. This is also known as silent or implicit implementation.[141] When the prohibited conduct in the Directive is already criminalised in national legislation, then the national legislator could avoid superfluous provisions by notifying the Commission that the Directive is already implemented. The option of implicit implementation has certain limitations. First, all the elements of criminal liability should be found in the pre-existing provisions to achieve correct implementation. Here, there is some room for interpretation. The sufficiency of existing provisions depends entirely on the application of the legality principle.

---

139 For example see Case 300/81 Commission v Italy, 1 March 1983.

140 Report from the Commission based on Article 14 of the Council Framework Decision of 28 May 2001 combating fraud and counterfeiting of non-cash means of payment, COM (2004) 346 final, 30.4.2004, point 1.2.2.

141 G. Corstens, J. Pradel, 'Het Europese strafrecht', Kluwer, 2003, pp. 494–557.

The second limitation of implicit implementation is the observance of the standards of foreseeability of national law. An example is Framework Decision 2001/413 on fraud with non-cash payment means, where one can see differences in the approach taken by the Netherlands, Austria and Germany.[142] Theft of credit cards, which was to be prohibited under the Framework Decision, was to be punished under the chapeau provision of theft in the Netherlands and no implementation was thus needed. The margin for application of this provision has been broadly expanded in recent decades; as explained before, the Dutch provision on theft was used to cover offences related to theft of electricity and computer crime.[143]

The Dutch Supreme Court, in particular, regards the theft of credit cards and their pin codes as a form of aggravated theft.[144] The problem with this is that the protected legal good/interest is not the card itself, but the bank account to which the perpetrator gains access. In other Member States, such as Austria and Germany, theft of credit cards was criminalised by specific provisions that were introduced into their penal codes (e.g. Article 266b GCC). Determining whether an implicit implementation respects the *lex certa* principle depends greatly on the national conception of the principle. Thus, the Commission did not criticise this practice.[145]

Another question is whether there is a requirement to indicate the European origins of the national criminal liability. That was implied by the ECJ as individuals can verify whether national legislation complies with the European instrument.[146] However, in criminal law, the added value of this is not clear. Due to minimum harmonisation, national criminal laws would be incorrectly implemented only if the scope was more lenient than the European instrument. Therefore, going beyond the scope of a Directive is not a violation of EU law. However, perhaps that requirement could be an improvement for foreseeability; individuals would be able to clarify the scope of the national criminal liability that implements a European instrument. Moreover, European instruments also contain the goals and underlying purpose of criminalisation, which contributes to clarify the scope of criminal liability.

Similarly, the obligation of conform interpretation prohibits national courts from interpreting the scope of criminal liability in an unforeseeable manner; however, it obliges courts to read the national text in light of the European instrument. It seems that individuals are burdened with the task of being aware of European norms, especially when these relate to their professional sphere.[147] Requiring national

142 Framework Decision 2001/413 of 28 May 2001 combating fraud and counterfeiting of non-cash means of payment OJ L 149, 2.6.2001, pp. 1–4.

143 Chapter IV para. 10.1.2.

144 See HR 19 April 2005 LJN AS9237 and Gerechtshof Arnhem 28 May 2001 LJN AD8989.

145 Report from the Commission based on Article 14 of the Council Framework Decision of 28 May 2001 combating fraud and counterfeiting of non-cash means of payment, COM (2004) 346 final, 30.4.2004.

146 C–345/06 Gottfried Heinrich, 10 March 2009, para. 46–47.

147 T–216/05 Mebrom NV v Commission of the European Communities, 22 May 2007, para. 103; Rechtbank Groningen 17 December 2007 LJN BC0351.

legislators to denote the European origin of a provision would contribute to foreseeability and accessibility.

4.6. Methods of implementation

When the national legislator chooses to implement explicitly, different techniques in implementing EU rules into national law could be employed. However, European criminal law does not distinguish or prefer any of these methods.

The first method is the so-called copy-paste. The legislator simply copy-pastes the European criminal law provision in the national instrument.[148] This method is ergonomic and fast, and the legislator easily might presume that correct implementation is safeguarded. Therefore, it is a very popular technique, yet given the abstract description of European provisions it can be problematic for *lex certa.* Moreover, it could create incoherence and inconsistency in the national system. The method is problematic only if the European definition of the offence is too abstract, has unfamiliar terminology, or is inconsistent with national legislation. Therefore, challenges may exist on a case-by-case basis.

The second method is the reference technique. In this method, the legislator does not draft a definition of criminal liability in national law, but refers to the relevant EU provision, for instance: *'violations of Article X of the Y Directive will be criminalised with...'.*[149] This technique is also very popular for its simplicity, especially in fields of law where there are multiple instruments frequently amended, such as health law Regulations. As with the previous method, the legislator does not concretise the definition of criminal liability. In addition, the individual is obliged to search and consult the Directive or Regulation. By choosing this method, the legislator avoids repetitions. The referred norm, namely the definition of criminal liability in the Directive, is considered an integrated part of the national criminal provision.[150] The reference method may present serious problems with *lex certa,* as the individuals are burdened with the task of searching for the definition of the prohibited act.

In national law, it is not considered against the principle of *lex certa*; however, as the referred norm becomes a part of national criminal law, both provisions need to fulfil the requirements of the legal certainty principle.[151] Therefore, European definitions of liability also have to be precise once the national criminal norm refers to them. Because Directives are prescribed purposefully with a level of abstractness to leave room for implementation, the *lex certa* principle cannot be reconciled with the reference method in many cases.

Especially popular in national law is the dynamic reference. As mentioned previously, this method is used at the European level, which presents some challenges

148 A. Klip, 'European Criminal Law: An Integrative Approach', Intersentia, 2012, p. 221.

149 Ibid.

150 H. Satzger, 'Internationales und Europäisches Strafrecht', Nomos, 2011, pp. 131–136.

151 Ibid.

in tracking the instruments. At the national level, these difficulties are further accentuated because there is a multi-level system of norms created. Moreover, distinguishing the dynamic and static technique can be challenging. The use of a dynamic reference by the national legislator has been criticised because it causes confusion.[152] The individual is obliged to track a number of European instruments that are frequently amended or interrelated with more European instruments.

Third, the translation method requires that the national legislator concretise the context of criminal liability and adapt it to the national system of norms.[153] It reflects the genuine concept of implementation, which is to concretise European norms to give full effect to their goals. As a technique, it is rather safe and respects the principle of *lex certa* to the extent that the national legislator performs tasks accordingly. Problems might occur with few misunderstandings of the concept of European norms, because the national legislator can understand the terminology used differently. Thus, this method could inhibit dangers for the fulfilment of European obligations because the national legislator may misunderstand European legislation. The ECJ could also give a different interpretation to criminal liability.

The fourth method is the European interpretation. With this method, the national legislator does not implement European norms, but the national courts interpret pre-existing legislation or follow a judicial practice that fulfils the goals of the European instrument.[154] This is not a method of implementation per se because the national legislator does not introduce any provisions. It is quite similar to the implicit/silent implementation; however, in this case, pre-existing national provisions could be only remotely related to the criminal liability norms of the European instrument. This is the only method that the ECJ has declared not only in violation of the *lex certa* principle but also as an incorrect practice of implementation. As mentioned, word-for-word implementation is not necessary, and the national legislator is allowed to use prior legislation. However, a mere practice or interpretation of the norm by the national courts cannot be used as an implementation technique.[155] The requirement of legal certainty cannot be met *'even where the settled case-law of a Member State interprets the provision of national law in a manner deemed to satisfy the requirements of a Directive'*.[156] It is unclear on how to demarcate the implicit implementation technique from the prohibited European interpretation method. The actual distinction between the two practices lies with the limits of the *lex stricta* principle. Whether there are indeed pre-existing criminal provisions that could cover the scope of the European criminal liability is a matter of interpretation and also a matter of limits of the conform interpretation.

---

152 Ibid., p. 133.

153 A. Klip, 'European Criminal Law: An Integrative Approach', Intersentia, 2012, p. 222.

154 Ibid.

155 Case 300/81 Commission v Italy, 1 March 1983.

156 C–144/99 Commission of the European Communities v Kingdom of the Netherlands, 10 May 2011, para. 21.

What is evident from this discussion is that the implementation of European instruments is a field in which uncertainty and confusion can easily arise. National legislators may take lightly the task of implementation, often motivated from the pressure to implement quickly. Here, two questions arise: how far should the European legality principle control national implementation, especially because of the existence of national standards of legality? For example, should the principle preclude certain dangerous techniques?[157] The second question is related to the first one. What criteria should guide the supervisory role of the ECJ in infringement proceedings involving incorrect implementation of criminal law Directives due to lack of clarity?[158]

5. Interpretation of criminal liability

The principle of *lex stricta* is the fourth element of the legality principle that sets limits on the interpretation tasks of a judge in criminal law. As an aspect of the legality principle, it is addressed to courts. Courts cannot interpret norms by extending criminal liability. This aspect is also recognised as a general principle of EU law.[159]

The ECJ integrates the jurisprudence of the ECtHR with regard to the *lex stricta* principle, according to which the principle of legality does not preclude the gradual clarification of the criminal liability by jurisprudence.[160] However, such interpretation should be foreseeable for individuals. The notion of foreseeability depends on the wording of the text, the field of law and the status of those to whom it is addressed.[161] In this regard, foreseeability can be achieved not only through the wording of the provision but also with appropriate legal advice.[162] In particular, professionals are expected to assess the risks of their activities and be fully informed of the legislative context.[163]

Therefore, an interpretation can violate the principle of *lex stricta* if it *'produces a result which was not reasonably foreseeable at the time when the offence was committed, especially in the light of the interpretation put on the provision in the case-law at the material time'*.[164] The prohibition of analogy is also found in European criminal law but it is not frequently cited by the ECJ.[165] This is perhaps

157 Chapter VIII para. 3.3.3.
158 Chapter VIII para. 3.3.2.
159 Joined cases C–74/95 and C–129/95 criminal proceedings against X, 12 December 1996, para. 25.
160 Joined cases C–189/02 P, 202/02 P, 208/02 P *et al.* Dansk Rørindustri A/S *et al,* 28 June 2005, para. 217.
161 Ibid.
162 Ibid.
163 Ibid., para. 219.
164 Ibid., para. 218.
165 T–99/04 AC Treuhand AG v Commission of the European Communities, 8 July 2008, para. 140; Opinion AG Colomer of 12 September 2006 in C–303/05 Advocaten voor de Wereld VZW v Leden van de Ministerraad, 3 May 2007, para. 102.

because of the influence of the ECtHR jurisprudence on EU law. As mentioned, although the ECtHR refers to the prohibition of analogy, it does not investigate analogical reasoning per se; it focuses on the foreseeability of the interpretation, not the method.[166]

5.1. Methods of interpreting EU law

In general, concepts of criminal liability in EU law receive an autonomous meaning, which may be at variance with national definitions.[167] Discovering such an autonomous meaning may be challenging. The interpretation of European criminal law faces different pitfalls than national law. The multilingualism and the level of ambiguity of the European instruments result in many interpretative problems. To solve these, the ECJ uses literal/grammatical interpretation and teleological interpretation, whereas historical interpretation is less frequent.[168] In particular, literal/grammatical interpretation represents the first step of interpreting the scope of a provision. Many Framework Decisions and Directives contain definitions of terms such as 'legal person' or 'unlawful'.[169] The ECJ frequently chooses to closely read the wording of European instruments. For example, in a case considering criminal procedure, specifically the standing of the victims in criminal proceedings, the Court chose to stay within the limits of the term 'victim', as defined by the European instrument and exclude legal entities from the definition.[170] Although grammatical/literal interpretation is the first step, the ECJ rarely uses only the wording of European instruments.

By far the favourite method of the ECJ is the teleological interpretation. In explaining this method, AG Bot has stated, *'The Court has consistently held that, in interpreting a provision of Community law, it is necessary to consider not only its wording but also the context in which it occurs and the objectives of the rules of which it forms part'*.[171] This method serves the effective application of EU law and it is self-evidently necessary especially for Directives, which are binding for the result to be achieved. It also assists the obligation of conform interpretation.

Given the diversity in national systems, clarifying the will of the European legislator plays an important role for the observation of Treaties. An example of teleological interpretation is found in *Grøngaard*.[172] The question was how

---

166 For instance ECtHR Kononov v Latvia, App. 36376/04, 17 May 2010, para. 185: *'the principle that the criminal law must not be extensively construed to an accused's detriment, for instance by analogy.'*

167 C–261/09 Gaetano Mantello, 16 November 2010, para. 38.

168 A. Klip, 'European Criminal Law: An Integrative Approach', Intersentia, 2012, pp. 148–150.

169 E.g. Directive 2008/99 of 19 November 2008 on the protection of the environment through criminal law OJ L 328, 6.12.2008, pp. 28–37.

170 C–467/05 criminal proceedings against Giovanni Dell'Orto, 28 June 2007, para. 54.

171 Opinion AG Bot of 1 March 2007 in C–76/06 P Britannia Alloys & Chemicals Ltd v Commission of the European Communities, 7 June 2007, para. 53.

172 C–384/02 criminal proceedings against Knud Grøngaard and Allan Bang, 22 November 2005.

Article 3(a) of Directive 89/592 on insider dealing should be interpreted. The provision exempted the disclosure of information when this occurs in the normal course of a person's exercise of employment from the prohibited insider dealing.[173] Grøngaard was an employee-representative on the Board of Directors of a company, where he learned about an imminent merger. He disclosed this information to Bang, the General Secretary of the professional union, who further passed on the news to other colleagues. The latter individuals successfully bought profitable shares in the stock market. The question was what the phrase in Article 3 (a) meant: *'unless such disclosure is made in the normal course of the exercise of his employment, profession or duties'.*

The Court investigated by considering the objectives pursued by the Directive.[174] It searched the preamble of the Directive, as preambles can be a very rich source of information, although they lack a binding effect. Given the sensitivity of the issue due to the imminent merger, the Court specified that Article 3(a) should be construed to prohibit such disclosure, unless there is a close-link with the exercise of Grøngaard's employment and the disclosure is strictly necessary.[175]

The teleological interpretation may lead to a stricter or more extensive scope of criminal liability. In most cases, this method tends to broaden the scope of national criminal liability. Interpretational questions that are presented to the ECJ involve discrepancies between national legislation and EU law and tough interpretative questions, which may require a closer look into the purpose of European instruments.

Historical interpretation was, in principle, used infrequently by the ECJ. The *travaux préparatoires* were not usually consulted for interpreting EU law. The most important reason for that was that these documents were not published. Therefore, the individual could not foresee the possible interpretative result.[176] However, gradually the importance of the *travaux préparatoires* has increased. This is especially because the *travaux préparatoires* of recent amendments of the Treaties have received more widespread publication.[177] It is argued that the more accessible these documents are the more the ECJ shall consult them.[178] Therefore, historical interpretation is expected to gain more importance in the future.[179]

---

173 Directive 89/592 of 13 November 1989 coordinating regulations on insider dealing OJ L 334, 18.11.1989, pp. 30–32.

174 C–384/02 criminal proceedings against Knud Grøngaard and Allan Bang, 22 November 2005, para. 32.

175 Ibid., para. 48.

176 Opinion AG Maduro of 25 May 2004 in C–384/02 criminal proceedings against Knud Grøngaard and Allan Bang, 22 November 2005, para. 33.

177 K. Lenaerts, J.A. Gutiérrez-Fons, 'To Say What the Law of the EU Is: Methods of Interpretation and the European Court of Justice', EUI Working Paper AEL 2013/9, pp. 19–24.

178 Opinion AG Kokott of 17 January 2013 in C–583/11 P Inuit Tapiriit Kanatami and Others v European Parliament and Council of the European Union, 3 October 2013, para. 32.

179 K. Lenaerts, J.A. Gutiérrez-Fons, 'To Say What the Law of the EU Is: Methods of Interpretation and the European Court of Justice', EUI Working Paper AEL 2013/9, p. 24.

One should also add the method of interpretation in conformity with the Treaties. The provisions should always be interpreted in conformity with the Treaties (including the general principles of EU law) in case of more than one possible interpretation in European secondary legislation.[180] This interpretation reflects the hierarchy of European sources of law. It is somewhat similar to the 'systematic' method of interpretation. An example can be seen in competition law. Article 101 para. 1 TFEU prohibits anti-competitive behaviour, and para. 3 of the same Article exempts from this prohibition the agreements that promote competition under specific circumstances. Here, the scope of both these paragraphs functions as communicating vessels; a broad interpretation of 101 para. 2 would deem para. 3 ineffective. Therefore, the Court has followed an interpretation that maintains the effectiveness of Article 101 para. 3 TFEU.[181] Another example is the case of insider dealing mentioned above. The exemption from the prohibition cannot be construed in a manner that would jeopardise the effectiveness of the prohibited conduct. The use of the systematic interpretation depends on how systematic and organised a system is.

5.2. Is the ECJ bound by the principle of legality?

One of the main problems with the European *lex stricta* principle is that individuals have no standing before the ECJ, apart from the short list of exceptions in the Treaties. Thus, one may wonder whether there is any point in applying the *lex stricta* principle to the ECJ. The only manner in which an interpretation of the ECJ can influence the position of the individual in criminal proceedings is in the context of preliminary rulings. In a preliminary ruling proceeding though, the ECJ cannot delve deeply into the interpretation of criminal liability because there is a distribution of tasks between the ECJ and national courts. Accordingly, the ECJ can only interpret European norms.[182] The ECJ is neither competent to decide questions regarding the compatibility of national legislation with European rules nor whether there is room for interpreting national legislation in conformity to EU law. Should the ECJ be addressed with a preliminary question on compatibility of national law, it usually rephrases the question and answers only on the interpretation of EU law.[183]

Therefore, the ECJ does not wish to bind itself with the *lex stricta* principle in the preliminary rulings proceedings. It stated clearly in *Grøngaard* that the interpretation of a Directive does not depend on the nature of the national

180 C–305/05 Ordre des barreaux francophones et germanophone and Others v Conseil des ministers, 26 June 2007.

181 T–112/99 Métropole télévision (M6), Suez-Lyonnaise des eaux, France Télécom and Télévision française 1 SA (TF1) v Commission of the European Communities, 18 September 2001, para. 74.

182 A. Klip, 'European Criminal Law: An Integrative Approach', Intersentia, 2012, pp. 126–127.

183 E.g. C–348/96 criminal proceedings against Donatella Calfa, 19 January 1999, para. 13–14.

proceedings as civil, administrative or criminal law.[184] However, would the Court insist on this approach if the European instrument were of criminal nature? If the interpretation of the ECJ does not depend on the nature of national proceedings, does it depend on the nature of the Directive if it criminalises behaviour?

In practice, the Court may often interpret Directives by considering the effect that such an interpretation could have for criminal liability at the national level. In Italy, unknown persons were charged with the pollution of the water as a consequence of the periodic destruction of aquatic fauna by extracting water. This resulted in an increase of the quantity of polluting substances above acceptable levels. The relevant Directive obliged Member States to protect designated waters. The national prosecutor faced the following problem: the act of extracting water, which eventually increased the polluting factors, did not explicitly fall under any of the national provisions. The national provision prohibited the discharging of polluting substances – a different act than the extraction of water. The national court was contemplating whether the relevant Directive would also cover the extraction of waters.

AG Mancini indicated that to give full effect to the Directive, not only the discharge of harmful substances but also water extraction should be prohibited.[185] He maintained that the act of extracting water is similar to the act of discharging polluted factors, because both these behaviours entail the harmful effect that the Directive wishes to avoid. The Directive seeks to protect the habitat of fish; therefore, any act that would result in the increase of harmful substances should be prohibited. However, the ECJ did not follow this approach. It recognised that such an interpretation, albeit in accordance with the goals of the Directive, would result in the extensive interpretation of national criminal liability (also providing a good example of analogy). Therefore, without even delving deeper into the interpretation of the Directive, the Court advised the national judges to give priority to the principle of *lex stricta*.[186]

On the contrary, there are cases where the ECJ is mute on the conflict between effectiveness and the *lex stricta* principle. In *Damgaard*, the Danish court dealt with the criminal proceedings brought against an individual who published information on his website touting the healing effects of an herbal remedy classified as a medical product under national law.[187] Under the existing (non-criminal law) Directive, the advertisement of medical products should be prohibited by national legislation.[188] Indeed, national legislation prohibited this act. The defendant's

184 C–384/02 criminal proceedings against Knud Grøngaard and Allan Bang, 22 November 2005, para. 28.

185 Opinion AG Mancini of 17 March 1987 in Case 14/86 Pretore di Salò v Persons unknown, 11 June 1987, para. 10.

186 Case 14/86 Pretore di Salò v Persons unknown, 11 June 1987, para. 19.

187 C–421/07 criminal proceedings against Frede Damgaard, 2 April 2009.

188 Directive 2001/83 of 6 November 2001 on the Community code relating to medicinal products for human use OJ L 311, 28.11.2004, pp. 67–128 (see subsequent amendments as well).

website not only praised the medical benefits but also informed the public of the sales in Sweden and Norway, where it was classified as a food supplement.

The national court was troubled with whether the Directive was also meant to prohibit advertising by independent third parties acting on their own initiative. The ECJ held that the Directive should capture this behaviour.[189] Although the ECJ did not refer to the foreseeability requirement, it nevertheless determined the scope of criminal liability by weighing the interests involved.

The allocation of tasks between the ECJ and national courts is not very clear. In some cases, the ECJ deals with the conflict between the effectiveness of EU law and the *lex stricta* principle, and it gives a clear message to the national court on which one prevails; in other cases, it does not do so.[190] Would the Danish court have the choice to reject this interpretation as unforeseeable? It is unclear if this discretion exists because it is not evident whether the silence of the ECJ should be interpreted as an agreement that there is no conflict with legality or whether the national court should determine this issue. In the end, it is not well-defined whether only the national court should apply the principle of *lex stricta* or it should also be considered by the ECJ as well in defining the scope of European instruments. If the latter is correct, then the ECJ's interpretation should also be in compliance with the legality principle.

This question, of whether the ECJ should be bound by the *lex stricta* principle, is vital for European criminal law instruments. For Directives pursuant to Article 83 TFEU, it is the European legislator who determines the dividing line between prohibited and not prohibited acts. Since the ECJ is entrusted with the task of defining the scope of these norms and since the legality principle *'is an inherent limit to the effectiveness of Community Directives'*,[191] one must wonder whether this principle should not also apply to the ECJ.

Hence, the main problems with the European *lex stricta* principle are the following:

- First, with regard to the vertical allocation of tasks between courts, while the nature of the preliminary rulings procedure entails that the *lex stricta* principle does not bind the ECJ due to the lack of investigation of merits, the distribution of tasks between the ECJ and national courts is not always clear. Often, the rulings given by the ECJ already include a pre-decision of whether the behaviour should fall within EU law and is thus criminalised. Therefore, a weighing of the interests involved is already indicated in the ruling, and without proper transparency in the arguments used by the ECJ or some binding force of the *lex stricta* principle, criminal liability can be interpreted arbitrarily in those situations.[192]

---

189 C–421/07 criminal proceedings against Frede Damgaard, 2 April 2009, para. 27–29.

190 Ibid.; C–60/02 criminal proceedings against X, 7 January 2004.

191 Opinion AG Colomer of 17 June 1996 in Joined cases C–74/95 and C–129/95 criminal proceedings against X, 12 December 1996, para. 54.

192 Chapter VIII para. 3.4.1.

- Second, with regard to the horizontal institutional dynamics between the ECJ and the European legislator, the ECJ revisits the legislative choices that are incorporated in the preliminary rulings. Apart from the well-known methodologies used, there are no further guidelines to ensure that the ECJ will not take over the legislative task of the European legislator.[193]

5.3. The obligation of conform interpretation

The obligation of conform interpretation is a method of interpretation that was promoted to ensure the effectiveness of EU law when the national legislators fail to implement correctly or when interpretative questions arise. The obligation to interpret national provisions in light of the European instruments was pronounced first for criminal law in *Pupino*.[194] The case was significant because of the intergovernmental character of the former Third Pillar. However, even before that, this obligation was discussed in criminal law matters.[195] The obligation of conform interpretation is based on the principle of sincere cooperation, according to which national authorities should ensure the fulfilment of their European obligations.[196] This method expresses the hierarchy of the European and national systems and the sources of legislation. It introduces a structural dependence of European and national criminal liability rules. Hence, it creates a certain burden and pressure on national courts to seek the fulfilment of European policies during interpretation. The actual application of this method is a matter of national law. Therefore, the scope of criminal liability and the scope of interpretation would be, in principle, for the national courts to regulate. However, the ECJ has provided some guidance as to how this obligation should apply.

First, it should be clarified that the obligation of conform interpretation applies to national implementing legislation and also to national legislation that touches on European issues.[197] Therefore, national courts should consider national law as a whole in order to assess the compatibility with Directives and the room for interpretation.[198] Whether the national legislation was adopted before or after the Directive is also irrelevant.[199] What matters is the time of enactment of the Directive, because during the implementation period the national court is not obliged to employ this method, unless the national legislator has implemented the Directive early.

193 Ibid.

194 C–105/03 criminal proceedings against Maria Pupino, 16 June 2005, para. 36–43.

195 Case 80/86 criminal proceedings against Kolpinghuis Nijmegen BV, 8 October 1987.

196 C–105/03 criminal proceedings against Maria Pupino, 16 June 2005.

197 Joined cases C–397/01, C–398/01 *et al.* Bernhard Pfeiffer *et al.* v Deutsches Rotes Kreuz, 5 October 2004.

198 Ibid.

199 C–212/04 Konstantinos Adeneler and Others v Ellinikos Organismos Galaktos, 4 July 2006.

Second, the ECJ has put two limits on this method. The first limitation is that the interpretation should not be *contra legem.* This means that interpretation should not be contrary to the wording of the national provision. Moreover, the interpretation should not violate the *lex stricta* principle, namely the national court should not interpret national norms in an unforeseeable manner.[200]

What this obligation actually entails remains ambiguous. A first obstacle is determining what constitutes a *contra legem* interpretation. Presumably, this is when the wording of the national provision excludes the behaviour prescribed in the Directive.[201] The next question is whether the obligation of conform interpretation requires national courts to actively avoid a *contra legem* interpretation. According to AG Sharpston, national courts must employ the available methods to construe the national provision to avoid conflicts with other national rules.[202] Thus, one way to approach *contra legem* is to ensure that the interpretation does not contradict other national rules and therefore safeguard consistency. Another approach is that the *contra legem* requirement could be an obligation of national courts to employ the accepted national methods to avoid a *contra legem* result.

However, a more in-depth consideration of the *contra legem* element shows that this requirement is rather confusing.[203] In EU law, there is an amalgam of different obligations when it comes to conform interpretation and the validity of national implementing laws. Accordingly, when a national provision is *contra legem* to the Directive, then the national provision should be set aside.[204] Moreover, and especially in the context of criminal law, the requirement of *contra legem* becomes redundant as its application coincides with the application of the *lex stricta.*

To explain this, consider scenario A, where the interpretation in conformity with a Directive would entail that the court must go against the wording of the national law, and this would be to the detriment of the accused. Such an interpretation would be against the principle of legality (the other limitation to the interpretation in conformity), and thus, the *contra legem* element is not particularly useful.

In scenario B, the interpretation requires that the court must go against the wording of the national law for the benefit of the accused. Based on the *Simmenthal* doctrine, the national court would be, in principle, obliged to set this rule aside because it is evident that it contradicts with EU law.[205] However, if the European instrument is a Directive based on Article 83 TFEU (minimum harmonisation), this rule cannot apply, as national legislators are entitled to prescribe more severe criminal liability.

---

200 C–105/03 criminal proceedings against Maria Pupino, 16 June 2005, para. 36–43.

201 Opinion AG Elmer of 14 March 1996 in C–168/95 criminal proceedings against Luciano Arcaro, 26 September 1996, para. 39.

202 Opinion AG Sharpston of 11 July 2003 in C–209/12 Walter Endress v Allianz Lebens-versicherungs AG, 19 December 2004.

203 A. Klip, 'Contra legem', European Journal of Crime, Criminal Law and Criminal Justice, vol. 22, 2014, p. 112.

204 Case 106/77 Amministrazione delle Finanze dello Stato v Simmenthal SpA, 9 March 1978.

205 Ibid.

Would the national court presented with scenario B be prohibited from following a *contra legem* interpretation even if it would benefit the accused or is the court simply not obliged to do so? AG Kokott has offered two alternatives for this conundrum:

> The court has repeatedly held that the obligation on a national court to interpret national law in conformity with EU law cannot serve as the basis for an interpretation of national law contra legem. However, it does not appear to me to be unambiguously clear as yet whether a prohibition on interpreting contra legem arises from EU law itself or whether EU law merely does not preclude a national prohibition on interpreting contra legem.[206]

If the first option were correct, this would mean that national judges are obliged to avoid a *contra legem* interpretation even if individuals would not be harmed by it, which seems rather absurd. In the second situation, the *contra legem* element again does not seem helpful. AG Kokott suggests that the first option is correct, but in any case, a *contra legem* interpretation should not be precluded from EU law, unless there is an aggravation of criminal liability. AG Kokott states:

> In any case, in a scenario in which the national law allows such an interpretation and this would not lead to a burden on the individual, for example, in the present situation it would not lead to a punishment being imposed or made more stringent, but on the contrary to a punishment being inapplicable, it is not apparent why that should be precluded by EU law.[207]

Therefore, one could debate whether there is any meaning in the *contra legem* element, or if the *lex stricta* principle makes it redundant.[208] One of the reasons for this incoherence is that the obligation of the conform interpretation method was transposed from the internal market context. In the absence of the requirement of the *lex stricta* principle in non-criminal law areas, the element of *contra legem* is of value in areas other than criminal law.

Reviewing the discussion of the ECJ's second limitation to this obligation – the *lex stricta* principle – the ECJ has given little guidance to national courts because it is a matter of national criminal law and an idiosyncrasy of national legal systems. The conform interpretation method in this regard is to be applied *'as far as possible'*.[209] German courts, who are strongly bound by the wording of legislation, will see less leeway for an 'as far as possible' interpretation in comparison to the Dutch or English judges. AG Elmer confirmed this in *Arcaro* that:

---

206 Opinion AG Kokott of 12 May 2011 in Joined cases C–483/09 and C–1/10 criminal proceedings against Magatte Gueye and Valentín Salmerón Sánchez, 15 September 2011, para. 29.

207 Ibid.

208 Chapter VIII para. 3.4.2.

209 C–105/03 criminal proceedings against Maria Pupino, 16 June 2005.

> [T]he task of courts is to determine the existing law and give judgement in accordance therewith. The adoption of national legislation, including legislation for the implementation of a Directive, is on the other hand a matter for the political authorities of the Member States. It is possible that in the individual Member States there are various rules and various traditions regarding whether and to what extent the courts can draw the attention of the press and the political bodies to the state of the law as determined in the judgements they give. Community law, however, contains no rules on that question and thus involves no restrictions on the use of such measures as may be available to the national courts under national law and the traditions of the individual Member States.[210]

National courts are guided by the presumption that the national legislator correctly implemented the EU measures; this method requires that they place the texts alongside each other in an attempt to interpret the national provision in light of the wording and the purpose of the Directive.[211] Therefore, teleological reasoning is necessary within the conform interpretation method. The obligation of conform interpretation naturally depends on the wording of the national provision. The more vague the wording, the broader the scope for discretion. Moreover, the EU legislation is significant because the text should express clearly the scope of criminalisation, which is not always the case. Given the fact that national legislators usually favour implementation techniques that preserve the wording of Directives, it might be necessary to resort to a preliminary reference to the ECJ. The preamble provisions can be of great use to national courts, because they can explain the purpose and the scope of criminal liability.

Problems with the conform interpretation method can arise in national law, especially because the fulfilment of European obligations can function as an additional motivation to save national legislation from infringement proceedings. This could generally be true although AG Elmer observed that: *'It must be immaterial whether the result of an interpretation concerning a penal provision is obtained on the basis of a Community obligation or other interpretative factors'*.[212] For example, in the case of fraud against the EU, in earlier years, the Greek legislator had made use of the method of implicit implementation. That obliged the national courts to interpret national provisions in conformity with EU law, although that interpretation raised concerns because it was an analogical reasoning.[213] Similar problems arose in the Netherlands with the provision of breaking trust in the Euratom Treaty.[214] In addition, whether the German definition of 'public

---

210 Opinion AG Elmer of 14 March 1996 in C–168/95 criminal proceedings against Luciano Arcaro, 26 September 1996, para. 36.

211 Ibid., para. 38; H. Satzger, 'Internationales und Europäisches Strafrecht', Nomos, 2011, p. 145.

212 Opinion AG Elmer of 14 March 1996 in C–168/95 criminal proceedings against Luciano Arcaro, 26 September 1996, para. 43.

213 Α. Χαραλαμπάκης, 'Η σχέση απάτης κατά του Δημοσίου και της λεγόμενης κοινοτικής απάτης', Ποινικός Λόγος, vol. 3, 2004, p. 978.

214 D.R. Doorenbos, 'EG-recht en strafwetgeving', Delikt en Delinkwent, vol. 22, 1992, p. 1044.

servants' in the criminal code would include also European public officials is contemplated in the academia.[215]

Moreover, the general nature of the conform interpretation is thought provoking. Is it a new method? What does it specifically entail? In fact, the conform interpretation obligation is not so much a method in itself, because it does not introduce a specific technique. It is rather a general guideline that steers judicial interpretation and coordinates the application of existing methods. Therefore, this obligation is more of a direction to national courts to consider, as much as possible, the *telos* of the European legislator. In this regard, it can also be considered as a form of a teleological method, where national courts should consider the will of two legislators who have legislated in a similar issue. The question is whether such obligation requires that, in addition to considering the *telos* of the EU act, it should be given priority over the *telos* of the national legislation.[216] In this instance, the principle of legality should become relevant. However, further guidelines on this issue are not provided by EU law.

6. Conclusion

The goal of this Chapter was to gather the fragments of the legality principle in EU criminal law. The Chapter began with a discussion of the status of the principle. From the picture that emerges, it is evident that the principle has a strong footing in EU law and that its design follows the ECtHR's approach where matters of foreseeability have more gravity than formalistic requirements. However, there are some evident lacunae, problems, and conflicts in its application. There are three types of complexities associated with this principle.

First, it is not evident what comprises the theoretical rationales of the legality principle in EU law. In principle, its theoretical rationales should support its application in EU law. However, there is no coherent view on the manner in which the principle should be interpreted. A proper understanding of the legitimising function of the legality principle in European criminal law is lacking.[217]

Second, it is unclear how the principle operates in a two-level system and whether it should distribute tasks between European and national authorities. Such a distributive function would inevitably depend on the theoretical basis of the legality principle. There is some guidance regarding the application of the *lex certa* principle to Directives and the obligations of national authorities; however, a more generalised view is absent. As discussed above, problems often arose because it was unclear whether the ECJ was bound by the legality principle or how strictly the national legislation must follow the European *lex certa* principle.[218]

---

215 H. Satzger, 'Internationales und Europäisches Strafrecht', Nomos, 2011, p. 100.

216 Chapter VII para. 4 and more specifically Chapter VIII para. 3.4.2.

217 Chapter VIII para. 1.

218 Chapter VIII para. 2.2.

The third issue relates to the specific normative role of the principle. Again, there are some lacunae or inconsistencies. For example, it is unclear whether criminal liability should always be based on a statute. The position of jurisprudence is also unclear. In competition law cases, a concept of *droit* is adopted; however, the exact status of jurisprudence is ambiguous. This is even more muddled when it comes to national implementation. Although an implicit implementation is not precluded, it is uncertain how this could be evaluated by the ECJ in future infringement proceedings.[219]

Moreover, some modes of application of this principle have been underdeveloped. For example, there are no specific criteria to ensure proper implementation or guidelines as to the supervisory role of the ECJ in infringement proceedings in case of a breach.[220] Some inconsistencies and paradoxes have been also noticed, for example the *contra legem* rule.[221] In the procedure of preliminary rulings procedure, there are problems of distribution between the ECJ and national courts for one and also the lack of more specific guidelines regarding the application of this principle to the ECJ's reasoning.[222]

More often, the legality principle has been developed within a legal system that has been legitimising itself via the mandate of Treaties alone. This is a rather limited and a too positivistic approach that follows the reasoning of 'the Treaties say so'. This is a casual answer to a more profound question that has never been openly posed: what legitimises European criminal law? Although the ECJ applies the principle in particular cases, there has not been an evaluation of what the principle protects, and more importantly, how did its existence within the European criminal justice system change it. Is the European criminal law system more legitimate now that the principle of legality exists? How so? What does it mean to have a legality principle in European criminal law?[223]

In summary, a review of the legality principle in European criminal law to date indicates that there are many questions regarding its theoretical basis, its interplay in a two-level system, the specific normative role of the principle, and its modes of application. The questions raised in the present Chapter will be revisited in the next two Chapters where these problems are examined from the perspective of the general nature of the European criminal justice system.

---

219 Chapter VIII para. 3.1.
220 Chapter VIII para. 3.3.
221 Chapter VIII para. 3.4.2.
222 Chapter VIII para. 3.4.1.
223 Chapter VII para. 5.

Chapter VII
The Legitimacy of European Criminal Justice

The fragmentary application of the principle of legality in European criminal law is a consequence of deeper deficiencies regarding the system's legitimacy. The attribution of criminal law competences to European institutions has been determined to be mainly a reflex to the negative consequences of abolishing internal borders, although an incremental shift towards a more principled criminal justice has been noted. Currently, principles such as *ultima ratio*, proportionality, legality and guilt are considered to govern European criminal law, at least in theory. However, the theoretical foundations of the European *ius puniendi* and what these principles represent remain unclear. Does European criminal law offer a form of protection to individuals against arbitrariness, and if so, what would be the nature of such protection? Questions about the instrumental finality are also in order. What is the rationale of combating cross-border crime or facilitating judicial cooperation? Often, boosting freedom of movement has been cited as the *raison d'être,* but just how far can this argument go? In principle, every harmonisation of criminal offences would serve this purpose.

This Chapter will discuss the legitimacy of European criminal law. As with national criminal law, the function of the legality principle in EU law depends on how criminal law is legitimised. It was explained in Chapter I that the legality principle has a legitimising function.[1] Criminal law legitimacy was defined as the justification of coercive power. To construct a theory for this principle in EU law, it is important to understand what type of legitimacy it should provide. However, the question of legitimacy is quite complex. The European criminal justice system presents various unprecedented particularities that create a matrix of interrelated problems.

First, in national law, the main focus of the principle of legality is the relationship between individuals and the state. But the relationship between the EU and individuals in the field of criminal law is not clear. The purpose and nature of the EU in the field of criminal law is also uncertain. European criminal justice forms a part of the European legal order to which its purpose and nature are strongly connected. The justice system also holds a strong attachment to European integration, but what is the nature of EU law? Is the EU a state? From where does this legal order derive its legitimacy? Thus, the discussion of the legitimation of European criminal law must be put into the more general context of European integration.[2]

---

1 Chapter I para. 1.

2 E. Herlin-Karnell, 'Europe's Area of Freedom, Security and Justice Through the Prism of Constitutionalism: Why the EU Needs a Grammar of Justice to Improve Its Legitimacy', Discussion Paper SP IV 2014–801, Wissenschaftszentrum Berlin für Sozialforschung, 2014, p. 2.

Second, the attribution of criminal law powers to European institutions challenges the traditionally exclusive relationship between criminal law and nation states. For example, instruments such as the EAW or the amendments brought by the Lisbon Treaty have prompted national constitutional courts to challenge the legitimacy of European *ius puniendi.*[3] Similarly, criminal law cases at the European level such as *Kadi* have opened up a debate regarding the nature of the European legal order *vis-à-vis* the United Nations.[4] Concepts of democracy, separation of powers, Rule of Law, individual autonomy, and citizenship receive dimensions beyond the nation state. However, it is unclear how these concepts influence the European *ius puniendi*.

Third, the European criminal justice system is based on the interrelationship between two levels of decision-making and legitimation. This complexity results in both practical and theoretical questions. Should a European legality principle protect individuals from their nation states, or is the legitimising function of European criminal law limited by national sovereignty? These questions have remained unanswered because of the current momentum of European criminal law as a system in motion. What needs to be discussed is the constitutional relationship between European and national legal orders, especially in the field of criminal law.

Consequently, these issues shall be addressed in this Chapter. It begins with an explanation of the relationship between the European legal order, integration, and criminal law and a discussion of the different tendencies involved in legitimising European criminal law. An investigation of the current theories regarding the co-existence of European and national legal orders follows, in which theoretical and practical consequences of every theory shall be analysed. I shall then propose a theory of European criminal justice by employing the conclusions of the previous Chapters. Specifically, I shall advocate for a relational model of European criminal justice and explain why it may solve the existing problems and provide the required legitimation. Based on the proposed features of European criminal justice as a theoretical framework, I shall use the final Chapter (Chapter VIII) to explain the nature and functions of the legality principle in EU law.

1. Three mind-sets for understanding the EU

A preliminary question is whether the European legal order is capable of acquiring legitimation. This is a basic meta-question that requires consideration of whether

---

3 J. Komárek, 'European constitutionalism and the European arrest warrant: contrapunctual principles in disharmony', Common Market Law Review, vol. 44, 2007, pp. 9–40.

4 C–402/05 P Kadi and Al Barakaat International Foundation v Council and Commission, 3 September 2008; J. Kokott, C. Sobotta, 'The Kadi Case – Constitutional Core Values and International Law – Finding the Balance?', The European Journal of International Law, vol. 23, 2012, pp. 1015–1024; M. Kumm, 'Rethinking Constitutional Authority: On the Structure and Limits of Constitutional Pluralism', in M. Avbelj, J. Komárek (eds), 'Constitutional Pluralism in the European Union and Beyond', Hart Publishing, 2012, p. 39.

the concept of legitimacy is a pure state concept. Can criminal law only exist in a legitimate manner within a nation state? Over the years, various theories developed that could be summarised into three different schools of thought that differ with regard to the level of openness and rigidity of concepts. It is important to understand the different mind-sets, as these will be recognisable in further analysis.

The first school of thought approaches constitutionalism as a state-centred idea in which any underlying principles, such as democracy or the Rule of Law, cannot be transposed to the European legal order.[5] This school of thought is rooted in the Westphalian model of the state; any transposal of constitutional concepts to the European level is illegitimate. Nation states maintain their monopoly as the sole political and legal model within which political communities are organised. The European legal order is not negated but is rather approached from a perspective of international law (as an international legal order instead of a constitutional one).[6] In particular, this school of thought attempts to confine any transformations of authority beyond the state as governed by old-fashioned international law ideas. In literature, such attitudes are usually found in assertions such as 'the Member States are the masters of the Treaties'.[7] Thus, any legitimation of post-national organisations derives from national constitutional law. Constitutional principles such as democracy, separation of powers and the Rule of Law are only attained at the national level, and any form of protection of individual autonomy is to be achieved solely by national constitutional orders. This trend also shows in theories about European criminal law that reflect a state-centred idea of constitutionalism and is often noted in literature, especially that belonging to the pre-Lisbon era.[8] The consequence for European criminal law is that it does not derive any legitimation from the European legal order and, as such, it cannot protect individuals. Therefore, a European legality principle must be constructed to solely promote national sovereignty with a bottom-up legitimation of European criminal law measures.

In the second school of thought, constitutionalism is 'a mobile set of ideals' that can be easily transposed on a post-national or supranational entity such as the

5 A. Klip, 'European Criminal Law: An Integrative Approach', Intersentia, 2012, pp. 28–29.

6 T. Schilling, 'The Autonomy of the Community Legal Order – an Analysis of Possible Foundations', Harvard International Law Journal, vol. 37, 1996, p. 389; J.H.H. Weiler, 'The Constitution of Europe', Cambridge University Press, 1999, pp. 292–298.

7 N. Walker, 'Postnational constitutionalism and the problem of translation', in J.H.H. Weiler M. Wind (eds), 'European Constitutionalism Beyond the State', Cambridge University Press, 2003, p. 29.

8 For example, M. Kaiafa-Gbandi, 'The development towards harmonisation within criminal law in the European Union – a citizen's perspective', European Journal of Crime, Criminal Law and Criminal Justice, vol. 7, 2001, p. 239; B. Schünemann, 'Alternative Project for a European Criminal Law and Procedure', Criminal Law Forum, 2007, pp. 227–232. More generally see E. Herlin-Karnell, 'The Constitutional Dimension of European Criminal Law', Hart Publishing, 2012, pp. 13–15.

EU.[9] The nation state model is not negated. On the contrary, this school of thought searches for features of national constitutionalism in the European legal order.[10] To some extent, this mind-set supports an automatic transposition of features from the national to the supranational regime.[11] Failures of transposition due to the different characteristics of the European legal order are determined to be lacunae, or deficits. For example, one may accept the ability to transpose the concept of the democratic principle to the EU level, but any incompatibility results in a deficit. Countless contributions investigate how national principles such as the Rule of Law, democracy, separations of powers and proportionality transpose to the European level.[12] For European criminal law, such an approach would imply that the legitimation of European criminal law powers is possible. Often, this mind-set involves an empirical understanding of European criminal law. A frequent tendency in scholarship is to systematise and structure European criminal law as an analogy to the existing features of national criminal systems.[13]

Both schools present certain problems. On one hand, the second school of thought, which easily accommodates the nation state model in the European legal order, encounters lacunae. The first school of thought (to some extent a reaction to the pitfalls of copy-pasting the national constitutional model onto the EU and avoid apologetic thinking)[14] is rather locked into the passé and parochial views of state-centric ideals that do not extend the dialogue much further.[15]

The third school of thought approaches the transposition of the state model to the EU with a more critical eye. Its starting point is the classic Westphalian model incorporating the value of a constitutional state. Concomitantly, any transposition of the state model to the EU requires a more critical and open-minded approach.[16] Any adaptation must therefore *'proceed through an examination of the common core values and of how they inform and condition the normative frame of constitutionalism in any particular context'*.[17] If the choice is to place European criminal law in this school of thought, then one is forced to question the legitimacy

9 N. Walker, 'Postnational constitutionalism and the problem of translation', in J.H.H. Weiler M. Wind (eds), 'European Constitutionalism Beyond the State', Cambridge University Press, 2003, p. 29.

10 Ibid., p. 30.

11 Ibid.

12 For example, W. van Gerven, 'The European Union – A Polity of States and Peoples', Hart Publishing, 2005, pp. 104–255.

13 L. Gröning, 'A Criminal Justice System or a System Deficit? Notes on the System Structure of the EU Criminal Law', European Journal of Crime, Criminal Law and Criminal Justice, vol. 18, 2010, pp. 118–119.

14 B. Schünemann, 'Alternative Project for a European Criminal Law and Procedure', Criminal Law Forum, 2007, p. 230.

15 F. Meyer, 'Strafrechtsgenese in Internationalen Organisationen', Nomos, 2012, pp. 643–652.

16 N. Walker, 'Postnational constitutionalism and the problem of translation', in J.H.H. Weiler M. Wind (eds), 'European Constitutionalism Beyond the State', Cambridge University Press, 2003, pp. 35–54.

17 Ibid., p. 52.

of criminal law in the European setting.[18] Therefore, to have any discussion on the legitimacy of European criminal law, one should be mindful of the potential necessity to re-evaluate the connection between the nation state and criminal law.[19]

The third school of thought does not nullify national sovereignty. It also does not aver that all protective guarantees of criminal law necessarily transfer to the European criminal justice system. It argues that, first, there is a possibility to recognise some constitutional values within the European criminal justice system, and therefore, the system could potentially legitimise itself. Second, constitutional principles underpinning European criminal law are not an automatic copy-paste from the national to the European level. For example, the interpretation of a European democratic principle would differ from that of a national democratic principle, but this does not necessarily decrease the legitimacy of European criminal law.

The third school of thought echoes the methodological discussion in Chapter II.[20] Any transposition of national criminal law principles to the European legal order requires adaptation. This methodology is now viewed with a more substantial context. The third school of thought offers the opportunity to comply with the chosen methodology of this contribution and creates a mind-set upon which further discussions of the constitutional features of the European legal order can develop.

2. Nature and legitimacy of the EU

Unlike nation states, the formation of the EU was an intentional, autonomous and voluntary act by its Member States in order to form an 'ever-closer Union'. The European legal order is a different political community, as *'when acceptance and subordination are voluntary, and repeatedly so, they constitute an act of true liberty and emancipation from collective self-arrogance and constitutional fetishism'*.[21] Historically, the EU's specific goals were peace and prosperity.[22] In contrast to its violent past, peace was promoted as an alternative future for the European continent through economic, cultural and social interaction. Prosperity

---

18 L. Gröning, 'A Criminal Justice System or a System Deficit? Notes on the System Structure of the EU Criminal Law', European Journal of Crime, Criminal Law and Criminal Justice, vol. 18, 2010, p. 128.

19 F. Meyer, 'Strafrechtsgenese in Internationalen Organisationen', Nomos, 2012, p. 642; E. Guild, 'Crime and the EU's Constitutional Future in an Area of Freedom, Security and Justice', European Law Journal, vol. 10, 2004, pp. 220–223; H Jung, 'L'etat et moi: Some Reflections on the Relationship Between the Criminal Law and the State', European Journal of Crime, Criminal Law and Criminal Justice, vol. 6, 1998, p. 208; C.J.M. Safferling, 'European as Transnational Law – A Criminal Law for Europe: Between National Heritage and Transnational Necessities', German Law Journal, vol. 10, 2009, pp. 1383–1398.

20 Chapter II para. 1 and 4.

21 J.H.H. Weiler, 'Europe's Constitutional *Sonderweg*', in J.H.H. Weiler, M. Wind (eds), 'European Constitutionalism Beyond the State', Cambridge University Press, 2003, p. 21.

22 J.H.H. Weiler, 'The Constitution of Europe', Cambridge University Press, 1999, pp. 286–323.

entailed the improvement of the European economy by way of the free movement of goods, services, capital and workers.[23]

In earlier days, the *telos* of integration was the ever-closer union between nations and the abolition of obstacles set by national legal orders. The method of integration was not unification, but rather less intense harmonisation. European integration did not pursue the formation of a political and legal unity but, instead, of a political and legal community. The EU is not a federal state comparable with the USA[24] – the latter aims at unity and canalises the excesses of state interests by creating a larger super-state.[25] On the contrary, European integration incorporates a supranational perspective; it promotes community (not unity) and does not seek to eliminate national statehood but to tame the maximisation of national interests within the community.[26]

A third goal, developed much later, was the achievement of supranationality itself by establishing European citizenship and the subsequent legislative competences in citizen-oriented fields of law, such as immigration and criminal law. Apart from the specific goals of integration for each of these areas, such supranationalisation generated a European legal order that antagonised national citizenship without negating it.

More precisely, belonging to a group of people defined by nationality is valued and protected within the EU. National citizenship can counterbalance the stretching and thinning tendencies of cosmopolitan Europe.[27] However, some legal rights and privileges that originate from national citizenship are challenged.[28] Non-discrimination and freedom of movement liberated human interaction from national borders.[29] European citizenship does not dissolve legal bonds between individuals and their nation states. In the absence of a unified European state, nation states are still necessary institutions for guaranteeing liberty and wellbeing.[30] However, national citizenship cannot provide any privileges with regard to other nationalities.

On a historical note, the EU may also be deemed as a vessel for the renaissance of Enlightenment ideas after their brutal nullification during World War II. While a European community was not a general project to revive the Enlightenment in European societies,[31] it did provide a vessel for re-expression of the

23 N. Walker, 'Postnational constitutionalism and the problem of translation', in J.H.H. Weiler M. Wind (eds), 'European Constitutionalism Beyond the State', Cambridge University Press, 2003, p. 46.

24 ECJ Opinion 2/13, 18 December 2014, para. 156.

25 J.H.H. Weiler, 'The Constitution of Europe', Cambridge University Press, 1999, p. 250.

26 Ibid., pp. 250–251.

27 N. Walker, 'Postnational constitutionalism and the problem of translation', in J.H.H. Weiler M. Wind (eds), 'European Constitutionalism Beyond the State', Cambridge University Press, 2003, p. 47.

28 J.H.H. Weiler, 'The Constitution of Europe', Cambridge University Press, 1999, p. 250.

29 Ibid., p. 252.

30 J. Habermas, 'The Crisis of the European Union – A Response', Polity Press, 2012, p. 42.

31 M. Ishay, 'European Integration: The Enlightenment Legacy', History of European Ideas, vol. 19, 1994, pp. 207–213.

Weltanschauung after World War II.[32] European values such as solidarity are an echo of the Enlightenment legacy. Many of these ideals, however, have been dissolving in recent political developments, in particular due to increasing deficiencies of the welfare state, the uneven development of market and social policies, the Commission-based bureaucracy that shaped European policies and, more recently, the anti-solidarity manner of dealing with the economic crises among the southern economies.[33]

Specifically, the handling of the recent economic crisis and its manipulation and instrumentalisation throughout European and national political arenas has presented important existential questions. Raising questions regarding the violability of the Eurozone, the desirability of membership and possible restriction on the freedom of movement may injure the EU.[34] The unprecedented dissatisfaction of citizens towards European institutions clearly registered in the 2014 European elections, characterised by the increasing popularity of nationalist political parties in many Member States and, most certainly, by the UK opt-out decision. The current political climate has been, to some extent, fuelled by political opportunism and exaggerated national political *zitaten* that might disintegrate sooner rather than later. Any political crisis and withdrawal of trust in institutional structures offers more opportunities than dead-ends. 'De-taboo-ing' basic principles such as solidarity and mutual trust offers the opportunity to present further constitutional and political narratives within the EU in a positive and constructive manner.[35]

The EU has a specific political mandate that translates into certain EU policies found in the Treaties. Four basic freedoms were established and include the freedom of movement of workers, capital, goods and services (Article 26 TFEU) – the freedom of establishment in conjunction with non-discrimination has often been referred to as a fifth freedom.[36] Furthermore, mutual recognition and harmonisation constitute two basic tools. These have complemented each other, with mutual recognition achieving the actual movement of products and harmonisation establishing common standards.

The achievement of European policies is not at the discretion of Member States. The EU – especially the ECJ – has long pursued the effective implementation of EU policies. In particular, the principle of sincere cooperation, which was initially developed judicially[37] and then codified (Article 4, para. 3 TEU), obliged national authorities to correctly implement European legislation, enabling individuals to

---

32 J.H.H. Weiler, 'The Constitution of Europe', Cambridge University Press, 1999, pp. 252–255.

33 J. Habermas, 'The Crisis of the European Union – A Response', Polity Press, 2012, pp. 101–139.

34 For example, C–333/13 Elisabeta Dano and Florin Dano v Jobcenter Leipzig, 11 November 2014.

35 J. Habermas, 'The Crisis of the European Union – A Response', Polity Press, 2012, pp. 101–139.

36 G. Comandé, 'The Fifth European Union Freedom: Aggregating Citizenship… around Private Law', in H.-W. Micklitz (ed), 'The Constitutionalisation of European Private law', Oxford University Press, 2014, pp. 61–93.

37 For example Case 68/88 Commission of the European Communities v Hellenic Republic, 21 September 1989.

invoke EU law and actively respond to any violation of EU rules.[38] This principle further generated additional legal principles such as the indirect effect.[39] Simultaneously, in defiance of national constitutional courts, the ECJ began pressing for supremacy. The four freedoms are applied strictly with a general tendency to accept exceptions only in a restrictive manner. The effective enforcement of EU law has been promoted as an institutional mantra.[40] Though it is difficult to classify this concept as a principle, standard or result,[41] it fashions itself quite frequently in the ECJ decisions most often in the form of effective judicial remedies; yet its interpretation is not limited to this form. Today, a governing constitutional principle of EU law, the effective application of EU law supports normative supranationalism – namely, the binding effect of EU measures in national law.[42] Accordingly, the EU has established infringement proceedings against Member States that fail to enforce EU law.

What is clear is a strong political will to implement European policies. The political mandate has always strived for increased integration and supranationalisation of the internal market. Simultaneously, the constitutional character of this seemingly market-oriented EU has been emerging. The European legal order was forced to recognise and protect important individual rights. Later, in the Treaties and the Charter, the EU formally proclaimed itself a constitutional legal order based on the Rule of Law, democracy and other similar constitutional values, and incorporated individual rights within its political mandate.[43] However, that the EU has not fashioned itself as a human rights organisation such as the Council of Europe should be noted. Individual rights are accorded attention only with regard to EU law (Article 51 of the Charter).[44] Thus, though the EU has lost its sole economic character, the competence of the EU to interpret and impose fundamental rights standards remains confined to the areas of EU law.

3. Tendencies in legitimising European criminal law

European criminal law officially materialised in result of the Maastricht Treaty; however, EU law did influence national criminal law prior to this Treaty. Because

38 A. Klip, 'European Criminal Law: An Integrative Approach', Intersentia, 2012, p. 76.

39 C–106/89 Marleasing SA v La Comercial Internacional de Alimentacion SA, 13 November 1990.

40 M. Ross, 'Effectiveness in the European Legal Order(s): Beyond Supremacy to Constitutional Proportionality?', European Law Review, vol. 31, 2006, p. 480.

41 Ibid., pp. 479–486.

42 M. Accetto, S. Zleptnig, 'The Principle of Effectiveness: Rethinking its Role in Community Law', European Public Law, vol. 11, 2005, p. 380; J.H.H. Weiler, 'The Community System: the Dual Character of Supranationalism', Yearbook of European Law, 1981, p. 271.

43 Case 294/83 Parti écologiste "Les Verts" v European Parliament, 23 April 1986; C–402/05 P Kadi and Al Barakaat International Foundation v Council and Commission, 3 September 2008.

44 As most recently reaffirmed with the 'welfare benefit tourism', C–333/13 Elisabeta Dano and Florin Dano v Jobcenter Leipzig, 11 November 2014.

of the principle of sincere cooperation, national legislators were compelled to set aside or amend criminal norms that were in conflict with the freedom of movement. Similarly, legislators were occasionally obliged to issue criminal legislation, especially in the field of European fraud.[45] Conversely, national criminal law has also influenced EU law, especially in the field of freedom of movement. Abstractly formulated exceptions in the Treaties, such as public policy, have often allowed some room to the Member States to justify specific criminal law policies.[46] With the Treaty of Maastricht, criminal law was officially included within the realm of European policies, albeit in specific areas and within the intergovernmental scheme of the Third Pillar, whereas with the Lisbon Treaty, criminal law officially joined the former First Pillar.

3.1. The spill-over theory

Overall, European criminal policy has been abstract. The prevalent justification for transferring criminal law competences to the EU has been the assumption that freedom of movement has an increasing spill-over effect on criminal law. The spill-over argument advocates that this is a necessary reaction to increasing criminal phenomena in a borderless EU and has been a popular theory in scholarship and early policy instruments.[47]

The creation of the AFSJ has been largely associated with the internal market and spill-over theory. The terms 'freedom', 'security' and 'justice' have featured strong connotations of freedom of movement, yet the exact interpretation at policy levels has constantly changed. Article 3, para. 2 TEU and Article 67, para. 1 and 3 TFEU read:

> The Union shall offer its citizens an area of freedom, security and justice without internal frontiers, in which the free movement of persons is ensured in conjunction with appropriate measures with respect to external border controls, asylum, immigration and the prevention and combating of crime.
>
> The Union shall constitute an area of freedom, security and justice with respect for fundamental rights and the different legal systems and traditions of the Member States.
>
> The Union shall endeavour to ensure a high level of security through measures to prevent and combat crime, racism and xenophobia, and through measures for coordination and cooperation between police and judicial authorities and other

45 Case 68/88 Commission of the European Communities v Hellenic Republic, 21 September 1989.

46 A. Klip, 'European Criminal Law: An Integrative Approach', Intersentia, 2012, pp. 64–126.

47 S. Douglas-Scott, 'The Rule of Law in the European Union – Putting the Security into the Area of Freedom, Security and Justice', European Law Review, vol. 29, 2004, p. 222; J. Monar, 'The Dynamics of Justice and Home Affairs: Laboratories, Driving Factors and Costs', Journal of Common Market Studies, vol. 39, 2001, pp. 754–756; Conclusions of the Presidency – Tampere European Council, 15–16.10.1999, para. 2, 5, 6.

competent authorities as well as through the mutual recognition of judgements in criminal matters and, if necessary, through the approximation of criminal laws.

Freedom has primarily been associated with freedom of movement and the spill-over theory. European criminal law protects enjoyment of freedom of movement.[48] This is conceptually different to the manner in which national criminal justice systems interpret freedom – namely, as protecting individuals from state arbitrariness. In the absence of direct enforcement, the four types of freedoms are the only connection between citizens and the EU. The protection of the more traditional form of freedom remains generally with the Member States, which undertake the task of enforcing criminal law measures regardless of whether these have EU origin. It is unclear how European criminal law protects freedom and how this freedom is defined. How does harmonisation of criminal offences protect freedom of movement?

European criminal law, particularly as it relates to terrorism, protects the freedom of individuals to cross borders, as potential victims of crime. This one-sided interpretation of freedom has received support primarily through the Hague Programme, wherein the concept of freedom is defined as 'freedom from crime'.[49] Security-oriented measures that include border checks, surveillance, biometrics and illegal immigration are mentioned under the title 'strengthening freedom'.[50] While freedom is first connected with European citizenship in the Hague Programme (para. 1.1.), only crime-control measures are included within this concept.[51] A more balanced interpretation of freedom is advocated in the Stockholm Programme, wherein freedom is still connected to freedom of movement but it is the relationship between state/individuals that is this concept's primary depiction. In the section 'Promoting citizens' rights: a Europe of rights', various political goals are set, including the promotion of fundamental rights, rights of individuals in criminal proceedings and the right of privacy.[52]

Security has also been approached in the light of the internal market. The security of individuals within Europe has been of high importance in political agendas, with the aim to afford a 'high level' of security for citizens. Such security is understood to promote the safety of individuals against crime. Combating cross-border crime has been of particular importance, especially since 9/11, and is

---

48 M. Fletcher, R. Lööf, B. Gilmore, 'EU Criminal Law and Justice', Edward Elgar Publishing, 2008, p. 23.

49 S. Carrera, T. Balzacq, 'The Hague Programme: the long road to Freedom, Security and Justice', in S. Carrera, T. Balzacq (eds), 'Security versus Freedom? A challenge for Europe's future', Ashgate Publishing, 2006, p. 5.

50 Ibid.

51 D. Bigo, 'Liberty, whose Liberty? The Hague Programme and the conception of Freedom', in S. Carrera, T. Balzacq (eds), 'Security versus Freedom? A challenge for Europe's future', Ashgate Publishing, 2006, pp. 36–37.

52 The Stockholm Programme – An open and secure Europe serving and protecting citizens OJ C 115, 4.5.2010, pp. 1–38, para. 2.

supported in the Hague Programme.[53] For example, a clear shift has occurred in the political focus towards a security-led agenda.[54] Security is deemed a public good, but, as with freedom, it is unclear why security would be of concern to the EU. Article 4, para. 2 TEU reaffirms the monopoly of Member States in safeguarding national security; the concept of security is comparatively more developed by the European institutions. For example, in 1998 the EU was already working to create a 'European Public Order',[55] to secure and maintain a safe environment for individuals, build stable relationships and create a political community.[56] In addition, even in 1977 the dialogue for the establishment of an *espace judiciaire européen* was in motion.[57] Further promotion of these goals materialised in the Stockholm Programme, which focused on the interests and needs of citizens.[58]

However, the European public order lacks definition. It is not clear whether it is anything more than simply the accumulation of common fears and what its relationship is to national security.[59] Furthermore, a profound difference exists with national security and how national criminal systems define their policy agendas. In national systems, the priorities of maintaining safety arise from common and shared values of the national *demos*. In the European legal order, the absence of a European *demos* results in lacking independent sources to draw cultural unity.[60] Excluding European bodies, relatively few forums permit European citizens to develop cultural connections and needs. This means that safeguarding security for such a soft society can be only responsive to problems when they become visible, e.g. human trafficking or narcotics, instead of anticipating potential problems as they emerged from shared common values.[61] Thus, in the Stockholm Programme, security has been conceptualised with milder terminology as 'a European Union that protects', with attention to specific areas of crime such as terrorism and trafficking.[62] However, confusion exists since the

53 The Hague Programme – Strengthening Freedom, Security and Justice in the European Union OJ C 53, 3.3.2005, pp. 1–14.
54 S. Carrera, T. Balzacq, 'The Hague Programme: the long road to Freedom, Security and Justice', in S. Carrera, T. Balzacq (eds), 'Security versus Freedom? A challenge for Europe's future', Ashgate Publishing, 2006, p. 5.
55 Commission Communication Towards an Area of Freedom, Security, and Justice, COM (1998) 459 final, 14.7.1998, p. 9.
56 D. Chalmers, G. Davies, G. Monti, 'European Union Law: Cases and Materials', Cambridge University Press, 2010, p. 588.
57 Proposal by Valéry Giscard d'Estaing for the establishment of an *espace judiciaire européen*, Bruxelles, 5 December 1977, available via www.ena.lu.
58 The Stockholm Programme – An open and secure Europe serving and protecting citizens OJ C 115, 4.5.2010, pp. 1–38.
59 D. Chalmers, G. Davies, G. Monti, 'European Union Law: Cases and Materials', Cambridge University Press, 2010, p. 590.
60 N. Walker, 'Policing and the Supranational', Policing and Society, vol. 12, 2002, p. 318.
61 Ibid.
62 The Stockholm Programme – An open and secure Europe serving and protecting citizens OJ C 115, 4.5.2010, para. 4.

notion of protection can produce different interpretations: *'The question is, whose security is at stake exactly and in what sense? Security in the sense of protection against criminality and terrorist attacks? Or in the sense of protection against (over) intrusive measures by law enforcement authorities? Or both?'*[63]

Justice is even more difficult to grasp. On one hand, justice may be merely a technical term such as efficient administration and access to justice.[64] In the Stockholm Programme, policy goals related to justice are those 'making the life of citizens easier' and include such concepts as efficient administration of justice, enhancement of mutual trust, approximation of criminal norms in conjunction with mutual recognition, and access to e-justice.[65] Conversely, especially in the Charter, justice serves as the title for individual rights such as the principles of legality, proportionality, fair trial, defence rights, and *ne bis in idem* (Title VI of the Charter, Articles 47–50). Therefore, an actual interpretation of this term at the European level is unclear. What is the justice that the EU wishes to achieve?

It is therefore apparent that, at least *prima facie,* the legitimacy of the AFSJ is characterised by a political subordination to the internal market. It is often criticised in literature that security takes primacy over freedom and justice.[66] In the absence of concrete definitions of these concepts at the political level, security (defined as protecting individuals from cross-border crime) is the only plausible justification for the European criminal justice system.

3.2. A default European instrumentalism

The dominance of the spill-over theory and absence of a definition of the triad of 'freedom, security and justice' results in an instrumentalist justification of the European criminal justice system. The legitimacy of European criminal law is, by default, instrumentalist. Criminal law is a means to safeguard freedom of movement and it is philosophically annexed to the internal market.

---

63 Editorial Comment, 'Two speed European Citizenship? Can the Lisbon Treaty help close the gap?', Common Market Law Review, vol. 45, 2008, p. 5.

64 S. Douglas-Scott, 'The Problem of Justice in the European Union', in J. Dickson, P. Eleftheriadis (eds), 'Philosophical Foundations of EU Law', Oxford University Press, 2012, pp. 426–427.

65 The Stockholm Programme – An open and secure Europe serving and protecting citizens OJ C 115, 4.5.2010, para. 3.

66 T. Spronken, 'A place of greater safety', Inaugural Lecture October 2003, Kluwer, 2005; D. Anagonostou, E. Psychogiotopoulou, 'Legal integration and EU governance in a multi-level systems: Can the post-Lisbon Union ensure a balance between freedom, security and justice? (EULEXIS)', Collaborative project, SSH.2011.5.2–2; T. Elholm, 'Does EU Criminal Cooperation Necessarily Mean Increased Repression?', European Journal of Crime, Criminal Law and Criminal Justice, vol. 17, 2009, pp. 191–226; A.K. Gibbs, 'Reasoned Balance in Europe's Area of Freedom, Security and Justice', European Law Journal, vol. 17, pp. 121–137; M. Anderson, L. Apap, 'Striking a Balance Between Freedom, Security and Justice', CEPS, 2002; S. Douglas-Scott, 'The Problem of Justice in the European Union', in J. Dickson, P. Eleftheriadis (eds), 'Philosophical Foundations of EU Law', Oxford University Press, 2012, pp. 424–459.

Furthermore, the AFSJ is also doctrinally annexed to the internal market, as illustrated by the careless copy-pasting of doctrines from the internal market to European criminal law. This practice has created well-documented theoretical problems, especially regarding the doctrine of mutual recognition.[67] Additional practical problems have developed with the transfer of the principle of indirect effect to criminal law, especially in relation to the concept of *contra legem*, as seen in the previous Chapter.[68]

European instrumentalism is also reflected in the manner in which European competences in criminal law have been exercised and interpreted. The competences for substantive criminal law – as laid down in Article 83 TFEU – imply a strong connection to the internal market. The Euro-crimes chosen for approximation in Article 83 para. 1 TFEU are areas *'of particularly serious crime with a cross-border dimension resulting from the nature or impact of such offences or from a special need to combat them on a common basis'*. Though it is understandable why crimes such as human trafficking or child pornography can be particularly serious or have a cross-border character, their selection has been influenced by a spill-over logic whereby crime-control is of pivotal importance. In the absence of a definition of safety arising from the shared values of European citizens, its specific content is neutral. Safety of the European public order is, therefore, determined by ephemeral crime-control goals and has resulted in a fragmented European criminal policy.

This fragmentation, in addition to the annexed and non-autonomous character of European criminal law, is acknowledged by European institutions themselves.[69] For example, the European Parliament *'[s]tresses the need for a more coherent and high-quality EU approach to criminal law and deplores the fragmented approach followed so far'*.[70] Specifically, the lack of autonomy of European criminal law policy, i.e. its autonomy and neutrality *vis-à-vis* the internal market, is criticised in literature: *'The European institutions making criminal policy decisions on a large scale have failed to acknowledge criminal policy as an autonomous European policy. As a consequence they do not follow a coherent concept of criminal policy'*.[71]

Here lies the problem with the legitimacy of European criminal law: the EU is not a state, at least not in the sense of nation states,[72] and its political mandate is

---

67 S. Peers, 'Mutual recognition and criminal law in the European Union: Has the Council got it wrong?', Common Market Law Review, vol. 41, 2004, pp. 5–36.

68 Chapter VI para. 5.3.

69 Draft Council conclusions on model provisions, guiding the Council's criminal law deliberations 16542/2/09 REV 2 JAI 868 DROIPEN 160, 27.11.2009; Commission Communication, Towards an EU criminal policy?: Ensuring the effective implementation of EU policies through criminal law, COM (2011) 573, 20.9.2011.

70 European Parliament Resolution of 22 May 2012 on an EU approach to criminal law (2010/2310(INI)), 22.5.2012, para. 11.

71 European Criminal Policy Initiative, 'A Manifesto on European Criminal Policy', ZIS, vol. 12, 2009, p. 707.

72 ECJ Opinion 2/13, 18 December 2014, para. 156.

specific and limited to the advancement of the internal market and the four freedoms. Its *raison d'être* is to achieve further integration in those fields.[73] The European criminal justice system is neither meant to replace national criminal justice systems nor take over full control on the achievement of the shield/sword finalities of criminal law. National security remains a matter for national authorities, and the same goes for the protection of individuals' *vis-à-vis* the state. Therefore, European criminal law cannot completely separate from the policies of the internal market, as this is the political justification for the whole of European legal order. Conversely, there is the need – and a growing tendency as will be explained in the next paragraph – to establish an autonomous nature for European criminal law by strengthening its protective character and providing transparency in the use of the European competences via principles such as subsidiarity, proportionality and *ultima ratio*. Reconciling these two antithetical points remains a fundamental question.

In this regard, the basic premise of the spill-over theory is that criminal acts such as those depicted in Article 83 TFEU are facilitated particularly by the abolition of borders. However, the lack of statistical or concrete proof of this claim has been criticised.[74] Observations in statistical and criminological analyses indicate that organised crime is facilitated by the transnational nature of all economic activity, which may or may not be associated with the abolition of internal borders within Europe.[75]

In addition, using the spill-over theory to justify European criminal law presents theoretical problems. The spill-over theory can be traced back to 1963, to its initial conceptualisation in the internal market.[76] A spill-over exists when there is a specific goal X for which the EU assumes competence A. Spill-over means that competence A necessitates that competence B also be assumed to achieve goal X. Applying this theory to European criminal law requires that the internal market and the AFSJ are both goal X.[77] This, however, is an instrumentalist perception of criminal law. European instrumentalism rests exactly on this idea, i.e. that achieving an AFSJ is simply another tool in the toolbox of European competences to serve the internal market and not a new goal in itself. Such an approach is characterised by the neutrality of the character of criminal law, as described in Chapter V.[78] Similarly, the spill-over theory is, in itself, neutral. Any measure may generate a spill-over to other areas of law.

Framework Decision 2008/913 on racism and xenophobia demonstrates this more concretely. Much of the criticism that this instrument received concerned the

---

73 Ibid., para. 172.

74 M. Fletcher, R. Lööf, B. Gilmore, 'EU Criminal Law and Justice', Edward Elgar Publishing, 2008, pp. 24–26.

75 Ibid.

76 Ibid., pp. 27–31.

77 Ibid.

78 Chapter V para. 5.1. and 5.3.

lack of proper legitimation in relation to the principles of subsidiarity and proportionality. According to the preamble, harmonisation of criminal liability on racism and xenophobia furthers judicial cooperation in criminal matters.[79] However, it is unclear how and why this is the case and how the principle of subsidiarity was observed. Supposedly, every single harmonisation instrument would, in principle, further judicial cooperation.[80] Additional justification of this instrument included the protection of certain groups across Europe.[81] However, this protection was not conceptualised within a more general policy of providing protection for minority groups or ensuring harmonious relationships across Europe. What is the theoretical purpose and basic value of the European criminal justice system that would require harmonisation of hate speech? Were the specific provisions in line with these values? The default European instrumentalism of European criminal law results in uncertainty of policy goals. European policies, values, principles, and rights become blended together without any hierarchy, separation, or proper weighing.

Interestingly, if any instrument could be justified in the shared values of European citizens, it would be this Framework Decision. Creating common behavioural standards of mutual respect and tolerance in a European multicultural society is a prerequisite for exercising freedom of movement and for harmonious integration of individuals into another Member State – a tolerant and multicultural Europe mandates that individuals not be treated as 'others' by their fellow citizens in their new Member State.

The definition of European criminal law policies, therefore, should be on the grounds of commonly shared values and not solely on crime-control arguments. Furthermore, justifying these policies is a different matter than determining whether to pursue them at the European level. The legitimacy of combatting racism as a European policy depends on whether this represents a commonly shared value throughout Europe. In contrast, determining whether such legitimation should be pursued at the European level is a different question and involves consideration of the subsidiarity principle. For example, one should consider whether the different national regimes regarding hate speech would be an obstacle to achieving this goal and whether encroaching upon national sovereignty would be in line with the general respect for national cultures: *'The argument which needs to be made and won in order to justify the internationalisation, or, in this case, Europeanisation of criminal justice, must relate to the weight attributed to national sovereignty contra*

---

79 Recital 4 of the preamble Framework Decision 2008/913 of 28 November 2008 on combating certain forms and expressions of racism and xenophobia by means of criminal law OJ L 328, 6.12.2008, pp. 55–58.

80 European Criminal Policy Initiative, 'A Manifesto on European Criminal Policy', ZIS, vol.12, 2009, p. 714.

81 Recital 5 of the preamble Framework Decision 2008/913 of 28 November 2008 on combating certain forms and expressions of racism and xenophobia by means of criminal law OJ L 328, 6.12.2008, pp. 55–58.

repressive effectivity'.[82] Therefore, defining European policies on additional grounds than that of combatting crime is necessary, and, further, these policies require separate measurement against principles such as subsidiarity and proportionality.

The instrumentalisation of European criminal law is amplified by Article 83, para. 2 TFEU, which provides the EU with competence to use criminal law (approximation of criminal liability rules) as a method for effective implementation of other policy areas. This type of competence has been quite eloquently termed *Annexkompetenz* by the German Constitutional Court.[83] This Article is the codification of the findings in *Commission v Council* on environmental offences.[84] According to the ECJ:

> [...] However, the last-mentioned finding does not prevent the Community legislature, when the application of effective, proportionate and dissuasive criminal penalties by the competent national authorities is an essential measure for combating serious environmental offences, from taking measures which relate to the criminal law of the Member States which it considers necessary in order to ensure that the rules which it lays down on environmental protection are fully effective.[85]

AG Colomer expressed this opinion in more explicit terms: *'The power to impose civil, administrative or criminal sanctions must be classified as an instrumental power in the service of the effectiveness of Community law'*.[86] According to this view, the character of criminal law is limited only to its punitive effectiveness.

During the hearing, national governments were opposed to this instrumentalisation. AG Colomer rejected these concerns as plain semantics in a footnote to his Opinion:

> The holder of that competence must, in theory, have instrumental competence. The representative of the Finnish Government stressed at the hearing that criminal law is not a tool, since it is substantive in its own right, although that proposition smacks of mere semantics, since, like any provision imposing punishment, a criminal provision exists for the sake of, and serves, a more far-reaching end.[87]

This one-sided view of criminal law is in contrast with the philosophical approach to criminal law in national legal orders. This has also been highlighted by the

---

82 M. Fletcher, R. Lööf, B. Gilmore, 'EU Criminal Law and Justice', Edward Elgar Publishing, 2008, p. 29.

83 BVerfG 2 BvE 2/08, 30 June 2009, para. 66 (Lisbon judgement).

84 C–176/03 Commission of the European Communities v Council of the European Union, 13 September 2005.

85 Ibid., para. 46–48.

86 Opinion AG Colomer of 26 May 2005 in C–176/03 Commission of the European Communities v Council of the European Union, 13 September 2005, para. 84.

87 Ibid., footnote 37 of the Opinion.

German Constitutional Court in the Lisbon judgement: *'The core content of criminal law does not serve as a technical instrument for carrying out international cooperation but represents the particularly sensitive democratic decision on a legal, ethical, minimum standard.'*[88]

3.3. Anti-instrumentalist tendencies and their limitations

Prima facie, it may appear that instrumentalism is an inherent feature of European criminal law. However, this is not necessarily the case. The origins of this system might be characterised by an instrumentalist mentality, however, this is a developing system. Facilitating the internal market and battling cross-border crime might be currently prevalent justifications for European criminal justice. Yet, against this default instrumentalism, there are fragments of an alternative legitimation for European criminal law. Incremental steps are taken for the protection of individuals *vis-à-vis* the state(s) – a tendency enhanced by the binding force of the Charter and the impending accession to the ECHR.

In this regard, the concept of justice has recently been construed in a broader manner than simply the administration of justice. Justice could have a distributive role, especially in relation with the other two terms, i.e. as a mediator between security and freedom.[89] Because of the prevalence of the spill-over theory, such mediation by justice arises as a 'secondary spill-over'. The Europeanisation of criminal justice brought about the necessity to enhance the protective role of criminal law for the rights of individuals/perpetrators.[90]

Current trends in scholarship attribute a philosophical and moral connotation to justice. The AFSJ includes various areas of law (immigration, asylum, criminal and civil law) with restrictive measures for individuals. In this respect, justice could assume a more symbolic meaning; for example, as an umbrella concept for reconstructing political theories and principles such as social justice, the Rule of Law and respect of fundamental rights envisaged in the Charter.[91] The idea behind these trends is to establish a reverse approach to the relationship between the internal market and the AFSJ. On one hand, the AFSJ can be politically annexed to the internal market; but, conversely, the internal market could also function *within* an AFSJ. These trends are relevant not only for criminal law but also for other

---

88 BVerfG 2 BvE 2/08, 30 June 2009, para. 358 (Lisbon judgement).

89 M. Fletcher, R. Lööf, B. Gilmore, 'EU Criminal Law and Justice', Edward Elgar Publishing, 2008, p 49.

90 Ibid., pp. 49–53.

91 S. Douglas-Scott, 'The Problem of Justice in the European Union', in J. Dickson, P. Eleftheriadis (eds), 'Philosophical Foundations of EU Law', Oxford University Press, 2012, pp. 424–459; E. Herlin-Karnell, 'Europe's Area of Freedom, Security and Justice Through the Prism of Constitutionalism: Why the EU Needs a Grammar of Justice to Improve Its Legitimacy', Discussion Paper SP IV 2014–801, Wissenschaftszentrum Berlin für Sozialforschung, 2014; N. Walker, 'Justice in and of the European Union', University of Edinburgh Working Paper, 2014/10, available at http://ssrn.com/abstract=2399026.

European measures. In the aftermath of the European economic crisis particularly, measures of an economic nature, such as those supporting the European Monetary Union, should also be in conformity with social justice.

The European Parliament has criticised the fragmented and inconsistent use of criminal law competences without any coherent common policy approach and instructed that the legitimacy of European criminal law competences be based on a weighing of policies, rights and principles with a transparent argument.[92] Further, it reaffirmed the special character of criminal law as a highly intrusive measure, reasserted the necessity to take under consideration different principles of criminal law such as legality and the principle of guilt, and reaffirmed the rights protected under the Charter.[93] While the political mandate for European criminal law remains closely connected with mutual trust and mutual recognition, this criticism is supplemented by the further justification that *'criminal law must constitute a coherent legislative system governed by a set of fundamental principles and standards of good governance in full respect of the EU Charter of Fundamental Rights'*.[94]

In principle, the protection of individuals from arbitrary coercive measures lies with its Member States. The national legislators and courts are responsible for applying European measures in line with individual autonomy and liberty, and the EU is also expected to respect individual rights in the sense that it should not prescribe measures that force national authorities to violate individual rights.

In recent years, the EU has incrementally assumed a more independent responsibility for protecting individuals from arbitrariness in criminal law. The Charter brought to the foreground the relationship between individuals and the EU as an institutional authority. European bodies are expected to assume and exercise their competences in line with the values and rights depicted in the Charter to the extent that those rights are better protected at the European level.

This independent responsibility is fragmentary and subtle, particularly in areas where individuals might face a form of 'transnational arbitrariness', i.e. arbitrariness arising from the subjection to transnational criminal proceedings or transnational legal orders. A distinction arises for two sources of transnational arbitrariness: a primary and secondary source.

The primary source of transnational arbitrariness comes from the divergent normative status of individuals in different legal orders; acts prohibited in one state may not be prohibited in another. Moreover, the degree of criminalisation may vary. Individuals who cross legal orders confront unfamiliar criminal rules, both substantive and procedural, and are expected to be familiar with diverging criminal legislation, often published in foreign languages and often difficult to access. The question presented is whether there is an obligation to protect individuals from

---

92 European Parliament Resolution of 22 May 2012 on an EU approach to criminal law (2010/2310(INI)), 22.5.2012, point 3.

93 Ibid., point 4.

94 Ibid., point H.

transnational arbitrariness. Is the protective role of European criminal law to shield individuals from transnational arbitrariness? Such obligation cannot go too far, especially in substantive criminal law. European competences in harmonising definitions of offences are limited both in subject matter and in their effect, as they establish only minimum standards. However, this does not preclude the fact that the existing competences cannot be justified on such grounds, especially if legal certainty is interpreted as having a minimum, rather than maximum, foreseeability. Harmonisation of criminal offences creates the expectation that those criminal offences shall be roughly similar in different systems; an expectation created not only for judicial authorities but also for individuals. Freedom of movement presumes the ability to exercise such freedom in a general climate of certainty.[95]

Examples exist for which European criminal law protects individuals from diverging status in different legal orders. One example includes the series of Directives harmonising procedural rights.[96] The main objective of these instruments is to increase mutual trust amongst judicial authorities and promote mutual recognition. However, the nature of protection afforded may transcend that goal. In particular, these instruments also safeguard the trust of individuals towards foreign judicial authorities and essentially promote freedom of movement. *'Such common minimum rules should also remove obstacles to the free movement of citizens throughout the territory of the Member States'*.[97]

Another example is the case of *ne bis in idem*, where the ECJ interpreted this principle in the light of freedom of movement. Freedom of movement creates expectations for individuals that they can move freely within Europe. This is evident in various cases,[98] especially in the controversial *Gasparini*[99] in which the interpretation of *ne bis in idem* as also encompassing barred prosecutions entailed that, once the prosecution is barred and recognised as barred in one system, other Member States would lose their right to prosecute.[100]

It would be fair to say that freedom of movement presupposes a respect of legitimate expectations, namely that there is a link to the possibility of a subsequent prosecution in another state and the exercise of freedom of movement. In EU law, *ne bis in idem* is applied differently than in the traditional national setting. In a

---

95 See further below para. 6.

96 Directive 2010/64 of 20 October 2010 on the right to interpretation and translation in criminal proceedings OJ L 280, 26.10.2010, pp. 1–7; Directive 2012/13 of 22 May 2012 on the right to information in criminal proceedings OJ L 142, 1.6.2012, pp. 1–10.

97 Recital 8 of the preamble of Directive 2013/48 of 22 October 2013 on the right of access to a lawyer in criminal proceedings and in European arrest warrant proceedings, and on the right to have a third party informed upon deprivation of liberty and to communicate with third persons and with consular authorities while deprived of liberty OJ L 294, 6.11.2013, pp. 1–12.

98 Joined cases C–187/01 and C–387/01 criminal proceedings against Hüseyn Gözütok and Klaus Brügge, 11 February 2003.

99 C–467/04 criminal proceedings against Giuseppe Francesco Gasparini and Others, 28 September 2006.

100 A. Klip, 'European Criminal Law: An Integrative Approach', Intersentia, 2012, p. 255.

transnational setting, this principle is implemented in a horizontal manner, namely between Member States, whereas the traditional *ne bis in idem* application occurs within the same legal order. To this extent, arguments have been made in literature that the ECJ's interpretation is based on the assumption that the European criminal justice area is a single and unified order.

More precisely, its *ratio* is not only the protection of liberty against arbitrariness but also essentially, the safeguarding of the 'social contract'.[101] Individuals are a part of a social contract, as they agree upon the terms based on which communities come together. In national law, subsequent prosecutions for the same offence create a vertical temporal inconsistency: individuals are first considered to continually be a part of the social contract (in case of a first acquittal), while in the subsequent prosecution (in case of a conviction), they are considered to have violated the social contract.[102] If one imagines a national legal system with more than one jurisdiction (two judgements about the same facts for example, by the courts of Amsterdam and Maastricht), it would constitute a horizontal structural inconsistency, as the individual would be simultaneously considered as having violated and not having violated the social contract.[103] Similarly, in EU law, it is precisely this horizontal structural inconsistency that is problematic. Therefore, the interpretation of *ne bis in idem* in the light of freedom of movement rests on the assumption that the AFSJ is a single area: *'The reference to 'an area of freedom, security and justice' in Article 29 of the Treaty on European Union must now be read so as to mean that the AFSJ constitutes a single social contractual unit within which there can be no divergences in the normative status of individuals vis-à-vis the collective.'*[104]

Does a unified European legal order mean that individuals should also be afforded foreseeability of criminalisation in a transnational setting? Could harmonisation of criminal offences be interpreted as ensuring foreseeability of criminalisation within Europe? In *Advocaten voor de Wereld*, the question was whether the principle of *lex certa* was violated as the elements of criminal liability were not defined in the list of offences in Article 2, para. 2 of the EAW.[105] The primary argument by the Court was that the EAW is not a harmonisation instrument, as Article 2 para. 2 EAW did not have a harmonising effect, and definitions of criminal liability elements could be found in national law. The arguments of the ECJ are reasonable. In principle, legal certainty was not violated since individuals could foresee criminalisation in the national legislation where the act was committed.

However, this case demonstrates the potential for different interpretations of legal certainty and foreseeability. A practical consequence of the abolition of double

101 R. Lööf, '54 CISA and the principles of *ne bis in idem*', European Journal of Crime, Criminal Law and Criminal Justice, vol.15, 2007, pp. 309–334.

102 Ibid., p. 322.

103 Ibid., p. 323.

104 Ibid., p. 325.

105 C–303/05 Advocaten voor de Wereld VZW v Leden van de Ministerraad, 3 May 2007.

criminality is that individuals must be aware of the laws of all Member States.[106] To avoid criminalisation and subsequent prosecution, they must know the substantive requirements of the list of offences in all legal systems. The abolition of double criminality for offences that were not harmonised at that moment, would be in breach of a 'transnational legal certainty' or 'transnational foreseeability'. Such abolition creates a more abstract obligation of maintaining familiarity with the legislation of all Member States and would inhibit freedom of movement or, at least, the potential exercise of such freedom, because the limitation of individual autonomy would be different in every Member State. Hence, the European Parliament has highlighted the need to harmonise criminal offences, which would facilitate mutual recognition, instead of merely expanding the scope of European criminal offences.[107]

The secondary source of transnational arbitrariness arises as a spill-over to the existing mechanism of cooperation. Especially in the field of mutual recognition, Member States are unable to afford protection to individuals against possible arbitrariness by another judicial system, as mutual trust prohibits states from challenging the execution of a request on those grounds. In principle, all national systems should be presumed to sufficiently protect individual rights. However, in practice, this can be less accurate. Secondary transnational arbitrariness may also encompass another problem: the nature of mutual recognition proceedings often complicates the distribution of responsibility between the involved Member States since mutual recognition is not seen as a holistic criminal process but, instead, as different procedures of varied Member States.

In light of the vertical relationship between state/individual, the question arises as to whether mutual recognition creates a regime of multiple relationships between individuals and the states that cooperate in criminal proceedings (individual v. issuing state, individual v. executing state) or whether it presupposes the existence of a single vertical relationship (individual v. issuing and executing state). Considering the obligations of mutual recognition as a form of exercise of the *ius puniendi* and not as a form of cooperation between authorities, mutual recognition obliges national criminal justice systems to execute requests (and thus utilise their 'sword' finality of criminal law) while prohibiting them from attaining the 'shield' finality, which is to be complied with by the issuing state.[108] Essentially, the judicial authorities of two states function as one. They share the *ius puniendi*, which is why mutual trust is so essential. The requested state should execute an arrest warrant, but it cannot double-check whether such a warrant is actually legitimate according to its laws.

---

106 E. Herlin-Karnell, 'The Constitutional Dimension of European Criminal Law', Hart Publishing, 2012, p. 27.

107 European Parliament Resolution of 22 May 2012 on an EU approach to criminal law (2010/2310(INI)), 22.5.2012, point 7.

108 M. Fletcher, R. Lööf, B. Gilmore, 'EU Criminal Law and Justice', Edward Elgar Publishing, 2008, p. 124.

Without presuming mutual trust, the efficiency of cooperation mechanisms would be doomed; but mutual trust also requires mutual responsibility. From an individual's perspective, mutual recognition is not cooperation between judicial authorities, rather it is cohabitation or sharing of *ius puniendi*. Therefore, to maintain mutual trust and protection of individuals, the way forward should be for the EU to assume responsibility for such protection.[109] The Directives harmonising procedural rights are certainly a step forward.

A further improvement would be the accession of the EU to the ECHR. Until now, the ECtHR has followed a split solution for determining the responsibility of individual rights violations during mutual recognition. As there are no proceedings initiated against the individual, the requested state is not responsible for violations of Article 6, para. 1 ECHR, but it could be responsible for Article 6, para. 3 ECHR regarding hearing witnesses for example.[110] The problem with this split solution can be observed in *Sari,* a case involving a non-EU state, where Denmark transferred the proceedings to Turkey.[111] The proceedings lasted for five years in each country, amounting to a total of 10 years. The ECtHR found no violation, as it considered the individual responsibility of every country, and determined that five years of proceedings were not considered excessive. Contrary to this split solution approach, the ECtHR maintained that, generally, the obligations under the Convention entail the collective enforcement, and practical and effective application of individual rights. This was applied in *M.S.S.,* where Belgium was found responsible for expelling an asylum seeker to Greece based on the Dublin Regulation without considering the inhumane conditions in the Greek facilities.[112] While for the ECtHR the character of rights as derogable or non-derogable is important in applying such an approach, the argument for collective enforcement and practical and effective application of individual rights is an invitation to approach cooperation amongst Member States as a collective process where states are 'their brother's keeper'.[113]

However, the Opinion of the ECJ regarding the proposal for the ECHR accession seems to adopt a stricter view regarding the allocation of responsibility between the EU and its Member States and amongst the Member States. *Inter alia,* the Court maintained that, especially in the area of Justice and Home Affairs, mutual trust precludes Member States from directing complaints against each other before the ECtHR.[114] Understandably, such possibility would imply that a Member State controls whether another Member State complies with fundamental rights, which is prohibited by the concept of mutual trust. However, given the fact that mutual

---

109 N.M. Schallmoser, 'The European Arrest Warrant and Fundamental Rights', European Journal of Crime, Criminal Law and Criminal Justice, vol. 22, 2014, p. 153.

110 EComHR Chinoy v United Kingdom, App. 15199/89, 4 September 1991.

111 ECtHR Sari v Turkey and Denmark, App. 21889/93, 8 November 2001.

112 ECtHR M.S.S. v Belgium and Greece, App. 30696/09, 21 January 2011.

113 A. Klip, 'European Criminal Law: An Integrative Approach', Intersentia, 2012, p. 427.

114 ECJ Opinion 2/13, 18 December 2014, para. 191.

recognition (and thereby mutual trust) is not an absolute notion, the Court's appreciation of this matter is rather strict. One could perhaps support the Court's view on the primacy of mutual trust if it was not for its assessment of the proposed co-respondent mechanism and the allocation of responsibility between the EU and Member States. The benefit of accession the ECHR would be that the EU as an entity would become accountable to individuals regarding human rights violations. Human rights concerns of EU instruments – also in criminal matters – could therefore be directed against the EU as an entity. This mechanism would offer the possibility for the EU and its Member States to be co-respondents but it would also require that the ECtHR must decide how to allocate the responsibility between the EU and the Member State. According to the Court, a decision of the attributability of an act or omission necessitates interpretation of EU law by the ECtHR, which violates the autonomy of EU law.[115]

In conclusion, the default legitimacy of European criminal law is based on a instrumentalist mentality. Though there are subtle tendencies of a more autonomous legitimation, various problems remain in that direction. Whether European criminal law has a protective function towards individuals is unclear, as uncertainty exists regarding what this protection comprises. Both the areas of mutual recognition and harmonisation maintain an echo of newly created arbitrariness. Mutual recognition creates dangers to individuals that Member States are unable to curtail, and harmonisation establishes certain expectations for legal certainty in moving freely throughout Europe. As the current justification for these measures rests solely on crime-control arguments, it is difficult to further expand on these topics without a more holistic account of the nature of European criminal law. Any such account should take into consideration the interrelationship between the European and national legal orders. Depending on how one approaches this relationship, different levels of protection for individuals will arise in European criminal law.

4. Interlocking legal orders: the relationship between European and national legal orders

In this section, the nature of the European legal order and its relationship with national legal orders shall be examined. As explained at the beginning of this Chapter, European criminal law challenges the traditional monopoly that nation states had on criminal law.[116] It is therefore important to take a look at how the existing multi-level system functions from a constitutional law perspective. The question of legitimacy of European criminal law depends on whether the EU constitutes a truly autonomous legal order and how the relationship between European and national legal orders informs multi-level law-making. In doing so, I

115 Ibid., para. 215–235.

116 F. Meyer, 'Strafrechtsgenese in Internationalen Organisationen', Nomos, 2012, pp. 643–652.

will discuss existing constitutional theories on this issue and their impact in criminal law.

The interrelation of legal orders can usually be conceptualised through two models: dualism and monism.[117] Dualism is premised on a plurality of legal systems, with each claiming sole authority over the definition of rules.[118] Dualism is inherently introverted, in that the legal order must be protected against interventions from other legal orders.[119] For the European and national legal orders, this model would dictate complete independence, and the superiority of one over the other is governed by mutual agreement so long as there is continuous will to do so.

Monism carries the assumption that the various legal orders are not independent but co-dependent, as they are parts of a greater legal order or community[120] and the universal legal order has superiority or the 'last word' on authority. To this extent, monism is extroverted as it accepts that there exist universal values beyond the nation state's legal order that underpin the global legal experience.[121] This would mean that the European legal order includes the national legal orders and as a single order it determines its own nature and authority in the case of conflict.

Although these models seem diametrically opposite, both are based on the same premise of positivism – the 'exclusivity of legal orders'. According to the latter, legal orders are either completely dependent or completely independent.[122] This premise is challenged in current actions by various accounts in international law in which legal orders do not function under the premise of exclusivity but are interrelated in complicated ways.[123] Examples can be seen throughout EU law. One such example is the principle of mutual recognition, in which legal orders are not mutually exclusive.[124] The principle of mutual recognition functions on the assumption that normative divergence and conflicts need not be resolved necessarily, but legal orders can establish mutual forms of coordination. Other relevant examples are the principle of conform interpretation, which prevents normative conflicts, and the doctrine of equivalent protection, which has been employed in EU law to avoid conflicts of human rights on a normative basis.[125] As the forms of interrelation of legal orders become intense and increasingly

---

117 M. Claes, 'The National Courts' Mandate in the European Constitution', Hart Publishing, 2006, pp. 169–173.

118 E. Cannizzaro, B.I. Bonafè, 'Beyond the archetypes of modern legal thought', in M. Maduro, K. Tuori, S. Sankari (eds), 'Transnational Law: Rethinking European Law and Legal Thinking', Cambridge University Press, 2014, p. 80.

119 Ibid., p. 79.

120 H. Kelsen, 'General Theory of Law and State', Harvard University Press, 1945, pp. 363–380.

121 E. Cannizzaro, B.I. Bonafè, 'Beyond the archetypes of modern legal thought', in M. Maduro, K. Tuori, S. Sankari (eds), 'Transnational Law: Rethinking European Law and Legal Thinking', Cambridge University Press, 2014, pp. 79–80.

122 Ibid., pp. 80–81.

123 Ibid., p. 81.

124 Ibid., p. 82.

125 Ibid., pp. 89–95.

complicated, the two models of monism/dualism are mere ideal artificial models that cannot be applied in their totality.

The assumptions of these two models, however, reflect in the current debate regarding the interrelation of European and national legal orders. Three theories exist in this regard: the theory of EU law supremacy, the theory of national constitutionalism or statism and the theory of constitutional pluralism. The first two represent a rough application of monism and dualism; constitutional pluralism is not a mixture of the other two but is based on a different approach to the law and legal orders. All three theories offer a solution to the question of which legal order (EU or national) has the legitimate authority to solve constitutional conflicts. Beyond that, they also depict different mentalities for the relationship between the European and national legal orders. The focus of this contribution is not on constitutional conflicts, therefore these theories shall not be criticised in their capacity to best resolve constitutional conflicts (although this might become relevant on occasion). They shall be approached as different mentalities for a legitimate coordination of the EU and national criminal law systems.

4.1. The theory (and principle) of EU supremacy

4.1.1. General characteristics

The supremacy of EU law has been supported by the EU institutions. The EU self-proclaimed itself as a new and autonomous legal order that is an integral part of the national legal system,[126] enjoying primacy over national (including constitutional) law[127] and binding national authorities to apply EU law. The ECJ view on the European legal order is consistent with legal monism, as both European and national legal orders are exclusive and autonomous while the European legal order forms a part of the national legal systems. The European legal order has primacy over national legal orders. In addition, it has attained its *Kompetenz-Kompetenz*, which is the power to determine the scope of its own competences and the manner in which they are applied.[128] Thus, while the EU was historically created by national legal orders, it has emancipated itself from their consent and will. The legitimation for legal monism and the superiority of EU law is based on a set of arguments. It would be impossible for the EU to achieve its goals if Member States were allowed to set it aside at will. The EU is not an ordinary international organisation as EU law has distanced itself from international law and the state

126 Case 26/62 NV Algemene Transport- en Expeditie Onderneming van Gend & Loos v Netherlands Inland Revenue Administration, 5 February 1963.
127 Case 6/64 Flaminio Costa v E.N.E.L., 15 July 1964.
128 M. Claes, 'The National Courts' Mandate in the European Constitution', Hart Publishing, 2006, p. 709.

consent.[129] This monistic view of EU law has been a solid foundation in European legal theory. The ECJ, however, departed from monism in *Kadi* when the Court stated that the European legal order is not hierarchically integrated to the greater international law order, which would mean that international law would be supreme to EU law.[130]

4.1.2. The theory of EU supremacy in European criminal law

Various consequences stem from such a theory on European criminal law. First, national constitutional principles or values cannot block or compromise the effective implementation of EU law. National legislators cannot deviate from the minimum scope of criminal liability prescribed in Directives, even if such a criminalisation is against their constitutional law. For example, in the case of the Framework Decision 2008/913 on racism and xenophobia, national legislators would not be able to refuse implementation of criminal liability regarding genocide denial even if such a criminalisation was against their constitutional values.[131]

Criminal legislating is a highly political process in that it is an imprint of the cultural and political appreciation of certain rights:

> Securing legal peace by the administration of criminal law has always been a central duty of state authority. As regards the task of creating, securing and enforcing a well-ordered social existence by protecting the elementary values of community life on the basis of a legal order, criminal law is an indispensable element to secure indestructibility of this legal order. [...] Every provision in criminal law contains a social and ethical judgement of unworthiness on the action which it penalises. [...] To what extent and in what areas a polity uses precisely criminal law as an instrument of social control is a fundamental decision. By criminal law, a legal community gives itself a code of conduct that is anchored in its values, and whose violation, according to the shared convictions on law, is regarded as so grievous and unacceptable for social co-existence in the community that it requires punishment [...].[132]

Essentially, EU primacy implies that European political decisions on which rights should be protected by criminal liability based on Article 83 TFEU are superior to

---

129 M. Kumm, 'Rethinking Constitutional Authority: On the Structure and Limits of Constitutional Pluralism', in M. Avbelj, J. Komárek (eds), 'Constitutional Pluralism in the European Union and Beyond', Hart Publishing, 2012, p. 45.

130 C–402/05 P Kadi and Al Barakaat International Foundation v Council and Commission, 3 September 2008.

131 Framework Decision 2008/913 of 28 November 2008 on combating certain forms and expressions of racism and xenophobia by means of criminal law OJ L 328, 6.12.2008, pp. 55–58. However, the Spanish Constitutional Court has declared the criminalisation of denying genocide as unconstitutional: Spanish Constitutional Court Judgement No. 235/2007, of November 7, (unofficial) translation www.tribunalconstitucional.es/es/jurisprudencia/restrad/Paginas/JCC2352007en.aspx

132 BVerfG 2 BvE 2/08, 30 June 2009, para. 355 (Lisbon judgement).

national parliamentary discourse. Any discretion afforded to the national legislator is determined solely by the instrument itself: national legislation can provide for stricter criminal liability (a wider scope of criminalisation) but it may not limit the scope of criminal liability. Moreover, national courts would also violate EU law if they were to disregard the preliminary rulings of the ECJ on the interpretation of a European instrument even if they find such an interpretation to be inconsistent with constitutional values.

The same is applicable for the constitutional principles or fundamental law principles of their system. The obligation to correctly enforce EU law cannot be compromised through the use of national principles such as *ultima ratio,* proportionality or the legality principle. A national legislator that wishes to provide a more concrete definition of criminal liability during implementation to comply with *lex certa* could face the result of an incorrect implementation. In those situations, national *lex certa* cannot compromise the implementation of a Directive. One could argue that even before the implementation process and during the EU decision-making process, Article 83 para. 3 TFEU could be of use, as it gives the possibility of an emergency brake for instruments that may affect fundamental aspects of the national criminal system. One could debate its use in cases of an extremely vague European instrument. However, it is unclear how the term 'fundamental aspect' is to be interpreted and how Member States will utilise it.[133] Is the emergency brake only for measures that might affect the criminal liability framework (for example, the introduction of minimum penalties for the Netherlands or of criminal liability of legal entities for Germany), or could it be used when Member States disagree with the substantial content of criminal liability?

A second consequence of the theory of primacy is that any application of criminal law rules that have a European origin must effectively enforce EU law. National courts become review courts and in a case of conflict they must review national legislation and, occasionally, set it aside.[134] A notable consequence is for the obligation of conform interpretation. As explained this obligation stems from the principle of sincere cooperation.[135] The theory on EU primacy also shapes this obligation. The ECJ determines the exact nature and limits of this obligation. This theory assumes that legal orders merge into one, and therefore, the Directive is to be approached the same as any other national legal instrument of higher importance in the light of which national criminal rules evolve and function. Viewing the obligation of conform interpretation from the light of EU primacy may also have an effect on the hierarchy of interpretational methods or arguments.[136] The effective enforcement of EU law can play a significant role in weighing interests during

133 House of Lords European Union Committee 10th Report of Session 2007–08, The Treaty of Lisbon: an impact assessment, Volume I: Report HL Paper 62–1, pp. 118–121.

134 M. Claes, 'The National Courts' Mandate in the European Constitution', Hart Publishing, 2006, p. 102.

135 Chapter VI para. 5.3.

136 M. Claes, 'The National Courts' Mandate in the European Constitution', Hart Publishing, 2006, p. 116.

judicial interpretation.[137] The idea of this obligation is that from various possible interpretive outcomes, national courts should give preference to the interpretation that best enforces the Directive. While such an obligation may not violate the principle of legality according to the ECJ,[138] as noted in Chapter IV, the limits of interpretation depend not so much on the methods employed but on the argument itself.[139] Does the supremacy theory entail that above all principles and interests that are of relevance during interpretation, national courts should assign more gravity to the effective enforcement of EU law?

If such is the case, the primacy of EU law would oblige national courts not to prioritise other individual rights or values over the policy of effectively enforcing EU law. In other words, the reasoning of their judgement should be influenced primarily by the necessity to comply with the Directive. In addition, as Directives form an integral part of the national order, individuals may face the argument that an interpretation in conformity with a Directive is much more foreseeable than an interpretation that does not consider European instruments. After all, a judicial interpretation consistent with existing rules in a legal system provides for more legal certainty than judicial interpretations that create fragmentation. To this extent, the theory of primacy is no longer just a theory of how legal orders interact; rather, it becomes a viable part of judicial interpretation and, more concretely, a superior policy that is by definition of higher importance to other principles/rights/values. If this were the case, judicial interpretation would be highly instrumentalised.

Third, according to this theory the content and scope of the European obligations for national authorities are also to be determined by EU law. However, such content is not always clear. The problem is more evident with national implementation. The criteria for correct implementation are, in accordance with the primacy theory, decided by the hierarchically superior EU law, by European secondary legislation and, also, by the ECJ in preliminary rulings and infringement proceedings.

Some criteria are already known as to what constitutes correct implementation. As discussed in the previous Chapter, Member States must comply with the legality principle requirements when they implement criminal norms.[140] This means that implementation by means of case law with a complete absence of a statutory basis is an incorrect interpretation. A complete lack of national legal basis further renders the Directive inapplicable to individuals. National implementation must be precise so that individuals can invoke their rights or know their obligations.

What is ambiguous, however, is the level of precision. How precise should national legislation be in order to be a correct implementation? As Directives lack direct effect, they are inherently more general; they are binding as to the effect to be achieved, which is why their implementation is necessary. Understanding the

137 J. Altena-Davidsen, 'De reikwijdte van de plicht tot conforme interpretatie in het strafrecht tegen de achtergrond van de verhouding tussen de Europese en de nationale rechtsorde', Ars Aequi, 2012, p. 555.

138 C–105/03 criminal proceedings against Maria Pupino, 16 June 2005.

139 Chapter IV para. 10.1.4.

140 Chapter VI para. 4.5 and 4.6.

scope of EU obligations for implementation, especially for instruments based on Article 83 TFEU, has, however, become increasingly difficult. The absolute 'must' is to create/amend a statute, when necessary, and not decrease the scope of criminal liability found in the Directive. However, in principle national legislators are also expected to set the description of criminal liability by using terms that fit the national system or by generally adapting the description of the behaviour to the systemic structure of national criminal norms. This is to achieve essential coherence of national systems and to ensure the effective use of that provision in national proceedings.

Here, national legislators must make use of the criteria for precision that stem from the European legality principle, as they cannot, under this theory, compromise effective enforcement of EU law with the use of national standards. However, how are national legislators to know the European threshold of precision? Is the threshold determined in the Directive? Is the description of criminal liability in the Directive already in compliance with the legality principle? Would it be safe to copy-paste the definitions in the Directive to national law?[141] One of the negative effects of monism is that it assumes the incorporation of national legal orders into the European legal order in a climate of familiarity and coherent vertical cooperation amongst institutions, which is not the reality.

Another example of unclear European obligations is the case of the obligation of conform interpretation. To maintain primacy and uniform application of EU law, principles and concepts must maintain an autonomous European interpretation distinguished from the national interpretation of similar principles. This autonomous meaning has led to the assumption that there must also be a horizontal coherence of these principles within the different areas of EU law. In this regard, the concept of conform interpretation was transferred from the internal market to European criminal law. In the internal market, this obligation has its limits in the *contra legem* and the *lex stricta* requirements as seen before.[142]

The ECJ has successfully translated the first limitation into criminal law as the principle of legality, and therefore, national courts should not follow an interpretation that violates the legality principle.[143] However, certain problems relate to the second limitation. The previous Chapter considered the redundancy of the *contra legem* requirement.[144] If a *contra legem* interpretation has been provided for the benefit of the accused, then this criminal norm should be set aside due to the *Simmenthal* doctrine and/or the *lex mitior* principle if it contradicts a maximum harmonisation instrument (for example, an internal market Directive implemented

141 Chapter VIII para. 2.2. and 3.3.

142 Chapter VI para. 5.3.

143 C–105/03 criminal proceedings against Maria Pupino, 16 June 2005; See generally K. Sawyer, 'The Principle of 'interprétation conforme': How Far Can or Should National Courts Go when Interpreting National Legislation Consistently with European Community Law?', Statute Law Review, vol. 28, 2007, pp. 165–181.

144 Chapter VI para. 5.3.

with criminal law). For a harmonisation instrument under Article 83 TFEU, which is a minimum harmonisation, the more lenient scope of criminal liability provided in the Directive cannot be invoked since national legislators have the discretion to have a wider scope of criminal liability. A *contra legem* interpretation that presents to the detriment of the accused is covered by the legality principle. In either case, the *contra legem* requirement provides no added value.

Conversely, the theory of supremacy may have consequently motivated national courts to engage in a more transparent and concrete justification of their decisions, especially since they may be reviewed by European institutions during infringement proceedings. To this extent, European supremacy may lead to a desirable controllability and transparency of judicial interpretation. Moreover, this theory also ensures the uniform application of EU law across legal orders and can essentially benefit individuals and provide for legal certainty in cross-border activities.

The most important impact of this theory on criminal law is that European criminal law measures are not optional. National systems lose their power to make autonomous choices in their decisions (legislative or judicial) that would depict a different system of values that the one depicted in the European instrument. This is only an impediment if one accepts that national sovereignty has a superior ethical value (as will be shown, this is to be debated).[145] National sovereignty has always been a rather politicalised concept, used as a means of regaining control.[146] What lies beneath, though, is the claim to mirror in legislation and judicial decisions social values and individual rights that may differ across Europe. On one hand, harmonisation of criminal provisions at the European level results also in the harmonisation of values, as it mirrors the level of protection of certain individual or social interests (such as children's sexual integrity or the protection of the economic systems). Conversely, harmonisation in criminal law, as noted, is not practised with such motivation at the European level; criminal law is a tool to battle crime and facilitate the internal market and not to shape common standards of living in accordance with the values and rights that should be fundamental in the European legal order. The consequence is that national legislators and courts could perhaps maintain a valid claim to provide the protection they see fit towards individuals, whether those individuals are potential victims or perpetrators.

4.2. The theory of democratic statism

4.2.1. General characteristics

The theory of statism denotes a dualistic approach. In democratic statism, the nation state law is supreme as it derives its authority and legitimation from the *pouvoir*

---

145 For a definition see N. Walker, 'Late Sovereignty in the European Union', in N. Walker (ed), 'Sovereignty in Transition', Hart Publishing, 2003, p. 6.

146 H. Lindahl, 'Sovereignty and Representation in the European Union', in N. Walker (ed), 'Sovereignty in Transition', Hart Publishing, 2003, p. 87.

constituant that establishes a democratic constitutional order.[147] Dualism represents that, although Member States may enter into cooperation or international institutions and these organisations may have their own legal order and rules, the national constitutions remain supreme and sovereign. According to this view, the EU is based on treaties created by states and is thus controlled and subject to the limits of national constitutions; in other words, the EU is not emancipated from the consent of Member States. While derogation from Treaty obligations may just as well be a violation of EU law and result in an increased responsibility of a state, such has no influence in the internal legal order. The democratic statism theory maintains that the national democratic state is superior to the European legal order, as the state is based on a constitution, which Europe lacks, and it is governed by strong bonds of democracy – an area in which Europe suffers.[148] Being a state is essential for this theory, and the EU is not one because it does not fulfil certain institutional, procedural and sociological requirements. For example, it lacks the capacity to legislate fully on certain core areas such as criminal law, taxes and social welfare and its creation was not accompanied by a ceremonial and highly participatory popular happening, and so it lacks the elemental democratic ethos of 'We the People'.[149]

This theory enjoys popularity amongst national constitutional courts. The German Constitutional Court followed this theory in its Maastricht and Lisbon judgements.[150] Under this theory, the scope of European competences cannot be determined by the EU itself since it does not have the *Kompetenz-Kompetenz*. For example, the German Constitutional Court noted in the Lisbon judgement that:

> Due to the fact that democratic self-determination is affected in an especially sensitive manner by provisions of criminal law and criminal procedure, the corresponding basic powers in the treaties must be interpreted strictly – on no account extensively –, and their use requires particular justification. [...] Democratic self-determination is, however, affected in a particularly sensitive manner where a legal community is prevented from deciding on the punishability of conduct, or even the imposition of prison sentences, according to their own values. This applies all the more the more closer these values are connected with historical experience, traditions of faith and other factors essential to the self-esteem of the people and their society. In these areas, it is therefore only permitted to a limited extent to transfer the competence for criminal legislation [...].[151]

According to the German Constitutional Court, the democratic legitimation of the nation state is of primary importance for the legitimation of criminal conduct.

147 M. Kumm, 'Rethinking Constitutional Authority: On the Structure and Limits of Constitutional Pluralism', in M. Avbelj, J. Komárek (eds), 'Constitutional Pluralism in the European Union and Beyond', Hart Publishing, 2012, p. 48.

148 Ibid.

149 Ibid., pp. 49–50.

150 BVerfG 2 BvR 2134/92, 12 October 1993; BVerfG 2 BvE 2/08, 30 June 2009.

151 BVerfG 2 BvE 2/08, 30 June 2009, para. 358 and 363.

National sovereignty here is a superior ethical value that requires protection from outsiders. Certainly, this can be debated. The EU also enjoys a democratic legitimation via the European Parliament, and also, there is the Charter; overall, it cannot be said that it lacks the capacity or the legal sources to protect fundamental values in the criminal law setting. National courts:

> [...] must increasingly be aware that they don't have the monopoly over rules and that they often compete with other institutions in their interpretation. They have to accept that the protection of the fundamental values of their legal order may be better achieved by another institution or that the respect owed to the identity of another legal order should lead them to defer to that jurisdiction.[152]

In any case, the democratic statist theory maintains that EU law may take primacy only as long as and in so far as national constitutions allow it. In fact, most constitutions have been amended to better enforce EU norms and this is reflected in the principle of constitutional tolerance of EU law.[153]

4.2.2. The theory of democratic statism in European criminal law

What would be the implications of this theory for European criminal law? A first and major impact of this theory is on the legitimation of European criminal law. In light of the inherent instrumentalism of the European criminal policy, applying democratic statism would result in less opportunism. With this theory, European criminal law and the competences of the EU to prescribe criminal offences are accepted and enforced so long as they do not contradict basic constitutional values. In the case where an instrument somehow violates these values, national courts/legislators would have a legitimate right to disregard it. Furthermore, criminal law competences must be based on a strict reading of the Treaties. More concretely, the *Kompetenz-Kompetenz* belongs to nation states and, as explained by the German Constitution Court in Lisbon, competences in criminal law are to be interpreted strictly and applied with great care and only as far as they can be justified.[154]

This would not only prevent the EU from exercising the *Kompetenz-Kompetenz* that would expand its competences without legitimation but it also restricts opportunism and instrumentalism in the exercise of the current competences. Thus, while the decisions on what to criminalise and how to concretise criminal liability belong with the European legislator (as prescribed in Article 83 TFEU), national authorities would in principle be able to deviate when constitutional rights are

152 M. P. Maduro, 'Interpreting European Law: Judicial Adjudication in a Context of Constitutional Pluralism', European Journal of Legal Studies, vol. 1, 2007, p. 18.

153 M. Kumm, 'Rethinking Constitutional Authority: On the Structure and Limits of Constitutional Pluralism', in M. Avbelj, J. Komárek (eds), 'Constitutional Pluralism in the European Union and Beyond', Hart Publishing, 2012, p. 51.

154 BVerfG 2 BvE 2/08, 30 June 2009, para. 362.

encroached by European criminal law legislation. It should be noted that democratic statism does not advocate that EU law does not have to be applied. Any derogation constitutes a violation of the Treaties and of the national commitments towards the EU. It states that there is no such constitutional claim of higher authority or European primacy. Therefore, any derogation will be weighed against other constitutional rights or important principles of criminal systems. Thus, pursuing an implementation based on the application of national standards of *lex certa* (so concretising further the criminal liability in order to meet national standards of precision) that would compromise effective enforcement would be in principle acceptable and would be weighed with the obligation to enforce EU law.

Hence, European policies and the obligation to effectively apply EU law would be only one of the arguments to be considered and would be weighed with other rights or policies. To this extent, the obligation of conform interpretation based on this model would be no different from any other interpretational method, including the obligation to interpret the laws in compliance with the constitution.[155] This certainly could raise the question as to whether the obligation of conform interpretation has any added value.

Despite the positive impact of this theory on certain important problems in European criminal law, serious deficiencies also remain. First, the importance and actual application of EU law would be greatly impacted. The uniform application of EU law would be jeopardised but this is only a problem if one considers that the European legal order has an ethical value. In this regard, one can approach the question of European supremacy as a more fundamental claim of European sovereignty.[156] EU law has something to offer to its citizens and to its Member States. If one entertains the idea of a European sovereignty, then there could be an ethical value in it, wherein the right guaranteeing freedom of movement represents a social *acquis*. With regard to the welfare of Europe, achievements include increasing interest in individual rights in criminal proceedings and a general interest in the protective finality of criminal law. A European social *acquis* includes the Letter of Rights;[157] the same can be said about freedom of establishment and equal treatment of European citizens. In other words, the EU has guaranteed rights to individuals that are unique and go beyond national sovereignty. Moreover, European citizens have an interest in living in peaceful societies where transnational crime is prevented. While this argument can be seen as dubious and too crime-control oriented, criminal law also has a horizontal dimension protecting individuals in their various capacities and interrelations.

---

155 J. Altena-Davidsen, 'De reikwijdte van de plicht tot conforme interpretatie in het strafrecht tegen de achtergrond van de verhouding tussen de Europese en de nationale rechtsorde', Ars Aequi, 2012, pp. 556–557.

156 G. de Búrca, 'Sovereignty and the Supremacy Doctrine of the European Court of Justice', in N. Walker (ed), 'Sovereignty in Transition', Hart Publishing, 2003, pp. 451–452.

157 Directive 2012/13 of 22 May 2012 on the right to information in criminal proceedings OJ L 142, 1.6.2012, pp. 1–10.

One can also add a further argument to this view relating to the protective finality of criminal law in its vertical dimension. Even a minimum harmonisation of criminal offences contributes to legal certainty and foreseeability regarding criminal law offences in different states. An argument by one of the complainants in *Advocaten voor de Wereld* was premised on the lack of foreseeability in its transnational cross-border dimension. This is an issue to which national sovereignty cannot contribute. This *cross-border foreseeability* has been of concern, particularly in the case of conflicts of jurisdiction in criminal matters. When individuals find themselves in another jurisdiction through the cooperation mechanisms, one has to wonder whether a lack of common standards on jurisdiction creates great uncertainty in the AFSJ. In national law the principle of legality does not usually apply to jurisdictional rules, which are often categorised as procedural. This implies that jurisdiction does not have to be foreseeable; this is to be expected, as national criminal systems operate without reference to other legal orders. However, transnational arbitrariness exists within Europe: if there are no harmonised standards on which state has jurisdiction over one's actions, which system's legislation should citizens expect to follow? The presumption of knowing the law functions well within one legal order but, within a plurality of legal orders, it is demanding too much of individuals. In this regard, the obstacles created for individuals and the multiple regulatory burdens are often criticised.[158]

Finally, there is also the argument of the European *demos*. If there is such a thing as a European *demos*, which is different than simply the accumulation of national *demoi*, then, as a consequence of the theory on democratic statism, the needs and values of this European *demos* would not be fully expressed. This is because with democratic statism, the national constitutional values of the national *demoi*, by definition, prevail over the European. The questions of what constitutes *demos*, whether Europe has one or needs one have been extensively debated. One may approach *demos* as a concept expressing the link between citizenship and democracy.[159] Weiler, for example, examined the different perceptions of a European *demos* by advocating that, within Europe, nationality and citizenship are decoupled, which entails that there exist multiple *demoi* in cohabitation.[160]

There are three manners to conceptualise the European *demos* according to Weiler. First, one could see it as concentric cycles of differing intensity. Here, European identity derives from similar sources of human attachment as with national identity. Someone is Dutch and, on a more abstract level, he is also European. The problem with this view is that it approaches the European *demos*

158 M. Luchtman, 'Choice of forum and the prosecution of cross-border crime in the European Union-what role for the legality principle?', in M. Luchtman (ed) 'Choice of forum in cooperation against EU financial crime: freedom, security and justice and the protection of specific EU-interests', Eleven International Publishing, 2013, pp. 12–26.

159 J.H.H. Weiler, 'The Constitution of Europe', Cambridge University Press, 1999, p. 337.

160 Ibid., p. 344.

from its national connotation.[161] Second, one could say that individuals belong simultaneously to two *demoi* but with different factors of identification. I am Dutch, as I share the cultural identification and values of the Dutch *demos*, but I am also European, as I share European transnational affinities such as non-discrimination on the basis of nationality and human rights by the Charter and the ECHR. The problem with this view is that it is not clear how the two affiliations differ. Are democracy, human rights and the like not also part of the Dutch *demos*? Thus, a European *demos* in this theory is a rather narrow concept.[162]

The third approach is similar to the previous one in that it also invites individuals to embrace their affiliation to two *demoi* with different sets of identifying factors. As one cannot be a part of the European *demos* unless one is a citizen of a Member State, this approach binds together the concepts of Member States' nationalities and European citizenship and, interestingly, promotes the idea of a social contract. The EU is not only an agreement amongst Member States but is also a social contract amongst nationals, according to which individuals shall see each other within the European legal order as citizens of a broader society. Individuals must accept the legitimacy and authority of decisions adopted by fellow Europeans.[163] To this extent, there exists an underlying, two-way perception of belongingness, according to which belonging is not only a passive value (to be accepted) but also an active one (to accept).[164] This theory of European *demos* promotes a view of EU as a cosmopolitan reality and includes a logic of inclusive oppositions.[165] The thesis on a European *demos* becomes part of an experimental protocol of how territorial ethnicities and nationalities with deeply felt historical conflicts can become open to a cosmopolitan reality.[166]

This third theory on European *demos* is also the point of confluence between two antithetical tendencies. First, national identity has always represented a valuable historical, cultural and territorial heritage that provides individuals a point of gravity with which they can associate their existential yearnings and personalities. *'The nation, through its myths, provides a past and a future'*.[167] Second, European citizenship, the '*supra*-national', represents the liberal effort to establish connections of loyalty and belongingness beyond the concepts of national identity. Thus, belonging to a European *demos* mirrors an education of the 'I' to reach the 'Other' and a willingness to submit aspects of our social ordering to a broader polity composed of 'others'.[168]Approaching the European *demos* in this way protects national identity from the future of a melting pot such as that of the

161 Ibid., pp. 344–345.
162 Ibid., p. 345.
163 Ibid., p. 346.
164 Ibid., p. 338.
165 U. Beck, 'Cosmopolitan vision', Polity Press, 2006, p. 172.
166 Ibid., p. 176.
167 J.H.H. Weiler, 'The Constitution of Europe', Cambridge University Press, 1999, p. 347.
168 Ibid., pp. 346–347.

USA,[169] while it also prevents uncivilised expressions of national identity, such as over-nationalism, intolerance and inhumanity.[170] This theory is not necessarily a concept of European identity to be pursued, as it supports a 'community of others' and not a 'community of brothers'. To this extent, the theory on multiple *demoi* and its conceptualisation with this third theory on European *demos* has given rise to theories of democracy that further internalise it, such as the theory on European 'demoicracy' that is short of mutual recognition of national identities.[171]

Accepting such a theory of European *demos* implies that both the national and European popular sovereignty, as these are expressed via criminal law policy, have an ethical value. If both expressions of *demos* must retain their validity within EU law then one must think of ways to mediate between them. This leads to the conclusion that perhaps a more pluralistic theory should be considered, which shall show how these inclusive oppositions should be balanced.

4.3. The theory of constitutional pluralism

4.3.1. General characteristics

The theory of constitutional pluralism is a relatively recent theory and, to date remains the most consistent theory depicting the current status quo of European matters. To this a theory, many variations contribute, such as the following few examples:[172] socio-teleological constitutionalism, epistemic meta-constitutionalism, cosmopolitan pluralism (and 'the best fit universal constitutionalism'), harmonious discursive constitutionalism, multilevel constitutionalism and pragmatic constitutionalism.[173] One can also speak of pluralism at different levels such as pluralism of legal orders, sources of law, values, and polities.[174] The idea was conceived as a reaction to the Maastricht judgement and continued after the Lisbon judgement of the German Constitutional Court,[175] although one can locate it as an ambiguous idea in previous legal theory.[176] The abstractness of this theory and its popularity has led to various

169 U. Beck, 'Cosmopolitan vision', Polity Press, 2006, p. 176.

170 Ibid., p. 172.

171 K. Nicolaïdes, 'The Idea of European Demoicracy', in J. Dickson, P. Eleftheriadis (eds), 'Philosophical Foundations of EU Law', Oxford University Press, 2012, pp. 247–274.

172 Here I follow the categorisations of M. Avbelj, 'Questioning EU Constitutionalisms', German Law Journal, vol. 9, 2008, pp. 1–26.

173 M. Avbelj, J. Komárek, 'Introduction', in M. Avbelj, J. Komárek (eds), 'Constitutional Pluralism in the European Union and Beyond', Hart Publishing, 2012, pp. 5–6.

174 M.P. Maduro in M. Avbelj, J. Komárek (eds), 'Four Visions of Constitutional Pluralism', EUI Working Paper LAW, no. 2008/21, p. 6.

175 W. Hulstijn, J.W. van Rossem, 'Het *Lissabon-Urteil*: Pluralisme op Duitse voorwaarden', in J.M.J. van Rijn van Alkemade, J. Uzman, 'Soevereiniteit of pluralisme', Wolf Legal Publishers, 2011, pp. 21–46.

176 N. MacCormick, 'Beyond the Sovereign State', Modern Law Review, vol. 56, 1993, pp. 1–18; M. Delmas-Marty, 'Towards a Truly Common Law: Europe as a Laboratory for Legal Pluralism', Cambridge University Press, 2002.

interpretations, as discussed, and is quite difficult to pin down. I shall not analyse all theories here, but I will limit the discussion to the basic features of this theory and their impact on European criminal law.

Constitutional pluralism is a theory in which legal orders are autonomous and separate but not hierarchically positioned. The view is one of a heterarchy rather than a hierarchy.[177] Rather than a strictly monistic or dualistic system, the European legal system is composed of different legal orders that are interdependent and porous; however, these are part of a unified European legal system.[178] The starting point of this theory is empirical, as constitutional pluralism best describes the current reality[179] and where the EU functions neither on the basis of an absolute European primacy nor on the basis of democratic statism. The theory was developed for resolving the challenge of competing constitutional claims.

The basic premise of constitutional pluralism is that both the EU and national constitutional orders may have legitimate claims.[180] This departs from the classic Kelsenian view of an ultimate theory of recognition. Thus, the idea of constitutional pluralism is that the answer to competing forms of constitutional authority *should* remain open to allow room for diversity, tolerance and accommodation.[181] To some extent, this theory aims to acknowledge that both national and European legal orders have an ethical reason to pursue their sovereignty. However, their interaction should be based on bonds of loyalty. As a response to European primacy, constitutional pluralism advocates a European legal system that is strengthened and becomes vivid by embracing diversity. In this respect, it offers an avenue to canalise expression of national interests. As a response to democratic statism, it objects to the introverted and defensive attitude of national authorities to the European project. Therefore, it presupposes that national actors perceive themselves not subordinate to European institutions and decisions but as actors in that system.

As a normative theory, constitutional pluralism does not generate any specific answer to the question of primacy (for solving constitutional conflicts). In reality, it does not differ much in its starting point from the European primacy theory that, in principle, EU law should have primacy. However, an important switch is that it introduces a different mentality, whereby derogation from such primacy can be legitimate even in the absence of discretion. From a normative perspective, constitutional pluralism focuses on the 'rules of mutual engagement', in other words, the guidelines with which national courts decide on constitutional

177 N. Walker in M. Avbelj, J. Komárek (eds), 'Four Visions of Constitutional Pluralism', EUI Working Paper LAW, no. 2008/21, p. 19.

178 M.P. Maduro, 'Three Claims of Constitutional Pluralism', in M. Avbelj, J. Komárek, 'Constitutional Pluralism in the European Union and Beyond', Hart Publishing, 2012, p. 70.

179 Ibid., pp. 70–71.

180 Ibid., p. 76.

181 Ibid., p. 73.

conflicts.[182] Essentially, there is a shift of focus from clear-cut answers to the reasoning and argumentation of decisions. For Kumm, for example, the ultimate authority of EU law should not be found in its 'effective and uniform application' but in basic constitutional principles of liberalism such as democracy and human rights. These principles are not bound together by sovereignty or by the positive law of the Treaties (as in 'the Treaties said so') but normatively through the idea of human dignity and the commitment of all actors to secure it institutionally.[183] Thus, the decision not to apply EU law would be legitimate if such a law would significantly disregard individual rights or principles such as democracy and subsidiarity.[184]

Maduro has developed constitutional pluralism further at the normative level and proposed the 'harmonic principles of contrapunctual law'. First, the principle of pluralism, according to which any legal order must respect the identity of the other and maximise participation (of more national courts and actors for example);[185] second, the principles of consistency and vertical/horizontal coherence which require that decisions must fit and be justified in relation to previous decisions (this principle also requires that national courts consider decisions made by other national courts to promote horizontal coherency);[186] third, the principle of universalisability, according to which the EU and national judicial bodies should reason their decisions in universal terms and in the context of a coherent and integrated EU legal order wherein such decisions must be based on doctrines that could be applied by any other national court in a similar situation;[187] and, fourth, the principle of institutional choice that entails that because of the plurality of forums for conflict resolution, mutual understanding of the systems' virtues and malfunctions is essential.[188]

4.3.2. Constitutional pluralism in European criminal law

Having briefly analysed some of the basic ideas behind constitutional pluralism, one must wonder how it would influence European criminal law. Although normatively this theory does not produce much, a democratic pluralism in European

182 M.P. Maduro in M. Avbelj and J. Komárek (eds), 'Four Visions of Constitutional Pluralism', EUI Working Paper LAW, no. 2008/21, pp. 20–21.

183 M. Kumm, in M. Avbelj, J. Komárek (eds), 'Four Visions of Constitutional Pluralism', EUI Working Paper LAW, no. 2008/21, p. 26; M. Kumm, 'Rethinking Constitutional Authority: On the Structure and Limits of Constitutional Pluralism', in M. Avbelj, J. Komárek (eds), 'Constitutional Pluralism in the European Union and Beyond', Hart Publishing, 2012, p. 65.

184 M. Kumm, 'The Jurisprudence of Constitutional Conflict: Constitutional Supremacy in Europe Before and After the Constitutional Treaty', European Law Journal, vol. 11, 2005, pp. 299–305.

185 M.P. Maduro, 'Contrapunctual law: Europe's Constitutional Pluralism in Action', in N. Walker (ed), 'Sovereignty in Transition', Hart Publishing, 2003, pp. 526–527.

186 Ibid., pp. 527–528.

187 Ibid., pp. 529–530.

188 Ibid., p. 530.

criminal law has consequences especially at the theoretical level, as it influences mainly the mentality of interaction between EU and nation states. Some of the problems identified in the previous theories on the primacy of EU law and democratic statism are, to some extent, less evident here.

At the theoretical level, a pluralistic theory for European criminal law system entails that supremacy of EU law over national orders is neither absolute nor always desirable. In criminal law-making where societal values and interpretation of individual rights are influenced by national communities, allowing the national communities to depict those in their legislation is essential. To some extent, this theory fits European integration in the field of criminal law especially because such integration is premised on shared competences, which require only minimum harmonisation and may be blocked by the emergency brake (Article 83 para. 3 TFEU). In effect, therefore, the picture of European integration across Europe in the harmonisation of criminal offences is more pluralistic than other areas of law. Such pluralism, though, is not due to the positive law arrangement of the Treaties but is also desirable. In this way, a European criminal law functioning within a pluralistic Europe would have a role of mediation in the conflicts of societal values by allowing flexibility.[189]

This has consequences on how European competences should be employed and with what justification. One of the advantages of constitutional pluralism is that it invokes the question of justifying political decisions. This would imply that the use of European criminal law powers should be legitimised on considerations other than the self-serving Treaties. Such an impact has been documented in literature, as there is a plea to justify European competences on principles such as proportionality and *ultima ratio*.[190] The drive of European integration in criminal matters to increase harmonisation can only be legitimised as long as it is based on weighing competing principles and should consider the following: the mutual respect of the identities of the different orders (Maduro's principle on pluralism), the coherency of the European legal order and of national legal orders,[191] the ability to reproduce similar balancing of these principles in future situations to avoid instrumentalism (or a form of casuistry in legislative reasoning) and the basic backbone of the European criminal law order that is grounded in individual rights and human dignity. Thus, the assumptions and exercise of criminal law competences by the EU should also reflect a loyalty to and respect for the national legal traditions and systems.

In this regard, national courts can also control European instrumentalism. Constitutional pluralism allows for more comprehensive dialogue in 'hard cases' than simple 'nationalistic' or 'EU primacy' perspectives, as it obliges both sides to

---

189 M. Huomo-Kettunen, 'EU Criminal Policy at a Crossroads Between Effectiveness and Traditional Restraints for the Use of Criminal Law', New Journal of European Criminal Law, vol. 5, 2014, p. 304.

190 Ibid., pp. 312–316.

191 European Criminal Policy Initiative, 'A Manifesto on European Criminal Policy', ZIS, vol. 12, 2009, p. 709.

consider the other's views and interests. It allows for diverse national views regarding criminal liability and the values to be discussed.[192] To this extent, it is not only European instrumentalism in criminal law that can be controlled by national courts when necessary but also national instrumentalism; national courts cannot refuse the application and validity of EU law on grounds of purely national interests alone but must convey in their decisions a reasoning that promotes coherence and considers the identity and interests of the European legal system. It is not enough for national courts to simply invoke national cultural or constitutional values. Rather, they must explain them, measure them and investigate the impact of their decisions on the European legal system in general.

Thus, one of the benefits of constitutional pluralism for European criminal law is that it shifts the focus from the 'who has legitimacy' to the 'why'. In this regard, Kumm's theory can be enlightening as it focuses on a balancing of individual interests and principles of justice. Neither of the theories above (EU supremacy and democratic statism) offers this balancing as an essential element of their doctrine. The European primacy theory bases the authority of EU law on the Treaties, while the national statism bases the primacy of national law on the ethical value of national democracies without investigating as to whether it serves the rights involved in transnational proceedings.

Constitutional pluralism entails that problems such as the obligation to enforce EU law even when it violates core constitutional concepts or the principle of *lex certa* in implementation can be solved by weighing rights, principles and policies in a transparent manner, rather than by imposing a solution that disregards the value of national claims (in the case of European primacy theory) or of European claims (in the case of national statism). Similarly, when it comes to conform interpretation the obligation to enforce EU law is not, by definition, a superior policy to govern judicial reasoning. The question focuses on the interpretation and balancing of rights that occur between the European and national legal orders. In that sense, there is a shift towards a pluralistic discourse on how individual rights that are protected through European criminal legislation ought to be interpreted within different political communities that are supposed to operate within a broader pan-European political community.

Conversely, a major setback of this theory is that it does not promote legal certainty; at least not in the way that a theory with a definite answer would have. From a normative perspective, constitutional pluralism does not offer a clear answer as to who has the authority of the last word in constitutional conflicts. Most supporters of pluralism argue that the EU is still the authority, at least in principle, to define how certain obligations should evolve such as the obligation to conform

---

[192] L. Gröning, 'A Criminal Justice System or a System Deficit? Notes on the System Structure of the EU Criminal Law', European Journal of Crime, Criminal Law and Criminal Justice, vol. 18, 2010, pp. 115–137.

interpretation or *lex certa*.[193] If one tries to draw normative claims from this theory then there is the danger of uncertainty. One of the most prominent counterarguments for constitutional pluralism is the chaos that it potentially creates and the challenge in its application when theory turns into practice.[194]

Pluralism, however, remains relevant. The legacy of the pluralistic movement is relevant because it requires both the EU and national institutions to take account of concerns of legitimacy from both the EU and national arenas. Thus, even if not as a strict normative theory, pluralism introduces a valuable theoretical mentality and it can be the starting point for the discussion on European criminal law legitimation. It has been suggested that, even if one wished not to accept a generalised theory of constitutional pluralism, certain pluralistic elements would still be necessary. For example, in preliminary rulings, national courts could be faced with an interpretation of EU law that essentially violates core concepts of their constitutional values or renders the pursuit of their national policies extremely difficult or impossible. In such a case, following the preliminary ruling could be considered disproportional, depending on the European interest in question and how this can be weighed with the national interest.[195] Similarly, if the national legislator was faced with a European definition of an offence that was completely against the principle of legality, the national legislator should be able to implement with stricter and more precise wording, even if this would compromise in principle harmonisation.

4.4. Conclusion

From the above analysis, it is apparent that the European criminal justice system possesses certain fundamental constitutional challenges. Concepts such as European *demos*, democracy, sovereignty and fundamental rights are essential for legitimising a European criminal justice system, yet these concepts are still largely undetermined and always evolving. It is very difficult to pick a theory for all these concepts that would reflect reality.

However, there are needs that must be fulfilled. First, European instrumentalism in criminal law must be controlled and subordinated to a theory of justice. Second, the protective finality of European criminal law must find a more concrete basis. One must understand what individual freedom the European criminal law is destined to protect. Third, any connections to constitutional theories on the interrelation of the European and national legal orders must be able to canalise

193 J. Altena-Davidsen, 'De reikwijdte van de plicht tot conforme interpretatie in het strafrecht tegen de achtergrond van de verhouding tussen de Europese en de nationale rechtsorde', Ars Aequi, 2012, p. 558.

194 G. Davies, 'Constitutional Disagreement in Europe and the Search for Pluralism', in M. Avbelj, J. Komárek, 'Constitutional Pluralism in the European Union and Beyond', Hart Publishing, 2012, p. 271.

195 Ibid., p. 281.

certain pluralistic claims while maintaining some level of clarity. Fourth, the *Rechtskarakter* of European criminal law must be defined with due care to the particular nature of the European criminal justice system and its relationship to freedom of movement rights and the internal market.

5. A relational model for European criminal justice

In this section, a relational model for the European criminal justice system shall be proposed. In principle, the relational model has proven to be capable of describing the nature and application of the legality principle in national law. It has also been argued that this model not only best describes reality but also has theoretical and normative value.[196] A relational model for EU criminal law, as it will be explained in detail further, is based on the premise that both horizontal and vertical aspects of protection of individual autonomy are inherent to the function of criminal law. Especially with regard to European criminal law the relational model of criminal justice, which embraces the interrelation between oppositions rather than exclusion, is an apt tool to approach the mediation of two interrelating conflicts, i.e. a conflict between two accounts of popular autonomy and a conflict between two accounts of individual autonomy.

First, there is conflict between the European and national legal orders. For criminal law, this is translated as a conflict between two expressions of popular autonomy, the European and the national. This is not a typical conflict found in national law. Hence the relational model shall be called to expand to deal with this situation. To do so, the theory of constitutional pluralism is a useful theoretical framework for investigating how the principle of legality can contribute to the legitimacy of European criminal law. As explained, pluralism introduces a relational mentality between European and national claims of legitimacy, where none of the two are automatically annulled. The premise of constitutional pluralism shall be used mainly at the theoretical level and more concretely for the interaction between national and European popular autonomy.

Second, there is the conflict between the two finalities of criminal law, the instrumental and protective. In European criminal law, this is translated in the conflict between battling cross-border crime and furthering European integration, and protecting individuals against arbitrariness. Thus, a relational model of European criminal justice provides the platform where one may examine how European criminal law – and the AFSJ – may exist autonomously and yet still in connection with the internal market.

However, before the characteristics of such a European criminal justice system are examined, one has to wonder whether the European criminal justice system would be significantly better with one of the other two models for criminal justice; namely, the instrumentalist model or the classical model.

---

196 Chapter V para. 6.4.

5.1. The insufficiency of the instrumentalist model

If one chose the justice model that best describes the current European criminal justice system, the instrumentalist model would be the obvious choice. As noted, one of the basic problems in legitimising European criminal law and supranationalising some of its notions is the genuine lack of a unified European criminal system functioning at either a federal level or at the level of replacing national systems.

Because of the prevalence of the spill-over theory and not only the historical but also the normative connections of European criminal law and the internal market, European criminal law is by default based on an instrumentalist mentality.[197] It is perhaps superfluous and repetitive to mention the many faces of European instrumentalism once more. However, it is worth recounting some of the basic features of European criminal law that are inherent to the instrumentalist model.

First, in an instrumentalist model, criminal law is neutral. European criminal policy is annexed to the internal market and, in the end, criminal law is not a goal in its own right but a neutral tool designed to promote other policies. The spill-over theory, as a legitimation doctrine for the political mandate of European criminal law, is by definition, instrumentalist as it approaches criminal law as just another competence for effectively achieving a broader policy goal. The instrumentalist model does not bring any change to European criminal law. In other words, it is the best model for describing the current situation without reforming it. Such a model, as shown in Chapter V, is governed by policies and it is the effective implementation of these policies that legitimises criminal law.[198] This is the case for EU law that makes ample use of the principle of effectiveness in criminal law matters. This gives criminal law a neutral character, one in which criminal law is seen as a means to an end. Since the early days of European criminal law, principles, such as the assimilation principle, have obliged Member States to adopt criminal norms with a view to the effective enforcement of EU law. This has led to a functional criminalisation.[199] Functional criminalisation, according to Mitsilegas, is a concept that explains the instrumentalist approach of European criminal law, as criminal law is not a self-standing policy.[200] Mitsilegas identified the dangers of over-criminalisation. These dangers are a consequence of the instrumentalist model of criminal justice. While such an approach can also set limits on criminal law, especially when national criminal norms may infringe upon the four freedoms,[201] such limits are influenced not by considerations of individual freedom but by EU policies.

---

197 P.–A. Albrecht, 'Securitized Societies', Intersentia, 2011, pp. 262–263.

198 Chapter V para. 5.1.

199 V. Mitsilegas, 'From Overcriminalisation to Decriminalisation – The Many Faces of Effectiveness in European Criminal Law', New Journal of European Criminal Law, vol. 5, 2014, p. 419.

200 Ibid.

201 Ibid., p. 422.

Second, in such a model criminal law is legitimised via crime-control policies and serving the social good. It has a security-oriented motivation. Moreover, the social good is an amalgam of different concepts: battling cross-border crime and ensuring safety for European citizens while furthering integration. One could say that the European criminal justice area has deep instrumentalist foundations, as even the policies and the social good are not well-defined but left to opportunity and *zeitgeist*. It is generally assumed that battling cross-border crime is much better served via the establishment of mutual recognition proceedings. However, this leaves the question of individual rights for Member States under the premise of mutual trust. Does mutual trust exist because it is assumed, or is it assumed because it exists? Such concepts, based on the general hypothesis of loyalty, are difficult to deal with. Mutual trust is a dynamic notion strengthened by time and proven in every case. Yet it also presumes a mutual responsibility. This means that fostering it should also be a part of crime-control policies. In this regard, goals such as judicial cooperation in criminal matters, would be better served through a system of transnational guarantees on individual rights.[202]

Third, in this model the vertical protection of individuals is not in itself necessary to legitimise criminal law. When the vertical protection is of concern, it is also approached as a policy with a specific mandate. To be clear, vertical protection would not remain outside the sphere of legitimacy necessarily in an instrumentalist model. Such protection would be justified though with reasons of effectiveness. For example, foreseeability of criminalisation makes the deterrence of cross-border crime more effective. This is not far from the primary justification for the protection of individual rights in cross-border proceedings, namely that it facilitates judicial cooperation. This was further seen in the conception of the terms security and freedom in European criminal law. Chapter VI also mentioned that the application of the legality principle as an implementation criterion aims at facilitating effective implementation of EU law.[203] The instrumentalist model of European criminal law approaches individuals not as bearers of rights but as security risks.[204] The nature of such law is embedded in the desire to battle cross-border crime; however, there is no assumption of responsibility to protect individual rights in a transnational setting unless it serves effectiveness. The vertical relationship between the EU and the individual is not inherent to this system. As such, protection of individuals in the vertical sense is not necessary within the field of European criminal law and it is instead left to Member States in most occasions.[205]

Conversely, this interrelation with the free movement rights implies that criminal law in Europe also boasts a horizontal dimension. It aims at building stable

---

202 L. Marin, 'Learning from the Lessons of 10 Years of Practice with the European Arrest Warrant', New Journal of European Criminal Law, vol. 5, 2014, p. 341.

203 Chapter VI para. 4.5.

204 S. Melander, 'Effectiveness in EU Criminal Law and its Effects on the General Part of Criminal Law', New Journal of European Criminal Law, vol. 5, 2014, p. 283.

205 Chapter V para. 5.1.

and anticipated relationships amongst individuals as they exercise their rights to freedom of movement. In other words, it aims to promote and support the European community and common behavioural standards. This horizontal dimension is highlighted in European criminal law and is a feature of the instrumentalist model.[206]

Why then, would one argue against an instrumentalist model? Despite the fact that an instrumentalist model best describes the European criminal law reality, the aim is not only to provide a descriptive model but one that genuinely legitimises European criminal law. The instrumentalist model fits the European criminal justice system but is not a desirable option.

As seen in Chapter V, the instrumentalist model fails to properly address the protective finality of criminal law in its vertical sense.[207] Although such protection may exist it is only applied when it increases effectiveness. This has been a prevalent manner in interpreting the relationship between the Charter and EU instruments.[208] There is a new form of arbitrariness within the EU, namely, transnational arbitrariness and it can be defined as legal uncertainty regarding the content of criminal norms across jurisdictions and the protection of individual rights in a transnational criminal legal procedure. This has been primarily evident in mutual recognition proceedings but also in the lack of harmonisation of rules on jurisdiction. What is therefore unattainable in this model is a proper concept of justice within the EU, which as observed has been greatly criticised. However, the horizontal dimension of individual autonomy is not properly addressed in this model either. In an instrumentalist model the horizontal dimension does exist but is confined to the crime-control finality of criminal law. Such crime-control does not translate more generally to commonly shared values amongst European citizens. An instrumentalist model presumes that European citizens have no substantial connections other than their accumulated fears for their safety.

Additionally, the instrumentalist model does not possess sufficient means for controlling instrumentalism. The problems of the consistency of criminal policy and legislation have been put forward by European institutions.[209] The only means is a general claim toward consistency, as was seen in Chapter V.[210] The instrumentalist model of European criminal law does require that European policies and competences be resolved in a consistent manner. To this extent, subsidiarity/proportionality and *ultima ratio* can remain relevant to the model, however, it is not necessarily important that these principles are part of the decision-making and policy. In this model, effective crime-control suffices as legitimation for criminal

206 Ibid.

207 See above para. 3.2.

208 N. de Boer, 'Addressing rights divergences under the Charter: Melloni', Common Market Law Review, vol. 50, 2013, pp. 1094–1096.

209 Commission Communication, Towards an EU Criminal Policy: Ensuring the effective implementation of EU policies through criminal law, COM (2011) 573 final, 20.9.2011.

210 Chapter V para. 5.1 and 5.2.

law. Hence, if competences of the EU can be justified sufficiently on crime-control grounds (or improving judicial cooperation and mutual trust), recourse to principles such as subsidiarity is redundant. The aim of consistency is neutral, as it is not enriched with ethical connotation. Such consistency may very well be achieved through the use of consistent policy analyses.

Yet, the general claim regarding the consistency of the instrumentalist model could have some advantages, especially in the field of judicial interpretation as it obliges both the European and national courts to strive for consistency in their reasoning. Yet, again, there is no protection from excessive instrumentalism. The instrumentalist model does not prevent the principle of effectiveness of EU law from becoming the main policy consideration superior to all other principles, values or individual rights in interpretation. On the contrary, keeping the policy of effective enforcement of EU law at a superior position is actually quite beneficial for consistency. As is noted in literature, the principle of effectiveness has the potential to significantly alter judicial interpretation.[211] It requires national courts to re-prioritise the interests involved in judicial interpretation and also influences the reasoning of ECJ judgements.[212] Thus, one of the benefits of the instrumentalist model is that it promotes consistency. However, a major disadvantage is that it does not require a distinction between principles, policies and rights and a hierarchical connection between them that reflects the basic values of the European legal order.

5.2. The anachronistic nature of the classical model

The classical model seems to be less fitting for European criminal law. It is not only difficult to explain European criminal justice within such a model but also it is incapable of curtailing instrumentalism.

The basic claim of the classical model is that the vertical protection of individuals from state arbitrariness is the sole legitimation of criminal law.[213] A classical model for European criminal law would entail that the *Rechtskarakter* of criminal law is founded on the protective guarantees of individual liberty. European criminal law would be forced to legitimise itself on protective principles of justice. The assumption and application of European competences on criminal matters, their implementation by national legislators and the judicial decisions by the ECJ and the national courts could not be justifiable via policy considerations, the primacy of EU law, or the effectiveness or battling of cross-border crime but, rather, on how well it protects individual rights in their vertical dimension. However, a horizontal dimension here is of little concern. The classical model does not promote the necessity to protect individuals in their horizontal relationships by providing

---

211 S. Melander, 'Effectiveness in EU Criminal Law and its Effects on the General Part of Criminal Law', New Journal of European Criminal Law, vol. 5, 2014, p. 289.

212 Ibid.

213 Chapter V para. 4.1.

common European standards on behaviour, upon which individuals could depend their freedom of movement rights. Policies such as freedom of movement, internal market, cross-border crime, and the facilitation of judicial cooperation cannot legitimise the use of criminal law at the European level. It follows that a large part of European criminal law *acquis*, which lacks any fundamental rights protection, would already be at odds with the classical model. All these instruments would require re-evaluation for their compliance with individual autonomy, which is certainly a positive step.

Conversely, this instrumental finality of criminal law is excluded from the *Rechtskarakter*. How can one reconcile this with the nature of European criminal law? The European criminal justice system cannot be entirely detached from the rest of the areas of the Treaties that create an EU with specific policies and goals. Unlike the national criminal law system, the European system has a rather limited and more concrete purpose defined by the restricted field of the Treaties. Once detached from these, it has no reason for existence unless it aims to replace national systems or create a federal criminal law system. In addition, how could this model control European instrumentalism? Even if one accepts that the *Rechtskarakter* of European criminal law is defined as focused only on the protection of individuals against arbitrariness and even if tools are developed to enforce this, how could this model then control and legitimise European instrumentalism? As noted in Chapter V, this is perhaps the major problem with the classical model.[214] What is necessary is not to exclude European instrumentalism but to subject it to a theory of justice and thus control it.

Further, the classical model advocates for maximum legal certainty. How can this be achieved in a multilevel transnational setting? On one hand, this would require that European criminal law assume *more* competencies to harmonise criminal offences in order to retain instruments of mutual recognition. Maximum legal certainty would be best achieved by establishing a federal criminal code or replacing all national systems with a European system. If maximum certainty is desirable, then one has to accept that, for individuals, a unified European criminal law system with a single criminal code is the best-case scenario. In a classical model, pluralism of values, legal orders and, especially, horizontal diversity and pluralism of sources of criminal liability cannot be accepted. Consequently, one of the problems of this model is that it cannot be reconciled with the current pluralistic model of the EU. Conversely, the classical model also has consequences on a more practical level such as the obligation of conform interpretation. In the classical model, this obligation is at odds with the legality principle. While such an obligation is supposed to be limited by this principle, one has to wonder how much margin in interpretation the judge might have. As noted in Chapter V, the classical model advocates for strict margins of appreciation, which do not allow courts to replace the will of the legislation with their own.[215] But is it not the purpose of the

214 Chapter V para. 4.3.
215 Chapter V para. 4.2.

obligation of conform interpretation to do just that, namely, to align national legislation to the goals and policies of the European instrument?

Finally, as shown, the classical model is locked into a very traditional approach regarding democracy, the separation of powers, and legal positivism in general.[216] How can one reconcile the classical model of European criminal law with the existence of a multilevel legal system that functions within a legal and cultural pluralism and where legal certainty cannot always be achieved? One problem is that European democracy, being multilevel and less representative in the traditional sense, would fail the test of the traditionally interpreted and procedural concept of democracy. The same holds for the separation of powers, particularly between European and national legal bodies. The classical model, in this respect, promotes less flexibility.

6. Characteristics of a Relational Model for European Criminal Law

A relational model of European criminal law is based on the premise that the inherent nature of criminal law is found both in its horizontal and protective dimensions. Infused with the theory of pluralism, such a model may also address the question of legitimacy of European criminal law *vis-à-vis* national legal orders. The *Rechtskarakter* of European criminal law should therefore be reconstructed around this idea. As explained, core elements of such a criminal justice system are the elements of transparency and controllability of legislative and judicial decisions.[217] These elements will be essential in understanding how the European criminal justice system should be legitimised. Transparency and controllability of political and judicial decisions ensure that EU law retains its mediating character between national and European sovereignty.

Furthermore, the protection of human dignity is central in such criminal justice. Such element is in line with the Charter but also with the ECHR. As seen in Chapter VI, the ECtHR jurisprudence has significantly influenced the ECJ's interpretation of the legality principle.[218] Especially with regard to the ECtHR's approach, this has been termed as the 'rights-conception'.[219] Its basic feature is to focus more on the concept of foreseeability and how this can be achieved rather than a mere examination of the cloak of the law. In particular, this trend is identifiable in the definition of legal certainty in the relational model of European criminal justice. Therefore focusing more on how decisions in European criminal law support the values of European criminal justice system (such as the European *demos*) is a

216 Chapter V para. 4.1.
217 Chapter V para. 6.1 and 6.2.
218 Chapter VI para. 1 and 2.
219 Chapter IV para. 9.1 and 11.

choice that builds upon, but also furthers, the ECtHR's 'rights-conception' of the legality principle.

6.1. The *Rechtskarakter* of European criminal law

The *Rechtskarakter* of European criminal law is composed of elements whose balance defines it. The inherent nature of European criminal law is to protect individuals. However, in the relational model, such protection is not only understood in its vertical dimension but also in its horizontal dimension, namely with regard to the protection of individuals against third parties. By redefining the protective finality of criminal law in a relational manner, instrumentality is subordinated to the protective finality. That is, crime-control – and any communitarian or utilitarian connotations it might have – cannot comply with the *Rechtskarakter* of European criminal law *unless* translated into the common shared values of the European community. The safety or security of the population, or attending to the greater good of society, should be based on common values such as tolerance, human dignity and other fundamental rights.

This influences the use of competences of European criminal law. The use of criminal competences cannot be legitimised only on the grounds of battling crime, improving judicial cooperation or furthering EU policies *unless* these policies translate into certain common values shared by the European *demos* that the European criminal law system must protect and respect.[220] To this extent, the relational model obliges the European legislator to justify the use of criminal law competences by paying attention to both vertical and horizontal aspects.

Regarding the vertical aspect, European criminal competences must be assumed and justified based on principles that mirror individual autonomy and dignity. Individual autonomy is assumed both in the concept of the European *demos* and in the concept of national sovereignty. In essence, the question is not about whether there ought to be 'less or more Europe', as the European legal order is about mediation between national and European sovereign rights.

In particular, in light of the interpretation given above of the European *demos* and constitutional pluralism, the EU must accept that the vertical protection of individuals in criminal law comprises a direct relationship between the EU and its citizens.[221] This means that exercising European competences must respect certain principles such as proportionality[222] and, most importantly, human dignity.[223] European citizens are not risks to security but carriers of rights and can claim that their human dignity be respected. In this sense, human dignity is the ethical

220 F. Meyer, 'Strafrechtsgenese in Internationalen Organisationen', Nomos, 2012, p. 726.

221 Ibid., p. 651.

222 S. Melander, 'Effectiveness in EU Criminal Law and its Effects on the General Part of Criminal Law', New Journal of European Criminal Law, vol. 5, 2014, p. 289.

223 M. Kumm, 'Rethinking Constitutional Authority: On the Structure and Limits of Constitutional Pluralism', in M. Avbelj, J. Komárek (eds), 'Constitutional Pluralism in the European Union and Beyond', Hart Publishing, 2012, p. 65.

minimum of the European legal order as is also demonstrated in the Treaties in Article 2 TEU. Such a direct vertical bond between individuals and the EU obliges the latter to take into consideration the impact of mutual recognition instruments and of harmonisation instruments for human dignity. The current blind spot regarding the emerging transnational arbitrariness is not legitimate criminal law. One may not consider Europe as a single legal order and single area of criminal enforcement but then disregard this very same element when it comes to the arbitrariness that this creates for individuals. In this regard, the relational model marks a plea for a major shift in the nature of European criminal law from a system of instrumentalism towards a system of relationism between individual rights and crime-control. It does not deny the character of the EU as a polity with a specific mandate but maintains that responsibility must be assumed, to protect individuals from arbitrariness.

The vertical protection of individual autonomy within the EU must also be conceptualised as a protection of national political communities and sovereignty. National sovereignty is not only a political term but also has an ethical value that allows expression for national identity and cultural bonds. The EU cannot disregard that political participation by individuals in the national political communities must also be respected. Individuals would otherwise be deprived of their rights to depict, in national criminal law, certain values relating to their cultural heritage. This entails not only that principles, such as subsidiarity, must receive substantial content but also that national political communities should be allowed to maintain certain basic cultural values as expressed in criminal law. In other words, the relational model mirrors the claim to pluralism of values.

Regarding the horizontal aspect, justifying European criminal competences on mere crime-control or on the efficient enforcement of European policies cannot be accepted. European criminal norms must be justified in terms of common values shared by Europeans. If one accepts that the European *demos* comprises the two aforementioned relational elements,[224] then European criminal law must translate its policies into common European values that enforce European cultural affiliations among individuals. This is why it is so important to subject instrumental policies to a broader protective *Rechtskarakter*: the crime-control dimension is not what justifies the existence of European criminal law. It is that European criminal law sets forth European values that are shared but not yet articulated or expressed. In this way, European criminal law promotes a European *demos*.[225]

The benefit of the relational model is that it does not deny the instrumental nature of European criminal law; it does, however, oblige the EU to justify whether these policies are in line with a set of common European values. Thus, the European criminal justice system is not separate from the internal market but, rather, requires its own justification and discourse. In this way, instrumentalism is controlled and curtailed. The *Rechtskarakter* of European criminal law therefore receives a much stronger vertical protection for individual autonomy than is currently recognised.

224 See above para. 4.2.2.
225 J.H.H. Weiler, 'The Constitution of Europe', Cambridge University Press, 1999, p. 337.

To this extent, European criminal law ceases to be a neutral instrument in the hands of the EU. Within a relational model, not just any European order is a European order ruled by *law*.

In this respect, one may notice a conceptual and theoretical connection between constitutional pluralism and the relational model of European criminal justice. Constitutional pluralism is a broader theory about the relationship between legal orders and proves to be more specific as it focuses on claims of authority. The relational model of criminal justice is an artificial theoretical model on the nature and legitimation of European criminal law. Therefore, these two theories concern different topics. However, both theories seem to have a similar approach towards law, as both hold that the law has an argumentative and mediating character. In essence, both theories are relational. The relational nature of the relational model lies in the mediation between the vertical and horizontal protections of individual autonomy in criminal law. The relational nature of constitutional pluralism is found in its focus on how European and national constitutional orders are engaged. Both theories focus on how antithetical claims should be balanced instead of how one is more valuable than the other.

However, there are also meeting points at the normative level. A pluralistic interrelation of legal orders presumes that both national and European legal orders have an ethical value. This value is found in the participation of cultural and political communities, both at the national and the European level. A relational European criminal justice system, guided by the democratic principle, also follows the assumption that individual autonomy is expressed both at the levels of national and European political communities. It also assumes that such autonomy must be protected from arbitrariness by both European and national institutions. Echoes of a pluralistic constitutional theory will be further noticeable in the application of the legality principle in European criminal law.

6.2. The principle of legal certainty

Legal certainty within this model has been conceived, as indicated in Chapter V, not as maximum legal certainty.[226] Maximum legal certainty is neither possible nor necessarily desirable because legal certainty comprises not only predictability but also acceptability. What is most important for individuals is that they can draw from provision behavioural standards that would allow them to rely on the law. Another feature of legal certainty is that it promotes transparency of judicial argumentation and trust from the individual towards the decisions of courts. What does this mean for European criminal law?

The purpose of harmonisation of substantive criminal liability must be understood to promote a climate of legal certainty in a transnational setting, albeit not at its maximum level. This fits quite nicely with the concept of minimum

226 Chapter V para. 6.1.

harmonisation. Even if national legislators go beyond the wording of a Directive, the creation of minimum standards of some offences guarantees that individuals can exercise their freedom of movement rights within a climate of legal certainty, even if this is not at its maximum level. Harmonisation of criminal offences has a symbolic effect, as it creates the expectation for individuals that national criminal offences are similar. However, there is another requirement here that concerns reliability and is especially relevant for rules on jurisdiction. While national provisions remain diverse and harmonisation creates a basic climate of legal certainty, one has to know which law to consider in order to properly rely on the law. The ability to rely on the law is vital in a relational model of European justice. Harmonising jurisdictional rules is, therefore, of primary importance.[227]

In addition, within the multilevel sources of criminal liability both European and national legislators must ensure that criminal liability complies with this requirement. As it will be discussed, the gravity of this obligation will vary. Legal certainty in European instruments is important, as the European legislator should not only abstain from requiring that national legislation is vague but must also assume responsibility for ensuring that national legislators are able to comply with legal certainty.[228]

In addition, legal certainty in this model requires transparency in judicial decisions. This is of particular importance, as it is in the interests of individuals to be able to trust that both the ECJ and national courts shall balance rights that respect individual autonomy and human dignity. Judicial decisions that balance principles instead of complicated legalistic and technical reasoning, which mask the evaluation of the court, are more intelligible for citizens.[229] In this regard, it is essential for the obligation of conform interpretation that courts reason their judgements with a transparent weighing of rights protected under the European instrument, European policies and principles, how rights are measured with respect to national legislation and, finally, how they are weighed and prioritised.

6.3. Counterfacticity of legal principles

Within this model, legal principles are counterfactual and require that, in European criminal law, principles remain open and responsive to European development.[230]

---

227 M. Luchtman, 'Choice of forum and the prosecution of cross-border crime in the European Union-what role for the legality principle?', in M. Luchtman (ed), 'Choice of forum in cooperation against EU financial crime: freedom, security and justice and the protection of specific EU-interests', Eleven International Publishing, 2013, pp. 12–26.

228 P. Asp, 'The Substantive Criminal Law Competence of the EU', Jure, 2012, p. 172.

229 A. von Bogdandy, 'Founding Principles of EU Law: a Theoretical and Doctrinal Sketch', European Law Journal, vol. 16, 2010, p. 103.

230 R. Foqué, 'Criminal Justice in a Democracy: Towards a Relational Conception of Criminal Law and Punishment', Criminal Law and Philosophy, vol. 2, 2008, p. 220; R. Foqué, A.C. 't Hart, 'Instrumentaliteit en Rechtsbescherming', Gouda Quint, Kluwer, 1990, p. 129.

Certain indeterminacy in principles is important, as principles only become sufficiently specific when they are applied in a concrete situation. Counterfacticity aims at preventing principles from receiving a crystallised meaning that would annul their mediating character. In EU law, principles should be constructed with a certain distance from ideological discourses in order to remain potential projection screens for divergent constructs.[231]

In addition, the counterfacticity of principles requires a clear distinction between policies, rules and principles. This is necessary during interpretation and also when criminal law competences are exercised to assure transparent identification of European policies, rights and principles (and their inter-relations). In principle, individual rights should always be prioritised over policies. Principles should also never become policies themselves. This requirement of the relational model brings the necessary transparency and consistency both for European criminal policy and for exercising criminal competences and adjudication in courts. Von Bogdandy, for example, advocated for a demarcation between rules, principles and policies in EU law. Principles are abstract and promote transparency as they are gateways for new convictions.[232] They should strengthen the autonomy of courts against European politics. Within the EU, one has to distinguish between principles and objectives/policies. The EU was founded on principles limiting the actions of state-actors. Objectives or policies stipulate intended effects in social reality;[233] the Charter offers the dimension of rights. Between policies and objectives, there can be also a distinction: policies, following Dworkin, are standards that set the goals to be achieved. Consequently, goals/objectives are political aims that have a collective nature, while policies are more ambiguous.[234] In European criminal law, the relational model advocates a clear demarcation between those elements and the prioritisation of rights over policies.

7. Protection of individuals in European criminal law

Within a relational model, protective finality is enlarged and includes vertical and horizontal dimensions. The European criminal justice system aims at protecting the individual *vis-à-vis* state arbitrariness. This finality is arguably underdeveloped, as previously explained.[235]

---

231 A. von Bogdandy, 'Founding Principles of EU Law: a Theoretical and Doctrinal Sketch', European Law Journal, vol. 16, 2010, p. 98.

232 Ibid., p. 101.

233 Ibid., p. 107.

234 R. Dworkin, 'Taking Rights Seriously', Duckworth, 1977, pp. 22 and 90–91; M. Huomo-Kettunen, 'EU Criminal Policy at a Crossroads Between Effectiveness and Traditional Restraints for the Use of Criminal Law', New Journal of European Criminal Law, vol. 5, 2014, p. 308.

235 See above para. 3.3.

The protective finality of European criminal law rests with the protection of individual autonomy as self-determination and human dignity, which translates into the protection of individuals from state arbitrariness. The concept of European citizenship has contributed to a political union where individuals do not orient themselves exclusively towards their national identities and that of their nation states. European citizenship, especially within the AFSJ, has fragmented application and is usually of concern when national criminal law measures are restrictive.[236] In the area of European criminal law, European citizenship has created a direct link between the EU and its individuals. Article 3, para. 2 TEU reads that the EU *'shall offer its citizens'* an AFSJ. However, this direct link has primarily expressed an obligation to provide security and protection from crime.[237] Yet the concept of European citizenship confers a protection of individual autonomy against nation states, as this has been demonstrated in the Charter itself and in more recent developments including procedural rights Directives; a *civis Europaeus* is therefore emerging in European criminal justice.[238]

The interpretation of the European *demos* explained above is actually relational as well; it is a mediation of the national and European identity, two poles of attraction that attempt to limit excessive national egoism whilst also limiting European chaos.[239] Thus, on one hand, it is vital to protect individual autonomy as expressed within national identity and its discourse. Individuals are members of their national communities that have different goals and cultures in a pluralistic Europe.[240] The EU is not a project of unity but of community, thus the protective finality of European criminal law must also express a protection of individuals as members of their national communities. Conversely, belonging to a European *demos* also means that individuals are invited to embrace the 'others'.[241]

The vertical dimension of the protective finality of criminal law may therefore be understood as follows. Individuals within the EU are entitled to be protected *vis-à-vis the EU's* and *vis-à-vis nation states'* arbitrariness *by the EU.* Such protection certainly exists within the scope of EU law and to some extent can relate to the protection of other individual rights as found in the Charter. This double addressability of the protective finality entails that a European legality principle

236 E. Muir, A.–P. van der Mei, 'The EU Citizenship Dimension of the Area of Freedom, Security and Justice', in M. Luchtman (ed), 'Choice of forum in cooperation against EU financial crime: freedom, security and justice and the protection of specific EU-interests', Eleven International Publishing, 2013, p. 124.

237 M. Luchtman, 'Choice of forum and the prosecution of cross-border crime in the European Union-what role for the legality principle?', in M. Luchtman (ed), 'Choice of forum in cooperation against EU financial crime: freedom, security and justice and the protection of specific EU-interests', Eleven International Publishing, 2013, p. 12.

238 Ibid.

239 J.H.H. Weiler, 'The Constitution of Europe', Cambridge University Press, 1999, p. 346.

240 L. Gröning, 'A Criminal Justice System or a System Deficit? Notes on the System Structure of the EU Criminal Law', European Journal of Crime, Criminal Law and Criminal Justice, vol. 18, 2010, pp. 118–119.

241 J.H.H. Weiler, 'The Constitution of Europe', Cambridge University Press, 1999, p. 346.

should generate guidelines both for European decision-making and for national implementation tactics.

Transnational arbitrariness necessitates individuals be protected against the negative effects of mutual recognition and against legal uncertainty. This vertical protection of individual autonomy is influenced by the interpretation of individual autonomy and liberty as a licence to cross borders. In particular, European criminal norms and their implementation should create a climate of trust for individuals regarding the potential criminalisation of their acts within Europe. Certainly, this is limited by the specific list of criminal offences for which there is competence. Yet, the European *ius puniendi* is supposed to create and protect a trust of individuals relative to the negative consequences of their acts throughout Europe. As was explained, the relational model does not require maximum legal certainty, not only because it is unattainable in practice but also because harmonisation in criminal matters is only a minimum harmonisation and because room should remain for national legal orders to express their values and choices in implementations of criminal law. As shown, this is a consequence of a pluralistic Europe.[242]

As in national law, criminal law is supposed to create foreseeability regarding criminalisation. In addition, the European *ius puniendi* aims at protecting individuals from an unequal and unforeseeable limitation of their individual autonomy by a foreign jurisdiction. In other words, the European *ius puniendi* creates some legal certainty and equality regarding criminalisation in order for individuals to be able to foresee the consequences of their actions.

This argument might seem a bit odd: Why is it important that potential human smuggler X in one Member State and potential human smuggler Y in another Member State should receive relatively equal conditions with respect to criminal liability? Is there a claim in this regard of equal treatment for European citizens? This claim is not easy to support, because harmonisation of criminal liability does not entail unification.[243] However, it at least eliminates differences. Because criminal law restricts the movement of individuals, harmonising offences with a strong cross-border background ensures that the four freedoms are restricted in a relatively equal manner. For the European citizen who moves freely, eliminating discrepancies between definitions of prohibited behaviour is of value. Here, I am referring to *cross-border foreseeability*. Knowing that all national legislations share certain common characteristics regarding, for instance, drug trafficking means that European citizens meet less difficulty in foreseeing criminalisation when they cross jurisdictions. This arms individuals with the confidence and trust necessary for the exercise of their European freedoms. Citizens feel secure that their interests are protected in all countries (as observed in the discussion of instrumental finality), while potential perpetrators are also deterred. The choices and possibilities that citizens of Europe have today to move, reside and work reflect

242 See above para. 6.2.

243 A. Klip, 'European Criminal Law: An Integrative Approach', Intersentia, 2012, p. 23.

remarkable progress in our societies and politics. The plurality of sources of law can be overwhelming:

> [L]egislation has to be clear-cut and easily understandable so that it becomes predictable for all whether an act amounts to a criminal offence or not. This holds even more so for Directives, since these have to be transposed into national law and any lack of clarity can lead to diverging interpretations, which can easily enhance confusion instead of reducing it.[244]

Conversely, the horizontal dimension entails that European criminal law also protects individual by third parties. As stated in reference to the relational model, the instrumental finality is subordinate to the protective finality and provides a horizontal dimension to protection. Any crime-control policies are subordinate and conceptually evaluated under the concept of horizontal protection. Thus, the protective finality in this model is enlarged and entails: (i) the protection of every individual *vis-à-vis* the state (vertical protection) and, (ii), the protection of every individual *vis-à-vis* third parties (horizontal protection).[245]

It was shown that the instrumental finality addresses the horizontal protection of individual autonomy (namely, the protection of individual autonomy in interpersonal relationships) and has two elements: the crime-control element wherein the state uses criminal law as a tool to battle crime and create a general feeling of safety, and the society-shaping element wherein criminal law is used as a tool to canalise human interactions, crystallise behaviours and impose certain common values that underpin expectations that individuals maintain about others' behaviours.[246] How should these two features of the instrumental finality be reconstructed?

The crime-control element has been quite prevalent in the process of European integration. Criminal law within the EU can be seen as a tool to combat cross-border crime or, generally, criminal offences that have been facilitated by the abolition of borders. Thus, in Article 83 TFEU the legal basis for prescribing substantive criminal law liability is that it is done *'in the areas of particularly serious crime with a cross-border dimension resulting from the nature or impact of such offences or from a special need to combat them on a common basis'*. The crime-control element, therefore, aims at creating a general feeling of security for individuals: *'An internal security strategy should be developed in order to further improve security in the Union and thus protect the lives and safety of citizens of the Union and to tackle organised crime, terrorism and other threats'*.[247] However,

244 European Parliament Resolution of 22 May 2012 on an EU approach to criminal law (2010/2310(INI)), 22.5.2012, p. 7.

245 J. Claessen, 'Misdaad en straf: een herbezinning op het strafrecht vanuit mystiek perspectief', Wolf Legal Publishers, 2010, p. 114.

246 Chapter V para. 2.

247 The Stockholm Programme – An open and secure Europe serving and protecting citizens OJ C 115, 4.5.2010, pp. 1–38, para. 1.1.

within this crime-control element there is another dimension, namely the facilitation of judicial cooperation in criminal matters. This is especially true for procedural rules, as explicitly stated in Article 82 of the TFEU. However, in the field of substantive law the driving force of early harmonisation of offences was to create mutual trust between national authorities in order to further criminal cooperation. In particular, such mutual trust is presumed to increase when national authorities know that certain offences are harmonised within the EU:

> [T]he harmonisation of criminal law in the EU should contribute[s] to the development of a common EU legal culture in relation to fighting crime, which adds up to but does not substitute national legal traditions and has a positive impact on mutual trust amongst the legal systems of the Member States.[248]

The society-shaping element is more substantive. At the European level, this element entails that criminal law is harmonised within the European legal order to create certain common preconditions of social interaction that allow individuals to exist in highly heterogeneous legal and social cultural environments with certain mutual expectations from their relationships.[249] European harmonised criminal liability becomes a point of reference for individuals to build autonomous relationships with each other, irrespective of the national jurisdiction in which they find themselves. This also shapes a European society so that individuals happily and eagerly exercise their right to freedom of movement. Framework Decision 2008/913 on racism and xenophobia is a strong example because it criminalised hate speech.[250] Regardless of how one may criticise this instrument from the viewpoint of national cultures, it shaped a European society within individuals can hope for respect by others regardless of their nationality or religion. This instrument created and mirrored very specific values within the European *demos* regarding equal treatment and mutual respect between individuals who find themselves vulnerable in foreign communities.

To some extent, the European *ius puniendi* may not simply bring more homogenous criminal law definitions but may also impose certain behavioural standards that mirror the founding principles of the European *demos* and the European political community. Thus, one may also say that harmonisation of criminal offences also aims at promoting European identity. Criminal law is a constitutive element for the identity of those that share its jurisdiction.[251]

---

248 European Parliament Resolution of 22 May 2012 on an EU approach to criminal law (2010/2310(INI)), 22.5.2012.

249 F. Meyer, 'Strafrechtsgenese in Internationalen Organisationen', Nomos, 2012, p. 693.

250 Framework Decision 2008/913 of 28 November 2008 on combating certain forms and expressions of racism and xenophobia by means of criminal law OJ L 328, 6.12.2008, pp. 55–58.

251 M. Hildebrandt, 'European Criminal law and European Identity', Criminal Law and Philosophy, vol. 1, 2007, p. 65.

> Criminal law is an important part of our legal traditions, because it entails constraints that we find crucial for the survival of our sense of self. Thus criminal law is interwoven with our identity as members of particular legal traditions, dependent on forms of local justice and on the monopoly of violence (sovereignty) to be both effective and legitimate.[252]

The European *ius puniendi* is also a tool to strengthen the European identity, as violation of the offences prescribed under Article 83 TFEU becomes a violation of the integrity of the EU legal order itself.[253] Thus, the harmonisation of the criminal offences *translates* those offences and the values that they represent into EU *law*.

Another dimension of the society-shaping element is Article 83 para. 2 TFEU, which prescribes the competence to approximate criminal liability to promote effective enforcement of other EU policies. In the relational model of European criminal justice, a proper use of such competence is not only meant to better enforce important EU policies but also to make them a part of the European identity and thus engrave them as important values of the European political community. If those values receive protection through criminal law, they shall pass into the European consciousness as important values. In *Commission v Council*, the ECJ employed criminal law merely as a tool to further other European policies and, in that particular case, environmental protection.[254] This blatant instrumental use of criminal law can be explained as a paradigm of excessive European instrumentalism. However, at the same time one could approach this judgement as intended to target the identity of European citizens with the hope that the protection of the environment *'becomes a shared value of citizens instead of an administrative task of government'*.[255] To this extent, the use of the competence in Article 83 para 2 TFEU should reflect such interpretation of the instrumental finality instead of being based solely on effectiveness-oriented reasoning.

8. Individual Autonomy, Democracy and Separation of Powers

8.1. Individual autonomy, human dignity and liberty

As the EU is based on the national legal systems and conceptually influenced by the ECHR, individual autonomy and human dignity are rooted in the heart of Europe. Within a relational model, human dignity is a core value. Thus, Chapter 1 of the Charter, entitled 'Dignity', provides the first fundamental right of the EU in Article 1: *'Human dignity is inviolable. It must be respected and protected'.* At the

252 Ibid., p. 76.
253 Ibid., p. 73.
254 C–176/03 Commission of the European Communities v Council of the European Union, 13 September 2005.
255 M. Hildebrandt, 'European Criminal law and European Identity', Criminal Law and Philosophy, vol. 1, 2007, p. 72.

same time, a more generalised right to freedom and security of someone's person rests in Article 6 of the Charter: *'Everyone has the right to liberty and security of person'.*

Yet one should point out certain interesting elements here. First, the wording of Article 6 of the Charter suggests two versions of individual autonomy; namely, that relating to liberty and that relating to security. Similarly, one can see this distinction depicted in the phrasing of Article 3 para. 2 TEU, in which the EU offers to its citizens an AFSJ. Again, the interpretation of these three elements may vary but, what is common with Article 6 of the Charter is that, individual autonomy is understood both as being sheltered by state intervention and from the intervention of others. This denotes both vertical and horizontal dimensions to the protection of individual autonomy. Nonetheless, there has been an unbalanced approach to these two elements within the EU.

A second element is the concept of freedom or liberty. As seen in Chapter III, the concept of liberty is different from individual autonomy, in that liberty is more connected with the idea of liberty as 'licence', which entails the freedom to act with no boundaries, as opposed to the concept of liberty as 'independence', which entails a concept of self-determination.[256] It is interesting that in EU law and under the current Treaties, the freedom to act (that is, liberty as licence) takes on a different interpretation than under national law. In particular, one may speak of a freedom of movement with no internal borders in an analogical manner, as with freedom to act. This can be seen again in Article 3, para. 2 TEU. Perhaps this is a far-fetched analogy, but it does seem that individuals are not only entitled to self-determination and to leading a dignified life, but they are also entitled to freedom from national borders.

This interpretation of individual liberty is further accentuated by the European interpretation of equality, which is seen as equality and non-discrimination on the basis of nationality. Again, the interpretation of a European equality aims to free the individual from another national border, namely nationality. Thus, European citizenship, equality and non-discrimination, and freedom of movement are connected:

> Promoting citizenship and fundamental rights: European citizenship must become a tangible reality. The area of freedom, security and justice must, above all, be a single area in which fundamental rights and freedoms are protected. The enlargement of the Schengen area must continue. Respect for the human person and human dignity and for the other rights set out in the Charter of Fundamental Rights of the European Union and the European Convention for the protection of Human Rights and fundamental freedoms are core values.[257]

---

256 Chapter III para. 2.1; R. Dworkin, 'Taking Rights Seriously', Duckworth, 1977, p. 262.

257 The Stockholm Programme – An open and secure Europe serving and protecting citizens OJ C 115, 4.5.2010, pp. 1–38, para. 1.1.

Thus, it can be concluded that interpretation of individual autonomy, liberty and human dignity within the EU has the following elements: (i) the respect of individual dignity and individual interests and projects regarding one's life and choices for self-determination; (ii) the respect of these rights *vis-à-vis* state-actors and other individuals; (iii) liberty from national borders, meaning the freedom to cross borders, and establish and move freely within the EU; and (iv) the claim to be identified as an equal individual and citizen of the European *demoi*, which implies respecting national identity and European civility.

8.2. A European democratic principle

The way in which democracy is understood at the European level is diverse. Transnationalism in combination with the various definitions of European *demos* poses significant questions.[258] The theory of European democracy has been such a popular topic that it is impossible to reproduce all elements of the discussion here in detail. Such a 'theory of everything' necessitates discussion at various levels, including civil society, identity, political theory and constitutional philosophy.[259] Moreover, any discussion regarding European democracy requires a starting point. One could either look for a model of European democracy that matches national democracy, or pursue an alternative post-national concept. There is discussion as to whether the EU has a democratic deficit. For those who approach European democracy with a national concept in mind, the EU is found to be in need.[260] For others, a European democracy does not need to necessarily be anchored to the national model. For example, several theories on post-national democracy have been presented such as that of deliberative democracy, cosmopolitan democracy[261] and associative democracy.[262] With respect to the EU, even more neologisms have been developed such as 'transnational democracy', 'compound democracy' and 'directive deliberate polyarchy'.[263]

In a relational model, the principle of democracy, together with the Rule of Law, takes a more substantive notion. This, as mentioned, entails not only a procedural aspect that focuses on procedures but also on certain substantive elements.[264]

258 M. Nettesheim, 'Developing a Theory of Democracy for the European Union', Berkeley Journal of International Law, vol. 23, 2005, pp. 358–400.

259 For an overview see, N. Deitelhoff, J. Steffek (eds), 'Was bleibt vom Staat? Demokratie, Recht und Verfassung im globalen Zeitalter', Campus Verlag, 2009, pp. 15–21.

260 R. Dehousse, 'Beyond Representative Democracy: Constitutionalism in a Polycentric Polity', in J.H.H. Weiler, M. Wind, 'European Constitutionalism Beyond the State', Cambridge University Press, 2003, p. 136.

261 D. Held, 'Democracy and the Global Order: From the Modern State to Cosmopolitan Governance', Polity Press, 1995.

262 V. Bader, P. Hirs, 'Associative Democracy: the Real Third Way', Frank Cass Publishing, 2001.

263 K. Nicolaïdes, 'The Idea of European Demoicracy', in J. Dickson, P. Eleftheriadis (eds), 'Philosophical Foundations of EU Law', Oxford University Press, 2012, p. 260.

264 Chapter III para. 5.

According to the latter, decisions are democratic if they transcend the values and ideas of the political community with respect to human dignity so that even dissenting individuals can feel that their human dignity has been respected. Democratic decisions are not only those based on democratic procedures but also those that truly represent the conditions under which individuals came into a community bound by a social contract.

With the establishment of European citizenship, individuals become members of a larger community – a European community – to which they come together under the conditions of a European social contract. Evidence of this social contract can be found via the equal treatment of individuals irrespective of their nationality, both from the state and from each other, the freedom to move across borders, the establishment of shared common values along with mutual respect of diverse cultural and political values, conditions of solidarity and support of each other's projects in life and the mutual respect of each other's individual autonomy and dignity in a diverse environment. Thus, European citizens belong to a larger, popular community beyond national communities. Citizens themselves should impose the relevant cultural, political and human values that play an important role in their ability to pursue their individual projects and dreams.

In this respect, European political autonomy of individuals cannot be franchised by the democratic procedures of nation states, as citizens must themselves participate in political discourses regarding the conditions in which they come together as a European community. Those conditions have to be evaluated, distributed and measured in a representative political body independent of national structures.

Thus, the concept of political autonomy and popular sovereignty in the EU receives a different and more hybrid interpretation than in the national context. Such interpretation comes directly from the TEU. Article 10 para. 2 TEU distinguishes between the representativeness of states and citizens:

> Citizens are directly represented at Union level in the European Parliament. Member States are represented in the European Council by their Heads of State or Government and in the Council by their governments, themselves democratically accountable either to their national Parliaments, or to their citizens.

An important element is that the very same individuals gain two political autonomies. The first is as members of the national political communities comprising the national popular sovereignty. The second is as members of the European political community comprising a European popular sovereignty.[265] Thus, in the EU citizens are represented both as members of their nation states through the Council (European peoples) and as members of the EU (EU citizens) through the European Parliament. The distinction between 'peoples of the Member States' and the 'citizens of the Union' is therefore vital to make any concept of

265 J. Habermas, 'The Crisis of the European Union – A Response', Polity Press, 2012, pp. 36–37.

democracy viable.[266] If one were to choose between one of the two, then the legitimation of criminal law could only be found either at the European level or the national level. Thus, a transnational democracy model can be built only if one accepts that *'[e]very citizen participates in the European opinion- and will-formation processes both as an individual European who autonomously says 'yes' and 'no' and as a member of a particular nation'.*[267]

A European legislator must carry the obligation to measure European policies in criminal liability with the ideals of dignity and equality between individuals as interpreted in EU law. For example, if the European legislator excessively broadened the conditions for punitively expelling European citizens from other Member State, that would violate the European democratic principle. This is not because such a decision would not be procedurally democratic but because it would hurt the European popular sovereignty which is based on strong values of non-discrimination of nationality and on freedom of movement. A transnational democracy is respected not only through the European and national elections and discourse but also when European decisions are measured *vis-à-vis* European collective consciousness.

Furthermore, the European legislator must ensure that criminal law decisions respect both the conditions under which citizens have formed a European social contract and justify how these decisions measure with respect to national social contracts. Thus, the substantial nature of the European transnational democracy is supported by the subsidiarity principle that requires that decisions at the European level be tested for their necessity and their impact on national political communities. For example, under Framework Decision 2008/913 on racism and xenophobia, one may question the democratic legitimacy of such criminal liability, not because it was not the product of democratic procedures (although in the pre-Lisbon regime the European Parliament had only a consultative role) but because it has not been made clear how this measure can be reconciled with the cultural diversities within the EU.[268] European citizens with their 'double hats' have (i) a right to enforce on their nation states the obligation to respect them as members of a European community with certain claims to freedom of movement, safety, equality and respect to human dignity; and (ii) a right to enforce the European legal order the obligation to respect the identities of their local communities. If one is to accept the value of both worlds, an evaluation of the manner in which the Council and the European Parliament respect the national and European political autonomies of European citizens must be regarded a part of European democratic legitimation of criminal law-making.

---

266 Ibid., p. 35.

267 Ibid., p. 37.

268 Framework Decision 2008/913 of 28 November 2008 on combating certain forms and expressions of racism and xenophobia by means of criminal law OJ L 328, 6.12.2008, pp. 55–58.

8.3. Separation of powers in the EU

The concept of the separation of powers, despite its importance not only in criminal law but also as a constitutional principle, has received relatively little attention at the European level.[269] One could debate whether the concept of separation of powers can be applied at this level. This is especially so because this principle has received various interpretations, as noted in Chapter III.[270] The problem is not only about how to separate the powers at the European level but also how to categorise the existing European actors to different *trias politica*. The European institutions are not similar to national institutions. Attempts to transport a classic and strict understanding of the separation of powers to the European setting may face several problems, especially concerning the role of the ECJ.[271] In particular, the ECJ is one of the most influential courts in the world, and its functions cannot be compared with the powers of a constitutional or a federal court.[272]

The European separation of powers is rather closer to the concept of 'checks and balances' as the cohabitation of various actors, national and European, makes any strong separation substantially difficult. This is accurate not only at the vertical level of multiple legal orders but also at the horizontal level. As it will be shown, the ECJ itself did not adopt a strict separation of powers doctrine but rather something more akin to that of 'checks and balances'.[273]

More concretely, four actors exist within the European criminal law system: two legislators (EU-national) and two courts (ECJ-national courts). All of these actors, each in its own capacity, handle criminal law powers. Whilst the tasks of everybody are distinct, it is in their best interests to protect against a potential monopolisation of power. One can look at the concept of the separation of powers in its 'checks and balances' interpretation in the European setting by distinguishing a vertical (between European and national state-actors) and horizontal (between the European legislator and ECJ, and the national legislator and courts) separation of powers.

8.3.1. Vertical separation of powers

The vertical separation of powers is understood as the distribution of tasks and the control of arbitrariness between the European and national state-actors. The reason

---

269 For example K. Lenaerts, 'Some Reflections on the Separation of Powers in the European Community', Common Market Law Review, vol. 28, 1991, pp. 11–35; L. Allio, G. Durand, 'Montesquieu Wakes Up: Separation of Powers in the Council of Ministers', Working Paper of the European Policy Centre, 02/2003.

270 Chapter III para. 4.

271 G. Conway, 'The Limits of Legal Reasoning and the European Court of Justice', Cambridge University Press, 2012, pp. 178–192.

272 Ibid., p. 192.

273 Y. Devuyst, 'The European Unions' institutional balance after the Treaty of Lisbon: 'Community Method' and 'Democratic Deficit' Reassessed', Georgetown Journal of International Law, vol. 39, 2008, pp. 247–325.

for a vertical separation of powers might not appear as evident. At the national level, the separation of powers protects the criminal justice system from the potential concentration of political power to one body and designates the distinctive tasks of each body. Why should there be a vertical separation of powers between the European and national legislators or between the ECJ and national courts?

There are two reasons. First, the current Treaties oblige a distribution of tasks between the vertical state-actors in European criminal law. Substantive criminal liability can be prescribed only by means of a Directive of minimum standards by the European legislator, which must be implemented by the national legislator. Such implementation also includes the possibility of going beyond the minimum scope of criminal liability. Similarly, the ECJ does not deal with the merits of criminal cases. There is no European criminal court. The interpretation of the facts and the appreciation of evidence are left to national courts. National and European courts share the load of interpreting criminal liability, and the national courts can interpret both European and national instruments, while the ECJ can interpret only European instruments in the preliminary reference procedure and review national implementing practices in infringement proceedings. Thus, it would be a violation of the Treaties if criminal liability were to be prescribed in a Regulation, and it would be a violation of the Treaties if the national legislator did not implement a Directive on criminal liability. Thus, a vertical separation of powers is to be explained by the current European constitutional order, as this is understood in the Treaties. A vertical separation of powers as a value and principle of the European legal order is a product of current institutional dynamics. Yet, there must be additional reasoning for this because current constitutional and institutional dynamics are always fluid and dependent upon amendment.

A second reason can be found in the constitutional and criminal law pluralism within the EU. A monopolisation of the *ius puniendi* by the European or the national legislator could breach the cohabitation of more than one political community within the European legal order. As individuals are identified through their participation in both their national and European political communities, they raise different claims towards the European and national legislators and courts. They expect the European legislator and courts to shelter their individual autonomy as freedom of movement throughout borders, their equality in terms of nationality and the European common values that they consider important in order to continue feeling that they are a part of a European *demos*. Most importantly, they expect from the European legislator and the ECJ a guarantee of respect of their human dignity when they exercise the European *ius puniendi*.

The national legislator and courts are expected to respect individual autonomy and local social values, to behave in line with the national cultural regime, and to protect the local community as they identify with it. The interest in preserving the involvement of national state bodies is partly to preserve culturally influential ways of living as a part of the national collective political community.[274] However, it is

---

[274] J. Habermas, 'The Crisis of the European Union – A Response', Polity Press, 2012, p. 42.

also important to ensure that individuals, as peoples of the Member States, have a justified right to demand from national state-actors that they be able to continue to perform – in their capacity as Member States of the EU – as guarantors of human dignity and to preserve the level of justice.[275] In this sense, the cohabitation of a European and national level of decision-making and adjudication should be an *asset* rather than a problem for European criminal law, as criminal liability passes through various checks, discourses and refinements that provide a further guarantee for human dignity.

Thus, a distribution of tasks between European and national state-actors is necessary. This entails that the legality principle should address this issue in European criminal law, while also focusing on how these actors interrelate. The challenge here is to arrange a distribution and complementary function between the European and national legislators and between the ECJ and national courts regarding the definition and interpretation of criminal liability.

8.3.2. Horizontal separation of powers

The horizontal separation of powers addresses the distribution and interrelation of state-actors within the same legal order; namely that of European legislator-ECJ, and national legislator-courts.

Concerning the horizontal distribution of tasks between European bodies, the ECJ has been the protagonist in furthering integration due to the cumbersome legislative processes at the European level. This can be seen not only in the development of the EU from an economic community to a citizen's union with the inclusion of the human rights dimension but also in the early abolition of the Third Pillar regime. Generally, it would be fair to say that the ECJ has been the prophet and the forerunner in the development of EU law: *'The transformation of the European legal system has turned the ECJ into probably the most influential international legal body in existence'.*[276] Its position could be compared with a common law court, given that European criminal law is case law oriented.[277] However, its contribution to the European system with the development of principles of justice could be seen as also comprising the function of a constitutional court.[278] The great interpretative role of the ECJ is of importance for the legality principle, as the latter reassures the limits of judicial interpretation *vis-à-vis* the legislator.

In EU law, one could say that separation of powers between the EU legislator and the ECJ is quite off-balance. The ECJ has been accused of being activist on

275 Paraphrasing, see ibid., p. 41.

276 K.J. Alter, 'Establishing the Supremacy of European Law', Oxford University Press, 2001, p. 229.

277 A. Klip, 'European Criminal Law: An Integrative Approach', Intersentia, 2012, pp. 10 and 479.

278 M. Claes, 'The National Courts' Mandate in the European Constitution', Hart Publishing, 2006, p. 399.

more than one occasion.[279] It is true that the ECJ produced many of the great and most successful ideas in EU law history such as the principle of mutual recognition. It was the ECJ's phrase *'provided that they have been lawfully produced and marketed in one of the Member States'* in *Cassis de Dijon*[280] that resulted in the Commission introducing the mutual recognition principle,[281] which was later transplanted to the criminal justice regime. The ECJ's powers are determined under Article 19 TEU as responsible for the interpretation and application of EU law; yet the Court is in close interaction with the European legislator, demonstrated not only in the above-mentioned case but also in the abolition of the Third Pillar regime.[282] In criminal law, it should generally be the case that the ECJ is more prudent when it comes to interpretational limits so that there is a balanced allocation of tasks between the ECJ and the European legislator. This has been addressed in other areas of law, but such academic discussions are scarce in criminal law due to the limited competences of the ECJ.

In this respect, EU law has adopted its own term for the separation of powers: the principle of institutional balance is a replacement for the principle of the separation of powers, according to which the institutes of the EU should remain within their role as prescribed in the Treaties.[283] This principle does not aim at creating some principled distribution of tasks between the European bodies but rather at ensuring that the Treaties will not be violated. The basis of this concept is purely normative and does not seem to be as strong as an ethical or 'Rule of Law' type of principle.[284] Applied inconsistently by the ECJ, its actual importance is debated in academia.[285] Thus, the Court has argued as follows:

> In that context, it is sufficient to state that the aim of the system of the division of powers between the various Community institutions is to ensure that the balance between the institutions provided for in the Treaty is maintained, and not to protect

---

279 There are numerous contributions published frequently in this topic, some recent examples: A. Arnull, 'Judicial Activism and the Court of Justice: How Should Academics Respond?', Maastricht Faculty of Law Working Paper, no. 2012–3 (available at http://ssrn.com/abstract=1986817); M. Dawson, 'The Political Face of Judicial Activism: Europe's Law-Politics Imbalance', Maastricht Faculty of Law Working Paper, no. 2012–1 (available at http://ssrn.com/abstract=1984636).

280 Case 120/78 Rewe-Zentral AG v Bundesmonopolverwaltung für Branntwein, 20 February 1979 ('Cassis de Dijon').

281 Commission Communication concerning the consequences of the judgement given by the Court of Justice on 20 February 1979 in 120/78 ('Cassis de Dijon') OJ C 256, 3.10.1980, pp. 2–3.

282 C–176/03 Commission of the European Communities v Council of the European Union, 13 September 2005.

283 J.–P. Jacqué, 'The Principle of Institutional Balance', Common Market Law Review, vol. 41, 2004, pp. 383–391.

284 G. Conway, 'The Limits of Legal Reasoning and the European Court of Justice', Cambridge University Press, 2012, p. 198.

285 See for an overview, M. Zwiers, 'The European Public Prosecutor's Office', Intersentia, 2011, pp. 179–190.

> individuals. Consequently, a failure to observe the balance between the institutions cannot be sufficient on its own to engage the Community's liability towards the traders concerned.[286]

In criminal law matters, the respect for proper institutional balance should certainly not have so much to do with the regime created in the Treaties as an authority or a convention, but rather with the legitimation of the *ius puniendi.* While the principle of institutional balance seems to be based on a rather institutional or pragmatic consideration, it must receive a more principled and legitimate context. The ECJ has played its role in observing the Treaties and has ensured the pivotal position of human rights within the EU. Conversely, this does not mean that the exercise of both legislative and judicial powers of the EU need not be based on a more philosophical understanding of their relationship. The mere fact that the Treaties provide the ECJ a large margin for discretion does not mean that it is legitimate in the field of criminal law. Therefore, in a relational model of European criminal justice, the principle of institutional balance must be understood not as an internal and technical principle of the system but as one that transcends a democratic legitimation and a 'balanced constitution'.

9. Conclusion

The aim of this Chapter was to discuss the legitimacy of European criminal law. The European criminal justice system is currently instrumentalist in nature; it has been and remains in transition and will do so for some time. This should come as no surprise given that this system was created with a more specific goal in mind and without taking into consideration the fact that its subordination to the internal market would turn at a certain point. It is, after all, 'the criminal law problem' that has led constitutional and supreme courts to well-discussed decisions.[287]

The problems identified are manifold. First, certain basic values underpinning criminal law lack a proper definition in the European setting. Principles such as democracy, legal certainty, *demos* and individual autonomy are usually defined with reference to their national connotations. This prevents the European criminal justice system from shaping its functions and establishing its legitimate basis. Second, legitimation of European criminal law is currently based on instrumentalism. The justifications for the existence and necessity of such system are only related to crime-control or furthering other European policies. This is to be expected as a European criminal justice system does not have a federal or super-state character. The current mandate to combat crime, facilitate judicial cooperation, and further European policies monopolises the character and legitimacy of

286 C–282/90 Industrie– en Handelsonderneming Vreugdenhil BV v Commission of the European Communities, 13 March 1992, para. 21–22.

287 See above para. 4.2.1.

European criminal law. Third, any protective role of this system is bound to be applied in a multilevel system. Often, protection of individual autonomy is left to national authorities. This becomes more complicated when one analyses different theories regarding the relationships between legal orders.

In this Chapter, a relational model for European criminal justice was proposed. In search of the *Rechtskarakter* of European criminal law, the following important elements have been identified and were placed within the auspices of the relational model.

First, individual autonomy, European citizenship, and freedom of movement are interrelated concepts that should be conceptualised together. Thus, protecting individual autonomy means: (i) self-determination, dignity and protection against state arbitrariness (vertical protection); (ii) protection from arbitrariness by third parties (horizontal protection); (iii) respect of political expression at the national level (member of the national *demos*); (iv) respect of political expression at the European level (member of the European *demos*) and (v) freedom from borders and the right to move freely throughout Europe within a climate of legal certainty and safety.

Second, European criminal law should be legitimised on the basis of protecting individual autonomy as defined above. This entails both vertical and horizontal dimensions. The vertical dimension is especially problematic, as this responsibility is shared by European and national institutions. The EU must assume protection of individual rights, especially in areas of European criminal law in which mutual trust is presumed. As explained, evidence of such tendency is already observed.[288] The strong protective character of European criminal justice assumes and promotes the idea that the European legal order is based on commonly shared values that should be further concretised at the European level and that should form the justification for political decisions made in criminal law.

Third, European instrumentalism can only be curtailed if the instrumental finality of criminal law is subordinate to the protective finality. European policies and goals, whether for battling crime, environmental protection or mutual trust amongst authorities, must be translated during the political process into rights and values that underpin or must underpin the European legal order. This is the only way in which one could evaluate their legitimacy, relevance and their acceptability by national legislators and courts. In this regard, a plea of transparency would go a long way with the constitutional conflicts of authority between national courts and the ECJ.

With these elements in mind, the next and final Chapter delves more deeply into the role and function of the legality principle in European criminal law. This analysis shall follow the features of the European criminal justice system within a relational model of legitimacy.

288 See above para. 3.3.

CHAPTER VIII
THE PRINCIPLE OF LEGALITY IN EUROPEAN CRIMINAL LAW

In Chapter VI, the fragments of the legality principle as it is currently conceived and applied in European criminal law were discussed. Certain questions, inconsistencies and lacunae were identified. In Chapter VII, the legitimacy of the European criminal justice system was discussed and a relational model was defended. How should the principle of legality function in a relational model of European criminal justice? In this final Chapter, a coherent doctrine of the legality principle for European criminal law will be presented. This Chapter is structured as follows.

In the first section, the values supported by the legality principle are addressed. Most of the theoretical foundations of the European criminal justice system were presented in the previous Chapter. The rationales shall be further concretised as they relate to the legality principle.

The second section will explore the nature and scope of the legality principle within European criminal law through two themes. The first theme addresses the role of the legality principle in legitimising the exercise of criminal law competences at the European level. In national law, the legislator is sovereign and decides what behaviours are criminal; however, this is not the case in European criminal law. Whether the legality principle should play a role in determining competences and how to justify this practice is also explored.

Another problem to be assessed is the application of the legality principle in a two-level system. Is this principle to be addressed to the European or national authorities, or both? As seen in Chapter VI, it is difficult to understand how *lex certa*, for example, would apply to Directives. Therefore, the distributive role of the legality principle shall be addressed.

The third section will delve deeper into the normative role of the legality principle, namely specific applications of the legality principle. Certain questions raised in Chapter VI are revisited here. For example, should case law be a formal source of criminal liability? If so, one would have to explain the features of each aspect of the legality principle.

General conclusions are presented in the fourth and final section, along with a recap of the initial research question and reflections on how it has been answered herein. The section concludes with further remarks, suggestions and questions for the future.

1. THEORETICAL RATIONALES OF THE EUROPEAN LEGALITY PRINCIPLE

In the previous Chapter, the European interpretation of different concepts such as *demos*, individual autonomy, democracy, arbitrariness and European primacy were discussed. European criminal justice is a very complicated matrix of constitutional principles, policies, and principles, all of which are interrelated. In particular, when it comes to the principle of legality, some clarity as to how these different concepts inform the discourse on European legality is in order.

1.1. *Rechtskarakter* and European criminal justice

The relationship between law and justice is not always clear. Law as an operative system is not always just, but it does promise justice.[1] Justice can also be associated with the Rule of Law.[2] As Fletcher puts it: *'Justice carries all the promise and the risks of a passionate love affair; the rule of law offers the stability of a loyal marriage'*.[3] Fletcher discusses a conflicting concept of justice, which simultaneously strives to protect individuals from arbitrariness (which he refers to as negative legality) and to protect individuals from each other (positive legality).[4] Much of what has been written about the interpretation of justice in the AFSJ is concerned only with the second dimension. The *Rechtskarakter* of European criminal law, as defined in the previous Chapter, notes that the intrinsic character of criminal law is the protection of individual human dignity in two separate dimensions, vertical (against arbitrariness) and horizontal (against other individuals).[5] Thus, what makes European criminal law a *law* is that it carries within it the ethos of human dignity. Therefore, the legality principle becomes an open concept within which different modes of respecting human dignity are guided. To some extent, the European legality principle promotes a fairer and more balanced concept of justice within the EU.

The legality principle's vertical protection against arbitrariness entails that individuals within the EU must be protected from any arbitrary infraction upon their human dignity by state authorities. Such state authorities may include both national and European bodies. The concept of human dignity has been extensively discussed and it has many expressions. It can take the form of foreseeability and reliability of legal norms, which indicates that the legality principle necessitates that individuals must be able to foresee the criminalisation of their behaviour. However, while such foreseeability cannot be achieved in its maximum, individuals must at least be able to identify the risk of criminalisation. Furthermore, it may take the form of political autonomy. The legality principle in this regard must safeguard the right of self-determination within communities.

---

1 P. Selznick, 'The Moral Commonwealth: Social Theory and the Promise of Community', University of California Press, 1992, pp. 443–444.

2 S. Douglas-Scott, 'Rethinking Justice for the EU', in M. Maduro, K. Tuori, S. Sankari (eds), 'Transnational Law: Rethinking European Law and Legal Thinking', Cambridge University Press, 2014, pp. 239–240.

3 G.P. Fletcher, 'Basic Concepts of Criminal Law', Oxford University Press, 1998, p. 206.

4 Ibid., p. 207.

5 Chapter VII para. 6.1.

Horizontal protection under the legality principle addresses the conditions under which individuals come together in the community. In other words, it protects the balance of rights among individuals' interpersonal relationships. Here, human dignity may be linked to the protections associated with basic human rights. Thus, it follows that European judicial bodies and legislators should ensure that legislation does not violate those basic rights. Furthermore, it reflects the mediation of rights, as an ethical minimum, which underpins the European legal order.

1.2. European *demos* and democracy

The principle of legality is also based on a relational interpretation of a European *demos*. European identity is a mixed concept.[6] Individuals find themselves belonging to different communities based on different affiliations. The EU is neither a mere accumulation of national communities nor a melting pot. The motto of the EU, 'United in Diversity' has a substantive meaning.[7] Individuals must be able to identify not only as members of their national *demos* but also as those of a European *demos*. The latter urges individuals to accept each other under conditions of tolerance and shared values. In this regard, the question of 'should there be more or less Europe' is often taken as meaning more or less Europeanisation as opposed to national regulation. This question is not genuinely valid as EU law *is* the mediator between purely national regulation and European unification. This so-called *sui generis* nature of the EU is not only descriptive but also normative.[8]

National criminal law traditions are not only of cultural importance. They include ethnical and historical values that are reflected in the national criminal system. Rules in a specific jurisdiction help constitute the identity of those that share this jurisdiction. In other words, there are national social contracts identified in national criminal codes.[9] These social contracts are a necessary constitutive element of a European *demos* and European identity. One cannot be European if he does not belong to one of the European nation states. This is a requirement for European citizenship; however, it also has a cultural connotation. The legality principle should offer protection for these national social contracts, as they are a necessary requirements for a European *demos*. It should therefore offer some room for pluralism. For example, the exercise of European criminal law competences should be guided by principles that protect national communities from losing their respective identities. On the other hand, the introduction of European legislation and policies in the national sphere gives European nations the opportunity to change and evolve.

---

6 J. Přibáň, 'Is there a Spirit of European Laws? Critical Remarks on EU Constitutional-Making, Enlargement and Political Culture', in V. Gessner, D. Nelken (eds), 'European Ways of Law; Towards a European Sociology of Law', Hart Publishing, 2007, p. 251.

7 http://europa.eu/about-eu/basic-information/symbols/motto/index_en.htm accessed 29/12/14.

8 ECJ Opinion 2/13, 18 December 2014, para. 158.

9 M. Hildebrandt, 'European Criminal Law and European Identity', Criminal Law and Philosophy, vol. 1, 2007, p. 64.

European citizens are also bound by a European social contract. The European community represents the sharing of certain common human rights, which are embedded in the European continent and are distinct from other world communities (such as Africa, the Middle East or the Americas), while also expressing a commitment to loyalty, tolerance and belonging to a broader culture despite one's nationality.[10] The legality principle should therefore promote a 'society-shaping' function. For example, the use of European criminal law competences should also be justified by the European values that they protect in order to make them a part of the European identity.[11] In other words, European criminal justice should be a space where European common values are born and shaped. These values should be respected by national authorities. For example, national courts should consider European values when they interpret the conformity of national criminal law with that of the Directives. Of course, one has to wonder what European values are; a question that remains largely unanswered. One could argue that these values are the human rights depicted in the Charter, although the Charter does not pay much attention to social rights. Another assessment would be that these values are an amalgam of human rights, common historical residues of the Enlightenment such as solidarity, and certain axioms depicted in European religions that have shaped European society.[12]

The European *demos* has an educational element as it helps individuals to learn to accept 'others'. In a liberal Europe, individuals should not be educated or patronised as to what the 'good life' should be. Certainly, the attainment of liberalism in a pluralistic Europe is a phenomenon that remains under debate.[13] Yet, the educational value of the European *demos* is not traced to utilitarian or communitarian values, but to the idea of tolerance. A social contract, by definition, has an educational purpose in the sense that it describes the conditions under which individuals have come into the community. Thus, it provides rules that cultivate behaviour for new members. To this extent, the European legality principle promotes a common European identity.[14] It also promotes a common understanding of EU law among its citizens.[15]

---

10 M. Delmas-Marty, 'Towards a Truly Common Law: Europe as a Laboratory for Legal Pluralism', Cambridge University Press, 2002, pp. 192–195; J.H.H. Weiler, 'The Constitution of Europe', Cambridge University Press, 1999, p. 346.

11 M. Hildebrandt, 'European Criminal Law and European Identity', Criminal Law and Philosophy, vol. 1, 2007, p. 72.

12 A. Supiot, 'Homo Juridicus: on the Anthropological Function of the Law', Verso, 2007, pp. 10–28; see more generally J. Habermas, 'Between Naturalism and Religion', Polity Press, 2008.

13 R. Michaels, 'On Liberalism and Legal Pluralism', in M. Maduro, K. Tuori, S. Sankari (eds), 'Transnational Law: Rethinking European Law and Legal Thinking', Cambridge University Press, 2014, pp. 122–142.

14 M. Hildebrandt, 'European Criminal Law and European Identity', Criminal Law and Philosophy, vol. 1, 2007, pp. 67–75.

15 A. von Bogdandy, 'Founding Principles of EU Law: a Theoretical and Doctrinal Sketch', European Law Journal, vol. 16, 2010, p. 103.

As far as democracy is concerned, a criminal law Directive does not lack democratic legitimacy simply because it is the product of European democratic procedures. As was stated in the previous Chapter, the principle of democracy is not a crystallised concept only realisable within the nation state.[16] Surely, there is always room for improving democratic procedures in European and national settings. A mixed concept of democracy incorporates both procedural and substantive elements. Accordingly, a criminal law Directive would lack democratic legitimacy if European democratic procedures were not respected. One example would be situations where criminal liability would be created by the ECJ. It would also be democratically unacceptable if a criminal law Directive did not recognise individual rights that define European citizenship, such as a criminal law Directive that was irreconcilable with the right to privacy, non-discrimination or freedom of expression.

1.3. Separation of powers

As explained in the previous Chapter, the concept of the separation of powers within the European criminal justice system is complicated.[17] It includes the traditional horizontal separation of the *trias politica* and the vertical separation between the European and national *trias politica*. The concept of the separation of powers has been interpreted in modern times as demanding a basic separation and control of powers by each other. This tension between separation and control can be seen as a co-operative mechanism wherein each power limits the other; however, this does not prevent each branch from exercising its tasks. The legality principle regulates this balance. Courts should be able to modernise anachronistic statutes or refine the bounds of criminal liability in a particular factual context. However, courts should not replace the function of the legislative branch.

A similar idea could be applied to the vertical distribution of power in EU law. The European legality principle in this context must regulate the allocation of tasks between the European and national *trias politica*. This is necessarily reflected in the Treaties, which already provided for such distribution. However, it is also essential because of the pluralistic cohabitation of European and national legal orders. It is important that national legislators do not compromise the effective application of European criminal law, as European criminal law provisions reflect European values and policies that stem from European democratic procedures. It is equally important that European legislation harmonising criminal offences does not prevent national parliaments from affording protection to individuals against arbitrariness. Similarly, the ECJ must provide in its preliminary rulings such an interpretation of criminal liability that articulates protected interests and rights in their European context, so that national courts may be able to adequately justify their decisions.

16 F. Meyer, 'Strafrechtsgenese in Internationalen Organisationen', Nomos, 2012, pp. 706–718; Chapter VII para. 8.2.

17 Chapter VII para. 8.3.

1.4. Legal certainty and foreseeability

As seen in Chapter IV, foreseeability has become the main feature of the legality principle.[18] This is especially due to the influence of the ECtHR jurisprudence to the interpretation of the principle of legality. As seen in Chapter VI, the ECJ has already incorporated the approach of the ECtHR with regard to the legality principle.[19] For a European legality principle, foreseeability has both a national and a transnational connotation. First, the European legality principle must ensure that national norms that implement European instruments communicate criminal liability in a foreseeable manner. The criteria of foreseeability should be of pivotal importance in judging the correctness of national implementation. As previously seen, legal certainty is already a part of the criteria that the Commission uses in its reports.[20] In future infringement proceedings, the foreseeability of legislation should not be brushed off as a requirement for the national authorities to comply with, nor should it be seen solely from the viewpoint of criminal law effectiveness. The criterion of effectiveness is neutral with regard to the protection of individuals *vis-à-vis* arbitrariness. The *Rechtskarakter* of European criminal law strongly requires a protective character. Whether the national implementation of European criminal law is foreseeable depends on various factors, such as the offence at hand, the norm addressees, the national system, its judicial language, the structure of its provisions and the specific sociological context wherein the criminal provision would operate. The criminalisation of hate speech in a homogenous society, such as in Greece for example, would require much more specification than in heterogeneous societies where there is more social experience in political correctness, such as in Germany or the Netherlands. Therefore, it is not possible to state in advance whether a higher national requirement of foreseeability should be applied if available, as this can be only decided on a case-by-case basis.

Second, foreseeability can also have a transnational application, namely, a *cross-border foreseeability*. Such foreseeability is an abstract concept that forms a part of the legitimacy of the European criminal justice system. It adds to the current justification for harmonising the elements of certain offences based on an amalgam of arguments: (i) the AFSJ creates a single area of justice;[21] (ii) with respect to freedom of movement, individuals expect a minimum climate of legal certainty in a single area of justice. This second argument has also been posited by the Commission to rationalise a climate of safety from crime. Furthermore, legal certainty is to be reinforced by the procedural rights Directives, according to the

---

18 Chapter IV para. 9.1.

19 Chapter VI para. 1.

20 Report from the Commission, Council Framework Decision of 28 May 2001 combating fraud and counterfeiting of non-cash means of payment, COM(2004) 346 final, 30.4.2004, point 1.2.2.

21 R. Lööf, '54 CISA and the principles of *ne bis in idem*', European Journal of Crime, Criminal Law and Criminal Justice, vol. 15, 2007, p. 325.

Commission;[22] (iii) harmonisation and cooperation instruments communicate a general legal expectation to individuals that criminal offences are punished similarly around Europe; and (iv) individuals can expect to identify common values in the European harmonisation instruments that reflect the European social contract. This argument does not address the reliability of the law, but rather its social acceptability. As explained, legal certainty and foreseeability entail two elements, namely the reliability to the law but also the acceptability of its interpretation.

Thus, foreseeability entails also that one reads criminal liability in the context of social values. For example, it would be inconceivable to read Article 2 of the Directive 2011/36 on human trafficking as criminalising proper employment relationships or legal transnational adoptions.[23] Considering that harmonisation of criminal offences is also justified by a more abstract concept of *cross-border foreseeability*, such criminal offences must depict a balancing of rights that corresponds to common and shared values. The concept of *cross-border foreseeability* remains at the abstract level as a justification for harmonisation, but it cannot be taken very far. If one wished to truly achieve *cross-border foreseeability*, all criminal norms would have to be harmonised or unified.[24] However, it could support some active measures to ensure reliability of the law, such as with the harmonisation of jurisdictional rules.[25]

2. Legitimising and distributive roles of the European legality principle

The legality principle is a general principle of EU law, as explained in Chapter VI.[26] According to a relational model of European criminal justice, principles should be distinguished from policies and rights. What does it entail that the principle of legality is a 'principle'? There are three elements to address in order to answer this question: the legitimising role of this principle regarding using European criminal law competences, its distributive role regarding the allocation of responsibility for protection against arbitrariness between EU and national authorities and the normative role, which is about the particular function of the principle's aspects.

---

22 Commission Communication, Towards an EU Criminal Policy: Ensuring the effective implementation of EU policies through criminal law, COM (2011) 573 final, 20.9.2011, p. 5.

23 Directive 2011/36 of 5 April 2011 on preventing and combating trafficking in human beings and protecting its victims, and replacing Council Framework Decision 2002/629/JHA OJ L 101, 15.4.2011, pp. 1–11.

24 H.G. Nilsson, 'How to combine minimum rules with maximum legal certainty?', Europättslig Tidskrift, 2011, p. 670.

25 See below para. 3.3.

26 Chapter VI para. 1.

2.1. Legitimation of European competences in substantive criminal law

The legality principle aims at legitimising the *ius puniendi*. One of its roles in national law is to define the source of criminal liability and set certain qualitative requirements. It determines what the legitimate use of *ius puniendi* is. Similarly in EU law, the European legality principle has such a legitimising function. National legislators have indefinite sovereignty to make criminal laws. However, this is not the case in European criminal law. The European legislator has competence in limited areas. One of the sources of European instrumentalism, as explained in the previous Chapter, is the opportunistic use of criminal competences.[27] This has a serious impact on the coherence of European criminal law, but it also poses questions regarding its compatibility *vis-à-vis* national sovereignty. Some of the values underpinning the legality principle include the European *demos*, which presupposes the protection of national identity, the protection of political autonomy of individuals *vis-à-vis* their own state and the EU, and finally the *Rechtskarakter* of European criminal law, which advocates against a neutral character. Therefore, the European legality principle is called to legitimise the use of European *ius puniendi* by defining the conditions under which European competences should be exercised for the harmonisation of criminal offences.[28] Thus, the legality principle has an attributive and legitimising character.[29]

Such competences are primarily controlled by a set of principles, namely, the principles of conferral, subsidiarity and proportionality. To these, one should add the principle of *ultima ratio*. Although *ultima ratio* is not depicted in the Treaties, it has been justified in European soft-law as an important part of the European criminal law framework.[30] Further criteria for the use of European competences are found in European legal instruments. For example, European criminal competences must be used for particularly serious cross-border crimes (Article 83 para. 1 TFEU) and for crimes that have a direct negative impact on European policies that have been subjected to harmonisation (Article 83, para. 2 TFEU). Moreover, according to the European Parliament, criminal provisions should focus on criminal conduct causing damage to society, groups or individuals.[31]

The legality principle in the relational model is a steering principle in that it obliges the European legislator to make decisions about criminal liability that are,

---

27 Chapter VII para. 3.2.

28 E. Herlin-Karnell, 'What Principles Drive (or Should Drive) European Criminal Law?', German Law Journal, vol. 11, 2010, p. 1119.

29 Ibid.; A. von Bogdandy, 'Founding Principles of EU Law: a Theoretical and Doctrinal Sketch', European Law Journal, vol. 16, 2010, p. 104.

30 European Parliament Resolution of 22 May 2012 on an EU approach to criminal law (2010/2310(INI)), 22.5.2012; Commission Communication, Towards an EU Criminal Policy: Ensuring the effective implementation of EU policies through criminal law, COM (2011) 573 final, 20.9.2011.

31 European Parliament Resolution of 22 May 2012 on an EU approach to criminal law (2010/2310(INI)), 22.5.2012.

as much as possible, aligned with existing legal principles and values of the legal order of Member States. As a steering principle, the legality principle safeguards legal transparency.[32] Its steering character does not result in the abolition of other principles, such as subsidiarity and proportionality. These principles have their own legitimising function and reflect different ideals. The European legality principle provides the platform upon which the above-mentioned principles and policies operate and are weighed, by guiding or steering their interrelations. An *ultra vires* or otherwise illegitimate use of the European *ius puniendi* (for example by not assessing adequately the subsidiarity principle) is a constitutional violation of the Treaties but, from a criminal law perspective, it is also a violation of the principle of legality. This is because the European produced Directive does not comply with a legitimate use of the European *ius puniendi.*

One of the premises of a relational model is that policies, principles and rights should be separated in European legal discourse, with European rights and principles having higher priority.[33] The weighing of all of these should respect the ethical minimum of the European legal order, which is human dignity. The European legality principle obliges the European legislator to identify policies that need to be pursued, such as battling cybercrime or environmental crime (in the case of Article 83 para. 2 TFEU). Similarly, the European legislator views individual rights from both the perpetrators' and the victims' sides and translates those rights into European values, such as the protection of privacy, the right to information on the internet or the right to a clean environment. The legality principle also requires the European legislator to consider the principles of subsidiarity, proportionality and *ultima ratio* in association with *both* European policies and rights, and to *be transparent* on how these potentially countervailing interests are weighed.

Transparent reasoning is of great importance in evaluating the legitimacy of European criminal norms. In particular, the distinction between European policies, principles and rights is essential. When statistics identify a problem area of cross-border crime, the rights that such criminalisation would potentially affect must reflect the balance that underpins the European legal order. A lack of transparency results in instrumentalism, which renders the function of principles such as subsidiarity redundant. Harmonisation of offences could facilitate judicial cooperation to stop cross-border crime more effectively. In an evaluation of the subsidiarity principle, national legislators should be able to identify whether they can defend and reconcile such criminalisation with their national legal order. National legislators, courts and European citizens, as members of their national and European *demoi*, must be able to identify their commitment, loyalty and belongingness in the European criminal justice system. Similarly, when it comes to Article 83, para. 2 TFEU, the principles of *ultima ratio* and proportionality can be respected if there is transparent reasoning on the necessity to use criminal law for

---

32 A. von Bogdandy, 'Founding Principles of EU Law: a Theoretical and Doctrinal Sketch', European Law Journal, vol. 16, 2010, p. 101.

33 Chapter V para. 6.2.

better enforcement of that particular European policy. However, such improved enforcement must also be conceptualised with reference to the individual rights interfered with by the criminalisation of a particular behaviour. If criminal provisions are to be created for a European policy outside the realm of the AFSJ, then it must be justified as to why they represent values that are considered vital in the European legal system and the European community.

2.2. Distribution of powers in the two-level European criminal justice system

As seen in Chapter VI, a fundamental question is whether the European principle of legality can be applied to European bodies and the extent to which it can be applied to national authorities implementing or interpreting EU law.[34]

For European bodies, the fundamental question is what would be the rationale for applying the legality principle to European actors? This is particularly problematic for the aspects of *lex certa* and *lex stricta*, because European legislation and the preliminary rulings of the ECJ do not directly concern individuals. As explained, the European legality principle is a dual norm;[35] as a general principle of EU law, it must be respected by both European and national authorities. Moreover, it is a ground of review for European instruments and for national legislation (such as infringement proceedings).[36] The starting point is that both European and national legislators are expected to follow the legality principle. However, the normative function of the legality principle must stem from the *Rechtskarakter* of European criminal law itself and not solely from positive law sources, such as the Treaties. The Treaties and the *acquis* may change, but the intrinsic nature of criminal law must be maintained.

In this regard, it is important to recall that the *Rechtskarakter* of European criminal law entails a direct relationship between individuals and the EU, where the latter assumes responsibility for the protection of the former. The EU has positive and negative obligations. The negative obligation is to refrain from legislation or interpretation of criminal liability that would oblige national authorities to violate the legality principle. The positive obligation is to ensure that Directives and preliminary rulings make the application of the legality principle attainable by national authorities.[37] As demonstrated, European legislation and interpretation of Directives do influence the quality of national implementation and interpretation by national courts. The lack of a direct system of enforcement and that of the direct effect of Directives does not diminish the responsibility of the European legislator

34 Chapter VI para. 4.1.

35 T.A.J.A. Vandamme, 'The invalid Directive: the legal authority of a Union act requiring domestic law making', Europa Law Publishing, 2005, p. 197.

36 T. Tridimas, 'The General Principles of EU law', Oxford University Press, 2006, pp. 244–246.

37 P. Asp, 'The Substantive Criminal Law Competence of the EU', Jure, 2012, p. 172.

to comply with the legality principle; it might affect the degree, but not the existence of the responsibility.

Considering the principle of separation of powers, the relationship of European and national legislators is a form of 'shared responsibility' to determine the scope of criminal liability.[38] The European legislator defines which rights should be protected and inflicted and the minimum scope of criminalised behaviour. The principle of legality would require that such criminalisation reflect a legitimate use of European competences as applied to criminal law. Moreover, the definition itself respects the qualitative requirements of the legality principle. In particular, it should be ensured that there is no retroactivity and that the definition provides sufficient clarity for national legislators to understand the minimum scope.[39] In other words, the minimum scope of criminal liability should already be sufficiently clear to draw a minimum regulatory behavioural standard. This is essential because national legislators must receive a clear mandate on what to criminalise. Thus, according to the European Parliament:

> [L]egislation has to be clear-cut and easily understandable so that it becomes predictable for all whether an act amounts to a criminal offence or not. This holds even more so for Directives, since these have to be transposed into national law and any lack of clarity can lead to diverging interpretations, which can easily enhance confusion instead of reducing it.[40]

Such a clear mandate would also facilitate a more transparent discussion at the national level as to whether a wider scope of criminal liability would be desired in accordance to the principle of proportionality.[41] It would also facilitate the legitimate exercise of European criminal law competences.

Regarding the application of the legality principle to the ECJ, the Court stated clearly in *Grøngaard* that the interpretation of a Directive does not depend on the nature of the national proceedings as civil, administrative or criminal law.[42] In Chapter VI, the question raised was whether this is in compliance with the legality principle.[43] This question must be answered in the negative. In fact, the ECJ has already stated that the interpretation given to a Directive should not result in the expansion of criminal liability.[44] One may wonder how the ECJ's rulings even

---

38 C. Peristeridou, 'The Principle of "Lex Certa" in National Law and European Perspectives', in A. Klip (ed), 'Substantive Criminal Law of the European Union', Maklu, 2011, p. 12.

39 J. Blomsma, C. Peristeridou, 'The way forward: a general part of European criminal law', in F. Galli, A. Weyembergh, 'Approximation of substantive criminal law in the EU: the way forward', IEE, 2013, pp. 123–124.

40 European Parliament Resolution of 22 May 2012 on an EU approach to criminal law (2010/2310(INI)), 22.5.2012, p. 7.

41 Ibid.

42 C–384/02 criminal proceedings against Knud Grøngaard and Allan Bang, 22 November 2005, para. 28.

43 Chapter VI para. 5.2.

44 Case 14/86 Pretore di Salò v Persons unknown, 11 June 1987, para. 19.

touch matters of substance and facts. The interpretation of Directives by the ECJ already includes an evaluation of the conflicting rights present in the European system and how the scope of criminal liability should be interpreted with respect to the existing facts. Preliminary questions such as, 'Can Article X be interpreted as precluding situation Y', indicate that the ECJ must consider whether the European norm could take such a meaning. While this interpretation may remain at the abstract level, it still involves an appreciation of the scope of criminal liability since this should still be applied to the relevant factual context. Therefore, the ECJ should take under consideration the criminal law nature of national proceedings, and therefore also of the legality principle, when it interprets European instruments.

A proper distinction of the tasks of the ECJ and the national courts is not only obscured in criminal law.[45] To make use again of the methodology of interpretation proposed by Sax,[46] the determination of the criteria for interpretation and the abstract interpretation of the relevant criminal liability norms with these criteria should be performed by the ECJ.[47] The relational model defended in the previous Chapter identifies the following requirements for the European legality principle.

First, the requirement of transparency entails that individuals (as members of the European *demos*) and national courts (as loyal courts belonging to the European criminal justice system) should be able to recognise the balance of interests, legal principles and policies in the reasoning of the ECJ. Second, the element of controllability requires that transparency in the reasoning of the ECJ gives individuals and national courts the opportunity to control whether they can defend and accept such an interpretation, and thus maintain their trust in European institutions.[48]

3. Normative role: the aspects of the European legality principle

In this section, the normative role of the legality principle will be discussed. I shall revisit certain questions raised in Chapter VI and discuss also certain further normative requirements that the legality principle should generate.

3.1. *Lex scripta*

In Chapter VI, a rather confused approach to *lex scripta* was identified.[49] On the one hand, the ECJ seems to recognise the parliamentary statute as the sole source of criminal liability. On the other hand, in competition law cases the ECJ has accepted

45 G. Conway, 'The Limits of Legal Reasoning and the European Court of Justice', Cambridge University Press, 2012, pp. 178–192.
46 W. Sax, 'Das Strafrechtliche "Analogieverbot"', Vandenhoeck & Ruprecht, 1953, p. 47.
47 See for the utilisation of Sax's analysis in Chapter IV para. 8.
48 E. Claes, 'Legaliteit en rechtsvinding in het strafrecht', Universitaire Pers Leuven, 2003, p. 467.
49 Chapter VI para. 2.

that the notion of *droit* can also give rise to liability in line with the ECtHR jurisprudence.

3.1.1. Should case law be a source of criminal liability?

Regardless of what happens in competition law, the answer for European criminal law must be in the negative. In a relational model, the principle of democracy is of pivotal importance. Particularly for European criminal law, the only popular institutionalised forum where individuals get to transform their needs and ideals into policy, detached from their national affiliations, is the European Parliament. In this regard, the legislative bodies of the EU, the Council and the European Parliament express different interests. The Council expresses the interests of the Member States and represents the different national political communities and their goals, while the European Parliament represents the interests of Europeans. European criminal liability can only be defined in a statute, namely, in the form of Directives.

Currently, despite some claims to the contrary, there seems to be no legal competence to define criminal liability in the form of Regulations.[50] Furthermore, national authorities are prevented from basing criminal liability solely on obligations found in Regulations. It is possible that a Treaty amendment could facilitate criminal legislation in the form of Regulations. Such an amendment would require important changes within the EU. First, such criminal law Regulations should clearly define criminal liability (and be non-retroactive). Second, a directly enforceable instrument in criminal law would require a re-interpretation of the European democratic principle and *demos*. Unlike competition rules, criminal law reflects a strong idea of national identity and values. Such a possibility would imply certain deeper changes in the European matrix of constitutionalism and a subsequent re-interpretation of the *Rechtskarakter* of European criminal law.

The position of case law is more difficult to grasp. In particular, for instruments harmonising criminal offences, the body of ECJ case law will only grow in number and intensity. Given the prevalent role of the ECJ within the EU and the (still) cumbersome legislative process, the ECJ certainly has the upper hand in 'filling up lacunae' or steering the law into different directions. Generally, the reasoning of the ECJ has always been meta-teleological, even in criminal law cases, and thus rather creative in interpretation.[51] The question of how to approach ECJ case law is not posed only with regard to criminal law. There is a large discussion as to whether

50 R. Sicurella, 'Some reflections on the need for a general theory of the competence of the European Union in criminal law', in A. Klip (ed), 'Substantive Criminal Law of the European Union', Maklu, 2011, p. 239; Article 325 TFEU, which has been discussed as a potential candidate for a criminal law Regulation, has been used as the legal basis for a Directive, see Proposal for a Directive on the fight against fraud to the Union's financial interests by means of criminal law, COM (2012) 0363 final, 11.07.2012.

51 G. Conway, 'The Limits of Legal Reasoning and the European Court of Justice', Cambridge University Press, 2012, p. 46.

and how ECJ jurisprudence is a part of the formal sources of EU law.[52] A majority of the scholarly views suggest that the influence of case law is fading.[53] However, the ECJ itself has treated its case law as a binding source of law.[54] The problem of accepting case law in an elevated position is that in a strictly positivistic system, sources of law are placed in a hierarchy. As in continental systems, a strict hierarchy can be challenging in practice, particularly because the legality principle cannot curtail casuistry.

It should be therefore accepted that in criminal law ECJ case law is neither a primary source, nor a secondary source. The ECJ cannot create new forms of criminal liability, but it can still determine its exact scope. As argued in Chapters IV and V, jurisprudence as an organism of law must be safeguarded from casuistry, which means that certain aspects of the legality principle should be applicable to case law as a source of law.[55] Demanding consistency in jurisprudence is a requirement of the legality principle in a relational system of criminal justice.[56]

This element has been mentioned in Chapter V as *lex methodologica*.[57] It obliges courts to ensure that the interpretation of a provision is consistent with prior cases and able to retain consistency by anticipating consequences in future cases. Could this element result in a doctrine of *stare decisis* for EU law? The ECJ does not have formal rules defining the force and binding character of past decisions.[58] Furthermore, it does not refer to its past decisions as 'precedent'. However, there is a *de facto* recognition of precedent.[59] In practice, prior case law is used as a justification from which an interpretation is drawn in an abstract manner, often using language identical to previous cases.[60] To reconcile this *de facto* precedent with the principle of *lex scripta*, one could distinguish between two types of precedent: precedent by solution and precedent by interpretation. In the case of precedent by solution, the judicial decision has a normative value and binding force *per se*, and it creates a new rule that resolves the conflict. In the case of precedent by interpretation, the judicial decision provides the best interpretation of existing law.[61] The ECJ's *de facto* precedent can be observed as a precedent by interpretation.[62]

---

52 J. Raitio, 'The Principle of Legal Certainty in EC Law', Kluwer, 2003, pp. 83–90.

53 Ibid.

54 Ibid., p. 88.

55 Chapter IV para. 10.1.4 and Chapter V para. 4.4, 5.2. and 6.2.

56 D.H. de Jong, 'Naar een common law-conceptie van legaliteit?', Delikt en Delinkwent, vol. 29, 1999, pp. 687–690.

57 Chapter V para. 6.3 and 7.

58 J. Raitio, 'The Principle of Legal Certainty in EC Law', Kluwer, 2003, p. 87.

59 G. Beck, 'The Legal Reasoning of the Court of Justice of the EU', Hart Publishing, 2012, pp. 237–251.

60 Ibid.

61 T. Tridimas, 'Precedence and the Court of Justice: a Jurisprudence of Doubt?', in J. Dickson, P. Eleftheriadis (eds), 'Philosophical Foundations of EU Law', Oxford University Press, 2012, pp. 307–330.

62 Ibid.

With such practices, the question is not whether ECJ case law can be a binding source of law but rather how it can achieve a continuum.[63] The requirement of consistency should be respected by the ECJ, particularly when interpreting instruments to harmonise criminal liability. The lack of formal precedent causes various problems. First, it is difficult to determine the *ratio decidendi*. Second, the ECJ often does not distinguish the material facts to which the *ratio decidendi* applies. This suggests that, in future cases revolving around different facts, the Court might depart from the *ratio decidendi* in an ambiguous manner. Third, the method of the ECJ is characterised by the use of 'building blocks', i.e. collections of prior case law cited repeatedly as authority, without further elaboration on how these are applied in the present case. While this may retain a measure of consistency, it obscures the development of jurisprudence because minor changes in the definition of terms arise in time but are not given proper consideration.[64]

For European criminal law, the legality principle should therefore generate more substance for developing the ECJ system of precedent. As seen in Chapter V, in a relational model of justice, the legality principle obliges courts to distinguish between the *in abstracto* interpretation of the norm from its application *in concreto*.[65] The ECJ should clearly identify the interpretation of a norm *in abstracto*, which would form the basis of the *ratio decidendi* that would be binding in future cases. The concrete facts that would give rise to the *ratio decidendi* should be made clear so that any distinction in the future is transparent, but also justified. The method of 'building blocks' is not necessarily an obstruction as long as the arguments behind the cases are revisited and incremental alterations in terminology in criminal liability are observed.

3.1.2. Lex parliamentaria and lex nationalis

As explained previously, the principle of democracy within the EU is one of the cornerstones of the European criminal justice system and of pivotal importance in a relational model of justice. Thus, a European legality principle would require that criminal liability be defined by democratic bodies, as these operate in the European setting.

Regarding national implementing legislation, as previously shown, there are various cases where this matter has been addressed by the ECJ. There is already a fragment of the European legality principle in existence, which is a *lex nationalis*. A *lex nationalis* indicates that national authorities would violate the European legality principle if they were to impose obligations on citizens through an unimplemented Directive. Moreover, the correct implementation of a Directive necessitates that this is performed by statute. The rationale for a *lex nationalis* goes

63 Ibid.

64 G. Beck, 'The Legal Reasoning of the Court of Justice of the EU', Hart Publishing, 2012, pp. 237–251.

65 Chapter V para. 6.3.

further than the nature of Directives as instruments requiring implementation. National implementation is also necessary to honour national popular autonomy, which is an indispensable requirement of European democracy. Furthermore, there is an additional function. With *lex nationalis*, the European legality principle protects individuals from arbitrariness by their national authorities. In this regard, the protective role of the EU in criminal matters also penetrates national systems.

3.2. *Lex praevia*

The European legality principle prohibits the prescription of retroactive criminalisation or the retroactive application of criminal liability to both European and national legislations.[66] Generally speaking, this aspect is well respected within the EU and does not present many problems.

An interesting question that came up in the inventory of the fragments of the European legality principle was whether the interpretation of national law in conformity with a Directive that did not exist at the time the offence was committed is prohibited by the *lex praevia*.[67] Such an interpretation is supposedly limited by the legality principle.[68] As long as the scope of liability is not expanded, there would be nothing to prevent a national court from interpreting national legislation in the light of a Directive issued after the commission of the act. Essentially, this becomes an issue of judicial interpretation rather than *lex praevia.* Here national courts should follow a dialectic and transparent interpretation of both the national and European instruments to identify which policies, rights, and principles are protected by the national legislation and which are protected by the European legislation. If there is a substantial difference between them, then the accused should not be confronted with an interpretation of national legislation that depicts different interests from ones he could have foreseen.

3.3. *Lex certa*

Before going into depth with the *lex certa*, it is important to remember that a maximum level of certainty is not attainable. European legality promotes foreseeability of legislation, according to which the law can draw a regulatory standard from legal norms. Moreover, the legality principle in a European relational model advocates for reliability of the law to promote trust in institutions and a climate of confidence towards the actions of the state and their own actions.

---

66 Case 63/83 Regina v Kirk, 10 July 1984.

67 Chapter VI para. 3.3.

68 C–105/03 criminal proceedings against Maria Pupino, 16 June 2005.

3.3.1. Accessibility of legislation

The accessibility of legislation is vital for defining the consequences of one's actions. The ECJ has prohibited the use of unpublished legislation for determining liability. Chapter VI identified two problematic issues in this regard.

The first issue is whether the European legality principle would also require national implementing legislation to be published in all European languages.[69] If the legality principle were to be interpreted in this manner, one would have to put exaggerated gravity on the concept of *cross-border foreseeability*. It would mean that this principle promotes maximum legal certainty in a cross-border setting, and it would also necessarily follow that EU criminal law competences must be expanded to all criminal offences. After all, the more harmonisation there is, the more foreseeable the criminal liability is when crossing jurisdictions.

Such an interpretation of the legality principle, though, is unacceptable, at least in the present state of EU law. It is one thing to justify *existing* harmonisation competences on the increased legal certainty in exercising freedom of movement in addition to other arguments. However, it is a completely different thing to argue that such rationale should function beyond the scope of European criminal law. That would necessarily lead to a unification of European criminal law or to a prevalent federalisation of criminal justice.

The problems of increased linguistic pluralism could be addressed in different ways. On a soft-law note, if one approaches legal certainty as a concept with less formal and more substantive connotations,[70] many jurisdictions already provide English translations of their criminal codes and selective case law, albeit they are not always official versions.[71]

An additional solution may come from the legality principle itself and its relationship to the principle of guilt. Chapter III touched on the difficulty of doctrinally separating the guilt principle from the legality principle, which could prove beneficial, as one principle could complement the other.[72] At the national level, there is an obligation for the individual to be familiar with the law, as 'ignorance of the law is no excuse'. This obligation is expressed in the doctrine of mistake of law. While ignorance of the facts can be used as a defence, ignorance of the law is not excused unless there are special and strictly interpreted circumstances (e.g. if the administration erroneously informed the individual on a legal matter).[73] Hence, one could wonder whether mistake of law can be applied in a cross-border

---

69 Chapter VI para. 4.2.

70 J. Raitio, 'The Principle of Legal Certainty in EC Law', Kluwer, 2003, p. 380.

71 The German Constitutional Court publishes some case law in English, for example, www.bundesverfassungsgericht.de/en/index.html accessed 6/11/2014 and there are more websites that provide English translations of national criminal codes. An example is www.gesetze-im-internet.de/englisch_stgb/index.html accessed 6/11/2014.

72 Chapter III para. 6.2.

73 J. Blomsma, 'Mens Rea and defences in European criminal law', Intersentia, 2012, pp. 469–474.

setting as an excuse. AG Elmer suggested that the mistake of law doctrine should not distinguish between national and EU laws in its application.[74] There have been some national cases in this regard. For example, an Italian working temporarily in Germany was excused for not knowing that in Germany shooting birds is illegal.[75] However, this excuse was not accepted in Germany, as the conduct was also punishable in the country of origin of the accused.[76] In non-professional spheres, there is room to suggest that mistake of law could be applied in some exceptional cases, particularly when national legislation opts for a much broader scope of criminal liability than the one depicted in the Directive, or when the character of the offence is very particular or technical. The European legality principle should not oblige national courts to bend the mistake of law concept for every European tourist who finds himself in trouble with the law. European citizenship and freedom of movement also create obligations for individuals. A case-by-case approach that would consider the exceptional nature of *ad hoc* circumstances is much more appropriate in this regard.

The second issue requires some hard law solutions. The most serious problem of accessibility of legislation relates to divergent rules regarding jurisdiction. National systems' jurisdictional rules and definitions of territoriality differ significantly.[77] This translates into a significant burden for individuals, as the European legal order cannot request individuals to do the impossible. In national law, jurisdictional rules usually escape the realm of the legality principle.[78] What is important is that the behaviour was criminal somewhere.[79] Jurisdictional rules are considered procedural rules to which the legality principle does not apply.[80] This interpretation of the scope of the legality principle is very nationally oriented. In national systems, the problem of knowing which jurisdiction applies to your conduct is of little concern, as national criminal systems are territorially confined. Yet in a transnational setting, this can be considerably more problematic as the question of jurisdiction becomes one of substantive law. Various provisions for the same conduct that exist horizontally result in inconsistencies regarding the content of the law, which is essentially a question of substance. This is a similar approach to the

74 Opinion AG Elmer of 14 March 1996 in C–168/95 criminal proceedings against Luciano Arcaro, 26 September 1996, para. 43.

75 J. Blomsma, 'Mens Rea and defences in European criminal law', Intersentia, 2012, p. 474.

76 Ibid.

77 A.–S. Massa, 'Jurisdiction in England and Wales and in the Netherlands: a Comparative Appraisal with a European Touch', in A. Klip (ed), 'Substantive Criminal Law of the European Union', Maklu, 2011, pp. 103–121.

78 M. Luchtman, 'Choice of forum and the prosecution of cross-border crime in the European Union-what role for the legality principle?', in M. Luchtman (ed), 'Choice of forum in cooperation against EU financial crime: freedom, security and justice and the protection of specific EU-interests', Eleven International Publishing, 2013, p. 23.

79 Ibid.

80 M. Böse, 'Choice of Forum and Jurisdiction', in M. Luchtman (ed), 'Choice of forum in cooperation against EU financial crime: freedom, security and justice and the protection of specific EU-interests', Eleven International Publishing, 2013, p. 80.

ne bis in idem principle, as these are horizontal inconsistencies of the same single European legal order. Borders are relevant only for the sake of enforcing judicial decisions. The view of the European legislator is that as soon as the criminality of the behaviour is foreseeable, there is no further problem with its foreseeability.[81] Freedom of movement entails that the EU grants its citizens the right to be subject to the legal order of their choice.

The choice to subject oneself to another legal order is the essence of free movement. A common view on jurisdiction is necessary to comply with the requirements of foreseeability and reliability. In this regard, the full potential of the consequences of one's actions should be foreseeable.[82] How can individuals be requested to simultaneously conform to laws of various legal orders, if it is not clear which state has jurisdiction over the conduct? It is one thing to request individuals to be familiar with local variations of the same criminal offence, and quite another to have no clear demarcation as to which national version of an offence will apply.

The requirement of *cross-border foreseeability* in this sense is no longer considered *in abstracto*, but as generating a normative obligation. This is not only because the lack of such harmonisation deprives individuals of legal certainty to an intolerable degree but also because such competence is envisaged in the Treaties (see Article 82 TFEU). The lack of proper initiative in this manner can only be attributed to the instrumentalist and security-oriented nature of the current European criminal justice system. The European legality principle, as defined by the *Rechtskarakter* of European criminal law, creates two obligations. First, jurisdictional rules must be harmonised and second, when there are conflicts of jurisdiction, the foreseeability requirement must be considered during negotiations, particularly when it comes to the jurisdiction to prescribe, and it should be given priority.[83] Such priority entails that it would be preferential to stick to territoriality or find further solutions that mitigate this problem.[84]

3.3.2. Precision of Directives and annulment proceedings

In Chapter VI, the discussion centred on the problems of vagueness in Directives.[85] At the beginning of this Chapter, explanations were developed on how shared responsibility to determine the scope of criminal liability should work between

81 M. Luchtman, 'Choice of forum and the prosecution of cross-border crime in the European Union – what role for the legality principle?', in M. Luchtman (ed), 'Choice of forum in cooperation against EU financial crime: freedom, security and justice and the protection of specific EU-interests', Eleven International Publishing, 2013, p. 27.

82 Ibid.

83 M. Böse, 'Choice of Forum and Jurisdiction', in M. Luchtman (ed), 'Choice of forum in cooperation against EU financial crime: freedom, security and justice and the protection of specific EU-interests', Eleven International Publishing, 2013, p. 81.

84 Ibid., p. 86.

85 Chapter VI para. 4.4.

European and national legislators. How should the ECJ deal with the possibility of applying *lex certa* to criminal law Directives?

In *Intertanko*, the ECJ passed the responsibility of complying with *lex certa* to national legislators.[86] The Court held that while Directives must meet the requirement of legal certainty, it is for the national legislators to actually enforce them. The problem of applying the legality principle to Directives has already been addressed.

Certain guidelines on how to apply *lex certa* to the harmonisation of criminal offences in Directives could include the following: (i) a vague determination is one that does not indicate with clarity the minimum scope of criminal liability that needs to be implemented; (ii) in principle, the level of precision in the definition of criminal liability should be of such clarity that should a national legislator choose to use the copy-paste technique, individuals would be able to ascertain the risk of criminalisation from the definition. In essence, the minimum scope of criminal liability should comply with *lex certa* as if it had direct effect. Indeed, it is often the case that national legislators use techniques that preserve the European definition of the offence and any possible uncertainty becomes a part of the national criminal norm. Moreover, the European legality principle requires the European legislator to ensure that national authorities can comply with the legality principle. Currently, if a definition of criminal liability has unambiguous terms, then national legislators can either introduce the definition as it is, and therefore violate *lex certa*, or they can alter the terms themselves and risk that their interpretation of the minimum scope of the Directive is not in line with the ECJ's view.[87]

Importantly, the European legislator should make clear whether there is a degree of latitude intended as far as the minimum scope of criminalisation is concerned. There is discretion to broaden the scope of criminal liability. However, there could also be discretion in drafting certain terms for the minimum scope of the offence. In this regard, the legality principle could require the European legislator to indicate whether the harmonisation effort intends a unified minimum scope of criminal liability. In the absence of any contrary indication, the presumption should be that national legislators are allowed to concretise certain ambiguous terms. An opposite presumption would prevent national authorities from complying with the *lex certa*. As emphasised above, there is a negative obligation to refrain from legislation that would frustrate the application of *lex certa* in the national setting.

In annulment proceedings, the ECJ should consider the above criteria, as it is crucial that European legislation does not make compliance with the *lex certa* impossible. In particular, if the minimum harmonisation is intended to create unified minimum standards, the definition of offences in the Directive should be as precise as if it had direct effect. Some additional points of reference should be the purpose or *telos* of the Directive, the seriousness of the offence, the possible

86 C–308/06 The Queen, on the application of International Association of Independent Tanker Owners (Intertanko) and Others v Secretary of State for Transport, 3 June 2008, para. 71.

87 P. Asp, 'The Substantive Criminal Law Competence of the EU', Jure, 2012, pp. 172–173.

interpretations that might occur, and whether these are incompatible with individual rights, the uniform application of EU law and the effectiveness of harmonisation.

3.3.3. Implementation, infringement proceedings and the supervisory role of the ECJ

The requirement of a European *lex certa* as applied to national authorities requires them to implement European legislation so that individuals can rely on criminal provisions. National parliaments should make sure that implementing legislation complies with the principle of legality. There are two questions to be discussed.

One question raised in Chapter VI was whether *lex certa* should require national authorities to use a specific technique.[88] Considering pluralism and the necessity to respect national legal orders, their systemic particularities and structures, it would seem difficult to reconcile this with the pluralistic character of Europe. National authorities must retain the right to introduce descriptions of criminal liability as they see fit. After all, what is inherent to the process of transposition is the internalisation of criminal liability prescribed from one legislative authority to another. Implementation further reflects the nature of national criminal justice systems, where national legislators should be given the opportunity to receive a description of criminal liability and make it 'their own'. Additionally, the choice of a technique for implementation might depend on the character of the offence and any relevant, pre-existing criminal offence.

In a minimum harmonisation scenario for unified minimum standards, discretion is more limited. One could claim that the copy-paste technique should be preferred for the legality principle in this context. However, such an interpretation of this principle would deprive national authorities of the ability to adjust European terms to their national systems. In Chapter VI, concerns were also raised about the dynamic reference technique.[89] In my view, this technique should be available only for criminal offences of a technical nature and depending on the norm-addressees. Such a technique should only be used with due caution with respect to the need to draft accessible and clear legislation. In any case, it is self-evident that both the reference and the copy-paste techniques should be used only when the definition of liability in the Directive satisfies already the requirement of foreseeability.

The second issue relates to the supervisory role of the ECJ. In case of infringement proceedings regarding *lex certa*, the ECJ should take note of the following considerations. First, the Court should consider the nature, severity and placement of the particular criminal offence in the national system of rules. Here the ECJ is called upon to understand why the national legislator preferred such implementation and how that stricter interpretation protects foreseeability. Furthermore, the ECJ should seek whether such implementation was conducted

---

88 Chapter VI para. 4.6.

89 Ibid.

because of a different appreciation of the interests, principles and values of national law and whether these values are a fundamental part of the national legal order. For example, a stricter implementation could be because of a higher consideration of the guilt principle, or because of the proportionality principle. The ECJ should also take note of existing national case law on the interpretation of this term to identify the application of this provision and the possible dangers of an overly open norm in that particular legal order. Additionally, the ECJ should review different translations of the Directive in different languages from which a divergent scope could arise.

The Directive itself should be scrutinised not only with regard to its purpose but also with regard to its quality and precision. In the absence of a specific indication regarding the discretion to define ambiguous terms, national legislators should retain the right to do so. Finally, an overall appreciation of the compliance with the legality principle must be pursued by the ECJ. The lack of a statutory basis results in infringement on the legality principle. More difficult is the case of silent implementation. In those circumstances, emphasis should be placed on the existing national jurisprudence and whether a conform interpretation of the existing norms could be in line with the requirements of foreseeability.

3.3.4. Is a European criminal code necessary?

Does the European legality principle require a European criminal code? This question did not arise in the inventory of Chapter VI but is relevant to the legality principle. Codification in one document, as observed in national law, serves many goals such as consistency, efficiency, accessibility and comprehensibility; some of these benefits may be associated with *lex certa*. An argument is that European legislation would be more accessible and comprehensible to individuals; however, in the absence of direct enforcement and as long as such legislation is depicted in statutes, the European legality principle does not require that the law be codified in a single document. Given the limited number of instruments, it seems both unnecessary and inefficient at present.

With respect to the elements of the general part, they are largely undetermined in Directives and are judicially developed by the ECJ.[90] A codification of the general part in this case would be much more important than that of the special part. Such definitions do not establish a separate basis of criminal liability but establish certain fundamental features of criminal liability that are applied to most special offences. Their formulation in the general part is with a certain *Rechtsgutsblindheit*, namely, they are stipulated in disassociation from the different protected interests.[91] The norms in the general part have a normative significance for criminal liability. The concepts of *actus reus* and *mens rea* determine the actual

90 S. Melander, 'Effectiveness in EU Criminal Law and its Effects on the General Part of Criminal Law', New Journal of European Criminal Law, vol. 5, 2014, pp. 274–300.

91 M. Fincke, 'Das Verhältnis des Allgemeinen zum Besonderen Teil des Strafrechts', J. Schweitzer Verlag, 1975, p. 90.

scope of criminal liability, as they are read together with the rules of the special part.[92] The true relationship between the general and special parts is not a *lex generalis-lex specialis* relationship, but a complementary relationship. One cannot do without the other.

The indeterminacy of these concepts in European legislation creates three problems for European criminal law. First, the minimum scope of criminal liability in the Directives is not achieved because the minimum scope can only be clear if these concepts also have minimum scope.[93] Second, harmonisation suffers from divergences that are not immediately apparent but tend to reveal themselves during application. Third, provisions of the general part are a manifesto of a criminal liability theory as they measure the stance of every system *vis-à-vis* the Rule of Law. For example, a system that distinguishes between different forms of participation respects the principle of proportionality to a different level than a system that does not. A uniform approach to these concepts in a system also reflects a coherent and principled criminal law theory. Determining autonomous concepts of elements of *mens rea* and *actus reus* for European criminal law is therefore a positive step for the observance of the legality principle. It should be reminded that the present contribution is part of a project to construe a consistent and coherent general part of criminal law for the European Union.[94]

Should these concepts be codified in a specific European instrument? It seems hard to suggest this, as Article 83 TFEU does not leave much room for the adoption of a Directive on the general part. Moreover, such a Directive would be hard to reconcile with the subsidiarity principle as it would follow that the national concepts of the general part would have to be completely replaced. In particular, when it comes to the general part, diversity has always promoted more dialogue on legal theory and reflection, which has provided an opportunity for some of these doctrines to remain open and develop further.[95]

However, Directives should give at least some general definitions.[96] National authorities could either change their general part accordingly, or provide diverging definitions of the general elements for the specific offences of the Directive when necessary. This solution would likely result in divergence and fragmentation in the national legal system. However, it is not the case that the concepts of the general part are separated completely from the specific offences to which they apply. Such a solution would facilitate the function of the emergency brake in Article 83 para. 3

---

92 Ibid.

93 J. Blomsma, C. Peristeridou, 'The way forward: a general part of European criminal law', in F. Galli, A. Weyembergh, 'Approximation of substantive criminal law in the EU: the way forward', IEE, 2013, pp. 123–124.

94 Chapter I para. 4.1.

95 J. Blomsma, 'Mens Rea and defences in European criminal law', Intersentia, 2012; J. Keiler, 'Actus Reus and participation in European criminal law', Intersentia, 2013.

96 J. Blomsma, C. Peristeridou, 'The way forward: a general part of European criminal law', in F. Galli, A. Weyembergh, 'Approximation of substantive criminal law in the EU: the way forward', IEE, 2013, pp. 135–136.

TFEU. Concepts of the general part often incorporate fundamental decisions on criminal law theory that defines the character of national systems. Examples are strict liability, forms of participation, and minimum sanctions. Should the ECJ be left with the task to concretise these terms, national parliaments could lose their power to block choices on criminal liability that encroach heavily on the foundations of their national systems.

3.4. *Lex stricta*

For *lex stricta* two questions raised in Chapter VI need to be addressed.[97] First, the application of the legality principle to preliminary reference procedures and its binding force for national courts, and second, the incoherence of the obligation of conform interpretation must be examined.

3.4.1. Preliminary reference procedure

The preliminary rulings of the Court are, in principle, binding for the referring court and the interpretation of the ECJ is binding *erga omnes*.[98] This is necessary to ensure legal certainty, legitimate expectations and uniform interpretation of EU law.[99] The first question is whether *lex stricta* should also bind the ECJ in the interpretation of Directives based on Article 83 TFEU. This should be answered in the affirmative. The rationale of applying the legality principle to the ECJ has already been explained. The legality principle in judicial interpretation is a steering principle. It guides the mediation of different arguments in the interpretation of criminal liability and works to legitimise judicial interpretation. An additional rationale is that such judicial interpretation allows national courts to not only properly understand the *ratio decidenci* but also confidently defend and incorporate it in *ad hoc* cases. There are some cases where the ECJ considers the particular facts of a case, which colour the interpretation of the European definition of the criminalised conduct. This is particularly the case where the national courts ask the ECJ whether a particular situation would fall under the definition of an offence. It is in those situations that the interpretation of the ECJ inevitably includes an appreciation of the legality principle. In this regard, the ECJ should ensure that such interpretations are foreseeable or that the ruling will not prevent the national court from ensuring a foreseeable interpretation.

Therefore, for the interpretation of criminal law definitions, apart from using the recognised methodologies (e.g. grammatical and teleological), it is vital that the ruling distinguishes between the European policies concerned (battling human trafficking), the individual interests involved (e.g. freedom of movement, protection

97 Chapter VI para. 5.2. and 5.3.
98 J. Raitio, 'The Principle of Legal Certainty in EC Law', Kluwer, 2003, p. 87.
99 Ibid.

of human dignity and sexual autonomy) and the principles concerned (e.g. proportionality and principle of guilt). In particular, the policies of the EU depicted in a Directive should be translated into values that underpin the European criminal justice system to curtail instrumentalism.

Another question is whether national courts could legitimately disregard the ruling of the ECJ if it would result in unforeseeable criminalisation. At present, despite political resistance to the ECJ's rulings, national courts and parliaments seem to bestow legitimacy on the ECJ's approach to EU law.[100]

Disregarding ECJ rulings would violate the primacy of EU law and its unified interpretation. However, in exceptional cases such a possibility cannot be excluded. To approach this problem in a modestly pluralistic tone, and considering Maduro's principles of 'contrapunctual law',[101] both the ECJ and national courts need to follow a more dialectic reasoning in their decisions. They should consider both horizontal and vertical coherence and translate their arguments in universal terms to which other courts can relate. Because of the sensitive nature of criminal law, national courts would be entitled not to subject themselves to the European legal order should they find that the interpretation given by the ECJ: (i) does not respect human dignity;[102] (ii) arbitrarily prioritises policies over principles or rights to an extent that violates the backbone of a national legal order; (iii) cannot ensure a minimum of foreseeable criminalisation in the application of the ruling to an *ad hoc* case; (iv) or provides such an interpretation that would result in an excessive openness of the norm, such that neither future nor past case law can be reconciled, and thus a legislative action would be in order. This last scenario would also indicate an incorrect implementation of the Directive.

3.4.2. *Obligation of conform interpretation*

There are two issues to address regarding the obligation to conform interpretation. The first is about the *contra legem* restriction. In a coherent European legality principle, such a condition makes very little sense as demonstrated above.[103] Therefore, this obligation should be reformulated in European criminal law as obliging national courts to interpret national law in conformity to a Directive as long as the legality principle is not violated. Whether such interpretation would be

---

100 T. Tridimas, 'Precedence and the Court of Justice: a Jurisprudence of Doubt?', in J. Dickson, P. Eleftheriadis (eds), 'Philosophical Foundations of EU Law', Oxford University Press, 2012, pp. 307–330.

101 M.P. Maduro, 'Contrapunctual law: Europe's Constitutional Pluralism in Action', in N. Walker (ed), 'Sovereignty in Transition', Hart Publishing, 2003, pp. 526–530.

102 M. Kumm in M. Avbelj, J. Komárek (eds), 'Four Visions of Constitutional Pluralism', EUI Working Paper LAW, no. 2008/21, p. 26; M. Kumm, 'Rethinking Constitutional Authority: On the Structure and Limits of Constitutional Pluralism', in M. Avbelj, J. Komárek (eds), 'Constitutional Pluralism in the European Union and Beyond', Hart Publishing, 2012, p. 65.

103 Chapter VI para. 5.2. and Chapter VII para. 4.1.2.

contra legem and what this would suggest is covered by the function of the legality principle.

Second, while in principle this interpretation should follow the national *modus operandi*, the European legality principle should oblige the national courts to follow certain criteria in their interpretation to increase the transparency and controllability of their reasoning. Thus, national courts should: (i) always identify and distinguish between the principles, rights and policies pursued in the European and national legislation, (ii) weigh and give priority to principles and rights over policies, (iii) avoid giving an open connotation to a norm that cannot be defended in the future in other cases; the legality principle in the relational model requires that elements of generalisation must be applied in future similar cases, (iv) recognise that the effective application of EU law is only one of the principles to be considered and does not necessarily enjoy superiority (otherwise, judicial interpretation would be instrumentally guided by the effective application of EU law) and (v) preserve the ethical minimum of the national legal order, namely, human dignity.

One could wonder whether the method of interpretation in conformity loses its intrinsic nature and becomes 'just another' method that interprets national legislation considering international or supranational instruments. As stated in Chapter VI, it is not clear how the nature of this method would be in any case different from an interpretation in conformity with international law instruments.[104] This obligation does not introduce a new technique, but a new direction to the national courts' reasoning.[105] What is different is its intensity as an obligation and its top-down origin. In particular, this method is imposed as an obligation from the European legal order and does not stem in a discretionary manner from the national legal order. Yet, as a method in itself it is not substantially unique. In any case, by removing the necessary prioritisation of the effective application of EU law as policy, it cannot be said that such method loses its character. This is because national courts are still 'obliged' to consider the European instrument for their interpretation and make efforts to bring national definitions in line with the Directive. This obligation entails that national courts look into the will of the European legislator in this regard and compare it with the *telos* of the national legislation. Whether the first one will be prioritised though is a question of the principle of legality. It could be that the principle of legality would preclude the application of the provisions in the Directive. However, this does not mean that the national court did not comply with its obligations, or that it did not apply the method of conform interpretation. The character of this obligation does not depend on its results.

If such interpretation creates an intolerable vagueness in national norms that jeopardises individual autonomy for future cases, there is little to be done by a court. A legitimate use of this method lies in the manner in which national courts consider European policies and rights depicted in the definitions of criminal

104 Chapter VI para. 5.2.

105 M. Claes, 'The National Courts' Mandate in the European Constitution', Hart Publishing, 2006, p. 116.

liability in the Directive. What proves the national courts' sincere cooperation and loyalty to the European legal order is not pushing the limits of criminalisation with the sole goal of compliance to the EU policies, but their transparent articulation and sincere engagement in translating European criminal law's conflicting interests into national interests.

4. Final conclusions

The concluding remarks open with a reflection on the main research question and end with a discussion of future perspectives. This research was undertaken to develop an interpretation of the legality principle of European criminal law. The main research question necessitated this principle be adjusted and internalised in the European criminal justice system. To this end, a bottom-up approach was followed, where the *ratio* and application of this principle in national law were first evaluated. The national nucleus of the principle was then reshaped in the context of European criminal law.

4.1. Reflection on the chosen methodology

The methodology was chosen on the basis of the assumption that the principle of legality may elicit different interpretations and forms depending on its theoretical rationales, broader theories of justice and systemic particularities of the legal order within which it operates.[106] Such an assumption was subsequently justified by conducting research at the national and European levels. The open character of the principle of legality, and of principles in general, required a transparent appreciation of its nature. Because the principle of legality is open to interpretation, transparency is essential in justifying the versions of its functions and meaning in criminal law. A dialectic approach was followed, wherein the principle was broken apart into its different rationales and protective functions.[107]

This was further demonstrated both in a comparison of national systems and with the adaptation of the principle to EU law. For national systems, it was noticeable that this principle has been influenced by historical developments and different interpretations of the Rule of Law.[108] While it did not exist as such in the early common law system, it was explained that this does not result in an absence of forms of equivalent protection. For example, it was demonstrated that a form of precedent could also curtail arbitrariness in judicial law-making.[109] A dialectic approach is an eye-opener, as it liberates the principle of legality from its systemic origins. There can be alternative manners with which this principle can be expressed.

106 Chapter II para. 1.
107 Chapter III and Chapter IV.
108 Chapter IV para. 2.
109 Chapter IV para. 8.

Essentially, the openness of this principle, as illustrated at the national level, was an indispensable methodological factor for its adaptation to the European legal order. If the legality principle could be adjusted in the common law setting, which would *prima facie* contradict its traditional roots, such an adaptation could become a possibility as well for more challenging supranational legal systems.

Furthermore, the assumption that this principle is 'open' requires one to justify its nature using broader theories of criminal justice and variants of its theoretical rationales. Certainly, there are various ways to discuss legitimacy in criminal law. The structural and methodological choices made in this book aimed at maximising transparency of doctrinal construction. An important structural choice was to discuss the theoretical rationales of the legality principle as these are approached in the mainstream legal philosophy at the beginning of the book. By explaining the different interpretations of the Rule of Law and democracy, one gains a better understanding of what problems the principle of legality faces in the purely formal or procedural approaches of these concepts in later Chapters.[110] In addition, it facilitates the construction of criminal justice models in Chapter V. An important methodological choice was to discuss legitimacy with the three models of criminal justice. These models define legitimacy differently but they are also based on different interpretations of the theoretical rationales.

Next to transparency, using models of justice also encourages constructive debate on the choices made. The illustration of the models of justice and their fundamental assumptions offer transparency for the mantras of the legality principle. For example, one may criticise the assumption of the relational model that legal certainty should not be achieved in its maximum. For this, one could draw inspiration from the different interpretations of the principle of legality certainty, as explained in Chapter III.[111] Such a criticism would also entail that legal certainty, understood as reliability, is a superior value to the acceptability of decisions. The consequences of such an approach were discussed in Chapter V.[112] By subjecting the legality principle to different models of justice, one may understand the theoretical and practical implications that different choices could face. While certainly disagreements may arise from the choices made in this book, the methodology chosen provides a better understanding of the *ratio* behind every suggestion.

4.2. Comparative analysis

National research was divided into three Chapters to investigate the principle of legality at different levels: the *ratio* of this principle, its application in national law and its theoretical justification within broader models of criminal justice.

---

110 Chapter III para. 7.
111 Chapter III para. 6.1.
112 Chapter V para. 4.3.

The principle of legality was demonstrated to have a different status and application between common and continental systems. In continental systems, this principle was a mechanism that enforced a more positivistic approach to the Rule of Law. However, in the common law tradition protective guarantees for individuals were expressed only as a self-reservation of courts and the belief that their judgements shall be legitimised on the basis of commonly shared arguments. To some extent, the systems have followed an opposite path and English courts have had a prevalent position. Nevertheless, the growing dissatisfaction towards judicial activism and the strong political position of the British parliament today have created tension. This is largely demonstrated by the normative conflict between statutory and common law offences. Common law offences reflect the power to create and develop criminal liability, whereas statutory offences are about demarcation.[113]

An opposite tendency is observed among the continental systems. There, the starting point was a strict division of tasks between the *trias politica* and distrust towards the courts, as reflected in a rigid principle of legality. Recent social and technological developments have been difficult to handle. Judicial interpretation is increasingly important, and courts are now powerful institutions. This institutional tendency is more prevalent in Germany with the German Constitutional Court. However, normatively, it is the Dutch principle of legality that is more dynamic, partly because of Dutch legal pragmatism and partly because of the progressiveness of Dutch society. Dutch scholarship raises questions about the reformation of this principle. A debate regarding the transparency of judicial reasoning, common law features of the doctrine and a reformulation of its protective nature are prevalent in Dutch literature. In more subtle tones, similar discussions can be observed in German law; however, German literature puts more weight on existential questions regarding the legality principle, such as its erosion.[114]

The principle of legality is in transition in all systems for the same reason. The questions are not new. How can judicial arbitrariness be curtailed? How can legal certainty and acceptability, legitimacy and justice be reconciled? While these questions have always been difficult to answer, technology and multiculturalism have accelerated the need for justice and effectiveness.

Today, most differences among traditions have been greatly diminished, particularly because of ECtHR jurisprudence. A common interpretation of the legality principle regarding the concept of foreseeability has been largely adopted by national legal systems. However, the ECtHR has not only promoted a common view of the legality principle but also a new view. A 'rights-conception' means that this principle functions as a human right.[115] It is claimable, and it must be generalised and measured against other individual rights. This approach introduces a horizontal dimension to individual autonomy coloured by human dignity. Such an

113 Chapter IV para. 3 and 5.
114 Chapter IV para. 10.
115 Chapter IV para. 9.

interpretation of this principle was further developed under the relational model of criminal justice.

The goal of this research was not to provide solutions for national legal systems. Such a goal would require a more thorough and broader investigation of the selected national systems. However, as the three models of justice in Chapter V are used to justify and explain the national nucleus of the legality principle, it is submitted that a relational model would be the best starting point for resolving the problems of this principle in national legal systems.

4.3. Theoretical rationales

The *ratio* of this principle is founded in the concepts of individual autonomy, democracy, separation of powers and the Rule of Law. Additional principles, such as legal certainty and the principle of guilt, may also support the principle of legality. It was argued that these theoretical rationales could elicit different interpretations. The main antithesis that streamlines the interpretation of all theoretical rationales is the conflict between vertical and horizontal appreciation of individual liberty and autonomy.[116]

Individual autonomy and freedom are understood as requiring protection against state arbitrariness, in addition to protection against violations by others. Individuals thrive in a climate of certainty regarding their own actions and the actions of others. While the protection of individual liberty in its vertical dimension is considered a given, more problems occur with the assumption that the state should take up such protection in a horizontal manner. Essentially, this horizontal dimension is depicted in the character of law to mediate between conflicting interests and establish stable rules of conduct.[117] To avoid excessive paternalism, it is important to base any protection of individual liberty on human dignity. This conflict between negative and positive individual autonomy and negative and positive protection is further depicted in the models of justice.

This conflict is also met in the Rule of Law and the democratic principle. The formal and substantive versions of the Rule of Law and the procedural and substantive versions of democracy essentially reflect a similar conflict.[118] To what extent should substantive evaluations of human rights be part of these concepts? Ultimately, this brings the discussion back to the question of whether the state plays any role in the protection of autonomy in its horizontal dimension. If one is to assume that democracy reflects certain ethical values of the community, then such a protective character of the law results in an interpretation of legal certainty, including not only reliability but also the acceptability of law. Similarly, the separation of powers leaves behind a rigid separation and embraces the balanced

---

116 Chapter III para. 2.

117 Chapter III para. 2.2.

118 Chapter III para. 3 and 5.

approach of the *trias politica*.[119] As explained, the danger with accepting that the state should protect both versions of individual autonomy is that it could lead to paternalistic and anti-libertarian policies.[120] This danger is well analysed in legal theory and this conflict is one of the most difficult philosophical problems. In essence, it is a conflict between 'I' and 'us'.

This is further depicted in European criminal law. There is on-going tension between national and European communities. Individuals should be able to embrace their national affiliation and, at the same time, reach out to 'others'. The solution to conceiving both expressions as legitimate is based on the assumption that the law eventually must mediate between the two instead of denying one or the other. Both expressions of individual autonomy and both expressions of European citizenship are valid and have an ethical value.[121] They are both needed for individuals to be recognised as dignified members of a community. Should one approach these concepts with a narrower view, the core of individual liberty and autonomy would be negated.

4.4. Relational model of criminal justice

A relational model of European criminal justice justifies and legitimises current practices. The main advantage of this model of European criminal law lies within its definition of protection, its *Rechtskarakter*. This is a tripartite concept: (i) individual autonomy is protected in its vertical dimension (state arbitrariness), (ii) individual autonomy is protected in its horizontal dimension (from third parties) and (iii) individual autonomy, as expressed in the integrity of the legal order, is protected by future forms of totalitarianism, dogmatic institutional and political structures or political theories that threaten to monopolise criminal law (counterfacticity of legal principles).[122]

The default European instrumentalism can only be curtailed with a theory of criminal justice that controls the instrumental finality. By translating any instrumental use of criminal law as a protection, one is required to justify how instrumental goals and policies can protect individual rights. Such policies are legitimised in so far as they can be based on rights that are accepted within the European legal order. This has consequences, particularly for the use of competences at the European level. A strong vertical protection is also introduced. The EU is directly accountable to individuals, and such a bond is based on the freedom of movement and the concept of European citizenship. The latter is interpreted as requiring individual membership to national communities and the EU to be respected.

119 Chapter III para. 4.
120 Chapter III para. 5.
121 Chapter VII para. 4.2 and 8.2.
122 Chapter VII para. 6 and Chapter VIII para. 1.

The third definition of protection, the 'counterfacticity' of legal principles entails that the general nature of law must remain open to the dynamism of legal systems instead of being crystallised in time.[123] The integrity of the law should be protected from its monopolisation by totalitarian or dogmatic political theories. The concept of constitutional pluralism is of relevance. In essence, both theories of pluralism and the relational model protect criminal law from its use as a tool to claim superiority of sovereignty.[124] Frequently, criminal law has been the area where both national and European institutions unfurl their claims to pass a message for their supreme sovereignty. However, European criminal law based on a relational model remains open, and thus ready to react to these tendencies. By accepting the pluralistic nature of European criminal justice, criminal law reflects the mediation of conflicts of primacy. Pluralism protects the European legal order from becoming a melting pot and, at the same time, from monopolisation by destructive over-nationalism.

Arbitrariness was defined as stemming from both European and national authorities.[125] It is important to recognise this to prevent interlocking legal orders from having a negative impact on the protection of individuals. For example, a European legality principle should prevent national authorities from implementing a Directive in a vague manner and, at the same time, oblige the European legislator to ensure that this is possible. A broader interpretation of arbitrariness was also argued regarding the single European area of justice. This was particularly relevant to legal certainty and foreseeability. The concept of *cross-border foreseeability* should also be considered to be one of the justifications for the harmonisation of European criminal offences.[126] Furthermore, it was demonstrated that this concept should not be interpreted beyond the realm of the Treaties. One of its applications is the problem of the divergence of rules on jurisdiction. Thereby, the principle of legality should require that the EU take positive action and harmonise rules on jurisdiction in criminal law.[127]

4.5. Principle of legality

As demonstrated in Chapter VI, the principle of legality in EU law has already had a strong standing, and various fragments were collected regarding its different aspects. Of pivotal importance is the jurisprudence of the ECtHR.[128] In Chapter VIII, a theoretical and normative reconstruction of this principle was presented and answered the questions raised. The European principle of legality defended herein is a steering

123 Chapter VII para. 6.3.
124 Chapter VII para. 6.1.
125 Chapter VII para. 6.1 and 7.
126 Chapter VII para. 6.2 and Chapter VIII para 1.4.
127 Chapter VIII para. 1.4.
128 Chapter VI para. 1.

principle to secure the foreseeability, transparency, and controllability of European and national state actions in European criminal law through three main roles.

The *legitimising role* is concretised particularly in the use of criminal law competences. It is vital that exercising these competences be based on a transparent reasoning that distinguishes between policies of the European criminal system, principles and rights protected. The European legislator cannot legitimise its harmonising measures based only on the better enforcement of European policies and the facilitation of judicial cooperation in the battle against crime. These are policies that are not self-evidently justifiable, but they must be based on a concrete appreciation of the rights they defend in each case, as well as on whether these rights should be protected by European criminal law measures. In this way, principles, such as subsidiarity and proportionality, can be considered in a more substantial manner.[129]

The *distributive role* of the legality principle lies within the allocation of the responsibility of protection between European and national authorities. One element to be mentioned here is the *ratio* to ensure the legal certainty of European instruments. The application of the legality principle to European actors is explained by the co-responsibility of European and national authorities to protect individuals. In the vertical separation of powers, it is important to separate such responsibilities as well as to understand how they are shared. European actors should be obliged to positively ensure national actors can comply with the legality principle. This entails certainly more concrete obligations for the ECJ and the European legislator. Simultaneously, they should also refrain from obliging national authorities to violate such principles.[130]

The *normative role* of the legality principle relates to the application of its specific aspects. For *lex scripta,* the main conclusions referred to the democratic legitimation of the sources of criminal liability, as well as the emergence of a *lex nationalis.*[131] The latter is justified not only in the nature of Directives but also in the broader desire to respect the political autonomy expressed within the auspices of national communities. What was also argued is the necessity to establish a concept of precedent regarding interpretations of the ECJ. Such precedent does not negate the prevalence of the statute as the source of criminal liability but curtails judicial activism and casuistry.

For *lex certa,* I advocated for the harmonisation of rules on jurisdiction, as this is necessary to reduce problems related to *cross-border foreseeability.* Additionally, it is crucial to have more concrete definitions of offences in Directives, an indication of a unified minimum harmonisation and a presumption that, in the absence of the latter, national legislators may concretise ambiguous European norms.[132]

---

129 Chapter VIII para. 2.1.

130 Chapter VIII para. 2.2.

131 Chapter VIII para. 3.1.1 and 3.1.2.

132 Chapter VIII para. 1.4, 2.2 and 3.3.2.

Accordingly, the ECJ's role in annulment proceedings of vague Directives should be guided by specific criteria.

Finally, regarding the principle of *lex stricta*, the ECJ should not oblige national courts to accept an interpretation that could compromise foreseeability. On the other hand, they should also make it possible for national courts to comply with this requirement. The European *lex stricta* should be interpreted as obliging the ECJ to ensure that preliminary rulings related to criminal definitions in Directives include a test of foreseeability when necessary. This is important as the interpretation of Directives is influenced by the concrete facts of the case.[133] Regarding the methodology of interpretation, it is important to provide transparent and controllable reasoning that national courts can defend and accept as legitimate. Regarding the obligation of conform interpretation, it is clear that a more rationalised understanding of this method is necessary. Accordingly, the requirement of *contra legem* should be best left only for areas outside criminal law.[134]

4.6. Future perspectives

Based on what was observed in this research, in my view, future legal research with respect to the legality principle in European criminal law should continue in two directions. The first would be to investigate future developments in the European criminal law arena with the introduction of a directly enforceable system, as well as the impact of European criminal law on the national interpretation of the legality principle. The second direction should relate to interdisciplinary research regarding the sociological, criminological, and legal nature of European criminal law.

The first interesting development is the establishment of the EPPO. A direct system of European criminal law could also influence the application of the legality principle. For example, the demarcation between fraud attacks on both the European and national budgets or defining what constitutes participation in fraudulent activities would require an interpretation of European and national instruments. At the moment of concluding this book, such an institution has not yet been established; therefore, it is difficult to anticipate exactly what its influence would be on the principle of legality. The current reluctance of national systems to accept this institution adds further to the difficulties and compromises that must be made. To a large extent, the competence of the European prosecutor will depend on the interpretation of European fraud. The danger is that the antagonism of *Kompetenz-Kompetenz* between national and European prosecutors may have a negative impact on the interpretation of European fraud. The broader its scope, the more competence the European prosecutor will have. A relational model of European criminal justice, as defined herein, will undoubtedly protect European criminal law from instrumentalism in this regard. However, the actual practical problems that could

133 Chapter VIII para. 3.4.1.
134 Chapter VIII para. 3.4.2.

arise are largely undetermined at this stage. Therefore, it is important that research on the principle of legality continues to keep pace with the rapid developments.

Second, it would be valuable to investigate the impact that the European criminal justice has on the national interpretation of this principle. National interpretations of the legality principle are ultimately influenced to some extent by the European conception. Such an approach would require a top-down investigation of particular legal systems. The responsiveness of national legal orders to Europeanisation is a complimentary investigation that should be pursued to clarify the actual interactions between European and national interpretations of the legality principle. For example, the different methods of implementation should be researched empirically. Insight should be gained as to how these methods are used in practice and how national legislators make choices. The same can be said about the actual application of the obligation of conform interpretation.

Third, penal climates around Europe differ in large and small ways. This research offered insight into the differences between three legal systems with regard to the legality principle, and into which features played a role in its modern characteristics. However, as demonstrated, the current stance of legal principles, rules, and procedures in national legal systems is influenced by a variety of parameters. Future comparative research should revisit the differences and similarities among legal systems in criminal law to promote a better understanding of the matrix of European criminal justice. Such research should not remain within the narrow limits of statistical analyses or impact assessments, but it should also delve deeper into the character of legal systems and the reasons they operate in a specific manner.

Finally, future research on European criminal law should also be focused on the underlying sociological values of criminal law in the European setting. One of the conclusions of this book is that there is a growing concept of a single European criminal justice area where the impact of common individual and human rights creates a collective ethical consciousness. To this extent, it is necessary to approach the interaction between criminal justice systems as a question of cross-fertilising social communities. This is particularly true because a European public opinion is steadily emerging. The European elections and the economic crisis have brought national politics to the European scene and divided European public opinion into different groups that support different levels of solidarity. As criminal law is a science that is deeply influenced by the character of societies, more transversal studies should be conducted on the topics of European criminal law, sociology, and criminology. A broader interdisciplinary account of European criminal law would provide a better understanding of its foundations and future.

Selected Bibliography

Accetto, M., Zleptnig, S., 'The Principle of Effectiveness: Rethinking its Role in Community Law', European Public Law, vol. 11, 2005, pp. 375–403

Adams, M., van der Schyff, G., 'Constitutional Review by the Judiciary in the Netherlands', ZaöRV, vol. 66, 2006, pp. 399–413

Albrecht, P.-A., 'Securitized Societies', Intersentia, 2011

Allan, T.R.S,. 'The Rule of Law as the Rule of Reason: Consent and Constitutionalism', Law Quarterly Review, vol. 115, 1999, pp. 221–244

Allan, T.R.S., 'Fairness, Equality, Rationality: Constitutional Theory and Judicial Review', in C.F. Forsyth and I. Hare (eds), 'The Golden Metwand and the Crooked Cord', Oxford University Press, 1998, pp. 15–37

Allio, L., Durand, G., 'Montesquieu Wakes Up: Separation of Powers in the Council of Ministers', Working Paper of the European Policy Centre, 02/2003

Allison, J.W.F., 'Transplantation and Cross-fertilisation', in J. Beatson, T. Tridimas (eds), 'New Directions in European Public Law', Hart Publishing, 1998, pp. 169–182

Altena-Davidsen, J., 'De reikwijdte van de plicht tot conforme interpretatie in het strafrecht tegen de achtergrond van de verhouding tussen de Europese en de nationale rechtsorde', Ars Aequi, 2012, pp. 552–561

Alter, K.J., 'Establishing the Supremacy of European Law', Oxford University Press, 2001

Anagonostou, D., Psychogiotopoulou, E., 'Legal integration and EU governance in a multi-level systems: Can the post-Lisbon Union ensure a balance between freedom, security and justice? (EULEXIS)', Collaborative project, SSH.2011.5.2–2

Anderson, M., Apap, L., 'Striking a Balance Between Freedom, Security and Justice', CEPS, 2002

Anthony, G., 'The Europeanisation of United Kingdom Public Law', in R. Harmsen, T.M. Vilson (eds), 'Europeanisation: Institutions, Identities and Citizenship', Editions Rodopi B.V., 2000, pp. 83–104

Archibald, B., 'Restorative Justice and the Rule of Law: Rethinking Due Process through a Relational Theory of Rights', 2013, available at http://ssrn.com/abstract=2395224

Arden, Mrs Justice, 'Criminal Law at the Crossroads: the Impact of Human Rights from the Law Commissions' Perspective and the Need for a Code', Criminal Law Review, 1999, pp. 439–459

Arnull, A., 'Judicial Activism and the Court of Justice: How Should Academics Respond?', Maastricht Faculty of Law Working Paper, no. 2012–3 (available at http://ssrn.com/abstract=1986817)

Ashworth, A., Horder, J., 'Principles of Criminal Law', Oxford University Press, 2013

Ashworth, A., 'Interpreting Criminal Statutes: a Crisis of Legality?', Law Quarterly Review, vol. 107, 1991, pp. 419–449

Asp, P., 'The Substantive Criminal Law Competence of the EU', Jure, 2012

Atiyah, P.S., 'Common law and Statutory law', Modern Law Review, vol. 48, 1985 pp. 1–28

Avbelj, M., Komárek, J., 'Introduction', in M. Avbelj, J. Komárek (eds), 'Constitutional Pluralism in the European Union and Beyond', Hart Publishing, 2012, pp. 1–16
Avbelj, M., 'Questioning EU Constitutionalisms', German Law Journal, vol. 9, 2008, pp. 1–26
Bader, V., Hirs, P., 'Associative Democracy: the Real Third Way', Frank Cass Publishing, 2001
Baker, E., 'The United Kingdom and its Protocol 36 Opt-out: Is Police and Judicial Cooperation in Criminal Matters within the EU losing Momentum?', European Journal of Crime, Criminal law and Criminal Justice, vol. 21, 2013, pp. 237–245
Beauvais, P., 'Le principe de la légalité pénale dans le droit de l'Union européenne', Thèse, Université Paris X Nanterre UFR, 1 December 2006
Beccaria, C., 'An essay on Crimes and Punishments', Branden Press Inc, 1983
Beck, G., 'The Legal Reasoning of the Court of Justice of the EU', Hart Publishing, 2012
Beck, U., 'Cosmopolitan vision', Polity Press, 2006
Beck, U., 'Risk Society – Towards a New Modernity', Sage, 1992
Beck'scher Onlinekommentar zum StGB, von Heintschel-Heinegg, 2011
Bell, J., 'Mechanisms of Cross-fertilization of Administrative Law in Europe', in J. Beatson, T. Tridimas (eds), 'New Directions in European Public law', Hart Publishing, 1998, pp. 147–167
Bell, J., Engle, G., 'Cross on Statutory Interpretation', Butterworths, 1995
Bellamy, R., 'The Political Form of the Constitution: the Separation of Powers, Rights and Representative Democracy', Political Studies, vol. 44, 1996, pp. 436–456
Bentham, J., 'Rationale of Judicial Evidences', 1843
ten Berge, G., Widdershoven, R., 'The Principle of Legitimate Expectations in Dutch Constitutional and Administrative Law', Netherlands Reports to the Fifteen International Congress of Comparative Law, Bristol, 1998, pp. 421–452
Bernardi, A., 'Nullum crimen, nulla poena sine lege between European law and national law', in M.C. Bassiouni, V. Militello, H. Satzger (eds), 'European cooperation in penal matters: issues and perspectives', Cedam, 2008, pp. 87–117
Berlin, I., 'Four Essays on Liberty', Oxford University Press, 1971
Besselink, L., Pennings, F., Prechal, S., 'Introduction: Legality in Multiple Legal Orders', in L. Besselink, F. Pennings, S. Prechal (eds), 'The Eclipse of the Legality Principle in the European Union', Kluwer, 2011, pp. 3–9
Beyleveld, D., Kirkham, R., Towend, D., 'Which presumption? A critique of the House of Lords' reasoning on retrospectivity and the Human Rights Act', Legal Studies, vol. 22, 2002, pp. 185–207
Bignami, F., 'Rethinking the Legal Foundations of the European Constitutional Order: the Lessons of the New Historical Research', American University International Law Review, vol. 28, 2013, pp. 1311–1335
Bigo, D., 'Liberty, whose Liberty? The Hague Programme and the conception of Freedom' in S. Carrera, T. Balzacq (eds), 'Security versus Freedom? A challenge for Europe's future', Ashgate Publishing, 2006, pp. 35–44
Lord Bingham, 'The Rule of Law', Cambridge Law Journal, vol. 66, 2007, pp. 67–85

Lord Bingham, 'A Criminal Code: Must we wait for ever?', Criminal Law Review, 1998, pp. 694–696
Blankenburg, E., 'Patterns of legal culture: The Netherlands Compared to Neighboring Germany', The American Journal of Comparative Law, vol. 46, 1998, pp. 1–41
Blomsma, J., Peristeridou, C., 'The way forward: a general part of European criminal law', in F. Galli, A. Weyembergh, 'Approximation of substantive criminal law in the EU: the way forward', IEE, 2013, pp. 117–138
Blomsma, J., 'Mens rea and defences in European criminal law', Intersentia, 2012
de Boer, N., 'Addressing rights divergences under the Charter: Melloni', Common Market Law Review, vol. 50, 2013, pp. 1083–1104
von Bogdandy, A., 'Founding Principles of EU Law: a Theoretical and Doctrinal Sketch', European Law Journal, vol. 16, 2010, pp. 95–111
Borgers, M.J., 'De communicatieve strafrechter', in W.J.M. Voermans, M.J. Borgers, C.H. Sieburgh, 'Controverses rondom legaliteit en legitimatie', Kluwer, 2011, pp. 103–185
Böse, M., 'Choice of Forum and Jurisdiction', in M. Luchtman (ed), 'Choice of forum in cooperation against EU financial crime: freedom, security and justice and the protection of specific EU-interests', Eleven International Publishing, 2013, pp. 73–88
de Búrca, G., 'Sovereignty and the Supremacy Doctrine of the European Court of Justice', in N. Walker (ed), 'Sovereignty in Transition', Hart Publishing, 2003, pp. 449–460
de Búrca, G., Gardner, G., 'The Codification of the Criminal Law', Oxford Journal of Legal Studies, vol. 10, 1990, pp. 559–571
Buss, S., 'Personal Autonomy', The Stanford Encyclopedia of Philosophy (Winter 2014 Edition), E. N. Zalta (ed), URL = http://plato.stanford.edu/archives/win2014/entries/personal-autonomy/
Cannizzaro, E., Bonafè, B.I., 'Beyond the archetypes of modern legal thought', in M. Maduro, K. Tuori, S. Sankari (eds), 'Transnational Law: Rethinking European Law and Legal Thinking', Cambridge University Press, 2014, pp. 78–96
Carrera, S., Balzacq, T., 'The Hague Programme: the long road to Freedom, Security and Justice', in S. Carrera, T. Balzacq (eds), 'Security versus Freedom? A challenge for Europe's future', Ashgate Publishing, 2006, pp. 1–32
Carter, I., 'Positive and Negative Liberty', The Stanford Encyclopedia of Philosophy (Spring 2012 Edition), E.N. Zalta (ed), URL = http://plato.stanford.edu/archives/spr2012/entries/liberty-positive-negative/
Chalmers, D., Davies, G., Monti, G., 'European Union Law: Cases and Materials', Cambridge University Press, 2010
Christiano, T., 'Democracy', The Stanford Encyclopedia of Philosophy (Fall 2008 Edition), E.N. Zalta (ed), URL = http://plato.stanford.edu/archives/fall2008/entries/democracy/
Christman, J., 'Autonomy in Moral and Political Philosophy', The Stanford Encyclopedia of Philosophy (Winter 2014 Edition), E.N. Zalta (ed), URL = http://plato.stanford.edu/archives/win2014/entries/autonomy-moral/
Claes, E., 'Criminal Justice, Legality and Human Dignity', in E. Claes, R. Foqué, T. Peters (eds), 'Punishment, Restorative Justice and the Morality of Law', Intersentia, 2005, pp. 15–56

Claes, E., 'Legaliteit en rechtsvinding in het strafrecht', Universitaire Pers Leuven, 2003
Claes, M., 'The National Courts' Mandate in the European Constitution', Hart Publishing, 2006
Claessen, J., 'Misdaad en straf: een herbezinning op het strafrecht vanuit mystiek perspectief', Wolf Legal Publishers, 2010
Cleiren, C.P.M., 'Evolueren naar meer horizontale en multi-dimensionale verhoudingen in het strafrecht', Kluwer, 2010
Comandé, G., 'The Fifth European Union Freedom: Aggregating Citizenship... around Private Law', in H.-W. Micklitz (ed), 'The Constitutionalisation of European Private law', Oxford University Press, 2014, pp. 61–93
Conway, G., 'The Limits of Legal Reasoning and the European Court of Justice', Cambridge University Press, 2012
Copi, I., Cohen, C., McMahon, K., 'Introduction to Logic', Pearson, 2011
Corstens, G., Pradel, J., 'Het Europese strafrecht', Kluwer, 2003
Craig, P., de Búrca, G., 'EU Law: Texts, Cases and Materials', Oxford University Press, 2011
Dahl, R.A., 'Democracy and its Critics', Yale University Press, 1989
Damaška, M.R., 'The Faces of Justice and State Authority', Yale University Press, 1986
Davies, G., 'Constitutional Disagreement in Europe and the Search for Pluralism', in M. Avbelj, J. Komárek, 'Constitutional Pluralism in the European Union and Beyond', Hart Publishing, 2012, pp. 269–284
Dawson, M., 'The Political Face of Judicial Activism: Europe's Law – Politics Imbalance', Maastricht Faculty of Law Working Paper, no. 2012–1 (available at http://ssrn.com/abstract=1984636)
Dehousse, R., 'Beyond Representative Democracy: Constitutionalism in a Polycentric Polity', in J.H.H. Weiler, M. Wind, 'European Constitutionalism Beyond the State', Cambridge University Press, 2003, pp. 135–156
Dehousse, R., 'Comparing National and EC Law: the Problem of the Level Analysis', American Journal of Comparative law, vol. 42, 1994, pp. 761–781
Deitelhoff, N., Steffek J. (eds), 'Was bleibt vom Staat? Demokratie, Recht und Verfassung im globalen Zeitalter', Campus Verlag, 2009
Delmas-Marty, M., 'Towards a Truly Common Law: Europe as a Laboratory for Legal Pluralism', Cambridge University Press, 2002
Devuyst, Y., 'The European Unions' institutional balance after the Treaty of Lisbon: 'Community Method' and 'Democratic Deficit' Reassessed', Georgetown Journal of International Law, vol. 39, 2008, pp. 247–325.
Dicey, A.V., 'Introduction to the study of the law of the constitution', Macmillan, 1959
van Dijk, A.A., 'Strafrechtelijke aansprakelijkheid heroverwogen. Over opzet, schuld, schulduitsluitingsgronden en straf', Maklu, 2008
Doorenbos, D.R., 'EG-recht en strafwetgeving', Delikt en Delinkwent, vol. 22, 1992, pp. 1041–1057
Douglas-Scott, S., 'Rethinking Justice for the EU', in M. Maduro, K. Tuori, S. Sankari (eds), 'Transnational Law: Rethinking European Law and Legal Thinking', Cambridge University Press, 2014, pp. 206–247

Douglas-Scott, S., 'The Problem of Justice in the European Union', in J. Dickson, P. Eleftheriadis (eds), 'Philosophical Foundations of EU Law', Oxford University Press, 2012, pp. 412–448
Douglas-Scott, S., 'The Rule of Law in the European Union – Putting the Security into the Area of Freedom, Security and Justice', European Law Review, vol. 29, 2004, pp. 219–242
Driver, J., 'The History of Utilitarianism', The Stanford Encyclopedia of Philosophy (Winter 2014 Edition), E.N. Zalta (ed), URL = http://plato.stanford.edu/archives/win2014/entries/utilitarianism-history/
Duff, A., 'Legal Punishment', The Stanford Encyclopedia of Philosophy (Summer 2013 Edition), E.N. Zalta (ed), URL = http://plato.stanford.edu/archives/sum2013/entries/legal-punishment/
Duff, A., 'Theories of Criminal Law', The Stanford Encyclopedia of Philosophy (Summer 2013 Edition), E.N. Zalta (ed), URL = http://plato.stanford.edu/archives/sum2013/entries/criminal-law/
Dupont, L., 'Beginselen van behoorlijke strafrechtsbedeling', Gouda Quint, 1979
Dworkin, R., 'Law's Empire', Hart Publishing, 2006
Dworkin, R., 'A Matter of Principle', Harvard University Press, 1985
Dworkin, R., 'Taking Rights Seriously', Duckworth, 1977
Editorial Comment, 'Two speed European Citizenship? Can the Lisbon Treaty help close the gap?' Common Market Law Review, vol. 45, 2008, pp. 1–11
Elholm, T., 'Does EU Criminal Cooperation Necessarily Mean Increased Repression?', European Journal of Crime, Criminal Law and Criminal Justice, vol. 17, 2009, pp. 191–226
Endicott, T., 'Vagueness in Law', Oxford University Press, 2000
Engisch, K., 'Einführung in das juristische Denken', W. Kohlhammer GmbH, 2005
Etzioni, A., 'The New Golden Rule', Basic Books, 1996
European Criminal Policy Initiative, 'A Manifesto on European Criminal Policy', ZIS, vol. 12, 2009, pp. 707–716
Fabienne, P., 'Political Legitimacy', The Stanford Encyclopedia of Philosophy (Winter 2014 Edition), E.N. Zalta (ed), URL = http://plato.stanford.edu/archives/win2014/entries/legitimacy/
Feuerbach, P.J.A., 'Lehrbuch des gemeinen in Deutschland gültigen peinlichen Rechts', 1801
Fincke, M., 'Das Verhältnis des Allgemeinen zum Besonderen Teil des Strafrechts', J. Schweitzer Verlag, 1975
Fletcher, G.P., 'Basic Concepts of Criminal Law', Oxford University Press, 1998
Fletcher, M., Lööf, R., Gilmore, B., 'EU Criminal Law and Justice', Edward Elgar Publishing, 2008
Foqué, R., 'Criminal Justice in a Democracy: Towards a Relational Conception of Criminal Law and Punishment', Criminal Law and Philosophy, vol. 2, 2008, pp. 207–227
Foqué, R., 't Hart, A.C., 'Instrumentaliteit en Rechtsbescherming', Gouda Quint, Kluwer, 1990

Franken, A.A., 'Casuïstiek en legaliteit in het materieel strafrecht', Delikt en Delinkwent, vol. 67, 2006, pp. 949–958

Fuller, L.L., 'The Morality of Law', Yale University Press, 1969

Gallant, K.S., 'The principle of legality in international and comparative criminal law', Cambridge University Press, 2009

Gardner, J., 'On the General Part of the Criminal Law', in A. Duff (ed), 'Philosophy and the Criminal Law: Principle and Critique', Cambridge University Press, 1998, pp. 205–256

Garland, D., 'The Culture of Control – Crime and Social Order in Contemporary Society', Oxford University, Press, 2001

Gay, P., 'The Enlightenment: The Rise of Modern Paganism', W.W. Norton and Company, 1966

Gearty, C., 'Principles of Human Rights Adjudication', Oxford University Press, 2004

Geitmann, R., 'Bundesverfassungsgericht und "offene" Normen', Duncker & Humblot, 1971

van Gerven, W., 'The European Union – A Polity of States and Peoples', Hart Publishing, 2005

Gibbs, A.K., 'Reasoned Balance in Europe's Area of Freedom, Security and Justice', European Law Journal, vol. 17, pp. 121–137

Goodhart, A.L., 'The Shaw case: the law and the public morals', Law Quarterly Review, vol. 77, 1961, pp. 560–568

Gottlieb, G.A.G., 'Relationism: Legal Theory for a Relational Society', University of Chicago Law Review, vol. 50, 1983, pp. 567–612

Green, L., 'Legal Positivism', The Stanford Encyclopedia of Philosophy (Fall 2009 Edition), E.N. Zalta (ed), URL = http://plato.stanford.edu/archives/fall2009/entries/legal-positivism/

Groenhuijsen, M.S., 'Enkele aspecten van rechterlijk 'prospective overruling' in het straf(proces)recht', in M.S. Groenhuijsen, J.B.H.M. Simmelink (eds), 'Glijdende schalen' (Liber amicorum J. de Hullu), Wolf Legal Publishers, 2003, pp. 185–202

Groenhuijsen, M.S., 'Verlenging of afschaffing van verjaringstermijnen in het strafrecht', Delikt en Delinkwent, 2002, pp. 813–822

Groenhuijsen, M.S., Wiemans, F.P.E., 'Van electriciteit naar computercriminaliteit', Gouda Quint, 1989

Groenhuijsen, M.S., 'Straf en Wet', Gouda Quint, 1987

Gröning, L., 'A Criminal Justice System or a System Deficit? Notes on the System Structure of the EU Criminal Law', European Journal of Crime, Criminal Law and Criminal Justice, vol. 18, 2010, pp. 115–137

Grote, R., 'Rule of Law, Rechtsstaat and 'Etat de droit'', in C. Starck (ed), 'Constitutionalism, Universalism and Democracy – Comparative Analysis', Nomos Verlagsgesellschaft, 1999, pp. 269–306

Grünwald, G., 'Bedeutung und Begründung des Satzes nulla poena sine lege', ZStW, vol. 76, 1964, pp. 1–18

Guild, E., 'Crime and the EU's Constitutional Future in an Area of Freedom, Security and Justice', European Law Journal, vol. 10, 2004, pp. 218–234

Gutwirth, S., 'Waarheidsaanspraken in recht en wetenschap', Maklu, 1993
Habermas, J., 'The Concept of Human Dignity and the Realistic Utopia of Human Rights', in 'The Crisis of the European Union – A Response', Polity Press, 2012, pp. 71–100
Habermas, J., 'The Crisis of the European Union – A Response', Polity Press, 2012
Habermas, J., 'Between Naturalism and Religion', Polity Press, 2008
Habermas, J., 'Between Facts and Norms', Polity Press, 1997
Hale, M., 'History of the Pleas of the Crown', vol. 1, 1736
't Hart, A.C., 'Recht als schild van Perseus', Gouda Quint, 1991
Hart, H.L.A., 'The Concept of Law', Oxford University Press, 2012
Hart, H.L.A., 'Punishment and Responsibility: Essays in the Philosophy of Law', Oxford University Press, 1968
Hassemer, W., 'Einführung in die Grundlagen des Strafrechts', Verlag C.H. Beck, 1990
Hassemer, W., 'Tatbestand und Typus', Carl Heymanns Verlag, 1968
Hayek, F.A., 'The Road to Serfdom', Routledge, 1976
Heidegger, M., 'Identität und Differenz', Pfullingen, 1957
Held, D., 'Models of Democracy', Stanford University Press, 2006
Held, D., 'Democracy and the Global Order: From the Modern State to Cosmopolitan Governance', Polity Press, 1995
Herlin-Karnell, E., 'Europe's Area of Freedom, Security and Justice Through the Prism of Constitutionalism: Why the EU Needs a Grammar of Justice to Improve Its Legitimacy', Discussion Paper SP IV 2014–801, Wissenschaftszentrum Berlin für Sozialforschung, 2014
Herlin-Karnell, E., 'The Constitutional Dimension of European Criminal Law', Hart Publishing, 2012
Herlin-Karnell, E., 'What Principles Drive (or Should Drive) European Criminal Law?', German Law Journal, vol. 11, 2010, pp. 1115–1130.
Hildebrandt, M., 'European Criminal law and European Identity', Criminal Law and Philosophy, vol. 1, 2007, pp. 57–78
Horkheimer, M., Adorno, T.W., 'Dialectic of Enlightenment', Stanford University Press, 2002
de Hullu, J., 'Materieel strafrecht', Kluwer, 2012
Hulstijn, W., van Rossem, J.W., 'Het *Lissabon-Urteil*: Pluralisme op Duitse voorwaarden', in J.M.J. van Rijn van Alkemade, J. Uzman, 'Soevereiniteit of pluralisme', Wolf Legal Publishers, 2011, pp. 21–46
Huomo-Kettunen, M., 'EU Criminal Policy at a Crossroads Between Effectiveness and Traditional Restraints for the Use of Criminal Law', New Journal of European Criminal Law, vol. 5, 2014, pp. 301–326
Jacqué, J.-P., 'The Principle of Institutional Balance', Common Market Law Review, vo. 41, 2004, pp. 383–391
Jähnke, B., 'Zur Erosion des Verfassungssatzes "Keine Strafe ohne Gesetz"', ZIS, vol. 7, 2010, pp. 463–470
Joecks, W., Miebach, K., 'Münchener Kommentar zum Strafgesetzbuch', Verlag C.H. Beck, 2011

Jones, A., Sufrin, B., 'EU Competition Law: Texts, Cases and Materials', Oxford University Press, 2011

de Jong, D.H., 'Naar een common law-conceptie van legaliteit?', Delikt en Delinkwent, vol. 29, 1999, pp. 687–690

Jörg, N., Kelk, C., Klip, A., 'Strafrecht met mate', Kluwer, 2012

Jung, H., 'L'etat et moi: Some Reflections on the Relationship Between the Criminal Law and the State', European Journal of Crime, Criminal Law and Criminal Justice, vol. 6, 1998, pp. 208–215

Juratowitch, B., 'Retroactivity and the Common Law', Hart Publishing, 2008

Ishay, M., 'European Integration: The Enlightenment Legacy', History of European Ideas, vol. 19, 1994, pp. 207–213

Israel, J.I., 'Radical Enlightenment, Philosophy and the Making of Modernity 1650–1750', Oxford University Press, 2001

Kaiafa-Gbandi, M., 'Approximation of substantive criminal law provisions in the EU and fundamental principles of criminal law', in F. Galli, A. Weyembergh, 'Approximation of substantive criminal law in the EU: the way forward', IEE, 2013, pp. 85–116

Kaiafa-Gbandi, M., 'Οι επιλογές του N 3943/2011 για την οριοθέτηση του αξιοποίνου των φορολογικών αδικημάτων: Μια ατυχής προσπάθεια αυξημένης προστασίας των περιουσιακών απαιτήσεων του δημοσίου', Ποινική Δικαιοσύνη, vol. 12, 2011, pp. 1307–1320

Kaiafa-Gbandi, M., 'The development towards harmonisation within criminal law in the European Union – a citizen's perspective', European Journal of Crime, Criminal Law and Criminal Justice, vol. 7, 2001, pp. 239–263

Kaufmann, A., 'Analogie und "Natur der Sache"', R. v. Decker & C. F. Mueller, 1982

Keiler, J., 'Actus Reus and participation in European criminal law', Intersentia, 2013

Kelk, C., 'Studieboek materieel strafrecht', Kluwer, 2010

Kelsen, H., 'General Theory of Law and State', Harvard University Press, 1945

Kent Wright, J., 'Jonathan Israel, Democratic Enlightenment: Philosophy, Revolution, and Human Rights 1750–1790', H-France Forum, vol. 9, 2014, pp. 1–25

Kiikeri, M., 'Comparative legal reasoning and European law', Kluwer, 2001

Kim, I.-S., 'Der Gesetzlichkeitsgrundsatz im Lichte der Rechtsidee', in B. Schünemann, H. Achenbach (eds), 'Festschrift für Claus Roxin zum 70. Geburtstag am 15. Mai 2001', De Gruyter, 2001, pp. 119–143

van Klink, B.M.J., 'Bedreigt rechtsvinding de rechtszekerheid? Een kritisch-hermeneutische visie op de rol van de rechter in het materiële strafrecht', Delikt en Delinkwent, vol. 31, 2001, pp. 685–710

van Klink, B.M.J., Royakkers, L.M.M., 'Analogie en rechtszekerheid in het strafrecht', Delikt en Delinkwent, vol. 29, 1999, pp. 977–997

Klip, A., 'Contra legem', European Journal of Crime, Criminal Law and Criminal Justice, vol. 22, 2014, pp. 105–113

Klip, A., 'European Criminal Law: An Integrative Approach', Intersentia, 2012

Knigge, G., 'Verandering van wetgeving', Gouda Quint, 1984

Kokott, J., Sobotta, C., 'The Kadi Case – Constitutional Core Values and International Law – Finding the Balance?', The European Journal of International Law, vol. 23, 2012, pp. 1015–1024

Kolb, R. 'Réflexions de philosophie du droit international', Editions Bruylant, 2003

Komárek, J., 'European constitutionalism and the European arrest warrant: contrapunctual principles in disharmony', Common Market Law Review, vol. 44, 2007, pp. 9–40

Koopmans, T., 'The Birth of European law at the Crossroads of Legal Traditions', American Journal of Comparative law, vol. 39, 1991, pp. 493–507

Krey, V., 'Keine Strafe ohne Gesetz', Walter de Gruyter, 1983

Kristen, F.G.H., 'Misbruik van voorwetenschap naar Europees recht', Wolf Legal Publishers, 2004

Kumm, M., 'Rethinking Constitutional Authority: On the Structure and Limits of Constitutional Pluralism', in M. Avbelj, J. Komárek (eds), 'Constitutional Pluralism in the European Union and Beyond', Hart Publishing, 2012, pp. 39–65

Kumm, M., in M. Avbelj, J. Komárek (eds), 'Four Visions of Constitutional Pluralism', EUI Working Paper LAW, no. 2008/21

Kumm, M., 'The Jurisprudence of Constitutional Conflict: Constitutional Supremacy in Europe Before and After the Constitutional Treaty', European Law Journal, vol. 11, 2005, pp. 262–307

Legrand, P., 'The Impossibility of Legal Transplants', Maastricht Journal of European and Comparative Law, vol. 4, 1997, pp. 111–124

Lemmel, H.–P., 'Unbestimmte Strafbarkeitsvoraussetzungen im Besonderen Teil des Strafrechts und der Grundsatz nullum crimen sine lege', Duncker & Humblot, 1970

Lenaerts, K., Gutiérrez-Fons, J.A., 'To Say What the Law of the EU Is: Methods of Interpretation and the European Court of Justice', EUI Working Paper AEL 2013/9

Lenaerts, K., Gutiérrez-Fons, J.A., 'The Constitutional Allocation of Powers and General Principles of EU law', Common Market Law Review, vol. 47, 2010, pp. 1629–1669

Lenaerts, K., 'Interlocking Legal Orders in the European Union and Comparative Law', International and Comparative Law Quarterly, vol. 52, 2003, pp. 873–906

Lenaerts, K., 'Some Reflections on the Separation of Powers in the European Community', Common Market Law Review, vol. 28, 1991, pp. 11–35

Lepard, B., 'Customary International Law: A New Theory with Practical Applications', Cambridge University Press, 2010

Lindahl, H., 'Sovereignty and Representation in the European Union', in N. Walker (ed), 'Sovereignty in Transition', Hart Publishing, 2003, pp. 87–114

Lööf, R., '54 CISA and the principles of *ne bis in idem*', European Journal of Crime, Criminal Law and Criminal Justice, vol. 15, 2007, pp. 309–334

Luchtman, M., 'Choice of forum and the prosecution of cross-border crime in the European Union – what role for the legality principle?', in M. Luchtman (ed), 'Choice of forum in cooperation against EU financial crime: freedom, security and justice and the protection of specific EU-interests', Eleven International Publishing, 2013, pp. 3–61

Luhmann, N., 'Rechtssystem und Rechtsdogmatik', Verlag W. Kohlhammer GmbH, 1974

MacCallum, G.C.Jr., 'Negative and Positive Freedom', Philosophical Review, vol. 76, 1967, pp. 312–334
MacCormick, N., 'Rhetoric and the Rule of Law', Oxford University Press, 2005
MacCormick, N., 'Beyond the Sovereign State', Modern Law Review, vol. 56, 1993, pp. 1–18
MacCulloch, D., 'A History of Christianity', Penguin Books, 2010
Maduro, M.P., 'Three Claims of Constitutional Pluralism', in M. Avbelj, J. Komárek, 'Constitutional Pluralism in the European Union and Beyond', Hart Publishing, 2012, pp. 67–84
Maduro M.P., in M. Avbelj, J. Komárek (eds), 'Four Visions of Constitutional Pluralism', EUI Working Paper LAW, no. 2008/21
Maduro, M.P., 'Interpreting European Law: Judicial Adjudication in a Context of Constitutional Pluralism', European Journal of Legal Studies, vol.1, 2007
Maduro, M.P., 'Contrapunctual law: Europe's Constitutional Pluralism in Action', in N. Walker (ed), 'Sovereignty in Transition', Hart Publishing, 2003, pp. 501–538
Marin, L., 'Learning from the Lessons of 10 Years of Practice with the European Arrest Warrant', New Journal of European Criminal Law, vol. 5, 2014, pp. 327–348
Markezinis, B., 'Judicial Style and Reasoning in England and Germany', The Cambridge Law Journal, vol. 59, 2000, pp. 294–309
Massa, A.-S., 'Jurisdiction in England and Wales and in the Netherlands: a Comparative Appraisal with a European Touch', in A. Klip (ed), 'Substantive Criminal Law of the European Union', Maklu, 2011, pp. 103–121
McIlwain, C.H., 'The English Common Law, Barrier against Absolutism', American Historical Review, vol. 49, 1943, pp. 23–31
Melander, S., 'Effectiveness in EU Criminal Law and its Effects on the General Part of Criminal Law', New Journal of European Criminal Law, vol. 5, 2014, pp. 274–300
Mertens, T., 'Nazism, Legal Positivism and Radbruch's Thesis on Statutory Injustice', Law and Critique, vol. 14, 2003, pp. 277–295
Meyer, F., 'Strafrechtsgenese in Internationalen Organisationen', Nomos, 2012
Michaels, R., 'On Liberalism and Legal Pluralism', in M. Maduro, K. Tuori, S. Sankari (eds), 'Transnational Law: Rethinking European Law and Legal Thinking', Cambridge University Press, 2014, pp. 122–142
Mitsilegas, V., 'From Overcriminalisation to Decriminalisation – The Many Faces of Effectiveness in European Criminal Law', New Journal of European Criminal Law, vol. 5, 2014, pp. 415–424
Monar, J., 'The Dynamics of Justice and Home Affairs: Laboratories, Driving Factors and Costs', Journal of Common Market Studies, vol. 39, 2001, pp. 747–764
Montesquieu, 'De l'esprit des lois', 1748
Muir, E., van der Mei, A.-P., 'The EU Citizenship Dimension of the Area of Freedom, Security and Justice', in M. Luchtman (ed), 'Choice of forum in cooperation against EU financial crime: freedom, security and justice and the protection of specific EU-interests', Eleven International Publishing, 2013, pp. 123–142

Murphy, C., 'Lon Fuller and the Moral Value of the Rule of Law', Law and Philosophy, vol. 24, 2005, pp. 239–262
Naucke, W., 'Über Generalklauseln und Rechtsanwendung im Strafrecht', JCB Mohr, 1973
Nettesheim, M., 'Developing a Theory of Democracy for the European Union', Berkeley Journal of International Law, vol. 23, 2005, pp. 358–400
Nicolaïdes, K., 'The Idea of European Demoicracy', in J. Dickson, P. Eleftheriadis (eds), 'Philosophical Foundations of EU Law', Oxford University Press, 2012, pp. 247–274
Nilsson, H.G., 'How to combine minimum rules with maximum legal certainty?', Europättslig Tidskrift, 2011, pp. 663–675
Nottingham J. (ed), 'Western philosophy, an anthology', Blackwell Publishing, 2008
Olsen, L.P., 'The Many Faces of Europeanization', Journal of Common Market Studies, vol. 40, 2002, pp. 921–952
Oppenheim, F.E., 'Dimensions of Freedom: An Analysis', St. Martin's Press, 1961
Ormerod, D., 'Smith and Hogan's Criminal law', Oxford University Press, 2011
Outram, D., 'The Enlightenment', Cambridge University Press, 2013
Packer, H.L., 'The Limits of the Criminal Sanction', Stanford University Press, 1968
Paunio, E., 'Beyond Predictability – Reflections on Legal Certainty and the Discourse Theory of Law in the EU Legal Order', German Law Journal, vol. 10, 2009, pp. 1469–1493
Pech, L., 'The Rule of Law as a Constitutional Principle of the European Union', Jean Monnet Working Paper 04/2009 (available at SSRN: http://ssrn.com/abstract=1463242).
Peers, S., 'Mutual recognition and criminal law in the European Union: Has the Council got it wrong?', Common Market Law Review, vol. 41, 2004, pp. 5–36
Peristeridou, C., 'The Principle of "Lex Certa" in National Law and European Perspectives.' in A. Klip (ed), 'Substantive Criminal Law of the European Union', Maklu, 2011, pp. 69–95
Peter, F.K., 'Streichung des §370a AO', Steuer und Studium, 2008, pp. 428–430
Peters, A.A.G., 'Het rechtskarakter van het strafrecht', Kluwer, 1972
Pocock, J.G.A., 'Historiography and Enlightenment: a view of their history', Modern Intellectual History, vol. 5, 2008, pp. 83–96
Příbáň, J., 'Is there a Spirit of European Laws? Critical Remarks on EU Constitutional-Making, Enlargement and Political Culture', in V. Gessner, D. Nelken (eds), 'European Ways of Law; Towards a European Sociology of Law', Hart Publishing, 2007, pp. 231–252
Quevedo, S.M., 'Formalist and Instrumentalist Legal Reasoning and Legal Theory', California Law Review, vol. 73, 1985, pp. 119–157
Radbruch, G., 'Statutory Lawlessness and *Supra*-Statutory Law (1946)' (translated in English by B. Litschewski Paulson and S. L. Paulson), Oxford Journal of Legal Studies, vol. 26, 2006, pp. 1–11
Raitio, J., 'The Principle of Legal Certainty in EC Law', Kluwer, 2003
Raz, J., 'The Authority of Law', Oxford University Press, 2009
Raz, J., 'The Rule of Law and its Virtue', Law Quarterly Review, vol. 93, 1977, pp. 195–211

Roef, D., 'Strafrechtelijke verantwoordelijkheid in de risicomaatschappij', in E. Vos, G. van Calster (eds), 'Risico en voorzorg in de risicomaatschappij', Intersentia, 2004, pp. 201–228

Ross, M., 'Effectiveness in the European Legal Order(s): Beyond Supremacy to Constitutional Proportionality?', European Law Review, vol. 31, 2006, pp. 476–498

Rousseau, J.J., 'The Social Contract, or Principles of Political Right', 1762, Book 1, Ch. 1 (republished by Wordsworth Editions, 1998)

Roxin, C., 'Strafrecht: Allgemeiner Teil Band I', Verlag C.H. Beck, 2006

Rozemond, K., 'Nogmaals de tongzoen', Ars Aequi, 2014, pp. 291–296

Rozemond, K., 'Beccaria's Dream on Criminal Law and Nodal Governance', in J. Blad, M. Hildebrandt, K. Rozemond, M. Schuilenburg, P. Van Calster (eds), 'Governing Security under the Rule of Law?', Eleven International Publishing, 2010, pp. 37–51

Rozemond, K., 'De casuïstische grenzen van het materiële strafrecht', Delikt en Delinkwent, vol. 36, 2007, pp. 465–495

Rozemond, K., 'Legaliteit in het materiële strafrecht', RM Themis, 1999, pp. 117–130

Safferling, C.J.M., 'European as Transnational Law – A Criminal Law for Europe: Between National Heritage and Transnational Necessities', German Law Journal, vol. 10, 2009, pp. 1383–1398

Sampford, C., 'Retrospectivity and the Rule of Law', Oxford University Press, 2006

Samuels, A., 'Comment: Why do we not have a Criminal Code', The Journal of Criminal Law, vol. 67, 2003, pp. 214–219

Satzger, H., 'Internationales und Europäisches Strafrecht', Nomos, 2011

Satzger, H., Schmitt, B., Widmaier, G., 'StGB – Strafgesetzbuch: Kommentar', Heymanns, 2009

Satzger, H., 'Die Internationalisierung des Strafrechts als Herausforderung für den strafrechtlichen Bestimmtheitsgrundsatz', JuS, 2004, pp. 943–948

Sawyer, K., 'The Principle of 'interprétation conforme': How Far Can or Should National Courts Go when Interpreting National Legislation Consistently with European Community Law?', Statute Law Review, vol. 28, 2007, pp. 165–181

Sax, W., 'Das Strafrechtliche "Analogieverbot"', Vandenhoeck & Ruprecht, 1953

Schallmoser, N.M., 'The European Arrest Warrant and Fundamental Rights', European Journal of Crime, Criminal Law and Criminal Justice, vol. 22, 2014, pp. 135–165

Schaut, A.B., 'Europäische Strafrechtsprinzipien', Nomos, 2012

Schilling, T., 'Beyond Multilingualism: On Different Approaches to the Handling of Diverging Language Versions of a Community Law', European Law Journal, vol. 16, 2010, pp. 47–66

Schilling, T., 'The Autonomy of the Community Legal Order – an Analysis of Possible Foundations', Harvard International Law Journal, vol. 37, 1996, pp. 389–409

Schmidt, J., 'Inventing the Enlightenment: Anti-Jacobins, British Hegelians, and the *Oxford English Dictionary*', Journal of the History of Ideas, vol. 64, 2003, pp. 421–443.

Schönfeld, K.M., 'Rex, Lex et Judex: Montesquieu and la bouche de la loi revisited', European Constitutional Law Review, vol. 4, 2008, pp. 274–301

Schönfeld, K.M., 'Montesquieu en 'la bouche de la loi'', New Rhine Publishers, 1979

Schönke, A., Schröder, H., 'Kommentar zum StGB', Verlag C.H. Beck, 2014

Schreiber, H.-L., 'Gesetz und Richter', Alfred Metzner Verlag GmbH, 1976
Schünemann, B., 'Alternative Project for a European Criminal Law and Procedure', Criminal Law Forum, 2007, pp. 227–251
Schünemann, B., 'Nulla poena sine lege? Rechtstheoretische und verfassungsrechtliche Implikationen der Rechtsgewinnung im Strafrecht', Walter de Gruyter, 1978
Shute, S. and Simester, A.P., 'On the General Part in Criminal Law' in S. Shute, A.P. Simester (eds), 'Criminal Law Theory: Doctrines of the General Part', Oxford University Press, 2002, pp. 1–12
Selznick, P., 'The Moral Commonwealth: Social Theory and the Promise of Community', University of California Press, 1992
Sicurella, S., 'Some reflections on the need for a general theory of the competence of the European Union in criminal law', in A. Klip (ed), 'Substantive Criminal Law of the European Union', Maklu, 2011, pp. 233–249
Sieber, U., 'Die Zukunft des Europäischen Strafrechts', ZStW, vol. 121, 2009, pp. 1–67
Simester, A.P., Spencer, J.R., Sullivan, G.R., Virgo, G.J., 'Simester and Sullivan's Criminal Law: Theory and Doctrine', Hart Publishing, 2013
Smith, A.T.H., 'Judicial Law Making in the Criminal Law', Law Quarterly Review, vol. 100, 1984, pp. 46–76
Smith, E., 'Give and Take: Cross-fertilisation of Concepts in Constitutional Law', in J. Beatson, T. Tridimas (eds), 'New Directions in European Public Law', Hart Publishing, 1998, pp. 101–124
Smits, J.M., 'The Harmonisation of Private Law in Europe: Some Insights from Evolutionary Theory', Special Volume in honour of Alan Watson, Georgia Journal of International and Comparative Law, vol. 31, 2002, pp. 79–99
Spencer, J.R., 'Nulla poena sine lege in English Criminal Law', The Cambridge-Tilburg Law Lectures, Kluwer, 1980, pp. 35–57
Spronken, T., 'A place of greater safety', Inaugural Lecture October 2003, Kluwer, 2005
Stephen, J.F., 'A History of the Criminal Law of England', Routledge/Thoemmes, 1996
Supiot, A., 'Homo Juridicus: on the Anthropological Function of the Law', Verso, 2007
Tamanaha, B.Z., 'Law as a Means to an End', Cambridge University Press, 2006
Tamanaha, B.Z., 'On the Rule of Law: History, Politics, Theory', Cambridge University Press, 2004
Tridimas, T., 'Precedence and the Court of Justice: a Jurisprudence of Doubt?', in J. Dickson, P. Eleftheriadis (eds), 'Philosophical Foundations of EU Law', Oxford University Press, 2012, pp. 307–330
Tridimas, T., 'The General Principles of EU law', Oxford University Press, 2006
Tversky, A. 'Features of similarity', Psychological Review, vol. 84, 1977, pp. 327–352
Valentin, V., 'Les conceptions néo-libérales du droit', Economica, Corpus Essais, 2002
Vandamme, T.A.J.A.,'The invalid Directive: the legal authority of a Union act requiring domestic law making', Europa Law Publishing, 2005
Verhoeven M., Widdershoven, R., 'National legality and European Obligations', in L. Besselink, F. Pennings, S. Prechal (eds), 'The Eclipse of the Legality Principle in the European Union', Kluwer, 2011, pp. 5–72

Voermans, W.J.M., 'Legaliteit als middel tot een doel', in W.J.M. Voermans, M.J. Borgers, C.H. Sieburgh, 'Controverses rondom legaliteit en legitimatie', Kluwer, 2011, pp. 1–101

Waldhoff, C., 'Recent developments relating to the retroactive effect of decisions of the ECJ', Common Market Law Review, vol. 46, 2009, pp. 173–190

Walker, N., 'Justice in and of the European Union', University of Edinburgh Working Paper, 2014/10, available at http://ssrn.com/abstract=2399026

Walker N., in M. Avbelj, J. Komárek (eds), 'Four Visions of Constitutional Pluralism', EUI Working Paper LAW, no. 2008/21

Walker, N., 'Late Sovereignty in the European Union', in N. Walker (ed), 'Sovereignty in Transition', Hart Publishing, 2003, pp. 3–32

Walker, N., 'Postnational constitutionalism and the problem of translation', in J.H.H. Weiler M. Wind (eds), 'European Constitutionalism Beyond the State', Cambridge University Press, 2003, pp. 27–54

Walker, N., 'Policing and the Supranational', Policing and Society, vol. 12, 2002, pp. 307–321

Watson, A., 'Legal Transplants', Scottish Academic Press Ltd., 1974

Weiler, J.H.H., 'Europe's Constitutional *Sonderweg*', in J.H.H. Weiler, M. Wind (eds), 'European Constitutionalism Beyond the State', Cambridge University Press, 2003, pp. 7–26

Weiler, J.H.H., 'The Constitution of Europe', Cambridge University Press, 1999

Weiler, J.H.H., 'The Community System: the Dual Character of Supranationalism', Yearbook of European Law, 1981, pp. 267–306

Westen, P., 'Two Rules of Legality in Criminal Law', Law and Philosophy, vol. 26, 2007, pp. 229–305

Wiarda, G.J., '3 typen van rechtsvinding', W.E.J. Tjeenk Willink, 1988

Williams, G., 'Criminal law – the General Part', Stevens and Sons Limited, 1953

Williams, G., 'Law and Language – III', Law Quarterly Review, vol. 61, 1945, pp. 293–303

de Witte, F. 'Sex, Drugs and EU law: the recognition of moral and ethical diversity in EU law', Common Market Law Review, vol. 50, 2013, pp. 1545–1578

Witteveen, W.J., 'Evenwicht van machten', W.E.J. Tjeenk Willink, 1991

Lord Wright, 'The Study of Law', Law Quarterly Review, vol. 54, 1938, pp. 185–200

Χαραλαμπάκης, Α., 'Η σχέση απάτης κατά του Δημοσίου και της λεγόμενης κοινοτικής απάτης', Ποινικός Λόγος, vol. 3, 2004, p. 978

Zerouki, D., 'La légalité criminelle: enrichissement de la conception formelle par une conception matérielle', Jean-Moulin Lyon 3, 2001

Zwiers, M., 'The European Public Prosecutor's Office', Intersentia, 2011

Dutch legislation

Act of 8 April 1971 Stb. 1971, 210

Act of 7 July 1994, Stb. 1994, 529

Act of 16 November 2005, Stb. 2005, 595

Act of 5 July 2006, Stb. 2006, 310

English legislation

Criminal Law Act 1977
Constitutional Reform Act 2005

Other national legislative documents

Commissie Franken, 'Informatietechniek en strafrecht', Rapport van de Commissie computercriminaliteit, Staatsuitgeverij, 1987
Law Com, no 177 (A Criminal Code for England and Wales, 1989, vol. 1)
Kamerstukken II 1990/91, 22 008, nr 2
Kamerstukken II 2000/01, 27 159, nr. 5
House of Lords European Union Committee 10th Report of Session 2007–08, The Treaty of Lisbon: an impact assessment, Volume I: Report HL Paper 62–1, pp. 118–121

EU legislation

Regulation 17/62 of 21 February 1962 implementing Articles 85 and 86 of the Treaty OJ 13, 21.02.1962, pp. 204–211
Directive 89/592 of 13 November 1989 coordinating regulations on insider dealing; OJ L 334, 18.11.1989, pp. 30–32
Joint Action 98/742/JHA of 22 December 1998 on corruption in the private sector OJ L 358, 31.12.1998, pp. 2–4
Regulation 1760/2000 of 17 July 2000 establishing a system for the identification and registration of bovine animals and regarding the labelling of beef and beef products and repealing Council Regulation (EC) No 820/97 OJ L 204, 11.8.2000, pp. 1–10
Framework Decision 2001/413 of 28 May 2001 combating fraud and counterfeiting of non-cash means of payment OJ L 149, 2.6.2001, pp. 1–4
Regulation 1049/2001 of 30 May 2001 regarding public access to European Parliament, Council and Commission documents OJ L 145, 31.5.2001, pp. 43–48
Directive 2001/83 of 6 November 2001 on the Community code relating to medicinal products for human use OJ L 311, 28.11.2004, pp. 67–128
Regulation 2580/2001 of 27 December 2001 on specific restrictive measures directed against certain persons and entities with a view to combating terrorism OJ L 344, 28.12.2001, pp. 70–75
Framework Decision 2002/475 of 13 June 2002 on combating terrorism OJ L 164, 22.6.2002, pp. 3–7
Regulation 1/2003 of 16 December 2002 on the implementation of the rules on competition laid down in Articles 81 and 82 of the Treaty OJ L 1, 4.1.2003, pp. 1–25
Framework Decision 2003/80 of 27 January 2003 on the protection of the environment through criminal law OJ L 29, 5.2.2003, pp. 55–58

Directive 2003/06 of 28 January 2003 on insider dealing and market manipulation (market abuse) OJ L 96, 12.4.2003, pp. 16–25
Framework Decision 2003/568 of 22 July 2003 on combating corruption in the private sector OJ L 192, 31.7.2003, pp. 54–56
Directive 2005/35 of 7 September 2005 on ship-source pollution and on the introduction of penalties for infringements OJ L 255, 30.9.2005, pp. 11–21
Regulation 1448/2006 of 29 September 2006 amending Regulation (EC) No 622/2003 laying down measures for the implementation of the common basic standards on aviation security OJ L 271, 30.9.2006, pp. 31–32
Directive 2008/99 of 19 November 2008 on the protection of the environment through criminal law OJ L 328, 6.12.2008, pp. 28–37
Framework Decision 2008/913 of 28 November 2008 on combating certain forms and expressions of racism and xenophobia by means of criminal law OJ L 328, 6.12.2008, pp. 55–58
Framework Decision 2008/919 of 28 November 2008 amending Framework Decision 2002/475/JHA on combating terrorism OJ L 330, 9.12.2008, pp. 21–23
Directive 2009/123 of 21 October 2009 amending Directive 2005/35/EC on ship-source pollution and on the introduction of penalties for infringements OJ L 280, 27.10.2009, pp. 52–55
Directive 2010/64 of 20 October 2010 on the right to interpretation and translation in criminal proceedings OJ L 280, 26.10.2010, pp. 1–7
Directive 2011/36 of 5 April 2011 on preventing and combating trafficking in human beings and protecting its victims, and replacing Council Framework Decision 2002/629/JHA OJ L 101, 15.4.2011, pp. 1–11
Directive 2012/13 of 22 May 2012 on the right to information in criminal proceedings OJ L 142, 1.6.2012, pp. 1–10
Regulation 216/2013 of 7 March 2013 on the electronic publication of the Official Journal of the European Union OJ L 69, 13.3.2013, pp. 1–3
Directive 2013/48 of 22 October 2013 on the right of access to a lawyer in criminal proceedings and in European arrest warrant proceedings, and on the right to have a third party informed upon deprivation of liberty and to communicate with third persons and with consular authorities while deprived of liberty OJ L 294, 6.11.2013, pp. 1–12

Other EU legislative and policy materials

Proposal by Valéry Giscard d'Estaing for the establishment of an espace judiciaire européen, Bruxelles, 5 December 1977, available via www.ena.lu
Commission Communication concerning the consequences of the judgement given by the Court of Justice on 20 February 1979 in 120/78 ('Cassis de Dijon') OJ C 256, 3.10.1980, pp. 2–3
Commission Communication Towards an Area of Freedom, Security, and Justice, COM (1998) 459 final, 14.7.1998

Conclusions of the Presidency – Tampere European Council, 15–16.10.1999
Draft Charter of Fundamental Rights of the European Union, Brussels, 11 October 2000, CHARTE 4473/00 CONVENT 49
Report from the Commission of the Council Framework Decision of 28 May 2001 combating fraud and counterfeiting of non-cash means of payment, COM (2004) 346 final, 30.4.2004
Commission Staff Working Paper, Annex to the Report from the Commission based on Article 11 of the Council Framework decision of Decision of 13 June 2002 on combating terrorism SEC (2004) 655, 8.6.2004
The Hague Programme – Strengthening Freedom, Security and Justice in the European Union OJ C 53, 3.3.2005, pp. 1–14
EU Network of Independent Experts on Fundamental Rights, Commentary of the Charter of Fundamental Rights of the European Union, June 2006 available at http://ec.europa.eu/justice/fundamental-rights/document/index_en.htm
Commission Guidelines on the method of setting fines imposed pursuant to Article 23(2)(a) of Regulation No 1/2003 OJ C 210, 1.9.2006, pp. 2–5
Commission Notice on Immunity from fines and reduction of fines in cartel cases OJ C 298, 8.12.2006, p. 17–22
Draft Council conclusions on model provisions, guiding the Council's criminal law deliberations 16542/2/09 REV 2 JAI 868 DROIPEN 160, 27.11.2009
The Stockholm Programme – An open and secure Europe serving and protecting citizens OJ C 115, 4.5.2010, pp. 1–38
Commission Communication Towards an EU criminal policy: Ensuring the effective implementation of EU policies through criminal law, COM (2011) 573 final, 20.09.2011
European Parliament Resolution of 22 May 2012 on an EU approach to criminal law (2010/2310(INI)), 22.5.2012
Recommendations to national courts and tribunals in relation to the initiation of preliminary ruling proceedings 2012 OJ C 338, 6.11.2012, pp. 1–6
Commission Proposal for a Council Regulation on the establishment of the European Public Prosecutor's Office COM (2013) 534 final, 17.7.2013

Case law

Dutch case law

HR 23 May 1921 NJ 1921, 564
HR 15 January 1952 NJ 1952, 242
HR 7 March 1972 NJ 1972, 348.
HR 11 May 1982 NJ 1982, 583
Hof Arnhem 27 October 1983 NJ 1983, 80
HR 2 April 1985 NJ 1985, 796
HR 28 February 1989 NJ 1989, 658

HR 3 December 1996 NJ 1997, 574
HR 17 December 1996 NJ 1997, 26
HR 7 January 1997 NJ 1997, 361
HR 6 January 1998, NJ 1998, 367
HR 21 April 1998 NJ 1998, 781
HR 21 April 1998 NJ 1998, 782
HR 1 September 1998 NJ 1999, 61
HR 31 October 2000 NJ 2001, 14
HR 5 December 2000 NJ 2001, 98
HR 12 December 2000 NJ 2002, 516
Gerechtshof Arnhem 28 May 2001 LJN AD8989
HR 18 September 2001 NJ 2002, 559
HR 20 November 2001 NJ 2003, 632
HR 25 February 2003 NJ 2003, 572
HR 7 March 2004 NJ 2004, 675
HR 19 April 2005 LJN AS9237
Rechtbank Groningen 17 December 2007 LJN BC0351
Rechtbank Leeuwarden 21 October 2008 LJN BG0939
HR 21 October 2008 NJ 2009, 108
HR 7 December 2010 NJ 2011, 81
HR 12 July 2011 NJ 2012, 78
HR 23 October 2012 NJ 2012, 616
HR 26 November 2013 NJ 2014, 62

Dutch AG opinion

Conclusie, Hoge Raad (Advocaat-Generaal), 12 January 2010, ECLI:NL:PHR:2010:BO6446

English case law

Case de Libellis Famosis [1606] 77 ER 250
Rowland ap Eliza [1613] 3 Coke Inst. 164
R v Sidley [1663] 82 ER 1036
R v Thurston [1663] 83 ER 312
R v Taylor [1676] 1 Vent 293
Lynn [1784] 100 ER 394
R v Higgins [1801] ER 269
Queen v Price [1884] 12 QBD 247
Queen v Stephenson [1884] 13 QBD 331
R v Manley [1933] 1 KB 529
Joyce v DPP [1946] AC 347 (HL)
R v Clarke [1949] 2 All ER 448
R v Newland [1954] 1 QB 158

Smith v Hughes [1960] 2 All ER 859
Shaw v DPP [1962] AC 220
R v Mayling [1963] 2 QB 717
Practice Statement [1966] 3 All ER 77 (House of Lords)
R v Reah [1968] 3 All ER 269
DPP v Bhagwan [1972] AC 60
Knuller v DPP [1973] AC 435
R v O'Brien (Edward) [1974] 3 All ER 663
Black Clawson International Ltd v Papierwerke Waldhof-Aschaffenburg [1975] AC 591
DPP for Norhtern Ireland v Lynch [1975] AC 653 (HL)
DPP v Withers [1975] AC 842
Haughton v Smith [1975] AC 476
Low v Blease [1975] Criminal Law Review 513
R v Shivpuri [1987] AC 1 (HL)
R v May [1990] 91 Cr App R 157
R v R [1992] 1 AC 599
Pierson v Secretary of State for the Home Department [1997] 3 All ER 577
R v Miah [1997] 2 Cr App R 12
R v Ireland [1998] AC 147
R v Bow Street Metropolitan Stipendiary Magistrate Ex p. Pinochet Ugarte (No.3) [1999] 2 WLR 827
R v Kansas [2001] 3 WLR 1532
R v Lambert [2001] 3 WLR 206
R. v Perrin [2002] EWCA Crim 747
R v C [2004] EWCA Crim 292
R. v Misra and Srivastava [2004] EWCA Crim 2375
Jackson v Her Majesty's Attorney General [2005] UKHL 56
National Westminster Bank plc (Respondents) v Spectrum Plus Limited and others and others (Appellants) [2005] UKHL 41
R v Rimmington and R v Goldstein (joined cases) [2005] UKHL 63
Thet v Director of Public Prosecutions [2006] EWHC Admin 2701
R v Hamilton [2007] EWCA Crim 2026
R v Jones (Margaret) [2007] 1 AC 136
Norris v Government of the United States of America [2008] UKHL 16
R v JTB [2009] UKHL 20
R v Sadique and another [2011] EWCA Crim 2872
R v Ideal Waste Paper [2011] EWCA Crim 3237
R v Evans [2014] EWHC 3803 (QBD)

German case law

RG Rep. 739/99, 01 May 1899 (RGSt 32, 165)
BGH NJW 1953, 473, 29 January 1953

BGH NJW 1954, 159, 5 November 1953
BGH NJW 1957, 1642, 12 September 1957
BVerfG 2 BvR 15/62, 3 July 1962
BVerfG 2 BvL 4/62, 25 July 1962
BGH NJW 1967, 116, 9 December 1966
BVerfG 2 BvL 15 and 23/68, 26 February 1969
BGH NJW 1975, 1934, 24 July 1975
OLG Düsseldorf NJW 1982, 1111, 9 November 1981
BGH NJW 1984, 675, 7 November 1983
BVerfG 1 BvR 1053/82, 23 October 1985
BVerfG 2 BvR 234/87, 22 June 1988
BVerfG 2 BvR 752/90, 23 June 1990
BGH NJW 1990, 2393, 28 June 1990
BVerfG 2 BvR 2134/92, 12 October 1993
BVerfG 1 BvR 718/89, 10 January 1995
BVerfG 1 BvR 1476/91, 10 October 1995
BGH NJW 1998, 833, 3 December 1997
BVerfG 2 BvR 1907/97, 9 February 1998
BVerfG 2 BvR 794/95, 20 March 2002
BGH NJW 2004, 2990, 22 July 2004
BGH NJW 2007, 524, 25 October 2006
BVerfG 2 BvR 2238/07, 1 September 2008
BVerfG 2 BvR 1980/07, 10 March 2009
BVerfG 2 BvE 2/08, 30 June 2009
BVerfG 2 BvR 871/04, 29 April 2010
BVerfG 2 BvR 1230/10, 16 May 2011

Other judicial decisions

Spanish Constitutional Court, Judgement 235/2007 of 7.11.2007, at www.tribunalconstitucional.es/es/jurisprudencia/restrad/Paginas/JCC2352007en.aspx)

ECJ case law

Case 26/62 NV Algemene Transport- en Expeditie Onderneming van Gend & Loos v Netherlands Inland Revenue Administration, 5 February 1963, ECLI:EU:C:1963:1
Case 6/64 Flaminio Costa v E.N.E.L., 15 July 1964, ECLI:EU:C:1964:66
Case 41/74 Yvonne van Duyn v Home Office, 4 December 1974, ECLI:EU:C:1974:133
Case 43/75 Gabrielle Defrenne v Société anonyme belge de navigation aérienne Sabena, 8 April 1976, ECLI:EU:C:1976:56
Case 106/77 Amministrazione delle Finanze dello Stato v Simmenthal SpA, 9 March 1978, ECLI:EU:C:1978:49
Case 98/78 A. Racke v Hauptzollamt Mainz, 25 January 1979, ECLI:EU:C:1979:14

Case 120/78 Rewe-Zentral AG v Bundesmonopolverwaltung für Branntwein, 20 February 1979 ('Cassis de Dijon'), ECLI:EU:C:1979:42
Case 300/81 Commission v Italy, 1 March 1983, ECLI:EU:C:1983:50
Case 63/83 Regina v Kirk, 10 July 1984, ECLI:EU:C:1984:255
Case 238/84, criminal proceedings against Hans Röser, 27 February 1986, ECLI:EU:C:1986:88
Case 294/83 Parti écologiste "Les Verts" v European Parliament, 23 April 1986, ECLI:EU:C:1986:166
Case 14/86 Pretore di Salò v Persons unknown, 11 June 1987, ECLI:EU:C:1987:275
Case 80/86 criminal proceedings against Kolpinghuis Nijmegen BV, 8 October 1987, ECLI:EU:C:1987:431
Case 68/88 Commission of the European Communities v Hellenic Republic, 21 September 1989, ECLI:EU:C:1989:339
Case 331/88 The Queen v Minister of Agriculture, Fisheries and Food and Secretary of State for Health, ex parte: Fedesa and others, 13 November 1990, ECLI:EU:C:1990:391
C–106/89 Marleasing SA v La Comercial Internacional de Alimentacion SA, 13 November 1990, ECLI:EU:C:1990:395
C–282/90 Industrie- en Handelsonderneming Vreugdenhil BV v Commission of the European Communities, 13 March 1992, ECLI:EU:C:1992:124
C–193/94 criminal proceedings against Sofia Skanavi and Konstantin Chryssanthakopoulos, 19 February 1996, ECLI:EU:C:1996:70
Joined cases C–74/95 and C–129/95 criminal proceedings against X, 12 December 1996, ECLI:EU:C:1996:239
C–348/96 criminal proceedings against Donatella Calfa, 19 January 1999, ECLI:EU:C:1999:6
C–144/99 Commission of the European Communities v Kingdom of the Netherlands, 10 May 2001, ECLI:EU:C:2001:257
T–112/99 Métropole télévision (M6), Suez-Lyonnaise des eaux, France Télécom and Télévision française 1 SA (TF1) v Commission of the European Communities, 18 September 2001, ECLI:EU:T:2001:215
C–228/99 Silos e Mangimi Martini SpA v Ministero delle Finanze, 8 November 2001, ECLI:EU:C:2001:599
Joined cases C–187/01 and C–387/01 criminal proceedings against Hüseyn Gözütok and Klaus Brügge, 11 February 2003, ECLI:EU:C:2003:87
C–108/01 Consorzio del Prosciutto di Parma and Salumificio S. Rita SpA v Asda Stores Ltd and Hygrade Foods Ltd, 20 May 2003, ECLI:EU:C:2003:296
C–112/00 Eugen Schmidberger, Internationale Transporte und Planzüge v Republik Österreich, 12 June 2003, ECLI:EU:C:2003:333
C–233/00 Commission of the European Communities v French Republic, 27 June 2003, ECLI:EU:C:2003:371
T–224/00 Archer Daniels Midland Company and Archer Daniels Midland Ingredients Ltd v Commission of the European Communities, 9 July 2003, ECLI:EU:T:2003:195
C–60/02 criminal proceedings against X, 7 January 2004, ECLI:EU:C:2004:10

Joined cases C–397/01, C–398/01 et al. Bernhard Pfeiffer et al. v Deutsches Rotes Kreuz, 5 October 2004, ECLI:EU:C:2004:584

C–457/02 criminal proceedings against Antonio Niselli, 11 November 2004, ECLI:EU:C:2004:707

Joined cases C–387/02, C–391/02 and C–403/02 criminal proceedings against Silvio Berlusconi *et al.*, 3 May 2005, ECLI:EU:C:2005:270

C–105/03 criminal proceedings against Maria Pupino, 16 June 2005, ECLI:EU:C:2005:386

Joined cases C–189/02 P, 202/02 P, 208/02 P et al. Dansk Rørindustri A/S et al, 28 June 2005, ECLI:EU:C:2005:408

C–176/03 Commission of the European Communities v Council of the European Union, 13 September 2005, ECLI:EU:C:2005:542

C–384/02 criminal proceedings against Knud Grøngaard and Allan Bang, 22 November 2005, ECLI:EU:C:2005:708

T–279/02 Degussa v Commission, 5 April 2006, ECLI:EU:T:2006:103

C–212/04 Konstantinos Adeneler and Others v Ellinikos Organismos Galaktos, 4 July 2006, ECLI:EU:C:2006:443

C–467/04 criminal proceedings against Giuseppe Francesco Gasparini and Others, 28 September 2006, ECLI:EU:C:2006:610

C–303/05 Advocaten voor de Wereld VZW v Leden van de Ministerraad, 3 May 2007, ECLI:EU:C:2007:261

T–216/05 Mebrom NV v Commission of the European Communities, 22 May 2007, ECLI:EU:T:2007:148

C–76/06 P Britannia Alloys & Chemicals Ltd v Commission of the European Communities, 7 June 2007, ECLI:EU:C:2007:326

C–305/05 Ordre des barreaux francophones et germanophone and Others v Conseil des ministers, 26 June 2007, ECLI:EU:C:2007:383

C–467/05 criminal proceedings against Giovanni Dell'Orto, 28 June 2007, ECLI:EU:C:2007:395

C–161/06 Skoma-Lux sro v Celní ředitelství Olomouc, 11 December 2007, ECLI:EU:C:2007:773

Joined cases T–101/05 and T–111/05, BASF AG and UCB SA v the Commission, 12 December 2007, ECLI:EU:T:2007:380

C–308/06 The Queen, on the application of International Association of Independent Tanker Owners (Intertanko) and Others v Secretary of State for Transport, 3 June 2008, ECLI:EU:C:2008:312

T–99/04 AC Treuhand AG v Commission of the European Communities, 8 July 2008, ECLI:EU:T:2008:256

C–402/05 P Kadi and Al Barakaat International Foundation v Council and Commission, 3 September 2008, ECLI:EU:C:2008:461

C–345/06 Gottfried Heinrich, 10 March 2009, ECLI:EU:C:2009:140

C–421/07 criminal proceedings against Frede Damgaard, 2 April 2009, ECLI:EU:C:2009:222

T–24/07 ThyssenKrupp Stainless AG v Commission of the European Communities, 1 July 2009, ECLI:EU:T:2009:236
C–45/08 Spector Photo Group NV and Chris Van Raemdonck v Commissie voor het Bank-, Financie- en Assurantiewezen (CBFA), 23 December 2009, ECLI:EU:C:2009:806
C–550/09 criminal proceedings against E and F, 29 June 2010, ECLI:EU:C:2010:382
C–224/09 criminal proceedings against Martha Nussbaumer, 7 October 2010, ECLI:EU:C:2010:594
C–261/09 Gaetano Mantello, 16 November 2010, ECLI:EU:C:2010:683
T–299/08 Elf Aquitaine SA v Commission, 17 May 2011, ECLI:EU:T:2011:217
C–501/11 P Schindler Holding Ltd and Others v European Commission, 18 July 2013, ECLI:EU:C:2013:522
C–333/13 Elisabeta Dano and Florin Dano v Jobcenter Leipzig, 11 November 2014, ECLI:EU:C:2014:2358
ECJ Opinion 2/13, 18 December 2014, ECLI:EU:C:2014:2454

ECJ AG Opinions

Opinion AG Mancini of 17 March 1987 in Case 14/86 Pretore di Salò v Persons unknown, 11 June 1987, ECLI:EU:C:1987:136
Opinion AG Cosmas of 8 June 1995 in C–63/93 Fintan Duff et al. v Minister for Agriculture and Food and Attorney General, 15 February 1996, ECLI:EU:C:1995:170
Opinion AG Elmer of 14 March 1996 in C–168/95 criminal proceedings against Luciano Arcaro, 26 September 1996, ECLI:EU:C:1996:107
Opinion AG Colomer of 17 June 1996 in Joint cases C–74/95 and C–129/95 criminal proceedings against X, 12 December 1996, ECLI:EU:C:1996:239
Opinion AG Sharpston of 11 July 2003 in C–209/12 Walter Endress v Allianz Lebensversicherungs AG, 19 December 2004, ECLI:EU:C:2013:472
Opinion AG Kokott of 14 October 2004 in joint cases C–387/02, C–391/02 and C–403/02 criminal proceedings against Silvio Berlusconi *et al.*, 3 May 2005, ECLI:EU:C:2004:624
Opinion AG Colomer of 26 May 2005 in C–176/03 Commission of the European Communities v Council of the European Union, 13 September 2005, ECLI:EU:C:2005:311
Opinion AG Maduro of 25 May 2004 in C–384/02 criminal proceedings against Knud Grøngaard and Allan Bang, 22 November 2005, ECLI:EU:C:2004:316
Opinion AG Colomer of 12 September 2006 in C–303/05 Advocaten voor de Wereld VZW v Leden van de Ministerraad, 3 May 2007, ECLI:EU:C:2006:552
Opinion AG Bot of 1 March 2007 in C–76/06 P Britannia Alloys & Chemicals Ltd v Commission of the European Communities, 7 June 2007, ECLI:EU:C:2007:128
Opinion AG Bot of 26 October 2010 in C–352/09 P ThyssenKrupp Nirosta GmbH v European Commission, 29 March 2011, ECLI:EU:C:2010:635
Opinion AG Kokott of 12 May 2011 in Joint cases C–483/09 and C–1/10 criminal proceedings against Magatte Gueye and Valentín Salmerón Sánchez, 15 September 2011, ECLI:EU:C:2011:297

Opinion AG Kokott of 17 January 2013 in C–583/11 P Inuit Tapiriit Kanatami and Others v European Parliament and Council of the European Union, 3 October 2013, ECLI:EU:C:2013:21

ECtHR case law

ECtHR Handyside v United Kingdom, App. 5493/72, 7 December 1976
ECtHR Sunday Times v United Kingdom, App. 6538/74, 26 April 1979
ECtHR Kruslin v France, App.11801/85, 24 April 1990
ECtHR Kokkinakis v Greece, App. 14307/ 88, 25 May 1993
ECtHR S.W. v United Kingdom, App. 20166/92, 22 November 1995
ECtHR C.R. v United Kingdom, App 20190/92, 22 November 1995
ECtHR Cantoni v France, App. 178662/91, 15 November 1996
ECtHR Hashman and Harrup v United Kingdom, App. 25594/94, 25 November 1999
ECtHR Coëme v Belgium, App. 32492/96, 22 June 2000
ECtHR Sari v Turkey and Denmark, App. 21889/93, 8 November 2001
ECtHR Kononov v Latvia, App. 36376/04, 24 July 2008
ECtHR Scoppola v Italy, App. 10249/03, 17 September 2009
ECtHR Kononov v Latvia, App. 36376/04, 17 May 2010
ECtHR M.S.S. v Belgium and Greece, App. 30696/09, 21 January 2011

EComHR decisions

EComHR X Ltd Y v United Kingdom, App. 8710/79, 7 May 1982
EComHR Chinoy v United Kingdom, App. 15199/89, 4 September 1991

Websites

www.bundesverfassungsgericht.de/en/index.html (accessed 6/11/2014)
www.gesetze-im-internet.de/englisch_stgb/index.html (accessed 6/11/2014)
www.gov.uk/use-of-the-common-law-offence-of-conspiracy-to-defraud—6 (accessed 01/12/2014)
http://iclr.co.uk/ (accessed 02/12/2014)
www.cps.gov.uk/legal/d_to_g/drafting_the_indictment/ (accessed 20/12/2014)
http://europa.eu/about-eu/basic-information/symbols/motto/index_en.htm (accessed 29/12/2014)

Summary

This book is about the principle of legality in European criminal law. It is divided into three Parts and eight Chapters. The first Part is introductory and it is comprised of two Chapters, where the research topic and the methodology are set out (Chapter I and II respectively).

Chapter 1 introduces and explains the central topic of this research. The principle of legality is a keystone doctrine of national criminal justice systems. In short, the principle means that there is no crime without *law*. It has two functions; it legitimises the use of criminal law powers by the state (legitimising function) and it influences the operation of criminal law normatively (normative function). This principle legitimises the use of state powers by defining the concept of *law* as opposed to state force. It concretises the application of other important values or principles, which are often considered the theoretical rationales of the principle of legality. These include the Rule of Law, the separation of powers, democracy, and the principle of individual liberty and autonomy. Chapter 1 highlights that this principle may elicit different interpretations, depending on how one defines its legitimising role. Normatively, the principle of legality defines the sources of criminal liability and it guides the use of the discretionary powers by state actors. Four prohibitions stem from it, namely the prohibition of customary criminal liability, of retroactive criminalisation, of vaguely prescribed behaviour and finally, the prohibition of extensive interpretation by courts.

Whereas the legality principle is fundamentally important for the criminal justice systems, its interpretation and application in European criminal law is incoherent and incomplete. European criminal law is an area still in progress and increasingly more criminal law powers are entrusted to European state actors. Chapter I explains further the realm of European criminal law. The existence and nature of these powers demand that they are employed legitimately. The current application of the principle of legality in EU law is fragmentary. Many of its normative functions have already been developed judicially but these do not apply coherently at all instances. More importantly though, there has been very little discussion on the legitimation of the European criminal justice system and the conditions under which European criminal *law* is distinguished from state violence. The research question is, therefore, to examine the interpretation and application of the principle of legality in European criminal law. In particular, the research aims at examining the possible legitimising and normative functions of the European legality principle. It is to be noted that this research does not aim at replacing national doctrines, albeit a degree of influence should be expected. Furthermore, some limitations of this research are addressed. In this book, I examine the principle of legality as applied to courts and the legislator and not to the executive. Its application to sanctions is also excluded.

Chapter II deals with the methodology, which follows the nature of this principle in EU law. The legality principle is a human right codified in Article 49 of the Charter but it is also a general principle of EU law. These are distinctive European principles that have a double pedigree; they stem from national constitutional traditions and standards from international instruments (mainly the ECHR). General principles of EU law are frequently built in a bottom-up manner while they are also seen as open doctrines that can be adapted to the European system. Essentially this approach is also followed in this book. To translate this approach into methodological terms, I employ the concept of legal transplant. This is a phenomenon where a principle, a norm or an institution is transplanted in another system and thereby adapted. In this Chapter, I concretise further this process by referring to the concept of cross-fertilisation. The latter is similar to legal transplants but as a methodological concept it focuses more on the adaptation of legal concepts and their dynamic evolution within the new legal order. I argue that by employing the concept of legal transplant, or the process of cross-fertilisation, the analysis of the legality principle at the EU level becomes transparent and open to critical analysis.

Next to this, I distinguish three methodological steps. The first step is the national comparative research, which includes three national systems: the English, the Dutch and the German. The aim of the first step is to identify how the normative and legitimising functions of this principle operate in the national systems. The *modus operandi,* problems, and different existing approaches are to be analysed. The second step is the examination of the existing fragments of the EU system. In this step, the principle of legality is expected to be fragmentary and therefore a more critical analysis of the lacunae and the existing questions is necessary. The third and final step is the internal adaptation, where the principle of legality is adapted to the European legal system. This step requires that one respects certain parameters that define this system, which conclude Chapter II.

Part II deals with the national comparative research and it includes three Chapters. In Chapter III, the theoretical rationales of the principle of legality are analysed. The principles of individual autonomy and liberty, democracy, separation of powers, the Rule of Law, legal certainty, and guilt are examined. The aim of this Chapter is two-fold. Its goal is to explain the foundations of the legality principle but also to explore their different interpretations. Different interpretations of these concepts may change the legitimising and normative role of the principle of legality.

Different theories regarding individual liberty and autonomy are presented, the most central being the distinction between positive and negative liberty. Negative liberty means the absence of obstacles, while positive liberty entails the presence of something, i.e. elements that improve the capacity of the individual to act. Negative liberty represents the traditional understanding of liberty, and criminal law is therefore a threat to liberty. The relationship between positive liberty and the state are difficult to regulate, however, I argue that balancing them is essential. The concepts of predictability and legal certainty are further discussed. Additionally, the vertical and horizontal dimensions of criminal law are discussed.

The analysis of the democratic principle focuses on the elaboration of its assumptions, such as equality and political autonomy, and the expositions of two modern approaches. The procedural concept of democracy means that democratic procedures suffice to secure political autonomy and self-determination of individuals and communities. The substantive concept holds that, next to procedures, a substantive respect of human dignity and minimum respect of individual rights is also important. Essentially a similar conflict is also presented for the Rule of Law, where there have been various substantive and formal theories. I argue that both practically and dogmatically a strict formalistic or procedural approach cannot be reconciled with modern legal systems.

For the notion of separation of powers, I present the theory of Montesquieu and its different interpretations. A strict approach of separating the powers cannot be reconciled with modern legal systems but also the theory of Montesquieu itself. A system of checks and balances, on the other hand, where no power gains overall control reflects better the doctrine of the separation of powers. I conclude that a model where courts have a moderate dynamism is preferable to systems where courts have no discretion at all, or absolute control.

This Chapter ends with the principle of guilt and legal certainty. Regarding the principle of guilt, which has been frequently mixed with the principle of legality, I argue that instead of trying to strictly demarcate these two principles, an appraisal of their doctrinal interaction is more pragmatic. It also prevents the distortion of the concept of foreseeability, which both principles essentially safeguard at different levels. Regarding the principle of legal certainty, I analyse its different interpretations and subdivisions. What should be highlighted is that this principle may be understood as requiring predictability (e.g. non-retroactivity or clarity of norms) but it may also require acceptability, namely that criminal law is what is expected and accepted to be.

In Chapter IV, the focus is on the interpretation and application of the principle to national law. The three different systems are presented in an integrative manner, as the aim is to identify the *modus operandi* of this principle in national law. The Chapter is divided into two main sections. In the first one, the differences and similarities of continental and common law countries are presented. It becomes evident that this principle did not exist as such in common law, however, this did not prevent this system from developing functionally equivalent notions. What is also striking is that arbitrariness is conceptualised differently in both traditions, next to key rationales such as the separation of powers. Regulating the sources of criminal liability is an important function of the principle in the continental traditions. However, this element was absent in the traditional common law. Having said that, it is also shown that both traditions have come closer together, especially under the influence of the ECHR. In particular, continental systems have developed certain *de facto* common law trends and the principle of legality is currently a doctrine of English law.

Analysis of the ECtHR's jurisprudence shows that it brought the traditions closer to each other, and most importantly, it advanced a novel interpretation of the principle of legality, which is also prevalent in national law. The 'rights-conception' brings to the foreground the human right nature of this principle. As a human right, its application depends on a variety of factors that are further explained in this Chapter, the most important being that the principle is weighed with other rights. This essentially brings within this principle a substantive connotation as foreseeable criminalisation depends on the individual rights that are protected with criminal law. In addition, the sources of criminal liability are less important in the 'rights-conception' of the legality principle where the focus is shifted to qualitative elements such as foreseeability. Evidently, the ECtHR's 'rights-conception' has been partly incorporated in national law influence in different ways the interpretation of this doctrine.

In the second section, further research of the current application of the legality principle is conducted. The analysis reveals that in national law the principle of legality is eroding as its different aspects do not consistently comply with their dogmatic expectations. Much attention is paid to the *lex certa* and *lex stricta* elements. It is shown that courts have much more powers than what the traditional interpretation of this principle would allow. In addition, the courts' activity demands further guarantees be established against possible abuse. This becomes especially evident in the prohibition of analogy. It appears that courts make use of different techniques to legitimise their decisions, such as an appreciation of legal interests involved and their proper balance within the legal order. In short, it appears that the principle of legality is lacking tools to properly address certain dangers. This problem is further traced to the theoretical construction of this doctrine.

In Chapter V, the principle of legality is critically discussed in the light of three models of justice. These models as analytical tools to reconstruct the doctrine of the principle in order to compensate for its failures as discussed in the previous Chapter. Each takes a different approach to the interpretation of the theoretical rationales as presented to in Chapter III and the function of the legality principle as presented in Chapter IV. The models reflect roughly the traditional conflict in legal philosophy between formalism, pragmatism, and relational theories.

The classical model of criminal justice adheres to legal formalism, i.e. the legitimacy of the law is found in past decisions. Law should not be adapted to current developments because legal certainty is important. Principles and rules are separate concepts. In the classical model, a strict separation of powers and a formalistic understanding of the Rule of Law and democracy apply. Criminal law is legitimate when the vertical relationships between the individual and the state are regulated. Therefore, it is mainly through its protective finality that criminal law finds legitimacy. In the instrumentalism model, criminal law finds legitimacy in its pragmatic contemporary relevance. The instrumental goals of criminalisation are the main source of legitimacy and the protection against arbitrariness does not play a role in the legitimacy of criminal law. Substantive interpretation of the Rule of Law and democracy apply, while courts have increased powers. Finally, in the relational model of criminal justice the legitimacy of criminal law is found in the mediation between the instrumental and protective finalities of criminal law. Transparency and controllability of decision-making is important so that decisions are tested for arbitrary balancing of rights. In this model, a less strict separation of powers doctrine is favoured.

The legality principle in these three models functions differently. A comparison between the three models shows that the relational model is a more defensible approach for criminal law's legitimacy. In a relational model the character of this doctrine as a principle is accentuated, as principles remain open doctrines that must be concretised. It is a steering principle that guides construction and interpretation of criminal liability. This entails that as a principle it includes the weighing of the relevant interests of criminalisation. Its functions are enriched with further elements, such as a claim towards transparency during interpretation where courts must follow a transparent reasoning by differentiating between principles, policies and rights. The masking of opportunistic policies as more legitimate elements is therefore avoided. In addition, within a relational model the principle of legality addresses the problem of casuistry of jurisprudence. It is further explained that courts can methodically improve their interpretation to avoid casuistic development of criminal liability. The Chapter concludes with a general evaluation of the legality principle in the chosen relational model and the usefulness of the models of criminal justice as analytical tools.

In the third Part the focus is shifted to EU criminal law. The aim of this last part is to analyse and reconstruct the principle of legality in EU law. Part 3 is divided into three Chapters. Chapter VI follows an analysis similar to Chapter IV where the *modus operandi* in EU law is assessed. It is important that one establishes the current nature and application of the legality principle but also pin-point its lacunae. The Chapter is structured following the different aspects of the legality principle. One of the main problems is the lack of appropriate theoretical support. The principle of legality is often associated with or considered a part of other broader doctrines, such as legal certainty or legal expectations. Some of its function cannot be explained without further theoretical analysis. For example, why would this principle apply also to Directives when these are not addressed to individuals?

Normatively there are some important lacunae and inconsistencies. For example, there is no unified approach regarding the sources of criminal liability in EU law, whilst there are certain elements such as implementation guidelines that are not yet developed. For example, the principle of conform interpretation presents certain dogmatic difficulties especially due to the *contra legem* requirement. What is also pointed out in Chapter VI is that this principle must function in a two-level system, which is rather challenging as the way in which national and European legal orders interact is not too clear. Special attention is paid to the dissemination of tasks between European and national institutions, namely the ECJ and national courts, and the European and national legislators.

After laying down the current problems of this doctrine in the inventory of Chapter VI, the analysis is taken at the theoretical level in Chapter VIII where the legitimation of EU criminal law and justice system is examined. The aim is to understand the constitutional and theoretical elements of the criminal justice systems within which a European legality principle should operate. Chapter VII is divided into two main sections. In the first section the legitimacy of the EU criminal justice system and its relationship to the national legal orders are discussed. In the second section, a relational model for European criminal justice is advocated. The Chapter begins with an analysis of the current legitimation patterns of the EU criminal justice system. Instrumental motivation plays an important role in the legitimacy of this system as its nature and justification is politically annexed to the internal market. This is shown through an analysis of the spill-over theory; namely that the AFSJ is necessary because the internal market had a spill-over on crime control. Essentially, crime control and security are of importance for such EU system. What is missing is the protective finality of EU criminal law. This has been slowly emerging and evidences are presented from the *ne bis in idem* principle and other areas of EU criminal law. Some problems of the protective dimension of EU criminal law are also presented. If there is such an aspect to this system, then what short of protection will the EU afford to its citizens?

The Chapter continues with an analysis of the interaction between the EU and national legal orders where three existing theories are presented. Within these theories several other relevant doctrines, such as European citizenship, democracy and the legitimation of criminal law are discussed. The theory of EU supremacy supports the superiority of the EU legal order over the national one. The theory of democratic statism advances the importance of national legal orders as the sole basis for criminal law legitimacy. They theory of constitutional pluralism suggests that both European and national legal orders have a claim of legitimacy. The latter theory values a relational approach of European citizenship where EU law becomes the means to mediate between excessive nationalism and excessive unification.

In the second section, the impact of the classical and the instrumentalist models is discussed and a relational model for European criminal justice is presented. Such model is based on an assumption of pluralism of legal orders and of sources of legitimacy and it represents a furthering of the ECtHR's 'rights-conception', an approach prevalent amongst EU and national legal orders. The main characteristics of this model are presented. The European protective dimension of EU criminal law is reconstructed. It involves a strengthening of the vertical aspect, where individuals are protected from arbitrariness from both the EU and the national authorities, and a horizontal aspect, where the crime control element is reinterpreted in the light of the European *demos*. Further elements, such as legal certainty and the justification of harmonisation of criminal offences are examined. The Chapter concludes with an appreciation of the theoretical rationales of the legality principle in EU law and the general features of such principle.

The function of the European legality principle within such EU criminal justice system (based on a relational model of justice) is further developed in the last part of this book. Chapter VIII focuses exclusively on the legitimising and normative function of the European legality. An additional element, the distributive function, is added as explained in Chapter VII. The legitimising function consists of guidelines regarding the use of criminal law competences by the European legislator. It highlights the steering character of this principle. Focus is paid to the currently opportunistic character of the systems. What is suggested from this is that the EU legislator must assess substantially the principles of subsidiarity and proportionality and make a distinction between policies and rights. EU policies are not excluded from the legitimation of EU criminal law but they should be distinguished and their possible translation to rights addressed.

The distributive function addresses the problem of justifying the current multi-level system and how the European and national authorities should divide their roles in constructing and interpretation criminal liability. The normative function delves deeper to the function of the aspects of the legality principle. Key questions raised in Chapter VI are answered here. An important feature is that the European legality principle supports the statute as a source of criminal liability, but it also recognises case law as an active participant. As a tool against casuistry, a form of precedence is suggested for the ECJ. Transparency in judicial interpretation is essential for both the ECJ in preliminary rulings and national courts. Especially with the principle of conform interpretation, the suggestion is to delete the problematic *contra legem* element. Finally, the aspects of *lex certa* are further analysed. A solution for the requirement of precision of Directives is suggested. In addition, the pressing need of harmonising rules on jurisdiction is analysed. The Chapter ends with conclusions that summarise key points of the book but also reflect upon certain choices made, such as the methodology of this book and the use of models of justice. Final conclusions include possible directions for further research in this field.

Curriculum Vitae Christina Peristeridou

Christina Peristeridou (born 1984 in Thessaloniki, Greece) studied law at the Aristotle University of Thessaloniki and human rights at the University of Macedonia, Thessaloniki, graduating in 2006. She obtained her Master in European and International Public Law from the University of Tilburg in 2007 (cum laude). She is admitted to the Bar of Thessaloniki since 2008.

In 2007, she joined Maastricht University as a PhD researcher and lecturer. She has taught courses on European criminal law, national comparative criminal law and procedure.

School of Human Rights Research Series

The School of Human Rights Research is a joint effort by human rights researchers in the Netherlands. Its central research theme is the nature and meaning of international standards in the field of human rights, their application and promotion in the national legal order, their interplay with national standards, and the international supervision of such application. The School of Human Rights Research Series only includes English titles that contribute to a better understanding of the different aspects of human rights.

For previous volumes in the series, please visit http://shr.intersentia.com.

Published titles within the Series:

66. Etienne Ruvebana, *Prevention of Genocide under International Law. An analysis of the obligations of states and the United Nations to prevent genocide at the primary, secondary and tertiary levels* ISBN 978–1-78068–273–0
67. Evgeni Moyakine, *The Privatized Art of War. Private Military and Security Companies and State Responsibility for Their Unlawful Conduct in Conflict Areas* ISBN 978–1-78068–281–5
68. Esther Janssen, *Faith in Public Debate. On Freedom of Expression, Hate Speech and Religion in France & the Netherlands* ISBN 978–1-78068–309–6
69. Stefanie Jansen-Wilhelm, *Accepting Assistance in the Aftermath of Disasters* ISBN 978–1-78068–329–4
70. Helen Beckmann-Hamzei, *The Child in ICC Proceedings* ISBN 978–1-78068–339–3
71. Karel De Meester, *The Investigation Phase in International Criminal Procedure: In Search of Common Rules* ISBN 978–17–806–8305–8
72. Nelleke Koffeman, *Morally Sensitive Issues and Cross-Border Movement in the EU* ISBN 978–1-78068–349–2
73. Roland Moerland, *The Killing of Death* ISBN 978–1-78068–351–5
74. Andrea Broderick, *The Long and Winding Road to Disability Equality and Inclusion* ISBN 978–1-78068–358–4

www.ingramcontent.com/pod-product-compliance
Ingram Content Group UK Ltd.
Pitfield, Milton Keynes, MK11 3LW, UK
UKHW051920100926
8556IPUK00021B/1275

9 781780 683577